STACKHOUSE

BY J. RICHARD GRUBER

MORRIS MUSEUM OF ART
1999

For Phyllis Stackhouse and Maxine Belger

This volume has been published in conjunction with the exhibition, "Robert Stackhouse: Major Works 1969-1999," organized by the Morris Museum of Art and curated by J. Richard Gruber, presented May 20 - August 22, 1999.

All works drawn from the Robert Stackhouse Collection
at the John and Maxine Belger Family Foundation, Kansas City, Missouri.

Exhibition Itinerary:
Morris Museum of Art, Augusta, Georgia
Western Michigan University and the Kalamazoo Institute of Arts, Kalamazoo, Michigan.
The University of Arizona Museum of Art, Tucson, Arizona.

Editor:	L. Keith Claussen, Morris Museum of Art
Design:	Jane Carter, Morris Communications Corporation
Color Separations:	Mark Albertin, Diann Giles
	Morris Communications Corporation
Printing:	Crowson Stone Printing, Columbia, South Carolina

On the cover: *Flexed Flyer*, 1995

ISBN: 1-890021-07-5

Morris Museum of Art
One 10th Street • Augusta, GA 30901 • (706) 724-7501
www.themorris.org

TABLE OF CONTENTS

Introduction and Acknowledgements

Robert Stackhouse rose to national prominence soon after the opening of his first one-man show in New York at Max Hutchinson's Sculpture Now Gallery in 1976, a show dominated by his large A-frame construction, *Running Animals/Reindeer Way*. Stackhouse, who had been teaching at the Corcoran Gallery School of Art since 1966 and had attained a reputation as an important sculptor in the Washington-Baltimore area, had moved to New York from Washington in 1975. Following this first New York show, which generated favorable reviews and articles in national art magazines, Stackhouse received commissions for projects including outdoor installations in Cleveland, at Artpark, at the Cranbrook Academy and at the Hudson River Museum. By the early 1980s, when major A-frame constructions had been installed in many outdoor and museum environments, and his diverse serpent and ship forms had become increasingly well-known, Robert Stackhouse was regarded as one of the country's most prominent young sculptors.

In 1982, looking back over his accomplishments of the preceding decade, he completed a series of four very large watercolors that incorporated the iconic images that had marked his career to that point. Trained as a painter at the University of South Florida, Stackhouse discovered that large-scale watercolors offered a new approach to painting that inspired him and offered a distinctive avenue for his painterly instincts. During the 1980s, as he explored new possibilities for sculptural forms, and as he received international commissions for sculptural installations in Canada, Australia and Brazil, Stackhouse continued to paint distinctive watercolors, often recreating the imagery of his temporary sculptural installations, on an increasingly ambitious scale. By the end of that decade, even though his drawings and large watercolors had been widely exhibited in galleries and museums across the country and internationally, he was still recognized more as a sculptor than as a painter.

Beginning in 1991 and 1992, Stackhouse explored an important new series of images, centered on historic luxury liners including the Titanic, the Normandie and the Queen Mary, and he discovered that large-scale watercolor painting offered the greatest medium for the expression of his feelings about these subjects. Reversing his earlier working pattern, based upon the creation of a temporary sculpture and the subsequent painting of that image, during the 1990s Stackhouse became a painter whose paintings inspired later sculptural forms. Ships, serpents and diverse architectural forms dominated his compositions, as they had in the past. Yet, increasingly during the 1990s, Stackhouse achieved recognition as a watercolor painter as well as a sculptor. During this same time, he increasingly loosened his ties to the New York art world, creating sculptural installations in diverse regions of the country and serving as a visiting artist and professor of art at colleges, universities and art schools across the country. Important exhibitions and installations in and around Kansas City, terms as a visiting artist at both the Kansas City Art Institute and Drury College and the support of private collectors and a major regional foundation, the Belger Family Foundation in Kansas City, all contributed to his recent decision to move to Kansas City.

This publication, and the retrospective exhibition it accompanies, both organized by the Morris Museum of Art working in association with the artist and the Belger Family Foundation, offer a comprehensive overview of Stackhouse's life and work to the present date. The exhibition, focused on works created during the first thirty years of his career, from 1969 to 1999, was planned to serve as a mid-career retrospective. And, for the first time in any publication, the importance of the artist's distinctive early life and his experiences in Manhattan and in Yonkers, at Peach Lake, New York, at Lundy's fish camp near Auburndale, Florida and at the University of South Florida are considered within the context of his later life and his professional career. This is also the first study of the artist's significant ties to the culture of the South, specifically to the culture of central Florida and the Gulf Coast region. Building upon this research, his rich formative experiences on Peach Lake in New York and on Lake Julianna in Florida are considered as influences upon the development of his iconic images, including the serpent, the ship and the open form, lath-sided architectural structures that have marked his career.

A research and retrospective exhibition project of this magnitude, extending over a period of more than four years, would not have been possible without the generous support and the enormous patience of the artist. Working with a prolific artist like Robert Stackhouse during these years in locations as diverse as Manhattan and Port Chester, New York, Kansas City and St. Joseph, Missouri, and Auburndale, Gulfport and Tampa, Florida, has been a challenging and highly rewarding experience. During this period, his art and his life have evolved in significant ways, as documented in this publication. His mother, Phyllis Stackhouse, has been equally generous with her time and her rich memories and recollections of the Stackhouse and the Holland family histories. Her records and family scrapbooks, the source of many of the photographs and illustrations used in the first chapters of this publication, proved to be highly valuable resources. As I learned almost from the beginning of this project, it is not possible to consider the development of this artist's career, and his distinctive iconic forms, without considering the rich and complex family history that nurtured him and his creative vision.

In Kansas City, the support and encouragement of Richard Belger, Chairman of the John and Maxine Belger Family Foundation, and Myra and Dennis Morgan, of the Morgan Gallery, have been invaluable. During the past five years, Dick Belger, who first acquired the artist's work for his own personal collection more than a decade ago, has assembled for his family's foundation the largest body of the artist's work that exists in any single collection, public or private, reflecting all phases of his career, in all media. Intended to serve as a major research collection reflecting the development and evolution of the artist's entire career, this collection has served as the foundation for the Morris Museum exhibition from its inception. As research indicated the newly comprehended importance of a certain period or of specific works, every effort was made to find and incorporate the relevant works into the collection, for this project and for future research and exhibition projects. For the artist, as for the author, involvement with such an enlightened patron, one who recognizes the importance of collecting and preservation, of conservation and archival framing, of research and documentation, of publication and exhibition, has been a memorable and highly rewarding experience. The sharing of these resources with broad public audiences, in the South and the Middle West, as well as in other regions of the country, will make it possible to see and to understand this artist in ways never before possible.

During these same years, the Morgan Gallery, directed first by Myra Morgan, then by her son, Dennis Morgan, assumed an increasingly important role in the advancement of the artist's work and his career. Although associated with the Morgan Gallery since the early 1980s, Stackhouse demonstrated that he had entered a new phase of his career with the presentation of his exhibition of major painted works at the Morgan Gallery in 1993. Encouraged by Myra Morgan to show these paintings first in Kansas City, not in New York or another East Coast gallery, he enjoyed one of his most successful exhibitions in years and was convinced of the correctness of his decision to move more fully into painting. Later, as visiting artist positions and sculptural commissions brought him repeatedly back to Missouri, and specifically to Kansas

City, the artist recognized that the focus of his artistic activity was shifting from New York to Kansas City. Throughout the years of this project, both Myra and Dennis Morgan have been highly supportive of all phases of activity, from the largest to the most mundane and tedious elements of such a project. The Morgan Gallery staff has been equally supportive.

In Augusta, the support of William S. Morris III, as always, makes it possible for the Morris Museum of Art to commit to long term research, publication and exhibition projects of this nature. By studying and exhibiting the works of artists of national and international stature, like Robert Stackhouse, whose ties to the South have not been explored or documented previously in any significant way, we are able to gain new insights into the careers and the works of such an artist, and into the cultural history of our region, and the nation. Keith Claussen, director of the Morris Museum, has supported this exhibition and publication during all phases of planning and production, serving also as editor of this publication. Valuable research assistance has been provided by Cary Wilkins, librarian and archivist at the Morris Museum's Center for the Study of Southern Painting. Catherine Wahl has handled the shipping and movement of a challenging body of work with her usual grace and diligence. Jim Tar and Robert Bazemore assisted in the planning and installation of the exhibition in major ways. And, as evident throughout the pages of this publication, Vince Bertucci and Jane Carter have created a unique book design that reflects the spirit of a distinctive artist and his works.

Finally, Sharon White Gruber has supported and been an important part of this project from its inception to its final fruition in this publication and the related Morris Museum exhibition.

J R G
Augusta, Georgia
November, 1998

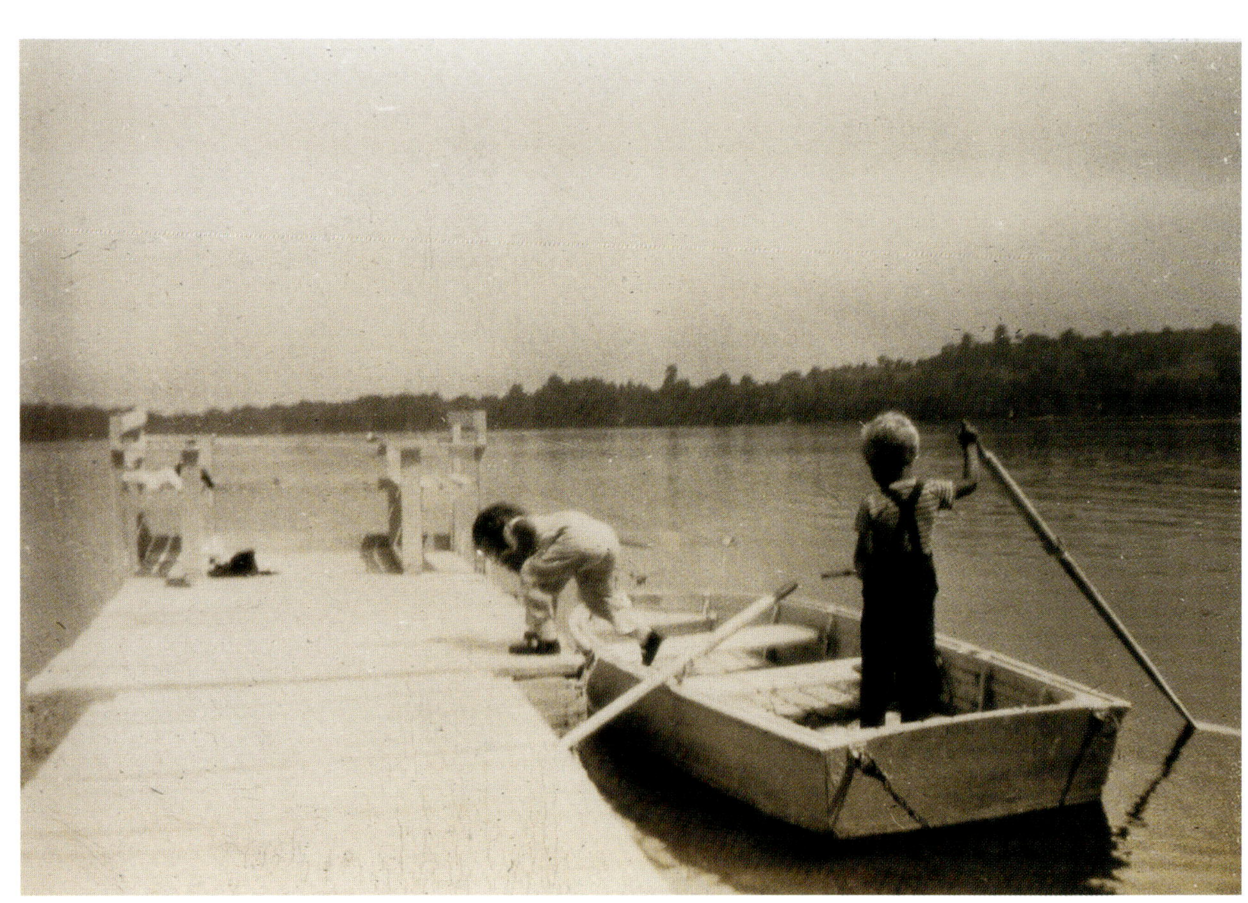

CHAPTER ONE

New York

Robert Stackhouse was born, the second of two sons, to Phyllis May (Holland) and Gerald Murry Stackhouse, on July 31, 1942. Like his brother, Kurt, he was born at Lawrence Hospital, in Bronxville. At the time, his parents' home was located on Seaman Avenue, in the Inwood section of Manhattan. At the time of his birth, not long after the surprise attack on Pearl Harbor on December 7, 1941, the nation was engaged in the process of transforming itself from the sluggish pace of the Depression era into a production-oriented, war-driven economy. On the day of that invasion, Phyllis Stackhouse, then pregnant with Robert, was vacationing with her husband, Jerry, her older son and members of her extended family on a beach at Fort Myers, Florida (Figure 1.1). It was her first trip to Florida, the state that later became her family's permanent home. His mother's presence along the West Florida shore, far removed from the turmoil of the day, was foretelling. Soon after his birth Robert would demonstrate that he was always most comfortable near water, a fact that would remain constant throughout his childhood and his adult years, one that significantly influenced the evolution of his mature art forms.

He was born between two of the most distinctive periods in American history, the Depression and the postwar, baby-boom era. The years that separated Stackhouse and his older sibling, who was born on December 30, 1936, proved to be significant for many reasons including his more complete immersion in a popular culture that was influenced by television, automobiles, jet planes, foreign wars, racial strife, the flight to the suburbs and a predominant American mood of optimism and expansion. Kurt, like other children of the late Depression era, grew up with a somewhat different childhood orientation than did Robert, whose earliest experiences and memories were more fully shaped by the boom mentality of the postwar era. The dispiriting symbols and realities of the Depression, with its breadlines, government employment programs and countless homeless figures, had little impact upon Robert's early years. And, although government war rationing of gasoline, tires, and foods including coffee, meat, fish and canned goods, went into effect during his first year, he experienced few of the deprivations associated with the Depression era or the war years. An early photograph, taken at the age of five weeks, shows Robert being held protectively by his father while his older brother looks on (Figure 1.2). By the age of nine months, an alert young Robert was photographed sitting upright in a carriage, wearing a well-made jacket, surrounded by vibrant neighborhood life in a street filled with high-rise apartment buildings, suggesting his immersion in the comforts of middle class urban life (Figure 1.3).

During the years between the births of Robert and Kurt, there were numerous indications of the transformations that were about to shape a new future for the average American.

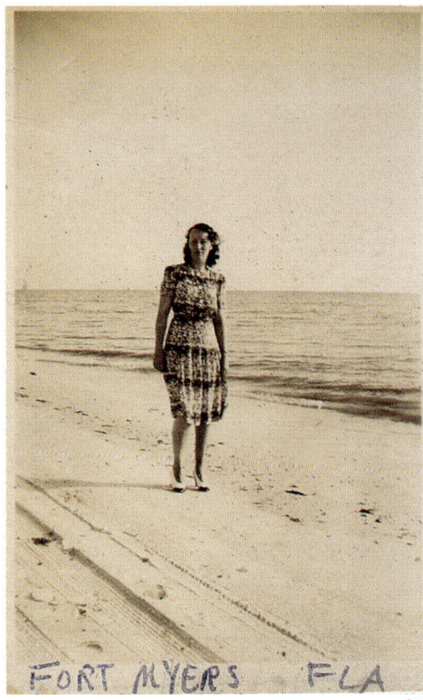

1.1

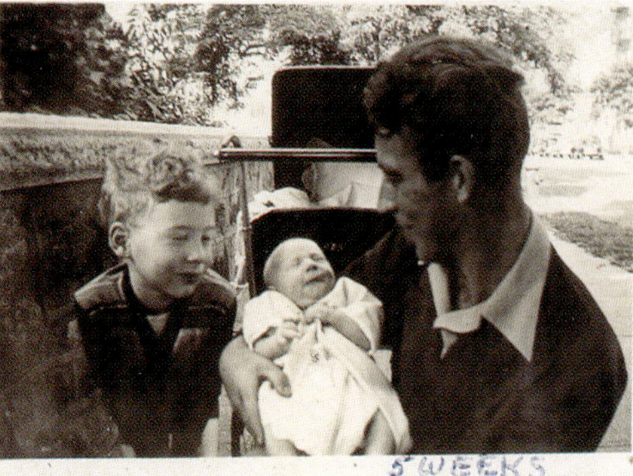

1.2

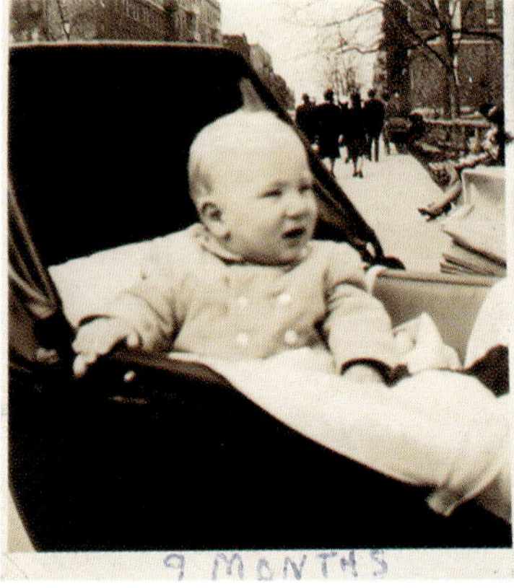

1.3

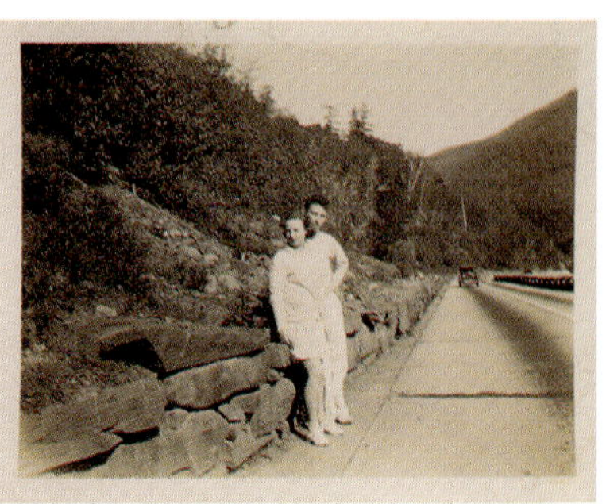
1.4

Phyllis Stackhouse on the beach at Fort Myers, Florida, December 7, 1941.

Robert Stackhouse, five weeks old, with brother, Kurt, and father, Gerald Stackhouse.

Robert at age 9 months, New York.

Robert's parents - Phyllis and Gerald Stackhouse - 1930s.

Many of these were incorporated into the plan and the design of the New York World's Fair of 1939 and 1940. The world's fair, dominated by modern architectural forms and the famous Trylon and Perisphere, was presented in Queens, only a short commute by car or train from the Manhattan home of the Stackhouse family. Phyllis Stackhouse remembers visiting this fair on numerous occasions, first with her husband and older son, then with different members of her New York family, and later, when she served as a tour guide for the many Ohio relatives who visited during both years of the fair's presentation. [1] As she, her relatives and countless others recognized, the lingering effects of the national Depression severely impeded the progress of the Machine Age, preventing average Americans from purchasing the homes, cars and manufactured products they desired. Yet, nothing prevented Americans from dreaming and planning for a better future. In fact, the popular movies, radio programs and print media of the 1930s had maintained visions of the brighter, consumer-oriented future that served as a focus of the fair. And, in the imaginative pavilions presented by General Motors, Ford, Chrysler, R.C.A., Firestone, Continental Baking (his grandfather's company) and other corporations, fair visitors were offered visions of a future filled with dream homes, streamlined automobiles and new consumer products and technological solutions to life's dreary routines.

Television, a vital medium in American popular culture as well as a significant element in the formative life of Robert Stackhouse, was introduced to the public on a massive scale at this fair. On April 30, 1939, President Franklin D. Roosevelt became the first president to appear on broadcast television when he officially opened the world's fair in a televised program transmitted by NBC. Phyllis Stackhouse remembers seeing television displays that were incorporated into many of the fair buildings, including those operated by RCA, Westinghouse, General Electric and Ford. The automobile, and futuristic new highway and commuter networks, figured prominently in the life of the fair. These displays made a lasting impression on the artist's mother, who still clearly remembers specific automobiles she saw at the fair and recalls the details of her visits to the Futurama pavilion. General Motor's Futurama, designed by Norman Bel Geddes, offered visitors a simulated flight over a futuristic American landscape dominated by automobiles and vast new highway systems. Democracity, presented inside the Perisphere, offered fair audiences a model American city, centered on a massive skyscraper and surrounded by expansive suburbs, from the year 2039. As contemporary scholars have shown, these displays at the 1939 fair accurately predicted many of the realities Americans associated with the suburban life of 1960, including many of the realities Robert Stackhouse and his family encountered in the cities and suburbs of Florida during the 1950s and early 1960s. [2]

Considering the evolution of Robert Stackhouse's career, it should be noted that art played a significant role in the fair. This was evident in the Gallery of American Art Today, which featured a survey of the American art world just prior to Robert's birth. As explained by Holger Cahill in "American Art Today," written for the exhibition's catalogue, 1200 works were selected from 25,000 submitted entries, creating "the most extensive and the most thorough winnowing of American art which has ever taken place."[3] Cahill wrote that visitors would see categories he called "The American Scene," "The Conservatives," "Modernists and 'Pure' Artists," "Neo-Romantics and Surrealists," "The Abstract Artists," "Social Content" and "Sculpture and Graphic Art." In 1939 and 1940, just as the American social and economic orders were poised on the brink of radical change, so too was the American art world. Artists who worked in a realistic manner dominated the American art world of the 1930s, just as they dominated the fair's exhibition. While abstract and nonobjective painting had fallen out of public favor during these years, a transformation was evolving, one that would profoundly alter the American art world of the 1940s and the 1950s, and would continue to be an influence into the 1960s, when Robert attended art schools in Florida and in Maryland. During these years Willem de Kooning, Jackson Pollock and others associated with the New York School created a new order in the American art world, an order that would later have significant implications for the development of Robert Stackhouse's art. However, it would be during his college years in Florida, not in New York, that Stackhouse first encountered these developments in a meaningful way.

Robert Stackhouse's artistic reputation is commonly associated with Manhattan and its art world. To the present day, he considers himself to be a New York artist. Until he moved to Florida at the age of 12, in 1954, he and his family lived in Manhattan and the greater metropolitan area of New York City. The earliest years of his life were spent in an apartment building on Seaman Avenue, located next to Inwood Hill Park, near the Hudson River and Sputyen Duyvil Creek. Later, his family moved to Yonkers, first to an apartment building on Midland Avenue, then to a nearby apartment on the Bronx River Road, close to his school, P.S. 14. Yonkers was a distinctive community at that time, the type of suburban metropolitan area that attracted many new residents in the years after the war. Robert and Kurt Stackhouse were raised in these urban settings within the environment of a large extended family, one dominated by his grandparents, Inez and Hoyt Holland, who charted the course of the family's life.

Robert's parents met in Toledo, Ohio, in July of 1934, when they attended a picnic and dance while on a blind date at a Lake Erie beach. Phyllis May Holland, who was born in Toledo in 1915, had moved with her parents to Mt. Vernon, New York, in 1927 when the expansion of her father's bakery business required his presence in the corporate headquarters in New York City. Gerald Murry Stackhouse, born in Toledo in 1913, had graduated from Toledo's Scott High School in 1932, then enrolled in classes at Toledo University. Both Phyllis and Jerry were only children; neither had brothers or sisters. Phyllis, who had graduated from New Rochelle High School in 1933, returned to New Rochelle with her parents in the fall of 1934, but she came back to Toledo that Christmas. On December 31, 1934, she and Jerry eloped, traveling about thirty miles to Monroe, Michigan, where they were married in the courthouse by a justice of the peace. They returned to Toledo in a driving snow storm. Because of their age, she was nineteen and he was twenty one, Jerry's lack of employment, and her defiance of her parents' plans for college and her future, they kept the marriage a secret until after she returned to New York (Figure 1.4). When she announced their marriage to her parents, they expressed their disapproval and disappointment, questioning Jerry's ability to provide the type of future they had envisioned for their daughter. They reluctantly accepted her new husband as a member of their family. Jerry soon moved to New York and was given an entry level job in one of her father's bakeries. Their first New York apartment, in Mt. Vernon, was located near the bakery and overlooked the lights of the George Washington Bridge.

The full Stackhouse and Holland families soon became a major part of the young married couple's life. As Jerry learned, he would live in the shadows of the successful Holland family for most of his married life. Not until 1972, when he and Phyllis moved to Gulfport, Florida, was he able to live alone with his wife, following the death of her mother. As Robert remembers, his childhood was spent surrounded by this extended family in diverse New York apartments and at the Hollands' summer home at Peach Lake, New York. Robert's family background was a mix of Scotch, Irish, English and Pennsylvania Dutch blood. Although organized religion was not a major aspect of family life, his parents attended the Crescent Place Reformed Church in Yonkers, and both Kurt and Robert were baptized at this same church. While his parents' families were tied to the Toledo area, members of both his mother's family, the Holland-Ewing-Millikan families, and his father's family, the Stackhouse-Murry family, also had ties to the South. His great grandmother, Mary Olive Ewing Holland,

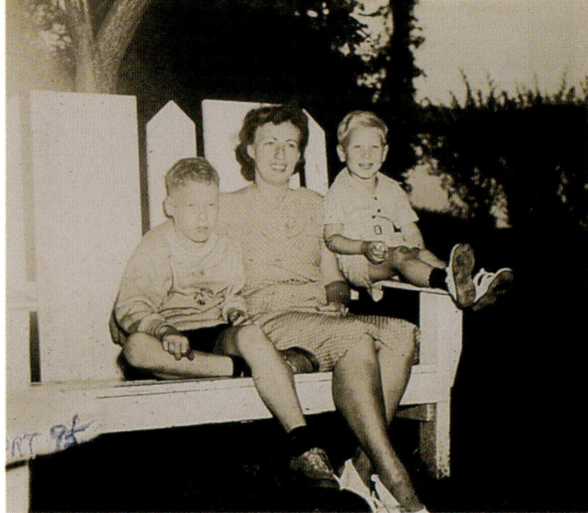

1.5

was born in Paris, Kentucky, and his great-great grandparents, the Millikans, were Quakers born during the antebellum period in North Carolina. David Carlos Stackhouse, his grandfather, originally came to Toledo from Virginia. The closeness (and the complexity) of this large family is illustrated in the way Robert relates to his second cousins, Susan and Janice Wood, whom he and Kurt regarded as sisters. Their mother, Rose Alice Millikan, was the youngest sister of Inez Holland (Robert's grandmother), who moved in with his mother and her parents when she was sixteen years old. Only a few years older than Phyllis, she was raised like a member of the family and was treated like Phyllis's older sister. When she later married Stanley Wood, he also worked for a time in the family's bakery business (including serving a stint as the night manager in the Continental Bakery pavilion in the 1939 New York World's Fair). Alice and Phyllis continued to regard each other as sisters, often traveling across the country with their children for family vacations and holiday gatherings.

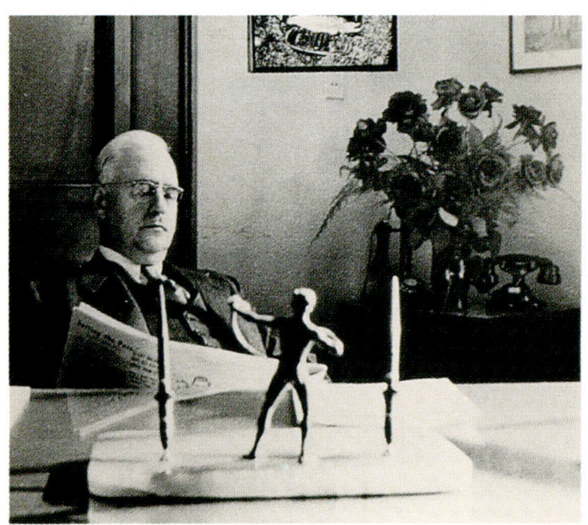

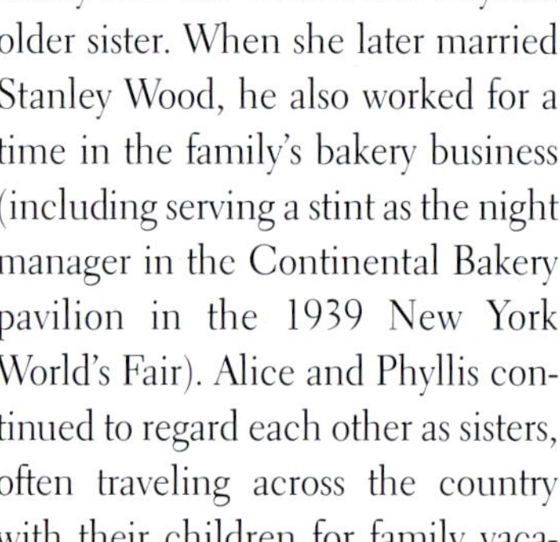

1.6

Kurt Stackhouse, Phyllis Stackhouse and Robert Stackhouse at Peach Lake, 1945.

Hoyt Holland in his Continental Baking Company office at Rockefeller Center at the time of his 35th anniversary with the company, February 15, 1947.

Surrounded by his family, urban life in Manhattan and Yonkers became increasingly influential upon Robert as he matured and eventually attended school. Another major influence, one that initiated a significant change in Robert's life, as well as in the life of his full extended family, began to develop when his grandfather Holland purchased a wooden summer home at Peach Lake, located outside Brewster, New York. Summers at the house and on the lake soon became a central part of the family's life together, creating a regular annual rhythm and a place of convergence for a diverse range of family and friends (Figure 1.5). Recently, the artist explained his grandfather's motivation for acquiring the lake house. "He purchased the cottage in 1944. My grandfather was an outdoors man and he thought Kurt and I needed that type of outdoor experience. He looked into the cost of sending two boys to camp and then decided to buy this house that he'd heard about from friends. It was just what he was looking for."

The location of the Peach Lake house made it possible for his grandfather to commute to his office at Continental Baking, located in Manhattan's Rockefeller Center. On the days of his commute during the summer, he took a New York Central train from Brewster into the city, then returned at the end of his work day. Robert still remembers the trains and the Brewster station: "They were all steam engines then. The tracks came around a hill. Brewster was an old coal mining town, located in the foothills of the Berkshires. When the train came in, you heard the engines, then you saw the train coming around the hill." His grandfather's personal life and his business schedule set the tone of the family's annual cycles during Robert's childhood. This continued through his high school years, after Robert moved to Florida with his grandparents.

Robert's grandfather and grandmother, Hoyt and Inez Holland, served as the patriarch and matriarch of the family and exerted a strong influence on Robert's early development. Hoyt's success in business supported the evolution of the family's life, even during the bleakest years of the Depression. Hoyt Holland and his brother, Wade, came from modest backgrounds in Ohio but achieved positions of prominence in New York and in the national business world. "He was," as the artist recently explained, "a self-made man. He left school when he was a junior in high school. He rose to the position of vice-president in charge of finance for the Continental Baking Company and was responsible for all new corporate acquisitions." And, as he explained, there were direct family connections in his business associations as well.

> *Hoyt was the brilliant one, Wade was the administrator. He and his brother rose through the ranks. Wade became the President of Continental Baking Company. They both had started with a little bakery, the Holland Baking Company then expanded and became the Toledo Bread Company. Then they developed the concept of Wonder Bread and called it that. Wonder Bread was their idea. Later Continental Baking purchased Wonder Bread. Eventually, however, the two Holland brothers ended up running Continental Baking.*

Peach Lake, as the artist recalls, served as an important center of escape and personal renewal for his grandfather, one that was literally reflected in his manner of dress during the day. "He went to New York every day, to Rockefeller Center, and he would return wearing a three piece business suit. He came back to Peach Lake, put on his old hat, then he would put on his sockless shoes and his L.L. Bean shorts, and go out to the garage to smoke a cigar and perhaps have a drink or two." A formal portrait photograph shows his grandfather seated at his desk in his office looking very much like a successful businessman (Figure 1.6). In contrast, a more casual family snapshot, taken at night on the family dock, shows him seated wearing a slouch hat, shorts and no shirt (Figure 1.7). While ambitious and successful in business, and equally aggressive and skilled as a sportsman, his grandfather also was an avid reader who remained interested in self education and cultural issues. As Robert remembers, "Often we would see him sitting around listening to the Bell telephone hour, to the opera, to classical music on the radio. If he was not reading magazines he would read the Encyclopedia Britannica or mysteries, including Mickey Spillane." In one family photograph, his grandfather is shown reading, sprawled in a floral pattern stuffed chair with one foot propped on a stool, wearing only his shorts and sockless shoes, surrounded by the wooden walls of the house, a table piled with reading materials, a reading lamp and a sideboard holding a radio and a fruit-filled silver bowl. (Figure 1.8)

The Peach Lake house was constructed of natural materials, using wood inside and out, with rough cut stone details in the fireplace and chimney as well as in the walks around the house (Figures 1.9, 1.10, 1.11, 1.12). It was a classic American vernacular lake house, with two wings containing the sleeping areas and the kitchen and bath areas, flanking a central great room, dominated by the fireplace, wooden walls and vaulted wooden ceilings. Most of the furniture was wooden as well, including a trussed dining table and its wooden benches. Numerous photographs, showing both the inside and outside of the house dominate the family scrapbooks, reflecting the stature of this house in the life and in the mythology of the family.

The importance of the Peach Lake house, as well as the social gatherings and family experiences he associates with the house and the lake, are critical to an understanding of Robert Stackhouse's development, as a person and as an artist. "Of all my family life," he recalls, "this is the only place where I have only fond memories. It was the one place where the family seemed to be harmonious." Here he developed and nurtured his close association with the natural world, swimming in the lake, floating and sailing in simple wooden boats, fishing, catching snakes, frogs and other wild creatures (Figure 1.13). His life study of snakes and other aquatic creatures, his use and appreciation of wood and natural materials, his awareness of the weathering effects of nature upon paint and diverse materials, his understanding of the effects of light upon man-made structures, his awareness of the principles of basic carpentry and appreciation of the forms of vernacular architecture—all were nurtured by his summer experiences at Peach Lake.

While remembering and describing the materials, the furniture and the related details of the Peach Lake house, including a reference to the "sanded and notched wooden ceiling" of the central room, Robert indicated how directly his memories of the house have affected the development of his art (See *Running Animals/Reindeer Way*, Figures 4.8 and 4.9).

> *Later, when I built the first A-frame sculptural form* (Running Animals/Reindeer Way, *1976), I had no idea of what it would be, of what it would look like or of how it would work. When I stood inside it, I did not know how important the interior view was. Then I realized that it reminded me of the beamed ceilings at Peach Lake. And I remembered that I had gotten a couple of deer antlers, someone had given them to me, so I went back to the studio to get them. I also recalled a stuffed pheasant and a coconut monkey being attached to the beams of the ceiling in the Peach Lake house. So I put them up in the sculpture one day, thinking that I would later take them down. But*

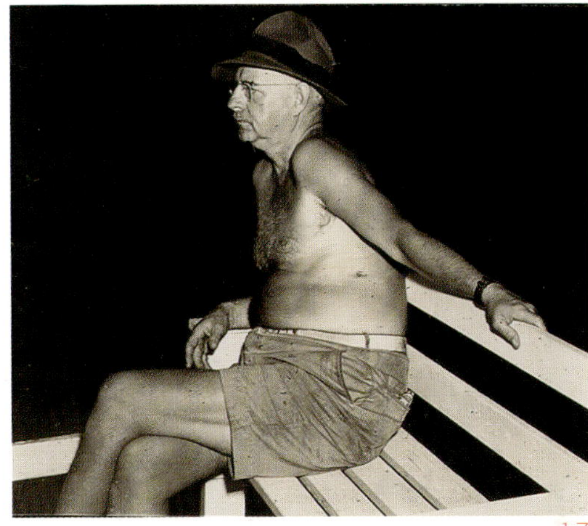

1.7

Hoyt Holland, in shorts and hat, seated on Peach Lake dock at night.

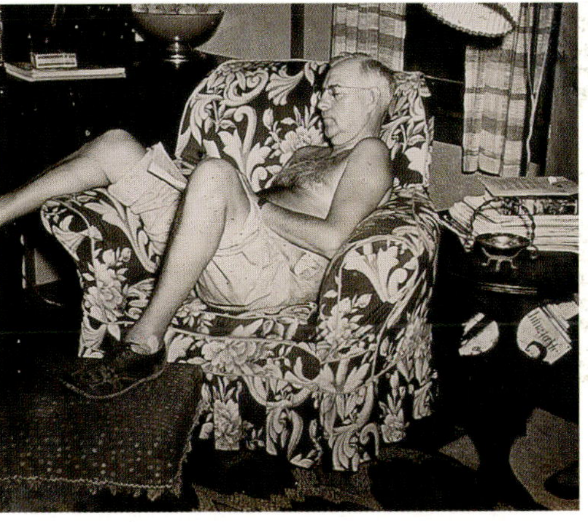

1.8

Hoyt Holland, Robert's grandfather, reading in a chair at the Peach Lake house.

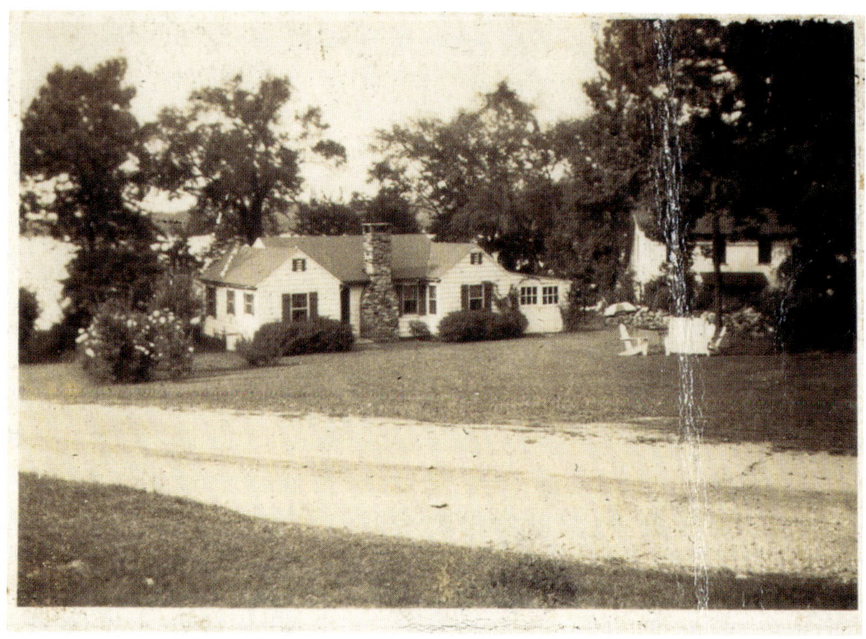

1.9

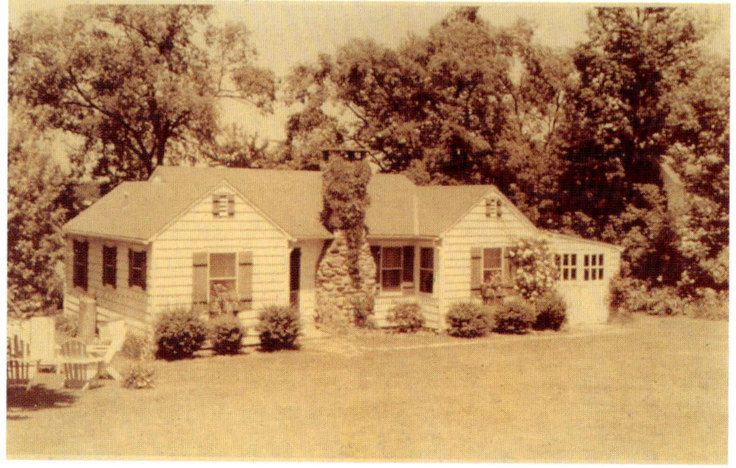

1.10

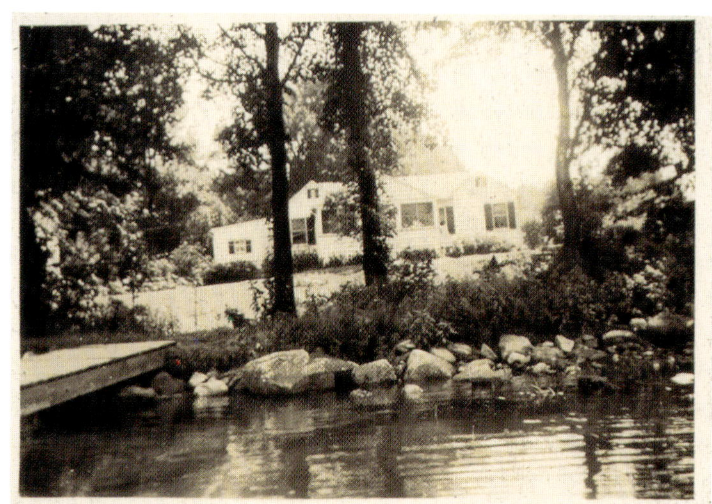

1.11

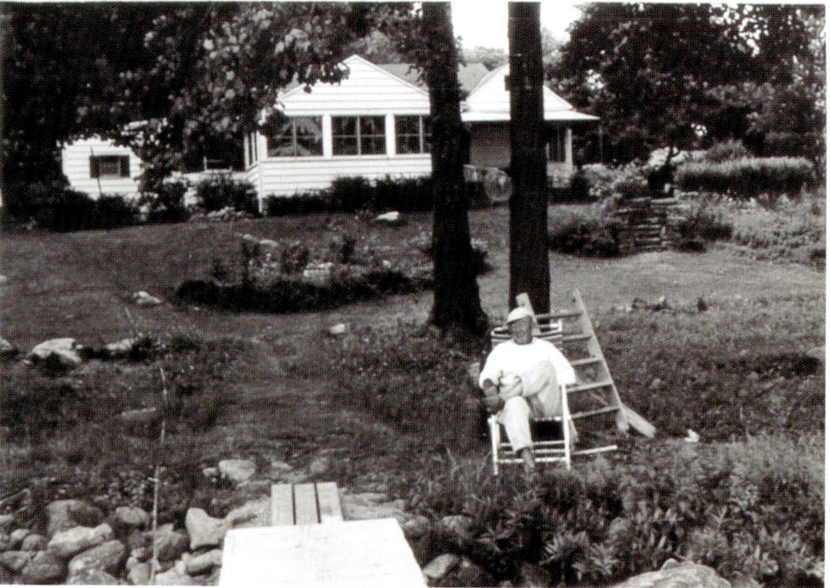

1.12

Views of the house at Peach Lake.

I never did. And I said that some people would see them there and others would not. It was something I immediately connected with those experiences at Peach Lake.

Robert's grandfather and a good friend, Pa Fuller, had experimented with designing racing boats. Their prized sailing boat, "The Wedge," was known as a cup winning racer on the waters of Lake Erie when Hoyt was a young man. Later, when Robert was about seven or eight years old, his grandfather designed another boat intended for fishing and sporting activities on the reservoirs of New York state. As the artist recalls: "I remember that it was basically one plank, the entire gunnel was one plank, about a twelve inch or a sixteen inch board. The boat was about sixteen feet long. It had very beautiful lines. It was very austere. It had a straight bow, like the Titanic. It was long and low." And as Phyllis Stackhouse remembers, her father wanted that one long board to fit to his boat design plans: "We spent the entire summer, with some of us on each side of that boat, holding the board, so it would not spring. Once it sprang loose with surprising power, and it was a miracle no one was injured. We all laughed about spending the summer building Gramp's boat together." He even designed a live bait bucket to fit under the seats. After it was completed, and painted a deep forest green color, Hoyt placed it on top of his car, drove off to a reservoir and no one ever saw the boat again.

In addition to the natural and the man-made environment of Peach Lake, Stackhouse recalls a rich and quite varied sense of social life, inside and outside the house. Relatives, friends and annual local summer residents who returned to the lake, many coming from Toledo, the Midwest and other parts of the country, mingled freely throughout the summer. Formality was left behind in the city. Dress, manners and social customs remained casual and relaxed. While Robert was well supervised as a young child he achieved increasing levels of freedom as he matured, which allowed him to explore the lake and the surrounding woods on his own, eventually using a wooden row boat that had been given to him. He loved life at the beach and on the lake, including sitting on the dock benches, floating in tubes and on rafts, learning to swim and to play on the water (Figure 1.14). Each year, his birthday parties took place out of doors, near the lake or around the family's summer house.

Daily life during summers at Peach Lake was dominated by the interests of both the men and the women of the family. As Robert recalls, his grandmother and the other women in the family played just as active a role as the men. "I was around a lot of men but I was raised mostly by women. But I was surrounded by a large group of men." His grandmother, the oldest of a large group of siblings, planned and structured daily life at the lake house each summer, inviting all the members of her family, even paying their way if traveling money became a problem. Everyone called her Aunt Inez. During the Depression, while many of her family members struggled to survive, she helped them in diverse ways until they regained their financial stability. Always known as a good cook, she organized the daily kitchen and meal planning activities, including preparing the fish and game that the men brought home, while maintaining a complex household that included large numbers of visitors. Her role as the family's matriarch extended far beyond the lake, back into their life in Yonkers and continued later, even while Robert was in college, when she dominated family activities in their new Tampa house during the 1960s.

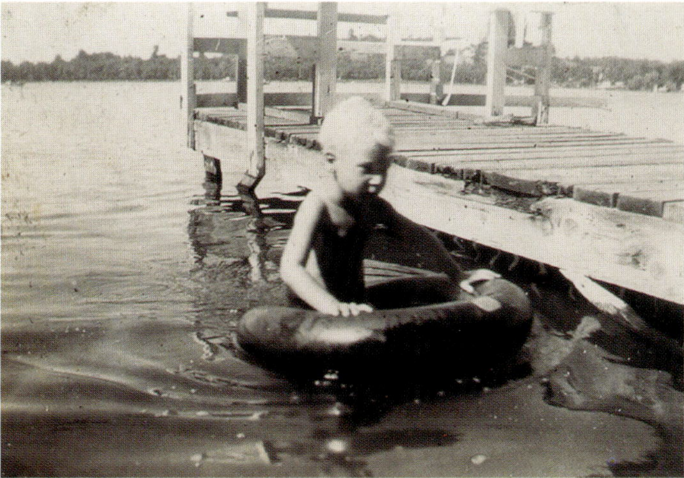

1.13

Robert Stackhouse floating in inner tube and standing in boat at dock on Peach Lake.

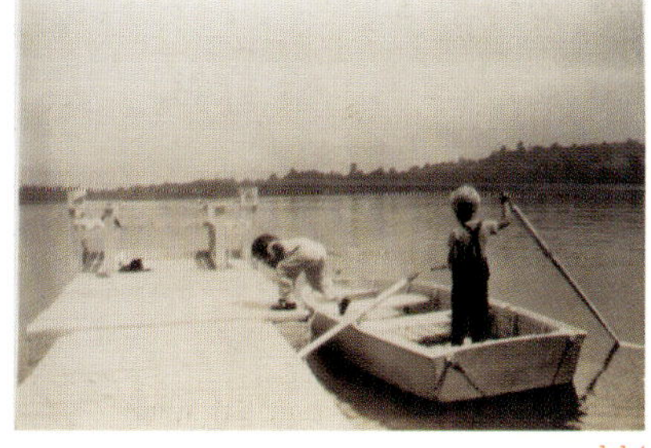

1.14

In contrast, a family snapshot seems to capture the attitude of the men as they stand together, half with shirts, half without, in a casual pose for the camera. (Figure 1.15) Looking at them recently, the artist identified each individual: his father, Jerry, his grandfather, Hoyt, John Connor, Stan Wood, Ray Blough, Homer Millikan Jr. As he later learned, his own father had grown up playing with Homer Jr. and the children of Ray Blough. Homer Sr., who was divorced and lived with Robert's grandparents until his grandfather died, paid his way during the summers by doing work around the Peach Lake property. He was a significant influence, often teaching the young boy the basics of carpentry.

He was a strong figure for me because he was very handy. And, he was often at war with my grandmother. She wanted me to have curls, he wanted me to have a butch cut. He had been a roustabout and a wanderer before the war. He actually worked in the pit lanes at the Indianapolis speedway. He told me about it and about how he had been a test driver for car companies and oil companies, sometimes even testing cars in the desert. So he was a practical man. He was also a loner who smoked and drank, cussed, fished and generally lived the "John Wayne" lifestyle.

And, as the artist's memories and family photographs suggest, his grandfather clearly enjoyed the company of such men, whether it was playing cards together while smoking and drinking in the small crowded garage (Figure 1.16), or fishing and hunting with them around the Peach Lake area (Figure 1.17). One of his grandfather's best friends, Don Ray, seen in both the card playing scene and seated before a car in a field, was a professional artist and outdoorsman who published paintings and illustrations regularly in *Argosy* as well as other sporting magazines. Don Ray was the first professional artist Robert Stackhouse knew. Fortuitously, he was a member of this rugged masculine circle who gathered around his family at Peach Lake. Art that was created by such a figure, a "regular guy," one who was immersed in the same type of activities as everyone else at the Peach Lake house, suggested that art could become a part of daily life (not just the museum world) and that it might be a suitable profession for a male member of their family. Ray even painted a watercolor image of the house, which he gave to Inez and Hoyt as a present (Figure 1.18).

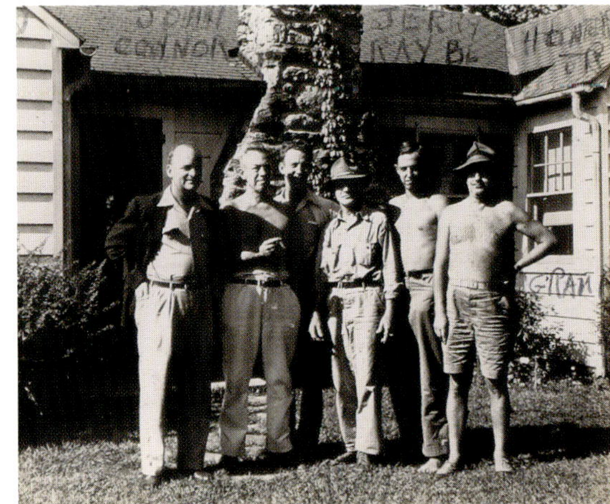

1.15

Robert's relatives at Peach Lake - Stan Wood, John Connor, Jerry Stackhouse, Ray Blough, Homer Millikan, Jr., and Hoyt Holland.

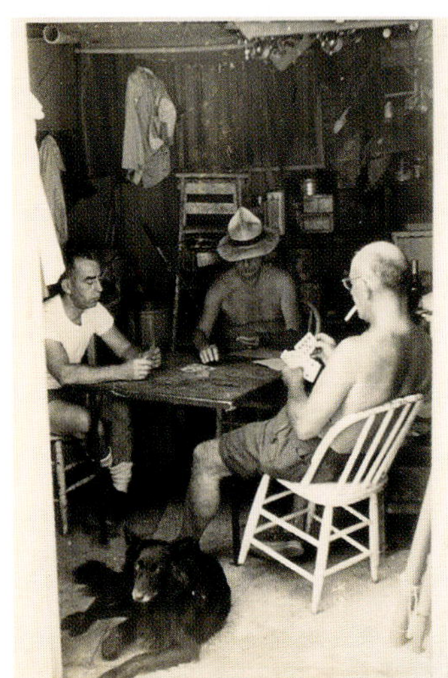

1.16

Hoyt Holland, Don Ray and Homer Millikan, Sr., playing cards at Peach Lake (with Blackie).

Stackhouse has lasting memories of Don Ray, recalling both his art and his reputation as an artist during the period. "He was very accomplished. He completed illustrations of fishing flies for sporting magazines. He also illustrated stories and other types of articles. He was, as I remember, mostly a wildlife artist." As a boy, Robert first learned that artists lived and worked in New York because of Don Ray. "He lived in New York, in downtown. Once I asked my grandmother where Don Ray lived. She told me he lived in New York City. And I asked, where was that, because my concept of New York City was just downtown, just buildings and stores. And she told me, in a disapproving manner, that I wouldn't like it where he lived. Which was ironic, since I ended up living in lower Manhattan." Don Ray's work was, in general, very realistic and reflected the natural environments he enjoyed. Robert later acquired one of Ray's watercolors (Figure 1.19) which incorporated his characteristic approach to painting and illustrations, and which also shows Ray's tendency to use the borders of a work for secondary illustrations. It was, as Stackhouse recently acknowledged, a distinctive approach to the borders that may well have influenced his own use of secondary and related images on the borders of his large scale watercolors. Stackhouse even paid a tribute to Ray in one of his works. "When I created the middle image in the *Ghost Dance* triptych, the profile of the deer, I thought of him all the time when I was doing that. I used one brush stroke for one piece of hair, the same way he would operate." (See *Drawing for Ghost Dance #2*, Figure 3.35).

The other person Robert regards as an important early artistic influence was his brother, Kurt. Kurt had a passion for drawing as well as for collecting and painting toy soldiers (something he later did professionally), as well as for building different types of models. Kurt drew constantly and was also a voracious reader on a wide range of topics, including military history. Although both brothers were blond and fair skinned, Kurt burned easily in the sun and could not stay out of doors to play for any length of time. Robert, on the other hand, tanned in the sun and flourished with his love of outdoor play. Kurt stayed inside at the camp, reading, drawing, listening to Broadway show tunes and staying busy with other activities. He and Kurt loved to draw and to design things, each often working on different yet related projects. They regarded it as one of their favorite forms of childhood entertainment.

When recently asked about his early memories of creating art, Stackhouse replied: "I did it for play. My first drawings were for play. My first specific memory of art is related to the time I decided to create some modern art—I don't remember if it was on a class trip or what—and I drew one legged, one eyed ducks, with the eye in the center of the head. I just made sort of Paul Klee or Arp-like shapes. I don't know where I might have seen those artists. I must have been 7 or 8 years old at the time. That is the first time I really remember drawing." His next real memory of drawing involved an experience with Don Ray. "I remember up at Peach Lake once. I was a little older, maybe

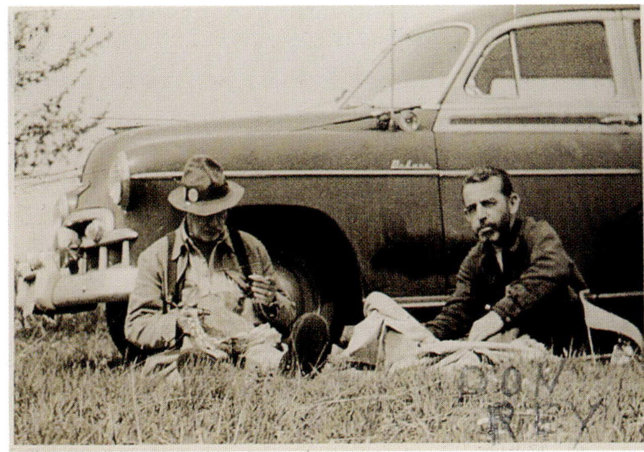

1.17

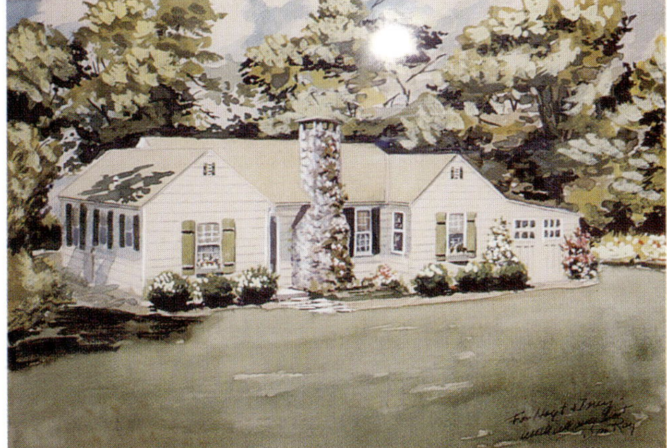

1.18

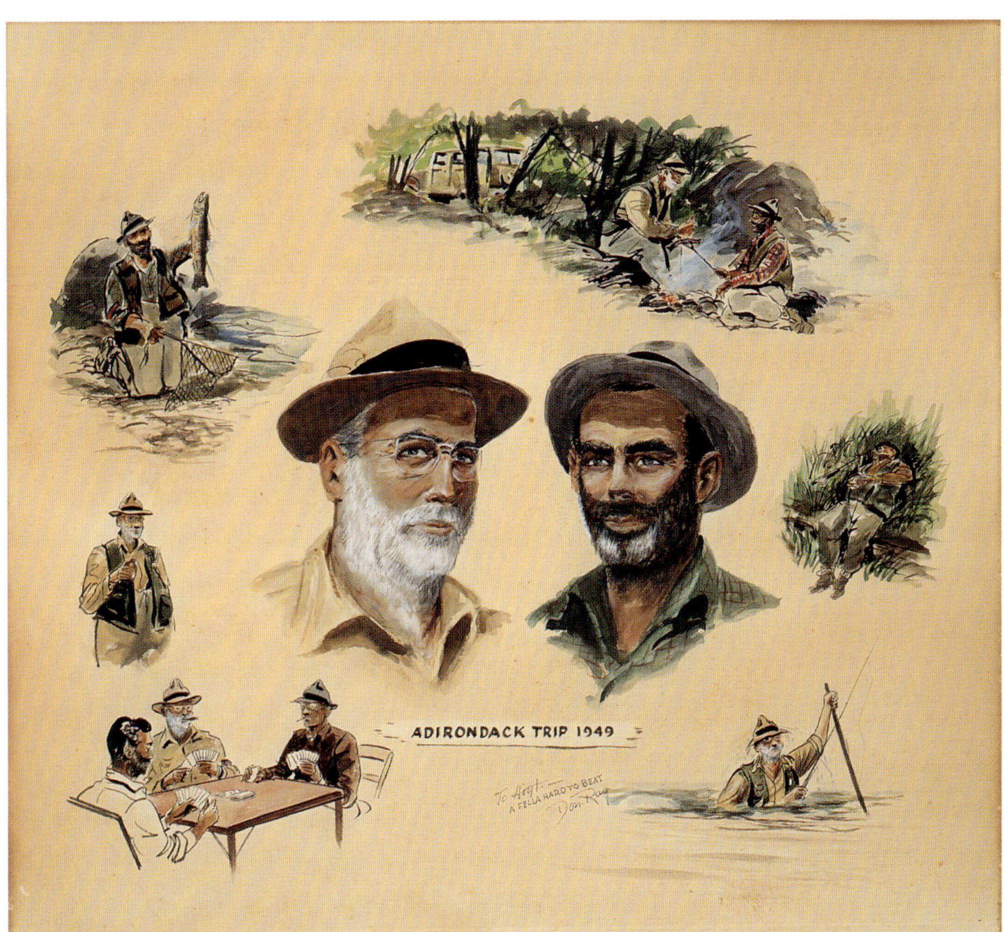

1.19

Hoyt Holland and artist Don Ray at Peach Lake.

Portrait of the summer house at Peach Lake by Don Ray.

Adirondack Trip 1949 by Don Ray, given to Hoyt Holland and inscribed "To Hoyt, A Fella Hard to Beat."

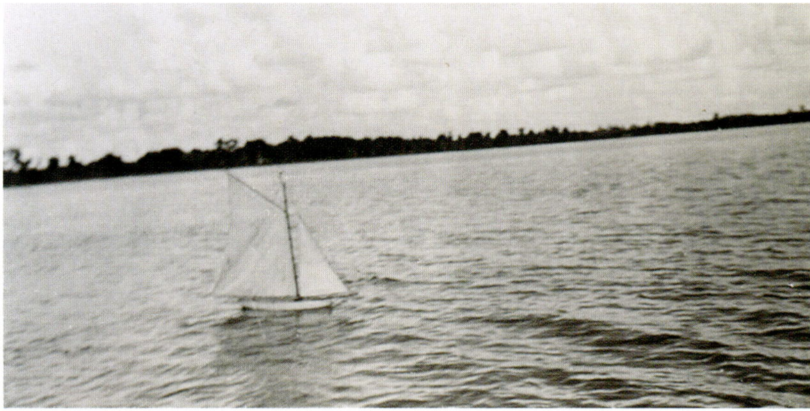

1.20

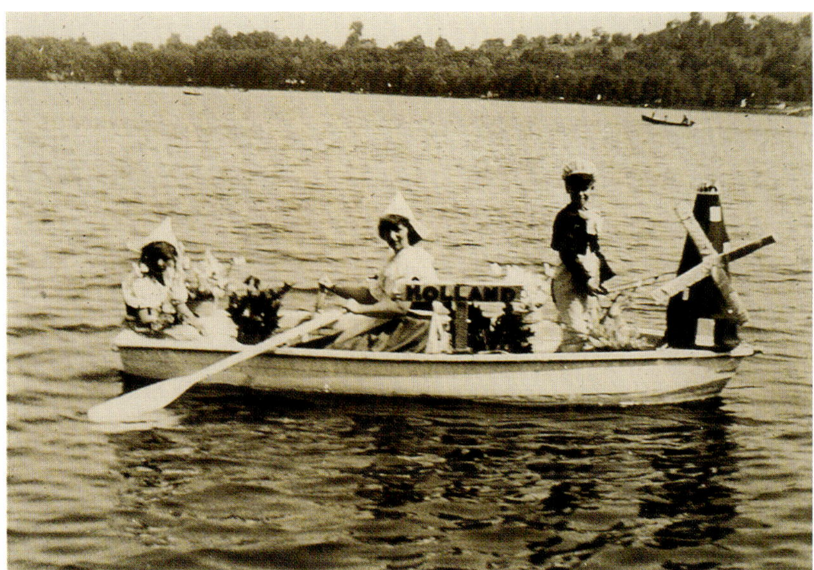

1.21

Robert Stackhouse's sail boat, "Pet."

Robert, his mother and relatives in their boat during the annual Peach Lake regatta.

ten or eleven. I copied a drawing out of *Argosy* magazine, an image of some soldiers, at night with shadows. And I drew that and of course, just drew the shadows as a solid. And Don Ray came up and looked at what I drew, which was good for my age, and said: 'No. No. You don't do that. There are things in your shadow.' Then he took a red crayon and drew over my drawing. It got me very upset. To this day, as an art teacher, whenever I teach drawing, I never correct anyone's art. That is the biggest affront. Tell me, don't show me." Later, Don Ray gave Stackhouse his first formal lesson in technique. "He gave me my first lesson in volume, and I learned it, I remember it. He drew the chest. He drew the chest in a volumetric way, showing me how the rib cage is formed and how to develop three dimensional contour."

"Art was," he now recalls, "part of my play. Every once in a while I would put down my toys and draw a picture. As a child in New York I remember making things. We always had plaster of Paris and papier mache, and I would make conglomerates of stuff. I once made a sponge of papier mache and rubber cement. I made dinosaurs out of clay. Mine were not as elegant as the more refined cardboard ones Kurt made. And I collected British-made animals and figures and I would sometimes make them myself." Through-out his early years he loved to build things, often using the most diverse of materials, depending on what was at hand. "I played with the *Encyclopedia Britannica* a lot and a Lincoln log set. I made a ship of war out of the encyclopedia, then I built the gunnels out of the Lincoln logs." From his childhood play, came an approach that informed the development of his mature art forms. "Later, in Florida, I made wooden models that were basically a piece of paper and some sticks. You glued the sticks down, onto the piece of paper, in a pattern. This is actually the first way I designed *Sleeping King Ascending*." I have a graph paper drawing of *Sleeping King Ascending* with a section of it, then I glued balsa wood sticks down on it, just like I would build a model airplane. The exact same method." (See Figures 3.28 and 3.29).

Underscoring the importance of these childhood experiences, Stackhouse recently stated: "The way I make my art today is not unrelated to the way I played as a child. Of course, seven years of art school training had a lot to do with where I am too." In addition to his experiences at Peach Lake, his creativity was reinforced by trips to the museums of New York City, particularly to his favorite institution, the Museum of

Natural History. "I remember looking at the swords and suits of armor, in the hall of armor, in the Metropolitan. But the Museum of Natural History was my favorite place to go." Despite his early interests, he was not excited by the possibility of visiting the city's art museums, as he recently recounted. "I remember we were going on a class trip to New York once and I thought—I didn't pay attention—because I thought all museums in New York were the Museum of Natural History. We went to the Met and I almost wouldn't get off the bus. I didn't want to look at paintings then. I wanted to see my favorite things, the skeletons of dinosaurs." His childhood interest in dinosaurs and skeletal structures anticipated the importance of the open skeletal structure in his later art forms, especially the wooden skeletal structures, created without surface layers or any type of skin, allowing light to enter and illuminate the work from multiple directions.

Another interest that can be related to his early years, one that continues to the present, is his love of the design and engineering of machinery and modes of transportation, especially boats, ocean-going ships, motorcycles and automobiles. Small boats, wooden row boats especially, were a part of daily life in his summers at Peach Lake. As he grew older he was given his own boat, which was named "Bobby." He also had a wooden model sail boat that had belonged to his grandfather and his mother, named "Pet," one that he recalls with great fondness (Figure 1.20). Summer pageants and holiday flotillas on the lake, complete with decorations and costumes designed and created by his mother and other relatives, transformed these simple boats into imaginative and often mythically suggestive vessels. With these elaborate trappings and conceptual programs, his entries into these boating competitions seldom netted him less than first place awards (Figure 1.21). Later, in Florida, his boating activities would become considerably more adventurous.

Robert also grew up around his family's automobiles, reflecting the great age of classic automobile design. An owner of BMW motorcycles and sports cars, now including a Porsche 944 Turbo, he speaks with fondness of these family vehicles. "I remember the cars. I loved the Buick. It was luxurious inside. It was my great uncle's, who bought it for my great grandmother, as a chauffeur driven vehicle. So it was more plush than a standard Buick. It was a limousine. The back seat was huge." (Figure 1.22) One of his grandfather's favorite vehicles was a specialized type of sporting wagon. "The Woody I loved. I can still smell it. Leather upholstery, the varnish on the outside and the beeswax ...my grandfather had that set up as a utility vehicle. He had a cot in the back and an old table if he needed to tie new flies and little boxes built into it and a rack above for his fly rods. He had tools. He had camping equipment in there. I remember that very fondly....I loved the Woody" (Figure 1.23). Another car that was part of his child-

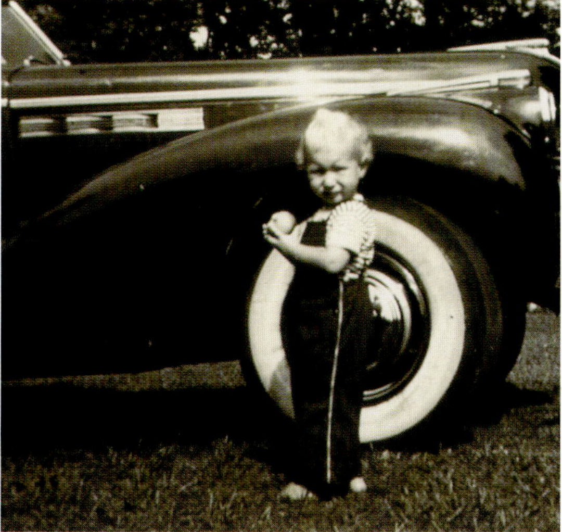

1.22

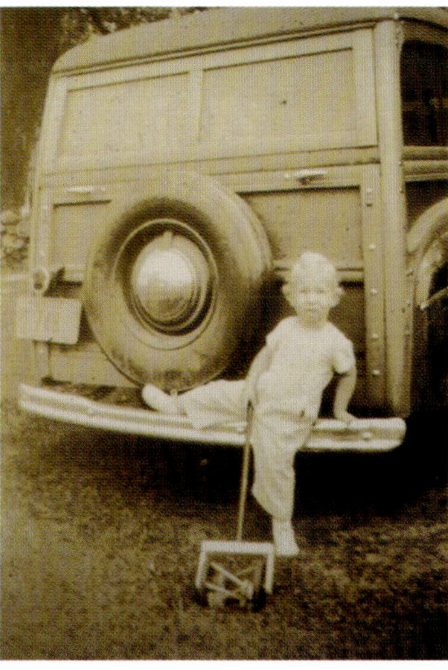

1.23

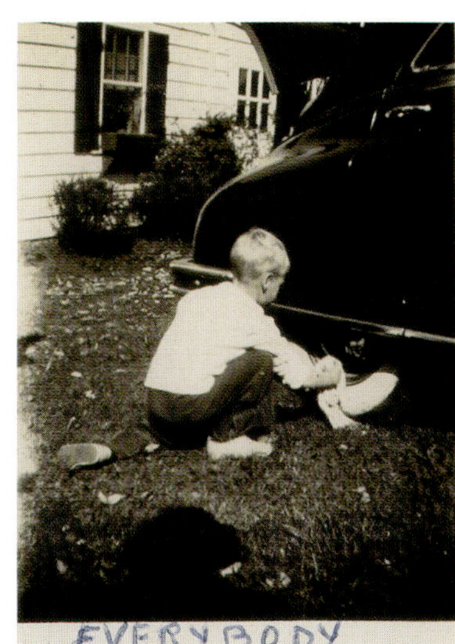

1.24

Robert with the family Buick at Peach Lake house.

Robert on Woody at Peach Lake.

Robert washing the family Packard at Peach Lake.

hood was a classic Packard. "The Packard was great because it looked like a gangster car. It was black and it had a sun visor, a black sun visor" (Figure 1.24). After the war, when automotive production resumed and updated designs and marketing contributed to new automotive sales across the nation, automobiles of the earlier era began to seem dated.[4] In the early 1950s, his grandfather sold his older cars and bought a 1952 Ford station wagon, an efficient vehicle with far less charm that became part of the family's adventures in Florida.

Every fall, the family left the lake and returned to life in the city. The school year began with shopping trips to fashionable department stores in Manhattan and White Plains, where his grandmother bought them new school wardrobes at Lord and Taylor's, Altman's and Arnold Constable's. During Robert's earliest years, his parents took him to see the Macy's Thanksgiving Day parade, usually watching along Central Park or in the Columbus Circle area. At Christmas, Robert's mother took the children, often accompanied by their cousins, to midtown Manhattan to see the holiday shows at Radio City Music Hall and the ice skating at Rockefeller Center. Robert fondly recalls childhood trips to Madison Square Garden for the circus and the rodeo. He also remembers the theater where he saw his first major Broadway stage production, *The King And I*, starring Yul Brynner. Later, as Kurt grew older and more independent, and as his love of theater developed, he sometimes included Robert on trips to see popular Broadway shows. Robert has many childhood recollections of New York City, yet one of his strongest memories centers on a specific trip when he was about eight years old. Riding in the back seat of one of the family's large cars, he remembers traveling along the dock areas of the West Side, on the Hudson River, from 59th Street to the area near Canal Street. Every dock they passed was filled with ships, each lined up, facing him, as their car drove down the highway. He still recalls the scale of these ships with perfect clarity, suggesting one possible precedent for his late paintings and sculptural projects inspired by classic ships including the Titanic, the Queen Mary and the Normandie.

Although he was always equally comfortable in the city and the country, Robert found that the return to their city home often required a period of adjustment. "It was always strange. But I had my friends there, I had more friends in the city. I had my bicycle. We lived on Bronx River Road, which was just a block away from school so I was always at the playground" (Figure 1.25). Not far from his home and nearby school he encountered a neighborhood that reflected the cultural and ethnic diversity that he associates with life in New York. "There was a one way street in Yonkers that stopped when it ran into a cliff, a straight solid wall of granite. I had about eight friends who lived in little houses there, each one was from a different country, including Richard Perrazo, Willie Specht and James Snider. The farther back into their houses you went the more their family's natural language was spoken. There was always a grandparent or great uncle who never spoke English at all. The kids I knew spoke English perfectly. Their parents spoke very broken English." The yards of these houses reminded him of just how far he was from Peach Lake. "I remember that the backyards were all cinder ashes because they all used coal fired furnaces and the cinders were just put out in the backyards. I didn't think anything about this because our playground at school was also cinders. We put on our gym clothes and played dodge ball and if you fell you would be picking cinders out of your elbow for weeks. It was like glass."

At times, Robert felt like he lived in two different worlds, both equally appealing to him, one in this urban context, the other in the world of nature. Like most urban children, he spent much of his time on the streets of the city. "The streets were unsupervised. I had a key and I was on my own much of the time. After school I dropped my books, grabbed my bicycle and went back out."

Throughout the school year he looked forward to the summers at Peach Lake and a return to the extended family who gathered there. Swimming, fishing, boating, picnics, his birthday party, costumed boating competitions and diverse other activities merged into the flow of the annual rituals of summer at the lake. Here he also reunited with his cousins, Susan and Janice, who came from their new home in the Midwest. As he grew older, his grandfather taught him to fly fish and to hunt squirrels. And, each summer, consciously and unconsciously, he experienced life in the natural world that surrounded him at the lake, absorbing a range of impressions that continue to filter into his art. During a 1998 interview in Kansas City, for example, while he flipped through a family scrapbook, he stopped at a photograph showing him on the family's boat dock and commented upon it. "See the wood on this dock? See the wood and how it is peeled? I can still smell that, the smell of sunbaked wood with drying out white paint on it, staying there until it starts powdering. If we go to the Kansas City Art Institute and look at my recent sculptural installation, K.C. Way, that is exactly it—the colors, the light, the use of wood. It offers a connection for me." (See Figure 6.23).

In 1954, Robert left his parents and his family's home to accompany his grandfather and grandmother to live in Florida. After his first year in Florida, he returned to Peach Lake, continuing the tradition that had become so much a part of his life. Many of his interests developed and were given form at Peach Lake. These experiences would be applied to a new environment in central Florida, as he has explained. "I was ready for Florida because of my upbringing in New York. I was a water rat and I fished all the time." Twelve year old Robert left his parents, his brother and his familiar environment with some reluctance, worried about how he would fare without them. Anxious about this transition, he nevertheless looked forward to traveling to the South and exploring the region with his grandparents. Robert would encounter a series of unexpected experiences, some seemingly far removed from the realities of 1950s America, when he moved, leaving behind urban life in New York, to live in one of the most remote places in the country, an isolated fishing camp hidden in the orange groves of central Florida.

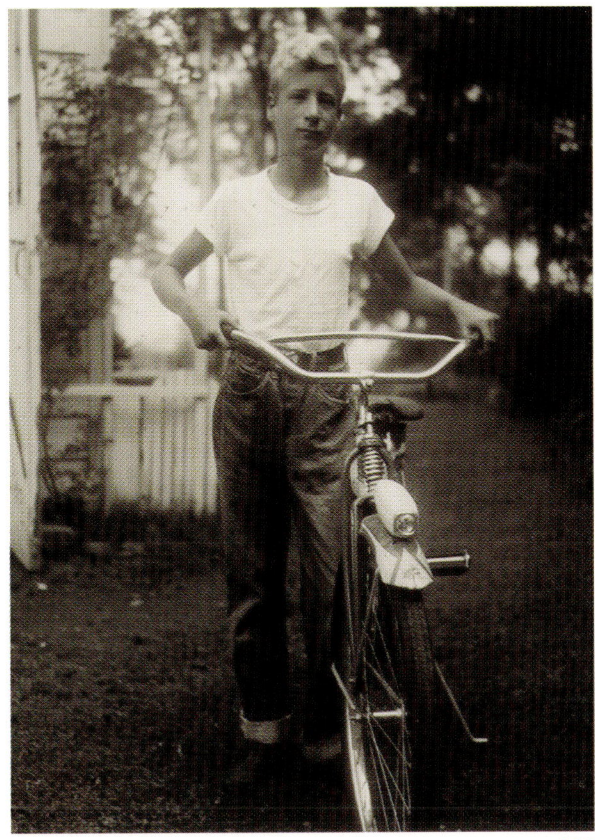

1.25

Robert Stackhouse and his bicycle, Yonkers, New York.

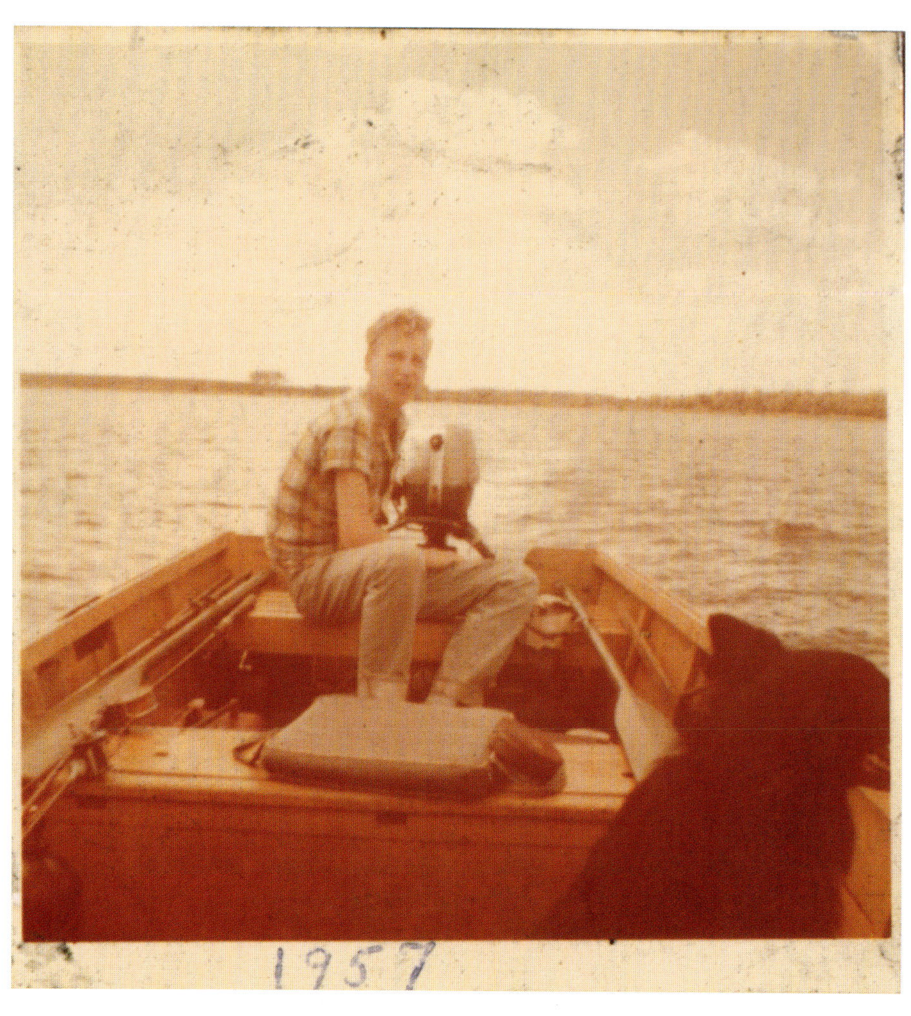
1957

CHAPTER TWO

Florida

For the majority of his first twelve years, except for summers spent at Peach Lake, Robert Stackhouse lived in an urban environment, most of it spent in high-rise apartment buildings. Manhattan, Yonkers and the metropolitan area of New York City served as the geographic center of his family's life. When he moved to rural Florida with his grandparents, he left these urban realities behind. When they departed from Manhattan for Florida, the city's skyline was still dominated by the Empire State Building and the Chrysler Building, icons of 1930s America. However, new steel and glass structures, including Lever House on Park Avenue and the United Nations' Secretariat on the East River, signaled the aspirations evident in New York by this time, architectural symbols that appeared along with the rise of the New York School in painting. Life in the New York metropolitan area, like his summers at Peach Lake with his family, had been crucial to the artist's early development.

At this early age, Stackhouse would not have realized that his experiences on the Hudson River and at Peach Lake had exposed him to the same environment that contributed to the formation of the first American school of landscape painting. The artists associated with the Hudson River School, including Thomas Cole, Asher B. Durand and Thomas Doughty, worked in the Hudson River Valley, and in the Adirondacks, the Berkshires and the White Mountains. Albert Bierstadt, Frederic Edwin Church and the later Hudson River School painters extended their focus to include the West, yet they maintained the earlier artist's reverential attitude toward the landscape. Thomas Cole summarized this philosophy. "Art is in fact man's lowly imitation of the creative power of the almighty." Nature, for these artists, was a reflection of the divine, a form of American Eden that man needed to understand and preserve, as Cole indicated. "We are still in Eden; the wall that shuts us out of the garden is our ignorance and folly." [5] Later, when Robert Stackhouse worked in sites favored by the Hudson River School painters, including Niagara Falls (*Niagara Dance*) and along the river at the Hudson River Museum (*Sailings*), he created works that, while informed by these artists' ways of seeing, were more directly inspired by the spirit and the unique qualities of these specific natural environments.

When he first discovered Florida and its Gulf Coast region in 1954, he did not realize that he had ventured into an area that once attracted artists who brought similar perspectives to the unspoiled landscape of Florida. For many artists active in the years from 1870 to 1930, including painters such as Martin Johnson Heade, George Inness, William Morris Hunt, Winslow Homer, Thomas Moran, Louis Comfort Tiffany and John Singer Sargent, Florida was viewed as a last frontier, a late American Eden. Countless artists traveled, sketched and painted there during these years, bringing the styles associated with the Hudson River School, Luminism, the French Barbizon

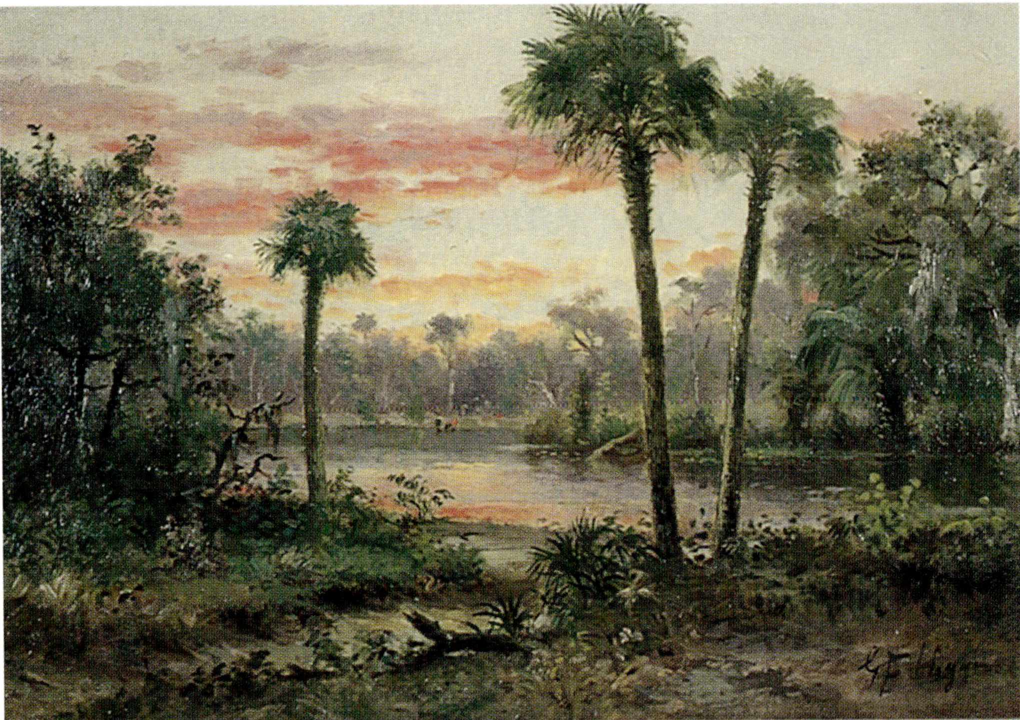

2.1

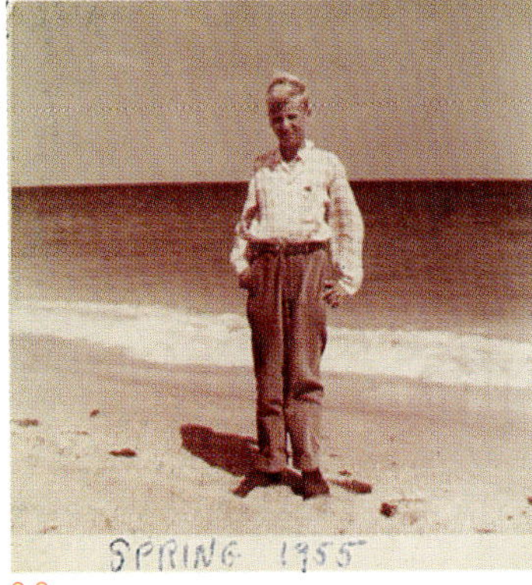

2.2

Palm Grove, Florida
by George F. Higgins
c.1875

Robert Stackhouse on the beach
in Florida, Spring, 1955.

School, Impressionism and Tonalism, responding to the natural beauties, the diverse foliage and the exotic wildlife they discovered in the state. George Inness, for example, known for his introspective and spiritually charged compositions, painted during the 1890s in Tarpon Springs. Winslow Homer visited Florida seven times from 1886 to 1909, painting along the St. Johns River in 1890 and around the Key West area in 1903.[6] The type of unspoiled landscape environment these artists discovered is reflected in *Palm Grove, Florida*, a work George F. Higgins completed in 1875[7] (Figure 2.1). The spirit and diverse realities of this environment influenced Robert Stackhouse's evolution, contributing in significant ways to the development of his mature aesthetic vision.

The environment Stackhouse encountered in the rural areas of central Florida remained essentially unchanged from the conditions known to these earlier artists. As was often the case across the South in the years from 1890 until 1945, change came quite slowly except in the major cities and the winter resorts. Conditions described in *Florida, A Guide to the Southernmost State*, published in 1939 by the Federal Writer's Project of the Works Project Administration, offer insights into the environment Stackhouse discovered in central Florida, conditions that evolved slowly from 1939 until the time of his arrival there. Auburndale, the Florida community where he completed junior high and high school, was concisely described in the 1939 guide. "Auburndale, originally named Sanitaria by the group of health seekers who founded it, was later renamed by settlers from Auburndale, Mass. Large frame residences, orderly groves, and two-story boxlike buildings line the principal thoroughfare." Beyond the city, WPA writers discovered conditions that would change notably in the postwar era. "Groves become less numerous, replaced by stretches of pine woods and lowlands dotted with small lakes. Small farms off the main highway are on paved county roads kept in condition by white and Negro prisoners from near-by county jails."

According to the guide, the nearby city of Lakeland "began with the coming of the South Florida Railroad in 1884; the town was incorporated the following year." Lakeland started as a railroad town and grew into a modern commercial city. "The metropolis of a region growing one-third of Florida's citrus fruit, Lakeland is executive headquarters of large producing and shipping companies...[and] ranks second in the state as a strawberry growing area, and stands high in the production of winter vegetables." Lakeland, the home of Florida Southern College, featured a notable architect's new campus plan that was, in some ways, parallel to the futuristic visions of the World's Fair. "An extensive building program has been laid out by the college, and designs for twelve units, connected by gardens and courts, have been made by Frank Lloyd Wright, one of the most individual of American architects." [8]

Robert arrived in Florida as the state entered an era of unprecedented growth. As a result of this influx, the types of urban and suburban models shown at the 1939 World's Fair would be reflected in the evolution of Florida's landscape environment over the next four decades. During the Eisenhower era, Robert traveled with his grandmother, visiting Florida's older cities, its historic sites and its major tourists attractions, stopping often to enjoy its unspoiled natural environment along the way. Much of what he and his mother now refer to as "the old Florida" they discovered then is gone. Sprawling metropolitan areas, suburban golfing and retirement communities, shopping centers and tourist complexes that annually attract millions of visitors to the state have appeared in their place. Nothing embodies this change more than the Orlando area, centered around Walt Disney World, located only thirty miles from Lundy's fish camp. For many modern tourists and visitors, the old Florida Robert discovered with his family is long forgotten.

The natural and the man-made environment of Florida changed in many significant ways during the years Robert lived in Florida. In 1965, for example, as he completed course work at the University of South Florida, Walt Disney announced plans for a new theme park near Orlando. The centerpiece, Epcot, his "Experimental Prototype Community of Tomorrow," reflected his belief in a future built upon a faith in technology. Epcot also reflected Disney's appreciation of the visions presented in events such as the 1939 World's Fair, as he suggested in 1966. "Epcot...will never cease to be a living blueprint of the future...a showcase to the world for the ingenuity and imagination of American free enterprise." [9] Disney died in 1966 and concepts for the park soon took a less philosophical turn. Since it first opened in 1971, Walt Disney World has served a reported 500 million visitors. [10] In 1996, after opening movie studios and resort hotels on this property, the Disney corporation unveiled Celebration, a new type of residential community that *The New York Times* described as a "post-neotraditional town." Celebration is regulated by "a strict design code that reflects the Southeastern vernacular architecture from the pre-1940s. There are deep porches, gables, dormers, loggia and large-columned porticoes." [11] Ironically, Celebration recreates, at great expense, the type of Southern natural and vernacular environment that was still common when Robert Stackhouse moved to Florida. [12]

Robert and his family participated in this expansive period of development in Florida. The family's move to Florida was prompted by his grandfather's retirement from Continental Baking as well as by a desire to find a more moderate, less stressful living environment. As Robert explains: "My grandmother and my uncle moved to Florida with my grandfather. My uncle and my grandfather went out fishing daily. The first winter there they went to about six different fish camps, on the ocean, on rivers and on lakes. My grandmother became upset and lonely. While they fished she was often left alone. At this same time, my mother was having trouble. She was working for Macy's Department Store in White Plains, not making much money. My father was unemployed at the time." Because of the financial and personal difficulties faced by his parents, health problems suffered by Robert and the isolated conditions endured by his grandmother, it was decided that he should join his grandparents in Florida. For most of his teenage years, Robert lived with and was raised by his grandparents, who became, in essence, his surrogate parents. Kurt, who was completing his last year of high school in Yonkers, remained at home there with his parents. The following year, almost immediately after his high school graduation, he enlisted in the United States Navy.

Initially, Robert lived with his grandparents in the Crystal River area. Soon after his arrival he joined his grandfather on fishing expeditions, an activity he recalls today with fondness. His descriptions of the unspoiled natural world they explored sounds remarkably like the accounts of the region rendered by artists and writers who traveled there at the turn of the century.

> *We went out in the Crystal River, which I dearly loved. Porpoises would come along and get on the bow of the boat, playing with us. We saw six foot long tarpon going up, into the air. We watched the porpoise fishing, diving down, then coming up with a fish jumping into the air with the porpoise following, catching the fish in the air. We looked under the boat and saw manatees underneath us. We saw them. It was called Crystal River for a reason. We went into the harbor near a commercial fishing area to buy cheap jumbo shrimp, then used them for bait. Later they put an atomic power plant on the river and it is all muddy now. But that was my first exposure to Florida.*

Three months after he arrived at Crystal River, his grandfather suffered a stroke. The family waited for him to recuperate,

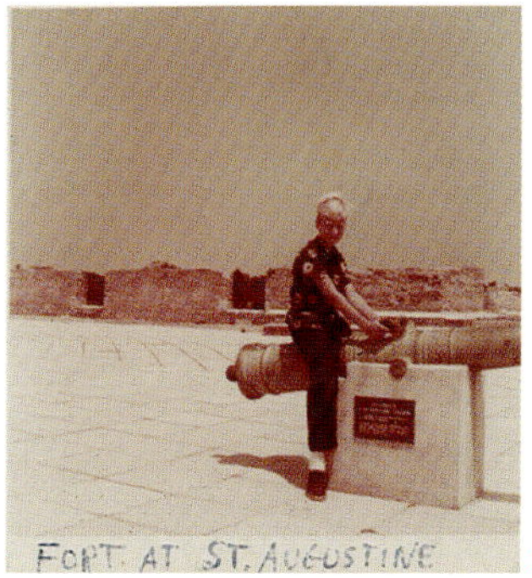

2.3

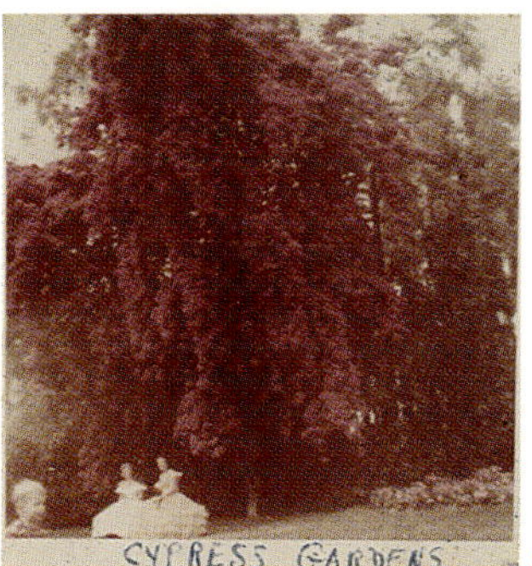

2.4

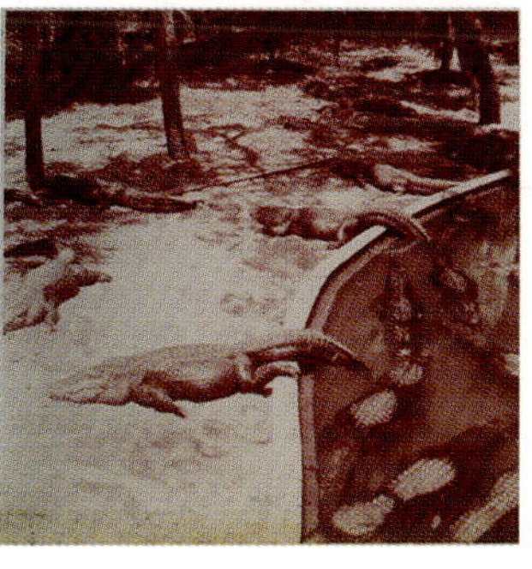
2.5

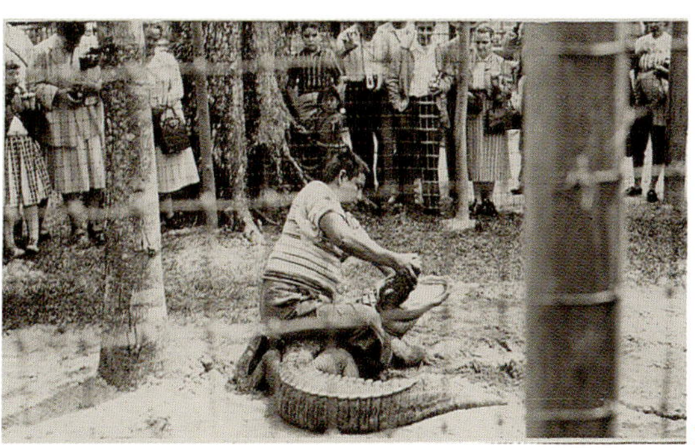
2.6

Snapshot views of Robert's early Florida trips –

St. Augustine
Cypress Gardens
Alligator Pond
Alligator Wrestling

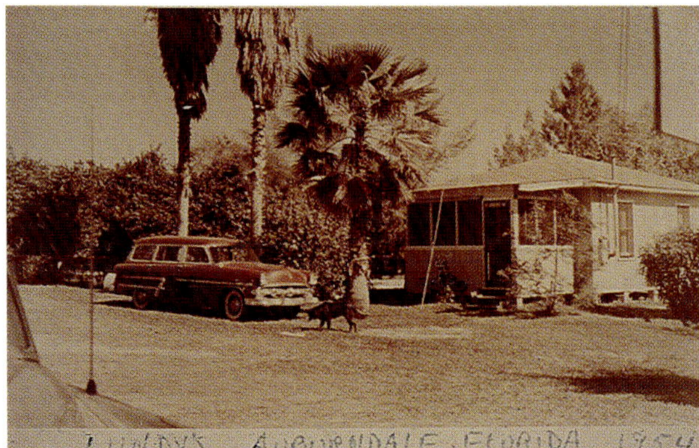

2.7

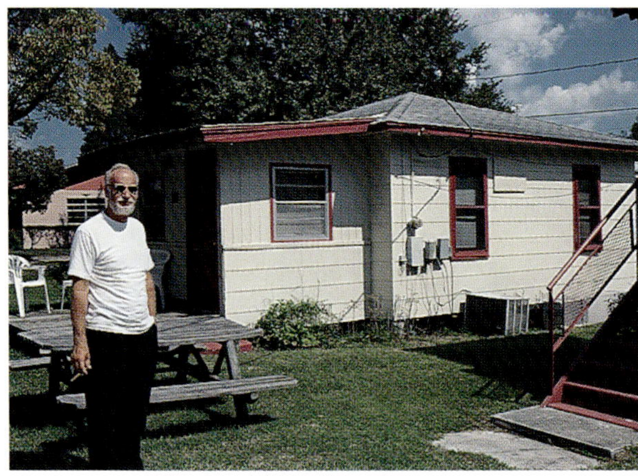

2.8

First House at Lundy's Fish Camp, near Auburndale, Florida, 1954.

Robert Stackhouse revisits first house at Lundy's Fish Camp in October, 1998.

then moved to Lundy's fish camp, located outside of Auburndale. After only a short time there, however, they moved to Palatka, on the St. Johns River. The stay in Palatka was quite brief, only about a month, so he was not enrolled in school there. Nevertheless, he attended two different schools during this first year in Florida. When it was decided that he would return to Florida the next year, his grandparents agreed to settle in one place so that Robert could have more stable educational life. During his first year there, he and his grandmother also visited many of the famous tourists sites in Florida. "We went all over Florida. Any vacation, any weekend, we would go off." The family scrapbook is filled with pictures from this period, the 1954-55 school year, including trips to Daytona Beach (Figure 2.2), St. Augustine (Figure 2.3), Satsuma, Cypress Gardens (Figure 2.4) and Marineland. As he grew increasingly familiar with the nature and the actual behavior patterns of the alligators he discovered around their fishing camp, he also saw alligators held in captivity at many of the most popular tourist attractions they visited (Figure 2.5 and 2.6).

Their first house, one of about twelve buildings located in Lundy's camp on Lake Julianna, was a simple wooden structure. A 1954 photograph shows this one-story wooden cottage with a screened porch, surrounded by palm trees and orange groves in the distance, with his dog, Blackie, standing near his grandfather's station wagon (Figure 2.7). Robert, his grandparents and his uncle Homer lived in this two bedroom house for several seasons. When the artist and the author returned to Lundy's fish camp, in the fall of 1998, this house still looked essentially the same (Figure 2.8). In fact, except for the addition of some new mobile homes, a combined store and bait shop, a small swimming pool and replacement concrete docks, the camp had changed remarkably little from his childhood. However, the orange groves are mostly gone now, replaced by new housing units. Across the lake, where avocado groves once stood in the distance, expensive new lakefront homes are being built. From this little house, located only about one hundred yards from the docks and the lake area, he set off every morning for school in Auburndale. And, every day during the school year, after the long bus trip back from Auburndale, he was dropped off on the main road and began the walk home.

> *I liked it. When I left the school bus I had a half mile to walk through an orange grove, down a dirt road—a truck path really. You never knew what you would encounter there. The fish camp had monkeys. They had a parrot. And, they had about three hundred ducks. Lundy also owned a bakery in Lakeland. He had a father-in-law from Arkansas, an old man, who also lived there. Every day, someone from Lakeland brought doughnuts from the bakery and the old man called the ducks, like they were pigs, to feed them. Suddenly, a white cloud would form across the lake as three hundred Muscovy ducks flew to be fed by him. However, I remember that by my third year there were only three ducks left. The alligators ate them during the night. You would be asleep and suddenly you heard the sound of ducks, then the sound of an alligator, finishing the kill. Wildcats also killed some of the ducks. We heard the terrible screams of wildcats at night as well.*

When he returned to the camp after school each day, he was primarily dependent upon himself for play and amusement. Unlike his life in Yonkers, where he had many friends and a wide variety of diversions after school, he was left on his own most of the time at the fish camp. There were rarely other children at the camp when summer ended, just the older residents, most of them of retirement age. As a result, he learned to make up games and to entertain himself. "I turned more to my imagination there. And, I did a lot of fishing. I often just went out in my boat, just to drift in the water, which I enjoyed." A regular activity centered around taking his rowboat out into the lake to hunt for snakes and alligators (Figure 2.9). Standing on a platform in the lake during the fall of 1998, he recalled a period when local hunters searched for a large, old renegade alligator, inspiring him to initiate his own alligator hunt, armed with a BB gun and his Brownie Hawkeye camera.

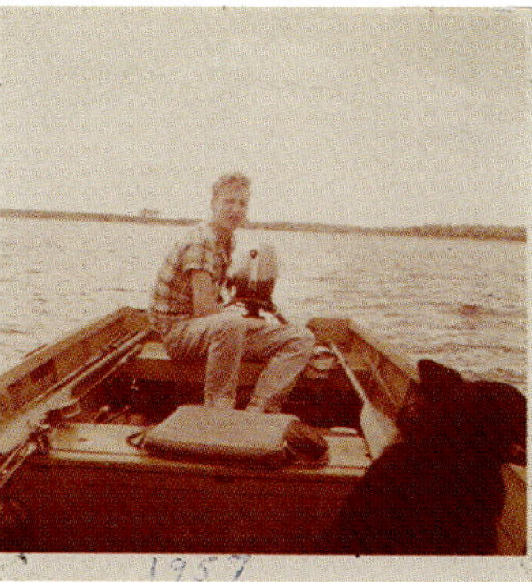
2.9

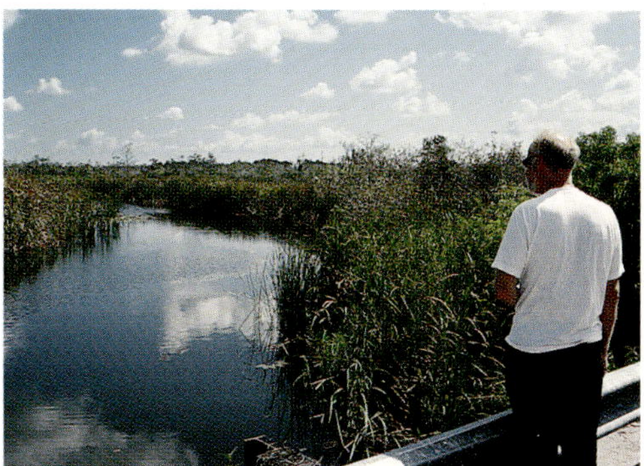
2.10

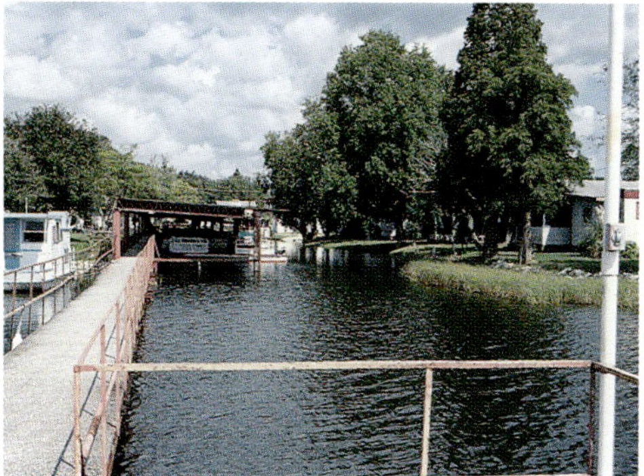
2.11

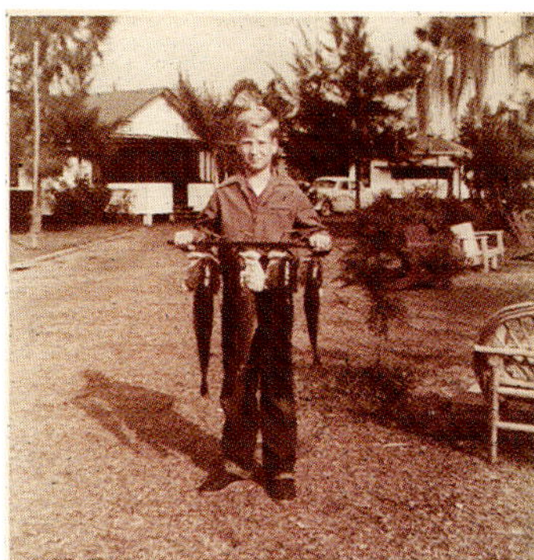
2.12

Robert Stackhouse, with Blackie, in fishing boat on Lake Julianna, Florida, 1957.

Robert Stackhouse at lake channel he initially created on Lake Julianna, October, 1998.

View of boat dock and adjoining marsh area, where snakes once flourished, at Lundy's Fish Camp in October, 1998.

Robert Stackhouse with fish at Lundy's Fish Camp.

> *That alligator lived across the lake and I knew where to find it. I always rowed my little boat to the far side of the lake, to where the alligator lived. Sometimes he would be on the left side of the boat, and I tried to row up close to him, to get a good picture with the Hawkeye camera, because it did not have a telephoto lens on it. Then he would disappear and I would continue looking for him and he would suddenly appear on the other side of my boat. He just stayed far enough away from me. I did this a countless number of times. I came home from school, jumped in the boat and rowed out there. It was almost always the same alligator, an old bull alligator, about twelve feet long. He was bigger than my boat. I did get my pictures of the alligator. And, as far as I know, they never caught that alligator, even though they used helicopters and air boats in their search.*

He became so obsessed with this alligator search that he decided to find its home by discovering a path or channel through to the adjoining lake, where he was convinced it lived and avoided the hunters. In fact, he spent almost one entire winter digging with his hands, in waters filled with snakes and baby alligators, through a thicket of water hyacinths and other plants, looking for the alligator's channel into the next lake. As he dug he discovered that bogs had developed around the plant forms, creating a type of natural dam, holding back the darker waters of the adjoining lake. Finally, after months of determined effort, he created a large channel, one that still exists, linking the two lakes (Figure 2.10). He remembers watching the much darker waters of the adjoining lake, created by the decaying of the old cypress trees in that lake, as it began to pour into Lake Julianna. His quest for this bull alligator, a determined search and series of encounters with this large and potentially dangerous creature, suggests much about Stackhouse's basic nature, including his later efforts to confront and understand snakes, the creatures he most fears, as well as his determination to confront barriers, often literally head-on.

If alligators form one significant part of his memories of life at the fish camp, water snakes formed an even larger, and more frightening aspect of his life there. Although he had known snakes at Peach Lake, they were usually not as poisonous or as dangerous as the snakes on Lake Julianna and in the central Florida region. He remembers growing up here and listening, every morning, as his uncle went down to the edge of the dock area and shot large cottonmouth snakes. Standing on the edge of that same dock recently, he looked into the water, describing the teeming water moccasins and cottonmouth snakes he regularly saw in this area, located next to the camp's only swimming beach. Then, pointing to a small marsh area just across from the dock (Figure 2.11), he recalled another incident that left a lasting memory.

> *One day I stood over there with my BB gun, at sunset, with the sun going down, when all the snakes began to come out of the breakwater. They were swimming in all directions and I was shooting at them with my BB gun. Of course you cannot hit them in the water with the BB gun, but I kept on shooting at them anyway. I was standing in the tall grass, just over there, and suddenly I realized that all the snakes*

were coming into the tall grass with me. I was wearing only a bathing suit, standing there barefoot. And I had to make a dash through this tall grass, that was now filled with snakes, some of them five foot cottonmouths. I was terrified. I held my breath, looked around and finally started running as fast as I could, hoping to get away. And I did. And I've never forgotten that experience.

Snakes became a constant, and often frightening, part of his daily existence. He once decided to fish on the rocks of the breakwater, located at the end of the dock, just across from the tall grassy area where his earlier confrontation with the snakes had occurred. "Once again, I had on only a swim suit. I sat there, fishing, and I sensed a movement just to my left, over my shoulder. I turned around and looked, and I was staring down the throat of a cottonmouth. I was about twelve years old and it was my first year here. Luckily, this snake was all wrapped up around a concrete block in the breakwater and could not rapidly untangle himself. His head was all that was available. So I looked down, saw him unwinding himself, and I got up and moved away quickly. It was part of my introduction to the wildlife of the area." Walking past his second home at the camp, he remembered another chilling incident. A small dirt road ran behind this house, between the house and the orange groves, near the camp's garbage dump, which attracted all kinds of animals. Pointing to the concrete block house before us, he described this event. "Each bedroom of the house had a back doorway, with a screen door, facing out toward this road. One night, in the summer, when we just had the screen door closed—luckily it was latched—the door started making a banging sound, a regular, rhythmic thumping sound. We went back, looked, and saw a large cottonmouth, stuck, half way in and half way out of the door. He couldn't go forward or backward. Fortunately, that door was locked."

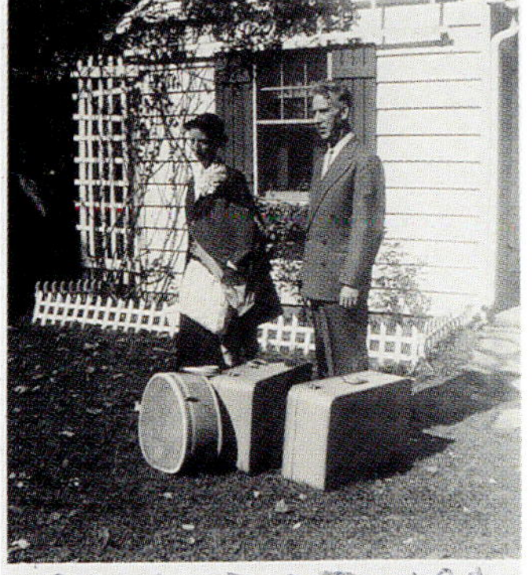

2.13

Robert Stackhouse's parents preparing to leave New York for Tampa, Florida, 1955.

As his school schedule allowed, he spent time fishing and getting to know his grandfather better. Because his brother Kurt was older, he had received more direct attention from his grandfather, who had always seemed somewhat aloof to Robert. Now, as the only child in his grandparents' environment, he grew closer to his grandfather and learned more about him, including how skilled a hunter and fisherman he actually was (Figure 2.12). He also grew more familiar with his grandfather's friends, including many of the famous baseball players, most of them from the Detroit Tigers team, who stayed in nearby Lakeland for spring training each year. He recalls, with humor, how he returned to the camp one day and saw his grandfather, still recuperating from his stroke, sitting with someone in a swing on the dock area.

I remember coming home from school one day and my grandfather was sitting in the swing, and Billy Martin was sitting next to him. They were both swinging on this little swing. My grandfather chewed tobacco, Beechnut, always Beechnut. And on the forward motion, about every ten times, he would spit into a little hole. Then, Billy Martin would alternate, and he would spit into the hole. And neither said a word. I was just vaguely aware of who Billy Martin was. I knew he was a notorious Yankee but he was with the Detroit Tigers then. I joined them on the swing and the three of us would be swinging, not saying a word. Finally, Billy said that he had to go to the ballpark, patted me on the head, and said "Great talking to you Hoyt. See you next time." And grandfather would nod, and spit into the hole, and kept on swinging. They were good friends.

After his first year at the Florida camp, Robert returned to Peach Lake with his grandparents and spent the summer with the rest of the family, maintaining their annual ritual at the summer house. There, as in the past, he enjoyed exploring the lake and the woods, as well as spending time with his cousins, relatives and his summer friends who continued to return to Peach Lake from across the country each year. His parents, his grandparents, his brother Kurt, all came together in these last summers on Peach Lake. After his first summer back at Peach Lake, there was another change in the family. His parents, after long discussions and much consideration, decided to move to Florida to be closer to Robert and to his grandparents. His mother and father left New York and moved to Tampa in October of 1955. As the summer season at the lake ended, his grandparents closed the house and loaded up their station wagon for the drive back to Florida.

His parents, who sold their furniture and most of their household goods, packed their luggage and prepared to embark upon a significant journey, one that would end their long years of living in New York. A family snapshot shows them dressed and ready for the journey, their bags before them, standing in front of the lattice and wooden walls of the Peach Lake house (Figure 2.13). Their new home, another wooden structure with lattice, was located at 1107 S. Albany in Tampa. After moving to Tampa, his parents found new jobs. His father located a position with another bakery and his mother went to work for a downtown department store, building upon her experiences at Macy's in New York. To maintain the stability of Robert's schooling in Auburndale, after his grandparents decided to remain at Lundy's camp, he continued to live with his grandparents. On weekends, his parents took a bus from Tampa to Auburndale, where they spent time with Robert and the rest of the family, establishing a commuting family relationship that was maintained throughout his high school years. Phyllis Stackhouse still remembers these long bus trips because of the racial encounters that occurred because of segregation. Blacks, who were required to ride in the back of the bus, were commonly threatened by the drivers if they crossed into the white section of the bus, creating a constant level of tension and conflict on these long rides to and from the city.

Even as Robert grew older and more independent, especially after he learned to drive and spent more time with his school friends, he continued to learn from his grandfather, especially about fishing, hunting and natural events. He recalls that once, after his grandfather's stroke, he took him out to watch an eclipse and, though it was difficult for him to talk, he tried to explain what was happening to Robert. In high school, after Robert started to hunt with his local friends, his grandfather asked about the nature of these hunting trips and about their safety precautions.

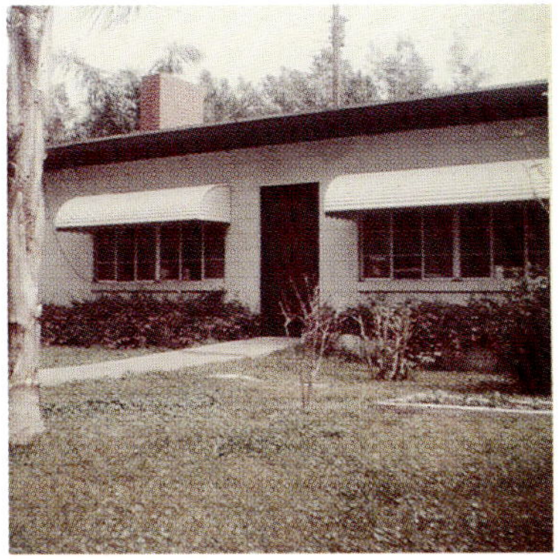

I told him that we hunted coots and doves. We hunted for coots in the water, and sometimes we stepped into a gator hole. I said that I worried about snakes and gators but the other guys didn't seem to mind, so I just followed along. He was concerned about that. And I also went dove hunting. He asked how I did that. I said that we went out into the fields, and we squatted down behind palmettos. He asked if anyone had been bitten by a rattlesnake. And I said that no one talked about it. The next day, when I came home from school, there was a pair of aluminum rattlesnake guards, the type that you fit from the knee down over your boots. And he told me to wear them because rattlesnakes thrived there. After one hunting trip, I came back and took my boots off. Then I took off the rattlesnake guards. When I looked down at them there was a double puncture mark and a stain coming down. I had been hit by a rattlesnake and didn't even know it!

2.14 Lundy's Fish Camp, second house.

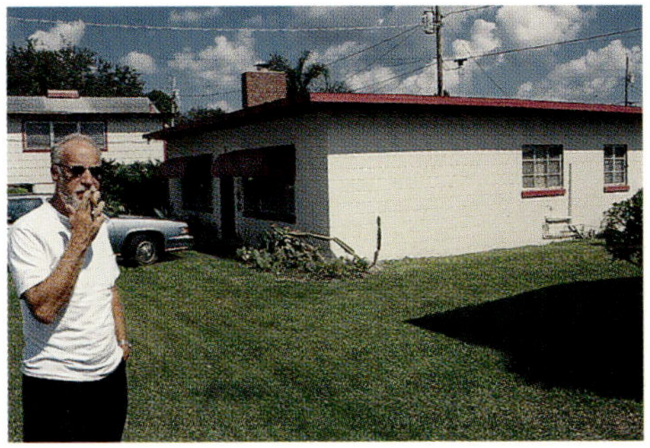

2.15 Robert at the second house in October of 1998.

After the first few seasons at Lundy's, and after the construction of a large new camp recreation hall, his grandparents moved into their second home there, the building that had formerly been the camp's recreation hall. This structure was made of concrete block and was larger than the first house, though it lacked the vernacular charm of that wooden structure. Here there was more room for them, though Robert continued to share a bedroom with Homer (Figures 2.14 and 2.15). The family lived in this building at the camp until Robert finished high school in 1960. And, although he could have gone to high school in Tampa, where his parents lived and the teachers were better, he was convinced by his family that it was best to complete the program in Auburndale. And, although he was in a seemingly remote location, the ability to drive when he came of age gave him a new sense of freedom and mobility. The ability to drive allowed him to cultivate friendships with other students and to develop a social life away from the older adults who populated the camp.

Like radio in the years before the war, television served as a way to connect the highly isolated regions of the South, linking viewers to news events and emerging issues in the nation's mainstream culture during the Eisenhower era. Robert remembers that when he first arrived at the camp the only television set was in the Lundy cottage, a fact that contributed to bringing the camp residents together to watch popular programs. He recalls seeing Elvis Presley's famous censored (from the waist down) appearance on the Ed Sullivan show on this black and white television in the Lundy cottage. Initially, television reception was limited where they lived. After the completion of the camp's new recreation building, and his family's move to the building next door, television became a more regular part of his life. The new building had a television he watched often, one he identified as the ABC set, because a new ABC affiliate station broadcast a signal strong enough to reach them at Lundy's. "We watched the ABC programs because they were more fun to watch. They had James Garner in *Maverick* and those types of shows. We watched variety shows and sports. I also became a Washington Redskins fan down here, because it was the southern-most football team broadcast on television. CBS carried football, so we saw every game the Redskins played." During their last years at the camp, he watched the console television his grandfather purchased for their house.

Like other members of his generation, television connected him, even in his isolated home in a Florida fish camp, to the same popular entertainment and cultural figures as the other children of his day. It also made it possible for him to become aware of the same popular heroes and the emerging icons of the baby boom generation. It also exposed him to developing national issues including presidential political campaigns and the emerging civil rights movement that was causing radical changes in the social patterns of the South. In 1954, when he came to the South, schools, libraries, parks, and other public facilities and amenities, including water fountains and restrooms, were still segregated. Signs designating "colored" and "white" were seemingly ever present. Like most children who attended public schools in his region, Robert was enrolled in a segregated junior high and high school in Auburndale. On the weekends, when his mother and father came to Lundy's from Tampa, they told stories about the ongoing tensions created by the segregation of passengers on the bus. Phyllis Stackhouse remembers the beginning of luncheon counter sit-ins and peaceful demonstrations by civil rights workers at the Tampa department store where she worked. While Robert was aware of these issues, he recalls that his life at Lundy's and at the high school in Auburndale seemed to have been little affected by them. However, both he and his mother remember having a difficult time understanding and adapting to the segregated system they encountered after they moved to Florida, especially because it was so different from the conditions they had known in New York.

During his senior year in high school (Figure 2.16) he purchased his first car, a 1954 Chevrolet convertible, with money

2.16

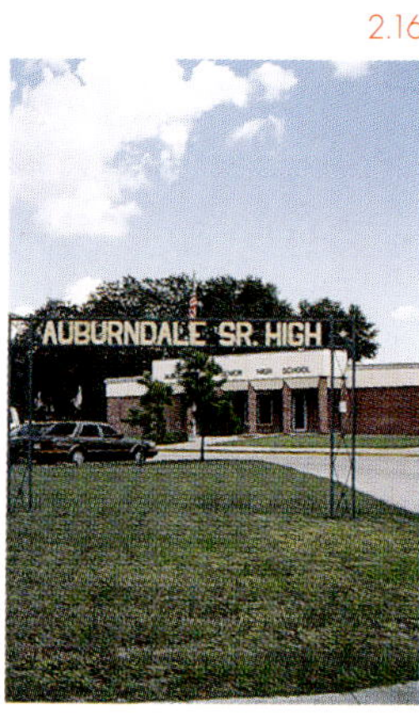

Auburndale High School, October, 1998.

2.17

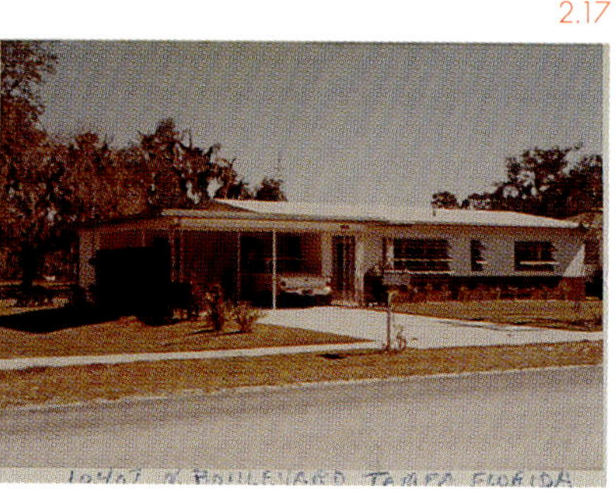

New house of Phyllis and Gerald Stackhouse, Tampa, Florida, 1960.

2.18

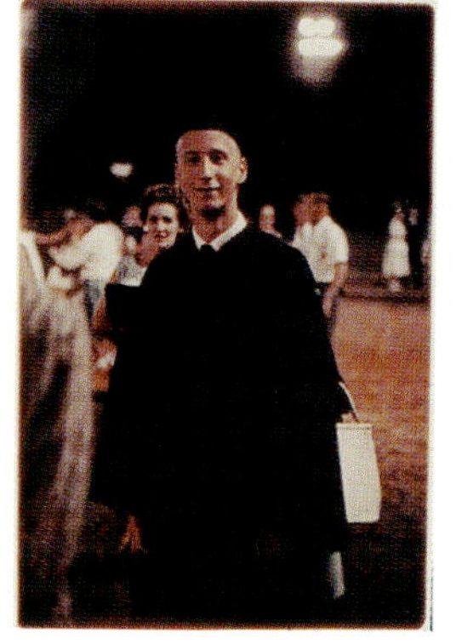

Robert Stackhouse high school graduation photograph, June 9, 1960.

2.19

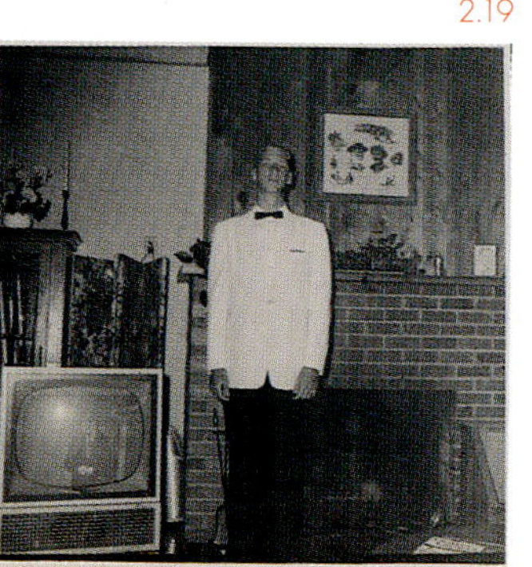

Robert Stackhouse prom night photograph at Lundy's Fish Camp house, 1960.

he made working with his friends at a Publix supermarket in Auburndale. Because of the car, he was able to become involved, for the first time, in after school activities including the Key Club, the junior Kiwanis club. He went out for the school baseball team because of the encouragement and continuing influence of his friends on the Detroit Tigers baseball team. To the surprise of his team, the equipment he used in high school baseball was of professional quality because he had been outfitted by his friends on the Detroit Tigers. With some prompting from other students, who knew about his abilities to draw, he also joined the school's yearbook staff, becoming its art editor. Earlier, when he was about sixteen, he had taken a shop class that included engineering drawing. Because it was the only class he got an A in during his high school years it caused his grandfather to plan the specific direction of his future college career.

> *My grandfather thought that I was architecturally inclined so he brought me a beautiful mechanical drawing set. Because my brother, Kurt, did not go to college—my grandfather was very disappointed in that—he was going to make sure that I went to college. So he said that he was going to sell the Peach Lake house and that the money from the house would be used for my college tuition. I was very upset over this. I didn't want him to sell it. But he thought I was going to be an architect. So I enrolled as an architect at the University of South Florida. And I was immediately told that I did not have the math required for the program. I was an architect for about two hours at the university. My advisor would not even allow me to sign up for the program. I didn't have the math.*

During the 1959-1960 school year, his senior year and his last period at Lundy's, change came quickly to Robert and his family. In November of 1959, his grandfather, who had a history of heart trouble, died following a heart attack at the fish camp. After his funeral, his grandmother began to consider a move from the camp and a reunification with her family in Tampa, after Robert's graduation. In January of 1960, his grandmother and his parents purchased a new ranch house in Tampa, the house where he would live during his college years. In many respects this house, located at 10407 N. Boulevard, was a Florida version of the type of suburban dream house so desired by Americans in these years. A low ranch house, constructed of concrete block, with an attached carport, it was surrounded by small front yard and a more expansive back lawn area. As evident in a scrapbook photograph, the move to this house, and the purchase of a new compact American car, a Ford Falcon, put his parents into the mainstream of contemporary American suburban life, marking how far they had come from their Yonkers apartment building (Figure 2.17).

On June 9, 1960, the family gathered for Robert's graduation from Auburndale High School (Figure 2.18). A snapshot of a tuxedo-wearing Robert, taken on the night of his prom, captures a quietly significant moment in his personal history. There, in the living room of the fish camp house, standing next to a console television set and a gun case filled with his grandfather's hunting rifles, before a fireplace with a Don Ray painting hanging over the mantle (now in his collection), he appears to be poised between a distinctive past and a very different future (Figure 2.19). Here, shortly before he and his grandmother left Lundy's, he paused between life at that rural fish camp and the transition to life in Tampa, where college and a return to living with his parents, in their new home, would change the pattern of his daily life.

During this period he had become much closer to both of his grandparents, and his grandfather would remain one of the most influential figures in his life. Building upon his earlier experiences at Peach Lake, the move to the fish camp had advanced his deep connections to the orders of the natural world, including his skills in boating, fishing and hunting. He also had advanced his appreciation of indigenous vernacular architectural forms, often similar in the rural South to those he had known at Peach Lake. During these years, with his grandfather's tutelage, he became increasingly knowledgeable about specific plants, animals, snakes, alligators and the other creatures indigenous to Florida and the Deep South. His observations in the natural world of Florida, including his awareness of its diverse light conditions, colorations and patterns, and the weathering effect of nature upon man-made structures, all influenced his mature aesthetic vision as well as his use of natural materials in his art. During these years, Robert Stackhouse came to a much deeper understanding of the natural world. At the same time, he also came to possess a much deeper understanding and acceptance of his own nature, an

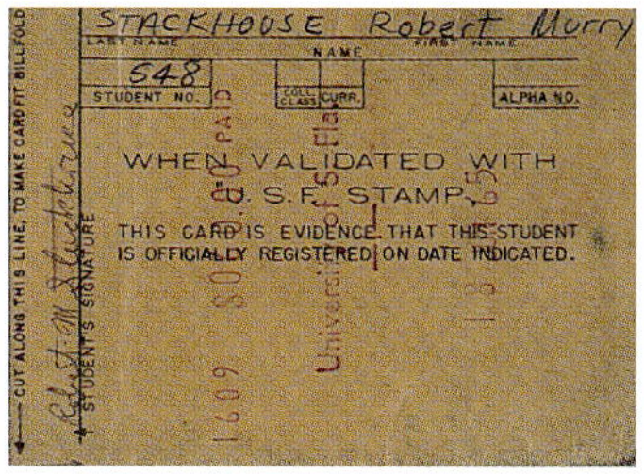

STACKHOUSE Robert Murry
548
WHEN VALIDATED WITH U. S. F. STAMP
THIS CARD IS EVIDENCE THAT THIS STUDENT IS OFFICIALLY REGISTERED ON DATE INDICATED.

2.20

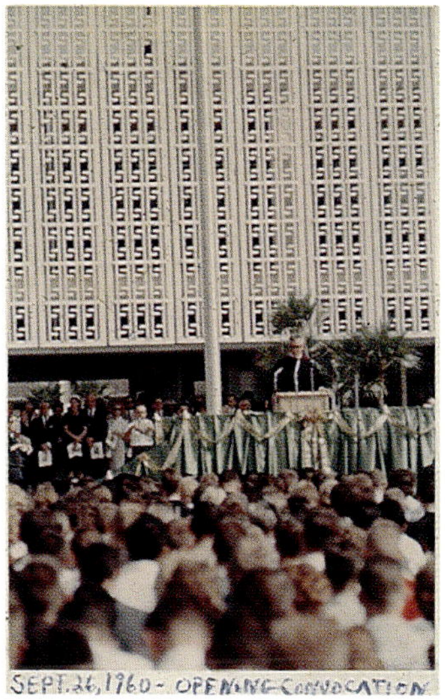

SEPT. 26, 1960 - OPENING CONVOCATION

2.21

Student identification card at the University of South Florida with charter student #548.

Opening convocation ceremony at the University of South Florida, September 26,1960.

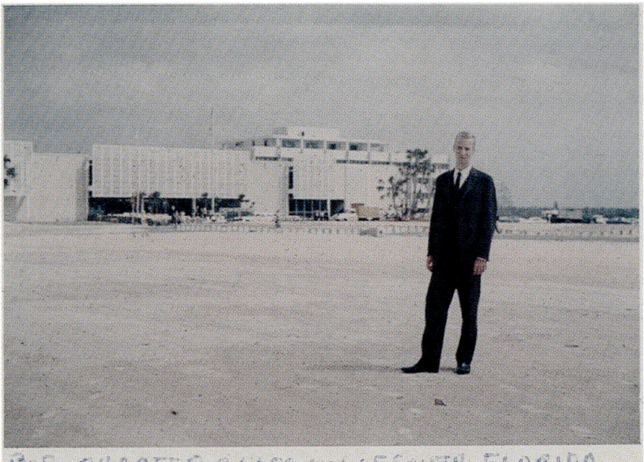

2.22

Robert Stackhouse at the University of South Florida, beginning of first academic school year, September 26, 1960.

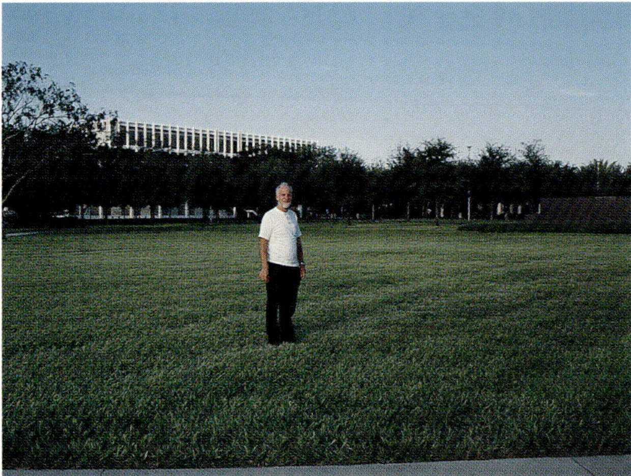
2.23

Robert Stackhouse at same location in October, 1998.

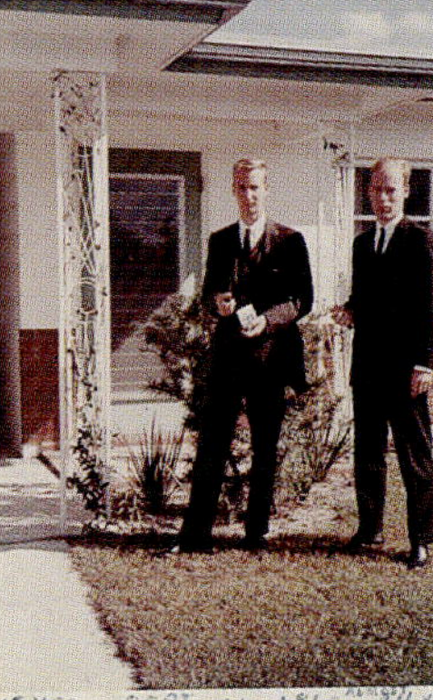
2.24

Robert and Kurt Stackhouse, Tampa, Florida, September 26, 1960.

understanding that would be used to significant ends in the evolution of his artistic and teaching careers.

When he enrolled in classes at the University of South Florida in the fall of 1960, he became a member of the university's charter founding class. In a uniquely contemporary moment in Florida's history, he entered college life at a totally new university, on a new campus, one that would expand during the years he spent there. He still prides himself on his student number, #548, reflecting his status as a member of the school's charter class (Figure 2.20). A snapshot taken at the convocation ceremonies on campus, on September 26, 1960, shows a crowd gathered before the school's contemporary administrative center (Figure 2.21). A second image shows Robert standing, wearing a dark suit, in a seemingly vast empty and treeless field, with this same building in the distance, suggesting a sense of the scale and the newness of the campus (Figure 2.22). A recent photograph of the artist in this same location shows the extent of the changes evident on the USF campus since 1960 (Figure 2.23). As he recalls, dress codes were stricter then, requiring USF students to wear sports clothing and dress shoes, even though the sidewalks were unpaved, causing female students to complain about the damage to their shoes and outfits as they plodded through sand and dust on the developing campus. On that same day in 1960, an historic one for both the school and the Stackhouse family, he posed before his parents' home with Kurt (then 24), who also wore a dark suit and white shirt for the occasion (Figure 2.24).

Robert's photograph on the grounds of the USF campus suggests the vast possibilities of a new university, and also captures a specific moment for the future artist. He stands, dressed in a three-piece suit, about to embark upon the freshman year at a new college campus, very much in the spirit of the era that would begin with the election of John F. Kennedy in November of 1960. During that fall, as the traditions of the Eisenhower era gave way to the beginning of the sixties, as the space race advanced at nearby Cape Canaveral, and as college students staged sit-ins and demonstrations across the South to protest racial inequality, it was clear that a new era was beginning. Within this context the absence of an established campus and a series of campus traditions, though challenging and quite different from older private and state universities elsewhere, offered distinctive opportunities to students who were interested in helping to shape the future of a new institution.

Robert Stackhouse was uniquely suited for the conditions he discovered at the University of South Florida.

After learning that his lack of skills in mathematics prevented his enrollment in the architectural program, Robert signed up for art courses at the university, seeking a way to apply his creative abilities in an appropriate alternative course of study. By the end of his first year at USF, he found himself surrounded by friends he described as individuals "who were more the creative side of the world rather than the pragmatic side." And, after his first year on campus, he discovered that he would be able to obtain a superb art education because of the arrival of a new leader for the art program. Harrison Covington, who became the head of the art department during his second year, was, as Stackhouse recalls, "the most surprising of all. He talked me into staying at USF, in the fine arts department. He talked me out of going to the University of Florida and getting a major in commercial art, because I was listening to my parents, who worried about how I might survive as an artist." Covington had come to Tampa from the University of Florida campus in Gainesville and had been charged with the responsibility of creating a first class university art program. He was, as Robert emphasizes today, the right person for the position and its responsibilities, and he would become a significant influence upon the evolution of Robert's artistic career.

> *Harrison was a painter. He always wore a suit and his hair was very closely cropped. He was actually a reserve Air Force pilot, a fighter pilot. He was also very Southern and offered me my first encounter with an educated, sophisticated Southern gentleman, from the Old South, from the old money South. He had the easy accent, the easy way of speaking that I find so melodious. Yet, he was also our tormentor. He didn't like beards or long hair and he could be very authoritarian. He could let us know, in no uncertain terms, his displeasure with us.*

Reviewing the evolution and the history of this art department, Harrison Covington recently recalled that when he arrived on the campus in 1961 the art classes were offered in a basement room in the student center, across from the pool room. Because all art classes were taught in the same room, the faculty had to move furniture in between classes, reconfiguring the room to fit all their teaching needs. And, because both members of the previous art faculty left after the first year, perhaps realizing the enormity of the challenge they faced, Covington and Wes Houk, the other new professor of art, founded a completely new program for the art department in the 1961-62 academic year. Covington based his program upon the art department model familiar to him from the Gainesville campus of the University of Florida, with certain modifications, recognizing that USF, as part of the same state system, was guided by an administrative structure similar to the one used in Gainesville. Designs for the art department building had been completed by state Board of Regents architects and construction was underway when he arrived. Consequently he had little voice, other than minor modifications, in the functional design of the structure that serves to the present day as the center of the university's art department.

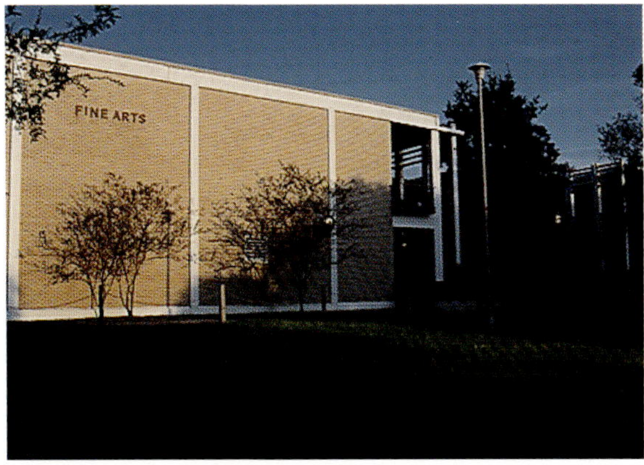

2.25

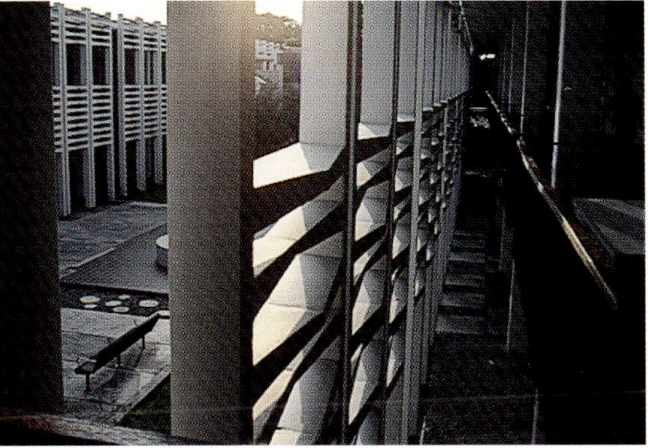
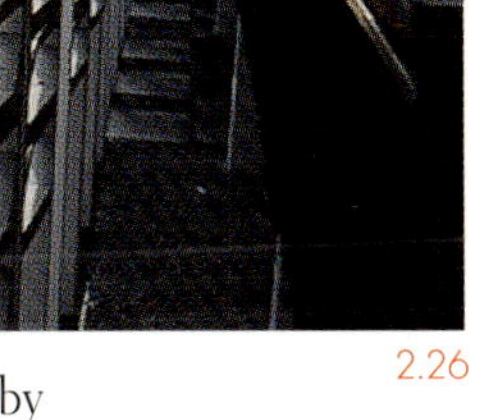
2.26

Art department building at the University of South Florida (exterior and courtyard views).

Covington is proud of the success of the art department, particularly because he envisioned the development of a program that would attract students from the region, many of whom lacked exposure to art or art museums. "One of the things that always made me feel good about the program," he recently explained, "is that as a native of Florida, in fact, as a native of the county, I knew that many of the students would never have been able to go to college. They never would have gone if the university had not been established. That was important to me because many of these people would have missed their chance for an education."[13] He also designed a program that was intended to take art students out of the isolated studio environment, exposing them to the offerings and intellectual stimulus of a broader university environment. "In this program, they had to get out and learn something in the other departments and programs on the campus. My feeling was that if you are not a reasonably well-educated person you will probably not have much to say as an artist. And I thought it really worked well. Right away, our students started winning every prize available in the state." Even as undergraduates in a new art department, his students were able to compete with the best in the state.

One unique aspect of this art program is the strength and consistency of the support it has enjoyed from the university's presidents, beginning with John F. Allen, the first president of USF, who was a very culturally oriented academic leader. This commitment was evident in the design of the original campus plan. The initial structures on the campus included the administration building, the student center, the library, the science building, the theater and the nearby art department building (Figures 2.25 and 2.26). Covington even recalls that Dr. Allen "called us his football team, meaning that we were to be the ones responsible for stirring up interest in the community, to serve as an outreach into the community. He thought that we could accomplish what most people expected from a sports program." Covington felt confident because of this support and was encouraged in his long range goals for the program. This included the initiation of a gallery program, at first in the library building, then later they obtained a dedicated art gallery. USF became, Covington recalls, the first university in the Florida state system to have a full-time gallery director and full gallery program.

The new fine art arts building was not completed until Robert's third year on campus, so he and his fellow students, including David Haxton, David Dye and Susan Tessum first studied art in the student center classroom. As they developed and as the program matured he and David Haxton were given keys to the art room by Covington, who also assigned them to serve as assistants in the first art gallery, located in the library. Covington and Wes Houk gave them increasing authority in the operations of the art gallery and its programs, including the planning and installation of exhibitions, as Robert remembers. "Many of the shows were those old ASA shows, packaged exhibitions. We got a Modigliani show once, and Covington told us to unload the truck, arrange the show, then hang it." From that point on, they were given keys to the new art department building and spent most of their time, day and night, working in the building. Because his parents lived close to the campus, Robert could not qualify for campus housing and was therefore unable to live on campus with his friends. However, they were all regular visitors to his family home.

One of Covington's primary teaching directives was, as Stackhouse remembers, for students "to find out what the latest thing in art was and then do it. For example, we would obtain current issues of *Arts* or *ARTnews* magazine, and search for specific subjects for our projects." A significant result of this process was that Stackhouse and his fellow students became, in spite of their geographic isolation from the New York art scene, quite well informed about current trends and directions in the contemporary art world. This became particularly important for Stackhouse after he left Florida and moved closer to the center of contemporary art activities. As Covington himself recently noted, his approach to teaching was not intended to encourage his students to work like him. He employed the principles and techniques of the Abstract Expressionists in his teaching, even though he worked as a figurative painter. "Basically, my approach used Abstract Expressionism because issues of structure were central for me, and that was my approach to using Abstract Expressionism. The reality of the material, the reality of the surface, the action of the painting—all of that was real, not illusional in painting. And we taught drawing, stressing the conversion of three dimensional objects to a two dimensional surface."

Covington felt that is was important for the students to be able "with authority, to put down what you see before you." He described a desired result in his methodology that would have lasting implications for Robert Stackhouse and his career. "To me, this is something that is an irreplaceable activity for an artist, this ability to understand the relationship between the three dimensional real object and the two dimensional reality of that two dimensional surface and the tension between them. To me, that is extremely important. And then to couple that with painting where you are allowed to concentrate on the reality of the materials, of the surface, with a combination of ideas. Then they could go off, in any direction they wanted to go." And, as he noted, Robert's movement into sculpture, and David Haxton's evolution toward computer imagery proved the flexibility of this teaching foundation. The last thing Covington wanted, he emphasized, was for his students to emulate his paintings. "What you gave them, hopefully, was the type of instruction that they could build upon, take off from or discard if they liked."

Robert concentrated on becoming a painter during his years at USF, finding that he had little interest in or patience for art courses in subjects such as ceramics and printmaking, as he recalls. "Of course, the context of the day was if you went to art school, you learned to paint. Everything else seemed minor." The teachers who were most influential upon his pursuit of this goals were Covington, Wes Houk, an artist who also taught the program's art history classes, and Robert Gelinas, a painter and jazz musician. Wes Houk's survey of art history, which used H.W. Janson's *History of Art* as a text, offered Robert a basic structure for understanding art history. However, rather than starting from the distant past, he and his friends found it more interesting to begin with a study of prominent contemporary artists and trace influences back from them. At first, they were more interested in de Kooning's work than Pollock's, because they were more oriented toward figurative painting, but then they began to explore issues in Pollock's art. "Because of our interest in Pollock, we became interested in Arshille Gorky, then Kandinsky, then Picasso, then Goya, then Titian, and then Carravaggio. There were certain artists we favored greatly, including Goya. If we liked an artist we went back into art history, searching for the artists who influenced those figures. In essence, we created our own approach to art history, finding reasons to study different directions and figures in the history of art." Later, Pop Art became an influence, followed, briefly, by Op Art as another influence. During his senior year, Robert Rauschenberg's combines and Rauschenberg's sense of structure interested Robert, as did the drawings and prints of Jasper Johns, especially those prints that used primarily black tones.

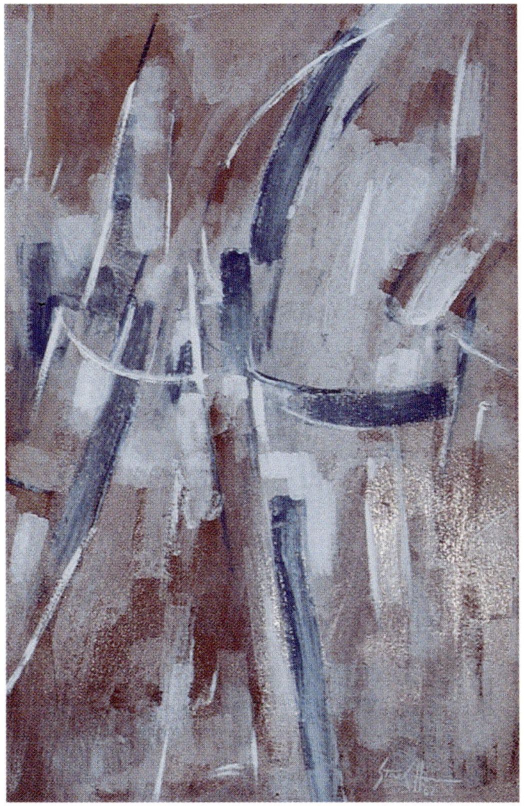

2.27

Robert Stackhouse, *Untitled* painted at the University of South Florida.

A distinct disadvantage to the newness of their school, and its location, was the difficulty that was encountered in bringing contemporary artists to the campus. After he had become dean of the school, Harrison Covington decided to create a reason for artists to come to the university. He arrived at an important decision, which Stackhouse described. "He and Donald Saff created Graphic Studio and gave artists a reason to come to Tampa. Covington and Donald Saff had everything to do with the founding of Graphic Studio. It was always Covington's dream. He said that this school would not work without visiting artists, and we have to have the very best." Two visiting artists that Robert remembers are the sculptor Richard Stankiewicz and the painter, Friedel Dzubas, who was involved in the activities of the New York School. Of the two, Dzubas made the more lasting impression. "He was part of that scene. He had a major impact upon us because he was a real, living artist. He could tell us stories about New York, and about the Bauhaus. He had been a student of Paul Klee at the Bauhaus." Stackhouse and the other students wanted him to tell them about the major figures of the New York school, rather than about his own work. But Dzubas did have an influence on Stackhouse. "He let us in to his studio, and he let us watch him paint. He told me that in a painting sometimes the most important activity took place right on the edge. That had an affect on me. I've always remembered that. And I think that is one of the reasons I take the borders of my works so seriously, because of Dzubas."

A teacher who had a significant impact upon Stackhouse and the other students, with both his art and his personality, was Robert Gelinas. "He came in and he was cool. He wore sun glasses at night. He wore a beret. He played a string bass. He was a jazz musician. He talked about art and music. He cross referenced. He was a perfect transitional figure from the beat to the hippie culture. He was in the center of the group there, between the faculty and the students." Gelinas taught at Memphis State University before coming to Tampa and, before that, completed graduate art studies at another Southern university, the University of Alabama in Tuscaloosa, with William Christenberry, a friend who would later become Robert's teaching colleague at the Corcoran school. [14] One of the greatest strengths of the art program in Tampa was a result of its intimacy, of the strong ties between the faculty and the students. If someone taught a great literature course, they all signed up and participated, becoming immersed in the subject, then discussing related topics at the "Scrounge Lounge," a room in the student center where many of them congregated. Professors and students intermingled, often crossing over into other departments, exchanging information, nurturing the true notion of a university environment, something Stackhouse still recalls with fondness. This type of teaching and faculty interaction would influence his own approach to teaching, and to his arts administration activities, when he went to the Corcoran.

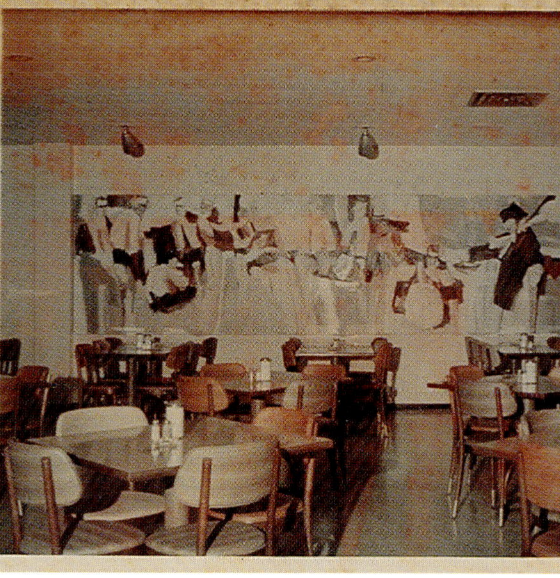

Mural painted by Robert Stackhouse in the student center at the University of South Florida, 1963.

2.28

Beginning in his sophomore year, Robert and his art student friends entered their art in a diverse range of local and regional art fairs and exhibitions, eventually competing around the state and in other parts of the South with a wide range of highly accomplished artists. In fact, the exhibition histories and the prizes these students amassed during their undergraduate years at USF was quite remarkable, contributing to Covington's pride in his students as well as to the growing regional reputation of the USF art department. In the spring of 1962, a photograph presenting Robert standing next to his award winning entry in the university's "Family of Man" competition was featured in the campus edition of the Tampa newspaper. This untitled montage, based upon a dream, won the $25 top prize in the competition's graphic arts division. Later that same month, one of his works, *Omega*, was included in the Young Floridians statewide competitive art exhibition. In July of 1962, the Campus Edition of *The Tampa Times* included two captioned photographs devoted to the art students' Botega Club summer exhibition and auction in the UC Gallery Lounge, one with Robert featured before his painting, and another reporting on the sale of their works, with mention that Robert sold three paintings. A short time later, a photograph of him appeared again in the paper, showing him accepting a $50 check for his first place winning entry in the "All University Painting Contest." [15]

In 1963, his work, titled *From a Coldwater Loft—Collage*, was one of 78 paintings selected from 786 entries for inclusion in the Florida State Fair Fine Arts Exhibition. The following year, two of his works, *Que and Blue It*, were featured in the State Fair exhibition. Notably, in 1966, when two distinguished New York curators, Dorothy Miller from the Museum of Modern Art, and Henry Geldzahler, from the Metropolitan Museum of Art, juried the exhibition, they selected two of his works for inclusion in the exhibition, *Early Joust on the Counterpayne* and *The Glories of Brien the Brave*. During 1964 and 1965, his last two years at the university, he was included in many exhibitions, received numerous awards and prizes and was often photographed and written about by the reporters and art columnists of the Tampa newspapers. A major award came in November of 1964, when his painting, *Wind Against Tomorrow*, was selected as the first prize winner in the Florida Golf Coast Art Center exhibition in Clearwater. The prize was accompanied by a $200 cash award (the equivalent of a semester's tuition at the time). By April of 1965, as he was completing his undergraduate program in Tampa, and as his work was hanging in the All-Florida Undergraduate Painting Competition at USF, along with his colleagues, Susan Tessum, David Haxton, and Michael Rowland, the arts writer for *The Tampa Times*, Hans Juergensen, offered one of his many numerous printed observations on the progress of these students' early careers. "As painters, Fonchon Lord (New College), Susan Tessum, Robert Stackhouse and David Haxton (USF) are rather well known through statewide exhibitions. These artists...have competed with the best painters in the Southeast and have done well." And, Juergensen concluded with specific praise for Robert's latest work. "Robert Stackhouse's *Circle-Three and Twelve Each*, a collage with delicate reds and blues on circular white design, is a personal favorite of mine." [16]

Most of these early works have been lost or destroyed over the years. One work that still survives, an untitled 1962 painting created over a political campaign poster backing, shows Covington's influence upon his work and his early experimentation with color, gesture and abstract composition (Figure 2.27). Looking at this work recently, the artist noted the suggestion of an A-frame like form in the painting, perhaps anticipating his well-known and widely reproduced A-frame structures and paintings of the 1970s and beyond. A popular gathering place on campus served as the site of Robert's first large public work of art, a painting that would leave a lasting impression on the USF faculty and students for years, in part because of its prominent location in the cafeteria in the student union. Another mural, also devoted to a jazz theme, was completed by David Haxton in an adjoining cafeteria area shortly before Robert began his project, the second of two murals designed for these spaces. Robert was commissioned to paint a site-specific mural for this space, a work that was 25' long, which he completed by the summer of 1963 (Figure 2.28). Its size suggested the scale that would become an increasingly significant element of his work, both in his later paintings and in his sculptural projects. He was paid $250 to create the mural which remained on view for almost fifteen years, until the cafeteria was remodeled with the rest of the student center. The mural disappeared at that time. Reflecting the influence of Gelinas and his appreciation of the jazz scene, Stackhouse used poets and jazz musicians as the subject of his mural. In a work that merged abstract and figurative elements, a drummer, bass player and pianist fill the right half of the composition, while a seated poet and a gathered audience fill the left half of the work.

In 1963, while discussing his mural concept with Lurlene Gallagher, a Tampa newspaper writer, he referred to the rapidly evolving history of the USF program, describing the campus "before it had sidewalks and grass." He also explained his love of art and his current painterly concerns. "Actually, there's more money in commercial art but my real love is creative art. I'm now particularly interested in action painting in which the artist uses violent brush strokes to express himself." [17] His reference to commercial art acknowledged his earlier inclination toward that field and also reflected his commercial activities at the time, including his creation of graphic images for the promotional materials of Edward's Pipe and Tobacco Shop in Tampa, an ongoing project that paid him with tobacco for his pipes. The USF mural was stylistically related to other easel paintings of the period, including two figurative works that combined the abstract, gestural brush work of the New York School painters, especially de Kooning, with a sense of the emerging Pop Art sensibility and a returning figurative tradition that was indicative of his own professors' paintings as well as California painters including David Park and Elmer Bischoff. One painting showed a seated female figure, shown from the rear (Figure 2.29). Another presented a clothed female, seated in a chair, with one leg crossed, facing the viewer (Figure 2.30).

During his undergraduate years, two other important influences emerged, both with significant implications for the evolution of his career. The first was his association with the University's theater department and his involvement in its theatrical productions, centering on his work on stage and set designs. In addition to taking many credit hours of theater courses, again mostly related to set design and lighting, he helped design and build many sets for the university's popular theatrical programs. From this he learned much about the creation of rapidly fabricated props, and, equally important for his own work, he learned the significance of designing projects that could be easily and rapidly disassembled for moving and storage. Here, away from the strong natural light of the surrounding

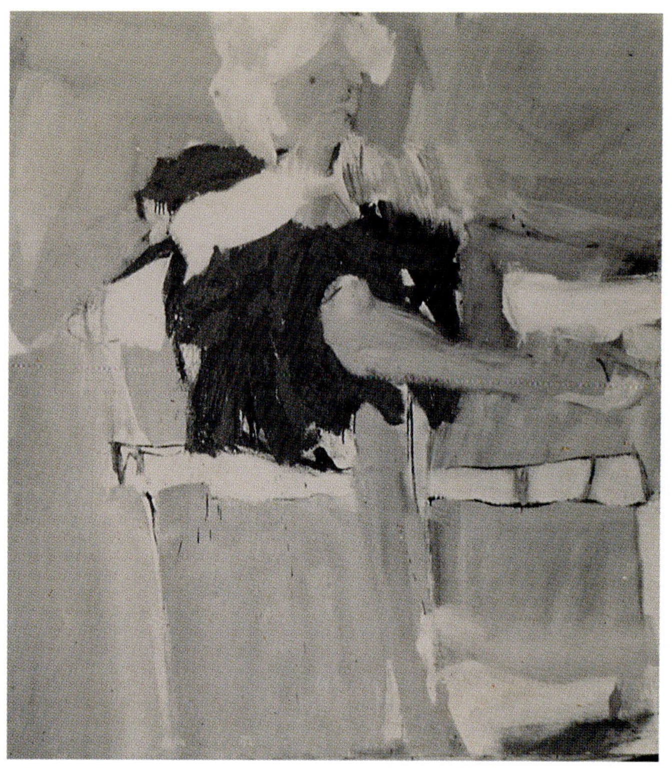
2.29

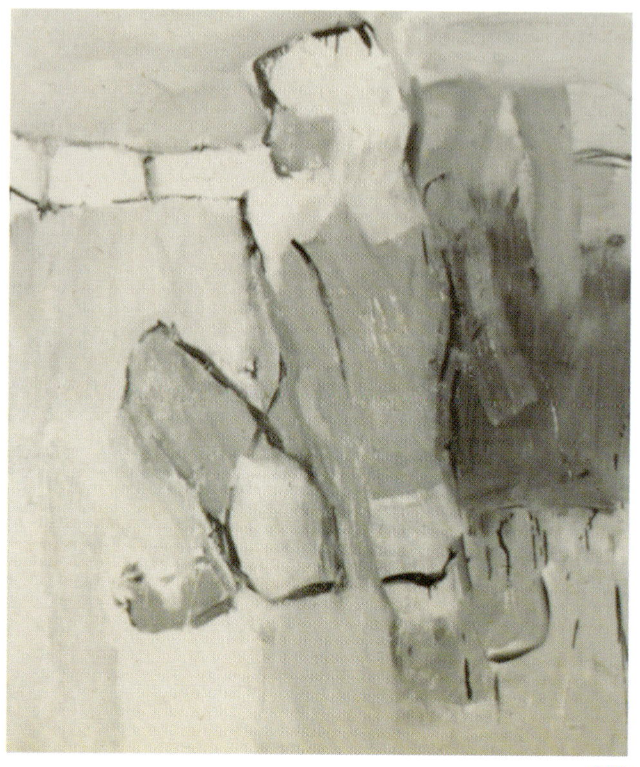
2.30

Robert Stackhouse untitled paintings, University of South Florida.

Florida environment, he learned much about the use and effects of artificial light and shadows, developing skills that would prove important in his later sculptural projects and the design of his gallery installations.

Robert's involvement with the theater department was also reinforced by the relationship he developed with Dolores Novoa, another undergraduate student who was studying to become a dancer, and who would become his wife after they moved to Maryland. Dolores had moved to Tampa from Washington, joining her father and her Cuban American family, who maintained strong ties to Tampa's Cuban American community, centered in the Ybor City area. With Dolores and her family, Robert expanded his previous explorations of Cuban culture in Ybor City and Tampa, learning much about the Cuban contributions to the cultural, social and economic history of Tampa and the Gulf Coast region. Ybor City had long served as the manufacturing center of the nation's cigar industry, and was known as an area where both Italian and Cuban immigrants came to work and live because of the cigar industry.[18] Dolores's interest in dance and performance art, along with Robert's experiences in theater, would contribute in significant ways to the development of his work with theaters and performances in Washington.

After Robert's class of art students, the first in the school's history, graduated and moved on to professional careers, the school continued to develop and expand under Harrison Covington's leadership. A graduate program in art was added. Building upon the success of the university gallery program, a University Art Museum was planned and completed, offering a center for the presentation of exhibitions and related activities. Today it is directed by one of Harrison Covington's former students, Margaret Miller. Over the years, Stackhouse has donated an example of each of his many prints to the collection of the university's Contemporary Art Museum, giving it a complete master set of his existing printed works. Additionally, nearby Graphic Studios continues to expand its operations and its national reputation, regularly bringing major national artists to the studio and to the campus of USF. Robert Stackhouse has created prints with Graphic Studio and has returned to the campus as a lecturer and a visiting artist, maintaining his strong ties to the campus and its art department as the school has grown to include a population of 35,000 students in 1998.

During the eleven years he spent in Florida much had changed, in his life and in the life of the state. His experiences at the fishing camp, at Auburndale High School, and at the University of South Florida all contributed to his personal and professional development. Although he would later return to New York to live and work in the SoHo area of Manhattan, and though he later became best known as a New York artist, Stackhouse's years in Florida were crucial to his evolution as an artist. (Figure 2.31) His family remained in Florida, where he spent as many years of his early life as he had in New York. Maryland and Washington, both locations on the northern fringe of the South, would serve as significant stops, as locations for important stages of his professional development, prior to his return to New York, in 1975.

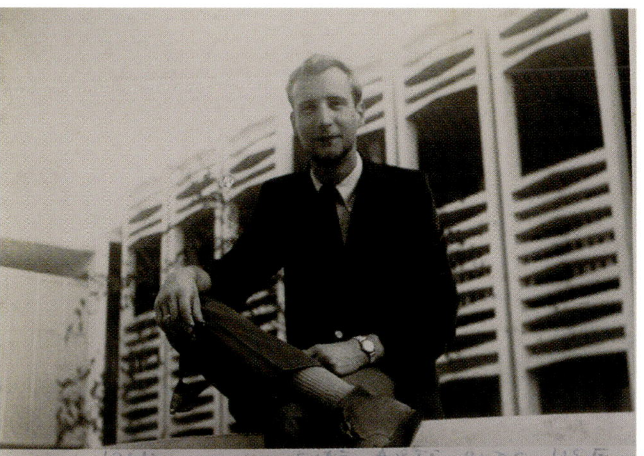

2.31

Robert Stackhouse seated before the Fine Arts Building at the University of South Florida, 1964.

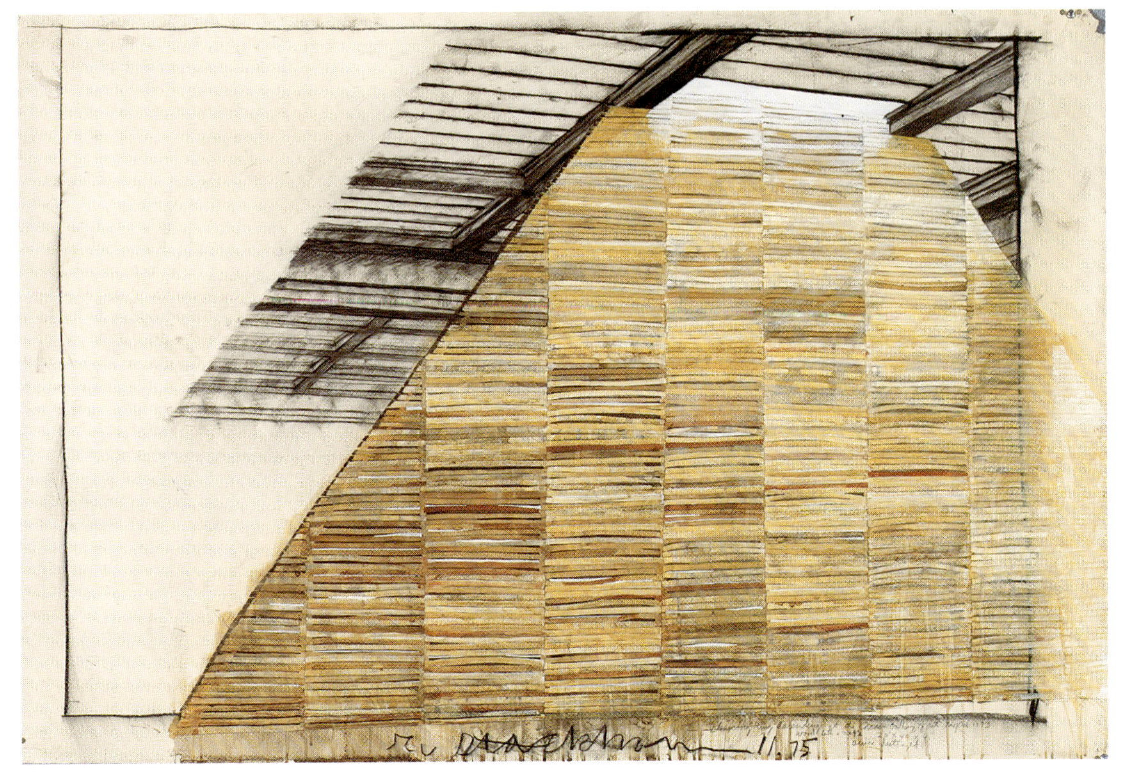

Sleeping King Ascending (watercolor) 1975

CHAPTER THREE

Washington and Maryland

When Robert Stackhouse left Florida and the environment that had nurtured him both personally and professionally for more than a decade, he was determined to find his own path into the mainstream of the American art world. And, as he knew from his studies and experiences at the University of South Florida, that art world was being transformed at an unprecedented pace. When he entered the university, in 1960, the influence of the first and second generation Abstract Expressionists was still dominant in the New York art world, as well as in many of the nation's art schools and university art departments. By that time, the New York School had become, to a significant degree, part of the new academic tradition. By 1960, however, the primacy of the Abstract Expressionists was challenged by artists of a younger generation, most significantly by Robert Rauschenberg and Jasper Johns. Pop Art, advanced by artists including Andy Warhol, James Rosenquist, Roy Lichtenstein and Claus Oldenberg, rose to prominence in New York in 1962 and continued during the years Stackhouse studied at USF, contributing to a rising interest in America's popular culture. Pop Art brought new attention to the signs and symbols that filled the urban and rural landscapes of the nation, including Florida, a state filled with so many billboards, destination signs and tourists attractions that the busiest parts of the state seemed to have evolved into a Pop Art landscape during Stackhouse's years in Florida.

However, before he moved to Maryland to begin his graduate program, a new approach to art, one often devoid of obvious subject matter or content, was become increasingly influential. By the fall of 1965, Minimal art, evident in the works of Donald Judd, Carl Andre, Dan Flavin, Tony Smith and others, had become a controversial new influence, one that baffled many museum and gallery visitors, including those who found Pop Art to be accessible and enjoyable. Minimalism raised challenges for critics as well. Barbara Rose addressed issues related to Minimal art in her influential 1965 essay, "A B C Art." She noted that the work of the minimalists was "critical of Abstract-Expressionist paint handling and rejects the brushed record of gesture and drawing along with loose painterliness," and observed that "as opposed to the florid baroque fullness of the Angst-ridden older generation, the hollow, barrenness of the void has a certain poignant, if strangled expressiveness." She also addressed the question of content in these works. "The simple denial of content can in itself constitute the content of such a work. That these young artists attempt to suppress or withdraw content from their works is undeniable. That they wish to make art that is as bland, neutral, and as redundant as possible also seems clear." [19] Lucy Lippard examined the relationship of Minimal art to the troubled state of contemporary painting in *Art International*, during the fall of 1965, just as Stackhouse entered this fractious art environment.

Although not an anti-art, the primary structure and structural painting are founded on a more negative premise than usual. They rather arrogantly reject almost all the tenets of both painterly and "post-painterly" abstraction....I still think it is important that most of the structurists were originally painters, and I still think of the real space of the structure as a means of escape, not from previous sculpture, which was hardly considered, but from the dilemma in which nonobjective painting finds itself. [20]

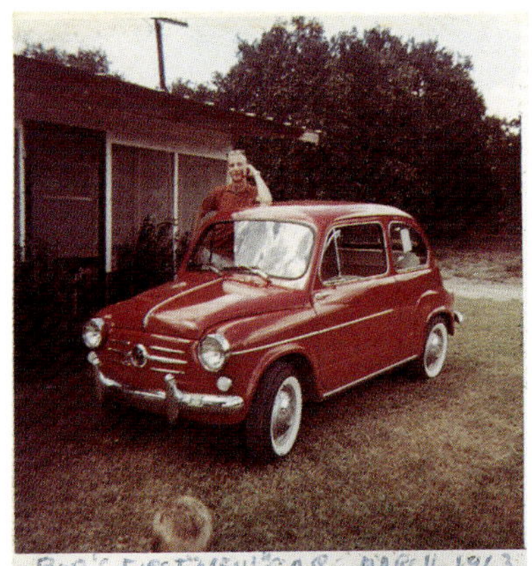

3.1

Robert Stackhouse's first new automobile, the same car he drove from Florida to Maryland to attend graduate school.

Trained as a painter under Harrison Covington in Florida, Stackhouse quickly learned that many of the nation's most advanced artists now questioned the relevance and continuing validity of painting, as well as the use of subject matter, leading critics and writers to speculate that painting was becoming a dying art form. Ad Reinhardt, a painter associated with the New York School, had offered a purist's approach to the future of painting as early as 1963. "The one object of fifty years of abstract art is to present art-as-art and as nothing else, to make it into the thing it is only, separating and defining it more and more, making it purer and emptier." [21] This critical dialectic was dominant in the progressive art world at the time Robert Stackhouse began his graduate studies at the University of Maryland. At this University, however, he discovered a faculty that was in many ways as attuned to the issues of the Depression era as it was to the contemporary one.

The first issue confronting Robert when he arrived in Maryland was a more practical one, how to pay the tuition and related costs for his graduate studies at College Park. He left Florida in his small red Fiat (Figure 3.1), with a wooden box filled with his paintings strapped to the roof, with very limited funds, hoping to find a way to enroll as an in-state student to reduce tuition costs. The graduate program at Maryland was in its second year when he arrived, and because, as he recalls, he was the first studio graduate student to enter from outside the undergraduate program at Maryland, he hoped for some form of tuition assistance. Much to his surprise, as he stood in the school's registration line, worried about how he would pay his fees, he was approached and told that the administrators of the art department wished to speak with him. In the art department office, because of higher than anticipated enrollments in the art program, he was offered a solution to this problem. Recognizing his past experience in Florida, the university offered him a teaching position in studio art with a salary, a waiver of all tuition costs, as well as a working studio space. Without hesitation, he accepted their offer. He was technically contracted to become a teaching assistant yet he, along with the other new teaching assistants, began to work like a member of the regular teaching faculty, including attending faculty meetings, while he was enrolled in the school's graduate program. And, like the other new members of the teaching faculty, all of them graduate students in art and art history, he had a studio located on the second floor, over the school's soccer team, in the war-era building they called the barracks, situated some distance down the hill from the regular art department building. As he and the other graduate students quickly learned, the older faculty did not like to come to the barracks, therefore they were commonly left to themselves, creating their own working collegial environment.

As he also soon discovered, many of the faculty members at Maryland had been actively involved with the WPA programs during the 1930s. His faculty advisor, Herman Maril, was a native of Baltimore, who, like Harrison Covington, remained in his native state and worked as a painter and art professor seeking to advance conditions for the arts in that state. As Virginia Mecklenburg has documented, Maril's reputation initially developed in the middle of the 1930s, when he began a series of New Deal government mural projects, and continued throughout his career. He became an instructor of painting at the University of Maryland after the war and remained there until he retired in 1977. Maril's mural study for the post office in Bethesda, Maryland, titled *The Growing Community* (installed in 1940), is part of the extensive body of New Deal art contained in the collections of the University of Maryland Art Gallery. [22] His painting, *Sunday at the Docks*, was a featured work in the Gallery of American Art Today at the 1939 New York's World Fair. [23] Maril's paintings were included in many exhibitions and served as the focus of a retrospective exhibition at the Baltimore Museum of Art in 1967, the year Robert completed his painting program at Maryland under Maril's direction. [24]

When Stackhouse met him at College Park, Maril was working in Baltimore during the academic year and spent the summers in Maine. Robert recalls that Maril typically painted the Maine coast in watercolor during these summer trips.

Despite his demonstrated painting skills and his national reputation, which Stackhouse respected and admired, Maril did not prove to be an effective teacher for him, because of his own very different art interests at the time and because he had flourished under the very different type of independent learning advanced by Covington's program in Florida. In contrast to Covington's approach, Stackhouse recalls that Maril expected his students to work in a manner more consistent with his own, and offered him specific criticisms regarding his use of colors. Stackhouse remembers that he and Maril quickly became indifferent to each other, and Stackhouse proceeded to teach courses and developed his own direction in contemporary painting. After enjoying the individual freedom and responsibility associated with Covington's style of teaching, Stackhouse felt it was too late for him to return to the older master and mentor approach to academic teaching. As a result, he continued on his own course, forming a close bond with a number of his fellow students, including Tom Green, Cynthia Bickley, Peter Bermingham and John Eaton. During his second semester at College Park, his good friend and fellow undergraduate from USF, Susan Tessum, transferred to the graduate program at Maryland from the University of Michigan, joining Robert in this program, bringing along her own interpretation of the Harrison Covington approach to art studies.

Another Maryland faculty member at this time was Mitchell Jamison, who, like Maril, had been an active WPA era artist. Jamison also had worked as a mural painter and had distinguished himself as a Navy combat artist during the war. By the time Stackhouse studied with him, Jamison was known for his work with NASA, including the portraits he painted of diverse figures associated with NASA and its programs. Robert studied drawing under Jamison and took several other courses with him as well. A significant aspect of the program at Maryland was its emphasis on the history of art and a related belief that students needed to be knowledgeable about the history of art. The University was developing a major program of study devoted to the art and artists of the New Deal era at this time, in conjunction with the National Collection of Fine Arts at the Smithsonian Institution (now the National Museum of American Art), based upon its collections, the presence of the New Deal artists on its faculty, and the interest of other members of its teaching faculty. Other than a general interest in his painting teachers' success as artists during the earlier period, he remembers learning little about the art of the New Deal era, or its emphasis on the public role of art.

Like so many of his contemporaries, Robert was more interested in the rapidly evolving influence of Minimalism and the related issues then current in progressive art circles in New York and Washington. One of the Maryland faculty members who did exert a lasting influence upon Stackhouse was Francis V. O'Connor, a newer member of the university faculty, who taught contemporary art history courses, including an advanced seminar in abstraction and surrealism that attracted Stackhouse. The presence of the New Deal era focus at Maryland reflected O'Connor's own research and publication interests. He was then assembling research materials on the WPA art and artist projects which resulted in publications including *Art For the Millions, Essays from the 1930s by Artists and Administrators of the WPA Federal Art Project*, which he edited. [25] Of greater interest to Stackhouse was O'Connor's research emphasis on Jackson Pollock, which became a featured part of the seminar he taught. O'Connor conducted extensive interviews with Pollock's surviving brothers, Charles, Marvin and Frank, and Pollock's famous teacher, Thomas Hart Benton, as part of his research for his influential 1967 publication, *Jackson Pollock*, which accompanied the major Pollock retrospective exhibition presented by the Museum of Modern Art. [26]

The seminar O'Connor taught was, as described by Stackhouse, "the most adult class" of his graduate school years. Robert, who had been intrigued by Pollock, de Kooning and the New York School since his days at USF and his discussions with Friedel Dzubas, found himself exposed to the most advanced research on Pollock at that time, including considerations of Pollock's creative methodologies. Discussions in this class explored issues such as Pollock's relationship to automatic writing, surrealism, Jungian therapy and his approaches to tapping the powers of the subconscious mind. Of particular importance for Stackhouse was the emphasis O'Connor placed on archetypes in the class. The concept of the archetype was a completely new subject for Stackhouse, one he found immediately fascinating. The discovery of Pollock's approach to unleashing the creative forces of the unconscious mind, nurtured by Jungian therapy, and particularly the notion of the archetype as it was revealed in this concept, was, he remembers, a "momentous event" in his artistic life, one that marked what he calls the "beginning of the beginning to see."

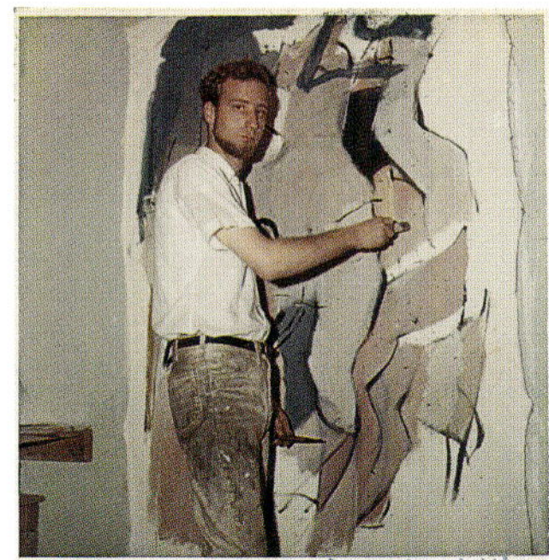

3.2 

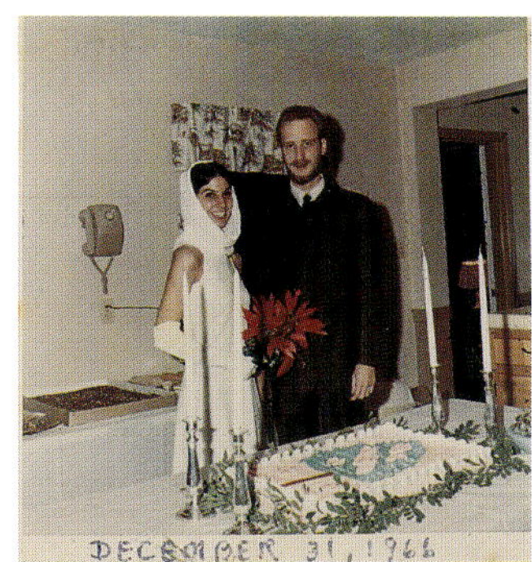

3.3

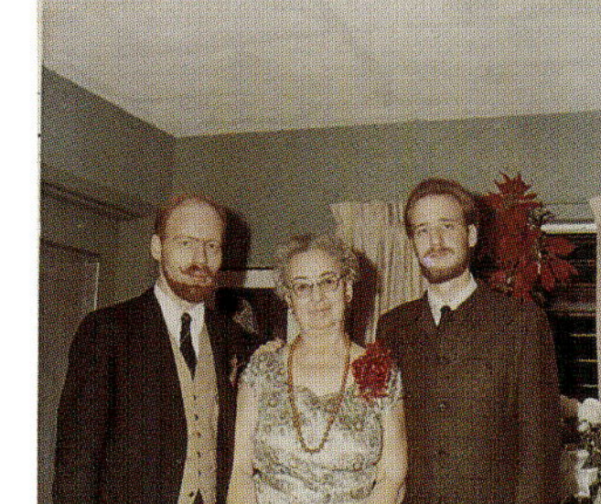

3.4

Robert Stackhouse in his studio at the University of Maryland.

Robert and Dolores Stackhouse wedding, Tampa, Florida, December 31,1966.

Kurt and Robert Stackhouse with Inez Holland, at the time of Robert's wedding in Tampa, December 31,1966.

Stackhouse's resulting fascination with the archetypal themes of myth and religion, including Carl Jung's theories, unleashed an intensive period of research and exploration which permanently altered the direction of his artistic career. This was explored in works he created at the University of Maryland and became evident in such seminal Stackhouse works as *The Great Rain Snake*, completed in 1969. During this period, he also developed new interest in contemporary American painters including James Rosenquist and Wayne Thiebaud. He recalls completing a research paper on Rosenquist's art, exploring his creation of abstract imagery inspired by the use of large scale images, including the creation of a billboard for the movie *Spartacus* and the related loss of a sense of scale and context in works of such enormous size. He discovered related elements in Pollock's canvases and in that artist's approach to the scale of his canvases. These discoveries informed Stackhouse's own approach to the use of large scale imagery, including his watercolors and his outdoor sculptural projects.

Throughout his graduate program at Maryland, Stackhouse continued to teach painting and drawing classes and served as a regular member of the school's faculty. In faculty meetings and related events, he came to know many of the senior faculty as peers even before he graduated. He also continued to paint in his studio in the barracks building, working alongside his fellow young faculty members (Figure 3.2). At the end of his first year at Maryland, he was given the opportunity to teach a painting course at the Corcoran Gallery School of Art in Washington. This possibility of teaching at the Corcoran in the summer of 1966 arose when a second year graduate student needed help with the course. Robert was happy to take the teaching position, which required him to teach a weekly Saturday painting class. He remembers being paid $12 per class for this three hour course, additional income which he welcomed as a supplement to his teaching salary at Maryland. By this time he and Dolores Novoa were living together in Maryland. Dolores had moved back to Maryland, rejoining her family in Washington, and was completing her undergraduate degree, initiated at USF, at the University of Maryland. One of the primary reasons Robert decided to attend graduate school at College Park was its proximity to Dolores. Not inconsequentially, Maryland was also the only graduate school that had granted him admission to its program.

During his time at Maryland, Robert took a trip to New York to visit museums and galleries with his friend and fellow student, Tom Green. He wanted to see a specific Georgia'O'Keeffe painting on view at the Whitney Museum of Art. When they arrived in the city they stayed with his brother Kurt, who had been living on the Upper West side of the city for some time. After serving in the Navy and working as a commercial photographer, Kurt had decided to combine his interest in military history with his artistic abilities to create a line of authentic, hand painted metal toy soldiers, which he sold to private collectors and to specialty shops on Madison Avenue. After Robert went to the Whitney and saw the O'Keeffe painting, he was ready to return to his studio in College Park, inspired by his response to the O'Keeffe. Before leaving the city, however, he and Tom Green visited a gallery on Madison Avenue. Upon leaving the gallery, Green asked him what he thought of its Giacometti sculpture. Stackhouse was surprised that he had overlooked the work of such an influential sculptor. His friend explained that, as was typical of Giacometti, the work had seemed large and substantial from the frontal view yet, from the side, where Stackhouse had been, the thin profile of the work made it practically invisible, almost like a line drawn in space. This notion intrigued Stackhouse and explained his oversight. He decided not to return to the gallery to see the piece. He was more taken with the notion of a major piece of sculpture that he had not seen, even standing near it, and pondered this idea for some time after the trip. Over time, this notion of a sculpture that was there, and yet not there, would have significant implications for many of his large works including *Sleeping King Ascending*, first seen in the atrium of the Corcoran Gallery.

At the end of this year, over the holidays, he returned to Florida with Dolores. On December 31, 1966 they were married in a private ceremony held at his parents' Tampa residence (Figure 3.3). About seventy people attended the ceremony and reception, including Dolores's father, who had returned to Tampa from Washington, about twenty five members of her family from the Tampa area, many members of Robert's family, including his parents, his brother and his grandmother, and a number of friends and neighbors. Before the ceremony, Kurt and Robert posed for a snapshot taken with their grandmother, who still lived in this house with their parents, remaining an important member of the family until her death in 1971 (Figure 3.4). Phyllis Stackhouse remembers designing and making a wedding bouquet for Dolores from poinsettias she had picked from her own yard. After spending time in Florida, they returned to Maryland where they were both completing academic programs. The following summer, they would travel together to Long Lake, Michigan, where Dolores was introduced to the members of his grandmother's family, the Millikans, who gathered at the lake for a large family reunion (Figure 3.5).

By the time Robert started teaching at the Corcoran, Washington had become established as a center for contemporary art, noted especially for the presence of the Washington Color School of painting. During the 1950s, art exhibition and activities at American University, the Institute of Contemporary Arts and the Washington Workshop contributed to advancing contemporary art in the city, often bringing art and artists from New York.[27] In 1965, the year he arrived in the area, the Washington Gallery of Modern Art presented a survey exhibition, "The Washington Color Painters," that examined the influence of this group. In the exhibition catalogue, Gerald Nordland wrote that "what has come to be called Washington Color Painting is the immediate descendant of the abstract expressionism of America's post-war artistic renaissance." In this essay, common elements used by these artists were noted, including the creation of optical effects by staining resin into raw canvas, the primary interest in color, and the use of geometric forms as the focus of a canvas. [28] Innovative uses of color became the hallmark of those associated with this group including Morris Louis, Kenneth Noland and Gene Davis.

Gene Davis, known for his striped paintings, often emphasized the importance of color, as when he once said that "there is no simpler way to divide up a canvas than with straight lines at equal intervals. This enables the viewer, more than in most paintings, to forget the structure and see the color for itself. [29] Davis was a long term faculty member at the Corcoran when Stackhouse arrived there and became a good friend to the younger artist. Over the years of their friendship, Davis offered him a direct connection to the issues associated with the Washington Color School and may have contributed, directly and indirectly, to Stackhouse's own distinctive sense and use of color, especially in his outdoor sculptural projects and in his paintings related to those projects.

In the spring of 1967, as he taught his last classes at the University of Maryland, Robert also completed his graduate

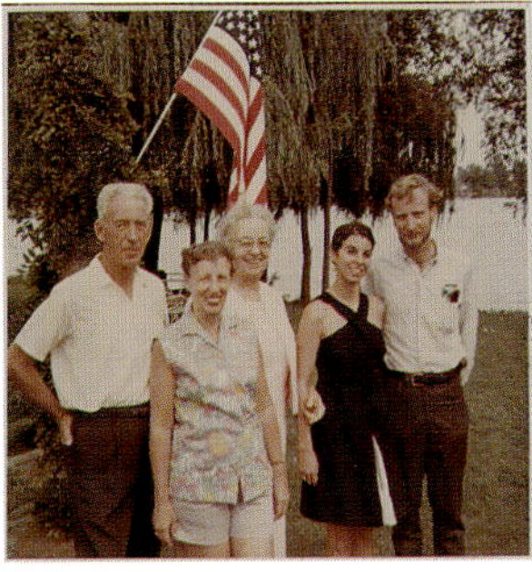

3.5

Robert and Dolores Stackhouse with Phyllis and Gerald Stackhouse and Inez Holland at Long Lake, Michigan, 1967

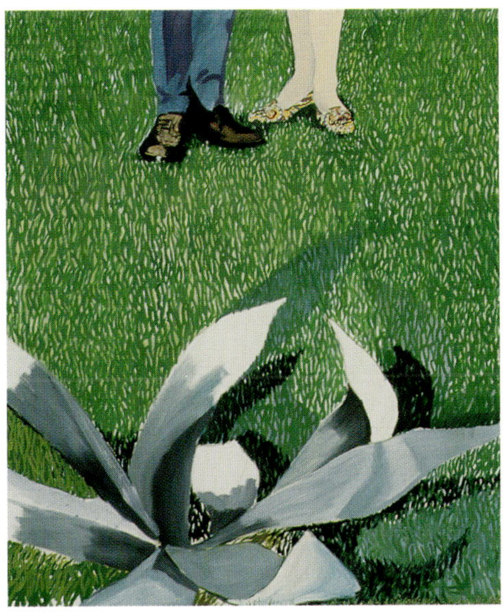

3.6

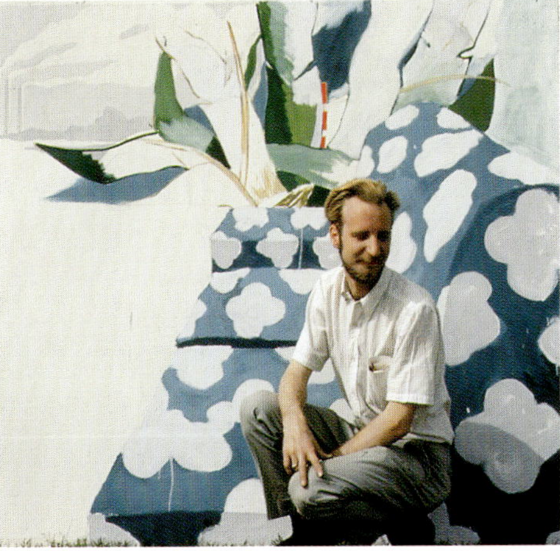

3.7

Two paintings from his M.F.A. thesis exhibition, *Wedding Painting* and *Couch & Plant.*

thesis project. Expanding his interest in archetypes, he created a body of work based upon a specific plant that regenerated itself by spitting up seeds. Working with little direction from the senior art faculty, he created a wide range of works that included canvases, shaped canvases and several three-dimensional objects, including a sculptural form that he described as a "Claus Oldenberg type of plant," that he placed in the center of his thesis exhibition installation (Figures 3.6 and 3.7). He remembers the faculty review of his thesis as being a fairly casual and unstructured event, more like teaching colleagues speaking with another colleague (which he was), with no specific questions asked about the plant form, either in its painted or sculptural state. His graduation ceremonies were held on June 3, 1966. Spiro T. Agnew, then Governor of Maryland, delivered the graduation address to the 5000 undergraduate and graduate students assembled for the ceremony in College Park. The following summer, Dolores would graduate from the same university with her undergraduate degree in English literature.

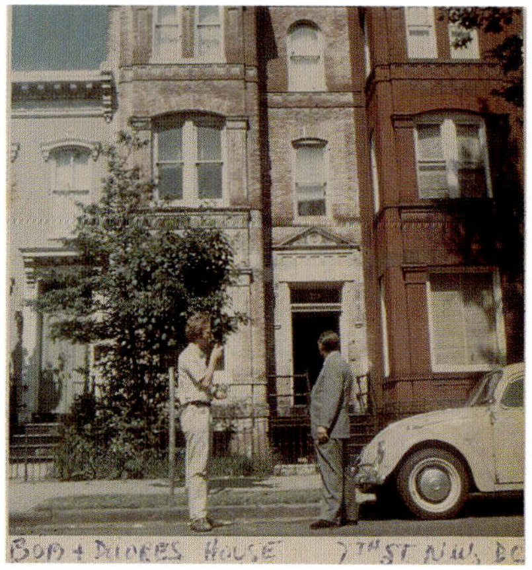

BOB + DOLORES HOUSE 7TH ST N.W. DC

3.8

Robert and Dolores Stackhouse home in Washington, 7th Street N.W..

Not long after graduation, he began to teach in the Corcoran's summer session. He was one of three artists on the painting faculty that summer, along with Thomas Downing and Sam Gilliam. After the summer session, he continued teaching at the Corcoran, joining a faculty that included Juan Downey and Ed McGowin, in addition to Davis, Downing and Gilliam. Already an experienced teacher, even though he had just completed his graduate degree, Stackhouse entered a faculty at the Corcoran that featured many of the region's outstanding artists. He came to the Corcoran in a period when sculpture was assuming a new primacy in the art world. In 1966, for example, the "Primary Structures" exhibition at New York's Jewish Museum, featuring the minimalist sculptures of English and American artists including Ronald Bladen, Carl Andre, Donald Judd, Robert Morris, Robert Smithson and Richard Artschwager, was described by Hilton Kramer, critic for *The New York Times*, as "one of those exhibitions that defines a period, and fixes it irrevocably in one's consciousness." [30] By 1967, only one year later, the rate of activity in the sculptural world caused even these works to look less than radical, as suggested by Irving Sandler in his reconsideration of the events of the "watershed year" of 1967.

> *The minimal sculpture of Donald Judd, Robert Morris, Dan Flavin, and Carl Andre, and its premises, had become familiar, at least to the art world, through shows in private galleries and in articles by Judd, Morris, Barbara Rose, Lucy Lippard, among others. This is not to say that minimal sculpture of high quality was no longer being made. On the contrary, much of the best was yet to come. But it had ceased to be in the vanguard. That role was assumed by a number of innovative late-minimal artists, such as Eva Hesse, Richard Serra, Robert Smithson, and Bruce Nauman. I use the term "late minimal" rather than "post minimal" because minimal art remained the aesthetic context of late minimalism, whereas postminimalism aimed to cut its throat.* [31]

At the Corcoran, Stackhouse was able to see some of the most exciting new works by many of these same artists, often projects designed specifically for the unique spaces of the Corcoran Gallery and the surrounding grounds, including the adjoining park facing the White House, the Washington Monument and the Washington Mall. During the late 1960s he was able to witness the construction and installation of major sculptural projects at the Corcoran by some of the most advanced artists of the period. Barnett Newman's influential *Broken Obelisk* was installed on the grounds outside of the Corcoran. Tony Smith's *Smoke*, a black tetrahedron fabricated of painted plywood, was constructed after Stackhouse had joined the regular staff at the Corcoran. And Ronald Bladen's two-story black *The X*, designed and constructed to fill the central atrium space at the Corcoran, made a significant impression upon Stackhouse, suggesting the possibilities of scale and site specificity that he would develop later in his monumentally scaled *Sleeping King Ascending*, designed specifically for the second floor atrium at the Corcoran. He was impressed by how these works energized the traditional spaces of the Corcoran and how they reflected the ability of painters like Newman and

Bladen to work three dimensionally on an architectural scale. And, although minimalist works implied a sense of machine made perfection and industrial seamlessness, he was fascinated by the poorly joined corners, splintered plywood edging and related finish flaws he found in the Bladen piece. Bladen's implication of perfection and the actual work's lack of perfection made a deep impression on Stackhouse, suggesting the ongoing struggle between the ideal and the real, the sacred and the profane, the industrial and the man-made that had become central to the evolution of his own compositions.

William Christenberry, who came to the Corcoran as a professor of painting and drawing in 1968, recently recalled that the years from 1968 to 1975 were the most exciting years of artistic activity he has witnessed during his thirty year tenure as a Washington artist and teacher. In 1968, the Corcoran changed leadership, marking a progressive shift at a venerable Washington institution. After teaching previously at the University of Alabama in Tuscaloosa, his alma mater, and Memphis State University, he had looked forward to joining the cosmopolitan art environment he discovered in Washington. [32] He found it to be "an exciting time," adding that "we all look back on 1968 as a pivotal year—at the Corcoran and in Washington." During his first years there he remembers a large David Smith exhibition, a major Robert Morris exhibition and a visionary architectural exhibition featuring the designs and works of Paoli Soleri. He too was impressed by Tony Smith's *Smoke* and by Ronald Bladen's *The X* installation at the Corcoran, recalling that "minimalism was heavy in the air." For Christenberry, the Corcoran was the most dynamic major cultural institution in the city, marked by innovative exhibitions and a highly talented teaching faculty, and filled with the best artists and teachers in the region. "I felt more like an artist," he noted, "than like a teacher of art."

Stackhouse, like Christenberry, was trained as a painter and, like Christenberry and other young painters then active in Washington, he was searching for new directions and materials for his ideas. Stackhouse taught and participated in this changing Washington art environment, absorbing the lessons of the Washington Color School while charting his own course among the emerging artists who were bringing sculpture to the forefront in the city. His earliest sculptural works suggest his awareness of the stylistic and theoretical elements of Minimalism. After moving to Washington with Dolores, to a Capitol Hill row house located on 7th Street S.E. (Figure 3.8), he constructed a sculptural sidewalk, literally making a curb and sidewalk out of plywood and paint. Embracing the Minimalist's notions of using industrial and prefabricated materials, he began to use aluminum downspouts as a basic fabrication material for his sculptural forms. During this time, he also used artificial turf panels as part of his projects. Lumber yards and building supply stores became major destinations in his search for new materials and art supplies.

In *Blades* (1968-1969), he used aluminum strips and acrylic fiber to create a system of interchangeable elements, designed to be flexibly aligned and stacked in diverse configurations, either inside or outside of the gallery or museum environment (Figure 3.9). *Blades* was the first of his works to be featured in a major museum exhibition, "Other Ideas," presented at the Detroit Institute of Art in 1969. His sculpture was featured with the works of established and emerging artists including Lynda Benglis, Carl Andre, Walter De Maria, Dan Flavin, Sam Gilliam, Michael Heizer, Hans Haacke, Ed McGowin, Nam June Paik and Richard Tuttle. Writing in the exhibition catalogue, Samuel Wagstaff referred to the appeal of sculpture for these artists. "Since Dada, at least, there has been a movement, one might almost call it, away from 'artness' to 'thingness,' away from remove to immediacy, an attempt to position reality or pieces of reality within the aesthetic....Process has become important, more important than style or idealization, part of the attempt to embrace reality firmly." And, in concluding, Wagstaff referred to the environment associated with the presentation of these art forms. "A portion of this exhibition moves out of the museum, away from the usual channels of presentation, as some work seems to be doing today. An idea can be manifest anywhere." [33]

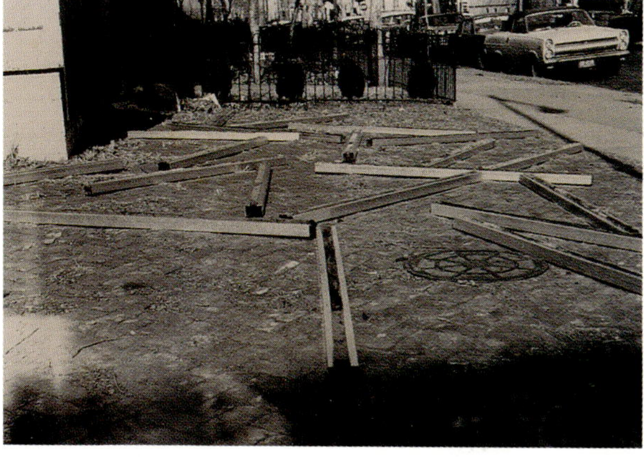

3.9

Blades

Blades also functioned on a very different level when it was incorporated into the design of a dance performance piece created by Dolores and Robert Stackhouse and presented at the Lisner Auditorium at George Washington University on April

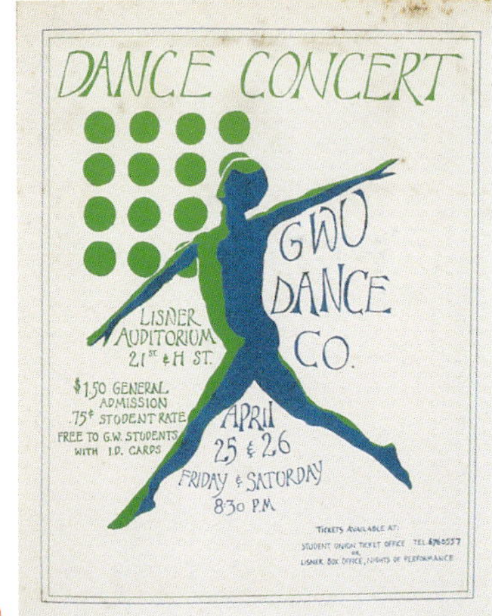

3.10

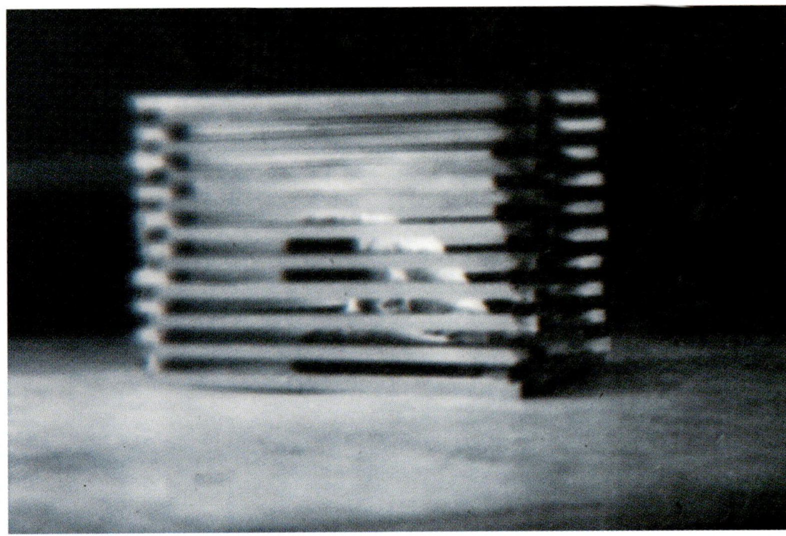

3.11

"Dance Concert" program cover for performance of *Blades* at George Washington University, April 25-26. 1969.

Blades as a Dance, 1969.

25 and 26, 1969. Dolores and Robert performed in the piece along with Dorothy Goodman O'Neal, Jim Cassell and Bob Clark, dancing to music based upon sounds taken from a Zen Buddhist temple. (Figure 3.10) A local newspaper writer, Robin Reid, described the piece. "The dance's movements are more a series of shapes and positions than actual dance steps and patterns. The impetus for movement is from an inner source, but the action is involved with a sculpture, which is assembled and dismantled several times on stage. This sculpture is made of long aluminum blades or rods with 'soft, green fuzzy stuff' (which greatly resembles the soft pile of a bathroom rug). These thirty aluminum pieces represent the blades of grass and of swords." Dolores noted that her ideas for the dance were inspired by watching Robert creating the sculpture, leading to a jointly choreographed performance, as she explained. "We deal with the sculpture...first with the physicality of it...then this physicality is removed....My solo which follows is sort of a lecture of what previously went on. It is the preparation for personal meditation" [34] (Figure 3.11).

The creation and performance of *Blades* demonstrated the collaborative abilities shared by Robert and Dolores and reflected Robert's theatrical experiences with the theater department at USF in Tampa. This was one of three performance pieces they presented during this period. These three pieces illustrated the continuing importance of theater, dance and music for the artist's work, and demonstrated how he consistently refused to limit the boundaries of his art forms. During the 1960s, numerous artists participated in the production of happenings, performance, dance and theatrical works, including Claes Oldenburg, Jim Dine, Alan Kaprow, Yoko Ono, Carolee Schneemann, Robert Rauschenberg and Robert Morris.[35] A second work created by Robert and Dolores was described by Paul Richard on the front page of the *Washington Post* Style and Art section, on October 28, 1969, titled "A Naked Art Form." Richard traveled to a place along the old C & O Canal, where he witnessed sixteen dancers, eight masked and naked men and eight masked and naked women, all participants in Dolores's class at the Corcoran, as they performed a choreographed dance using sheets of mylar in a wooded environment before a film class crew directed by Ramon Osuna. As Richard explained, "The Corcoran's student government had commissioned a dance designed by Mrs. Stackhouse, a dance to be performed before an audience at the

Corcoran Gallery of Art. The movie to be filmed near the farm house would be shown behind the living dancers as a kind of moving set." The Corcoran dance performance was to be presented in the Gallery's atrium in December of 1969, "when the dancers' bodies will be concealed and constrained by leotards and clothes. The figures moving on the screen—and the private memories of the dancers—will evoke the freedom that was learned by newly sensitive bodies moving over the newly discovered landscape through the cold October air." [36] The third work, *Game Opera No. 1*, was created with Loran Carrier, and consisted of a large series of bladed Styrofoam forms, lights and electronic circuits incorporated into a performance presented in December of 1969 at the Smithsonian's Museum of Natural History.[37]

The performance pieces were created during a year of significant change and experimentation by Robert and Dolores Stackhouse, experimentation that was consistent with the spirit and philosophies of the period. Earlier that year, Robert and Dolores had given away most of their possessions, except those that would fit into a white 1969 Volkswagen bus, which they bought brand new for $2600 cash (with financial assistance from Dolores's father), and departed on a journey to California and the West (Figure 3.12). Their trip was described in another *Washington Post* article written by Paul Richard, published in September of 1969. "They kept only what their small bus would hold and drove through Colorado and through Arizona. They searched the desert for semi-precious stones, and found them, and they bathed in mountain streams." The trip, as explained to Richard, caused a profound shift in Stackhouse's perceptions. "While he traveled, it seemed to Stackhouse that the things he thought and the things he did and the things he found had fused. Building a fire was building sculpture and preparing a meal step by step was a special kind of dance. The traveling and the shifting landscape changed his life and changed his work as well."

Although this newspaper description made it sound like Robert and Dolores had joined countless others of their generation traveling across the country on diverse journeys of discovery, including the famous central figures of the movie *Easy Rider* (released in July of that same year), they had, in fact, planned the trip as part of their relocation to the Bay Area following Robert's acceptance of a new teaching position in California. However, much to his surprise and disappointment, when he arrived at the California College of Arts and Crafts, he learned that changes in the school's leadership had scuttled his opportunity for teaching there, leaving them in an awkward position. They decided to see California (Figure 3.13), then drove back to the Washington area, where Robert later returned to teaching at the Corcoran. When they first returned, they had no place to live, except in their van, until Tom Green offered them the use of a chicken coop that he was converting to studio and living quarters. They accepted and moved into the chicken house and worked on the conversion during the rest of the summer and into the fall, a process that was described in Paul Richard's article. "The materials that Stackhouse finds and takes and then transforms are not just wood and stone. He works with window screening, too, and plastic and with sunlight, for he sees the chicken coop he lives in as a complex piece of sculpture. He sees the furniture he's made and the window system he's designed and even the vegetables he grows as things he's found, guided and controlled and somehow made his own." This article, presented in a two page layout with large photographs of their temporary home (Figure 3.14), generated significant interest in the Washington arts community. [38]

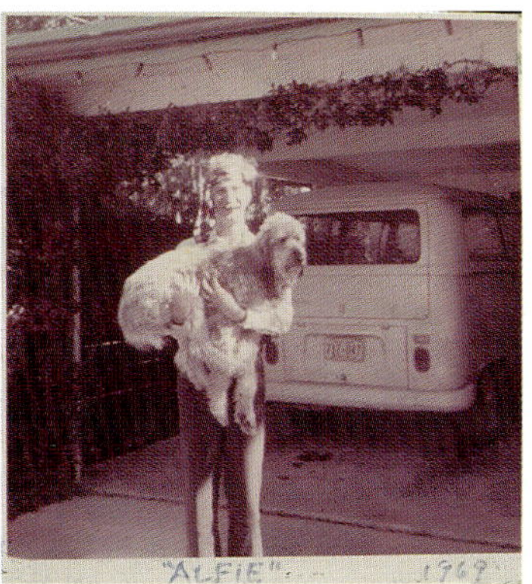

3.12

Robert Stackhouse and his dog, Alfie, before new Volkswagen bus.

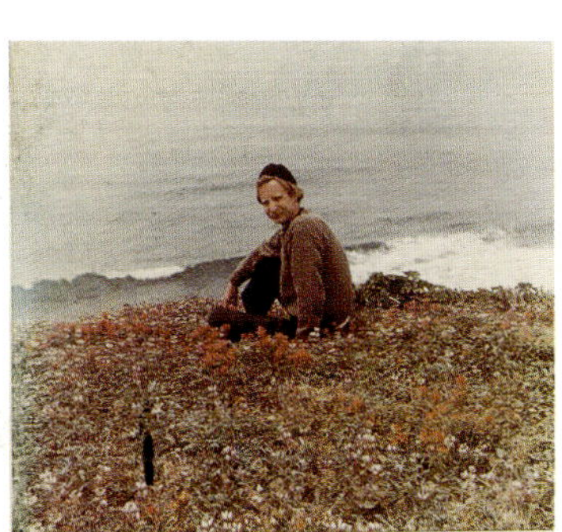

3.13

Robert Stackhouse on the beach in California.

Two seminal works initiated in 1969 reflect the significance of these explorations and experimentations, demonstrating the impact of these experiences upon the foundations of his mature art forms. In the process of creating *Great Rain Snake*, initially planned to be a minimalist wooden piece, he discovered the possibilities of a new approach to his creative process, one that, like Pollock's Jungian inspired experiences with the collective unconscious, unleashed archetypal sources and possibilities for Stackhouse. This work was originally conceived as another uniformly structured wooden composition, built with a more regular, machine-like

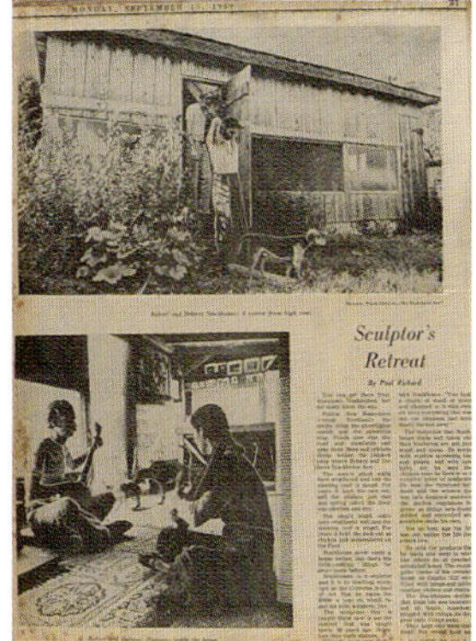
Sculptor's Retreat

3.14

"Sculptor's Retreat" article on Robert Stackhouse. ©1999, The Washington Post. Reprinted with permission.

use of straight lines and hard edges. However, while walking through a snowstorm with his dog, Alfie, in the woods near his house near Williamsport, Maryland, he was almost hit by a falling oak tree. After a significant ordeal that carried ritualistic overtones, he managed to drag the tree through the woods, back to his house. Not long after this, when he and Dolores separated, prior to their divorce in 1970, he returned to Washington, then decided to share a working studio space with Anne Truitt. Using the wood from the fallen oak tree in his new Washington studio, he began carving and discovered a distinctive shape emerging from the wood, one he had not intended to create. Trusting his instincts, and following what he regarded as direction from the wood itself, he continued to carve, releasing a form that he recognized as a snake (Figure 3.14). Prior to the creation of this work, completed during the period of his divorce from Dolores, he was immersed in research on archetypal imagery and symbols. And, he had spent the year participating in dance and theatrical performances, including a dance performance in the Maryland woods, had disposed of most of his belongings to travel and camp in diverse locations across the country in a van, and had spent an extended period living and working in a converted chicken house. He had, in essence, spent the year in what appears to have been a shamanistic process, shedding himself (in a snake-like fashion) of possessions and ties to the material world, exploring the inherent powers of the world of nature, immersing himself in the development of contemporary dance performances using his own painted and sculpted forms. Then, after the separation and eventual divorce from Dolores, he moved through to a new level in his life.

Great Rain Snake, 1969

As he later said, reflecting upon the evolution of this piece, "I thought of myself as a Minimalist then and I wanted this to be a sculpture like a pencil line. It became a snake because it insisted on it." The important transitional nature of this work has been described by Carter Ratcliff. "The object's presence is undeniably serpentine, as the artist acknowledged by calling it

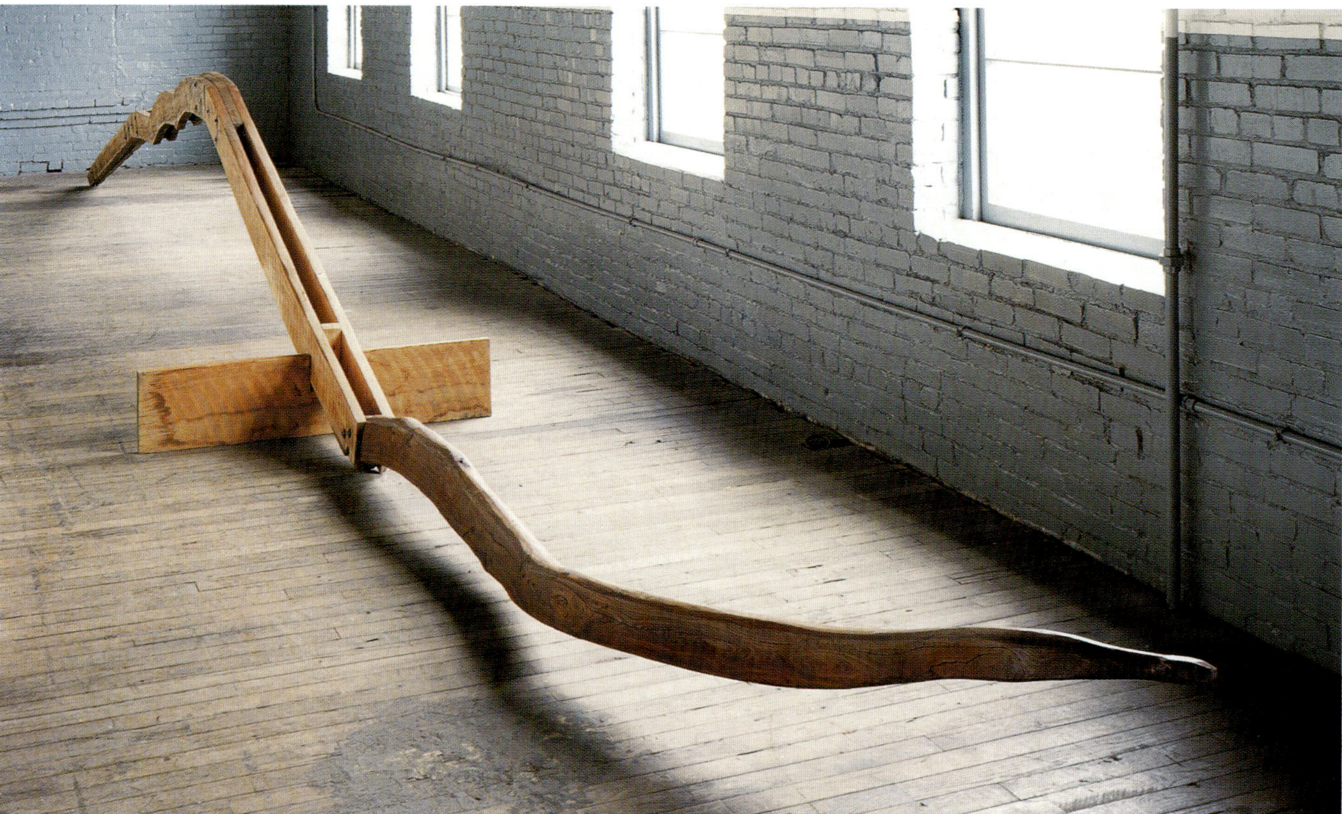

3.15

Great Rain Snake. Until now, Stackhouse had been a literalist who saw strips of gutter as strips of gutter....With *Great Rain Snake*, his literalism gave way to the oblique tactics of allusion and evocation. Stackhouse became a conjurer, an artist who summons meanings from elusive sources." [39] And, as became apparent during the making of *Great Rain Snake*, he discovered that the snakes he believed he had left behind, at Lake Julianna in Florida and at Peach Lake in New York, were still with him, transported in his psyche, coiled in the deepest layers of his inner being. In *The Wisdom Of the Serpent, The Myths of Death, Rebirth and Resurrection*, Joseph Henderson describes the snake as "a particularly significant symbol for the life of the unconscious," and refers to one aspect of this symbolism that seems particularly related to the process Stackhouse used to create his carved serpent form. "In its sinuous, unpredictable movement it frequently illustrates the indirect, non-rational approach to the unconscious, most necessary if anything new is to be learned." By this time, Stackhouse's own reading and research would have led him to understand the associations Henderson described in his 1963 publication.

> *The snake as a symbol of rebirth following death is an ancient, yet ever-present conception which can be traced through endless patterns of sculpture, painting, verse, and the myths of gods, demi-gods, or heroic mortals. This is so because during its yearly period of hibernation the snake sheds its skin and reappears as if renewed. The wisdom of the serpent, which is suggested by its watchful lidless eye, lies essentially in mankind's having projected into this lowly creature his own secret wish to obtain from this earth a knowledge he cannot find in waking daylight consciousness alone. This is the knowledge of death and rebirth forever withheld except in those times when some transcendent principle, emerging from the depths, makes it available to consciousness.* [40]

And, in that same year, *Sky Song* combined Minimalist sculptural forms with a drawing on paper, exploring the transitional possibilities of using mixed media as a way to document the increasingly complex nature of his exploration of archetypal imagery (Figure 3.16). A simple wooden "T" form, suggestive of ancient symbols including a truncated crucifix, constructed to reflect primitive joinery as well as his interest in Japanese architecture, is surmounted by a distinctive black and white drawing. In this image, taken directly from a book of traditional Japanese architectural forms, he focused on a detail of a sod roof that was topped by the curving form of a bamboo vent, placed beneath a cloud-filled sky. Floating, mysteriously, in the clouds above is an eye-like apparition, cut from Mylar and collaged to the surface of the drawing, that had appeared to Stackhouse in a dream, initially at the time he was completing the earlier sculpture, *Watchings*. This ambiguous dream image, suggesting both an archetypal eye and the profile of his later sculptural boat forms, became a recurring motif in his later works. The curving wooden structure, like the profile of the eye/boat form, predicts the direction of his future art forms, including the A-frame constructions that became his signature imagery in the middle 1970s. By 1974, when *Sky Song* was included in the exhibition, "Contemporary Religious Imagery in American Art," organized by the Ringling Museum of Art in Sarasota, his work was increasingly recognized for its spiritual intent as well as its resonance with viewers. As suggested in the catalogue for that exhibition, his work could be classed within a larger continuum of religious and spiritual imagery.

> *What binds these artists together is their use of visual symbolism to give their vision of the world, whether that symbol be representational, as in the work of Leonard Baskin and Rico Lebrun, or abstract, as in the work of Barnett Newman or Adolph Gottlieb, who have sought a universal sign in the collective unconscious. The desire for momentous content which touches the heroic base of each man's nature has informed the work of all these artists, whether they use the stories of the great religions, or an abstract symbol, to stand for the unseeable and the unknowable. The work*

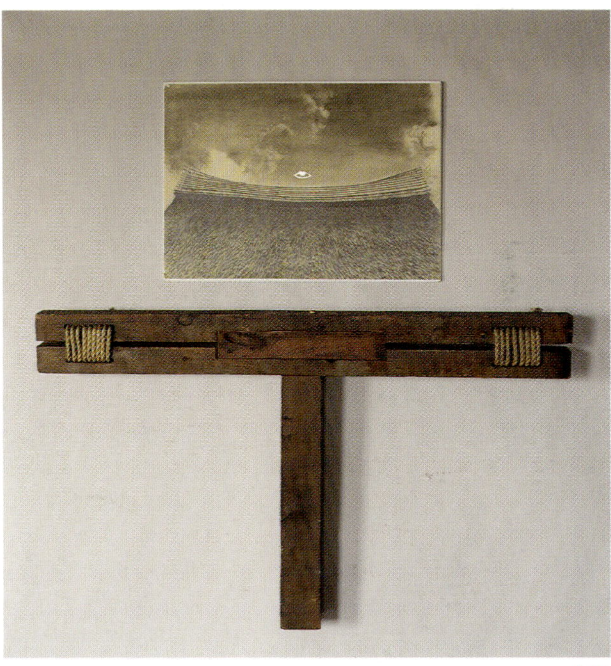

3.16

Sky Song (Drawing Element)
Sky Song (Sculptural Element)

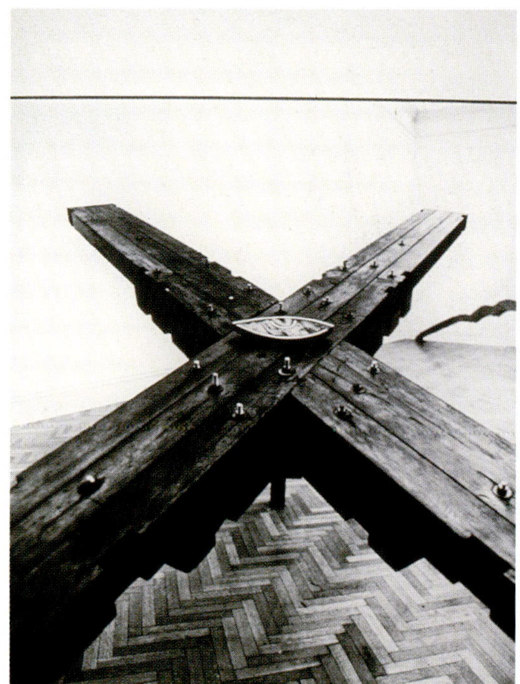

3.17

Watchings
(image of installation at The Corcoran Gallery)

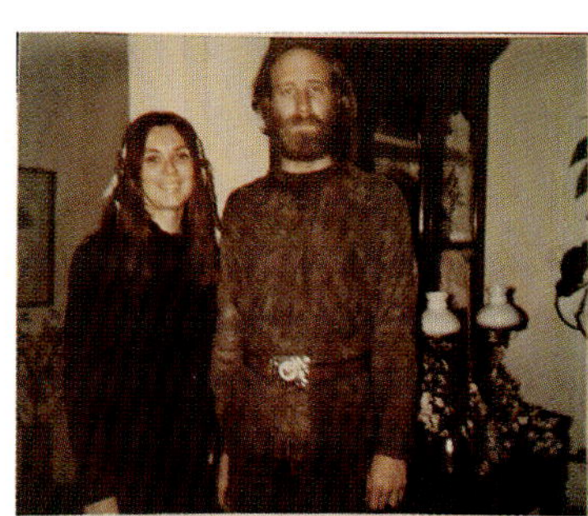

3.18

Robert Stackhouse and Mary Beth Edelson, Washington, 1971.

of art then seems to take on the ecstatic and redeeming characteristics of the religious experience itself. [41]

In 1970, Stackhouse and William Christenbery were both featured in two significant exhibitions presented in the Washington and Baltimore area. The previous year, they had both been included in the exhibition, "Art Now," presented at the University of Alabama. "Washington: Twenty Years," presented by the Baltimore Museum of Art from May 12-June 21, 1970, offered a survey of major established and emerging artists who had been active in Washington from 1950 to 1970. Artists included, in addition to Stackhouse and Christenberry, were Leon Berkowitz, Donald Corrigan, Gene Davis, Juan Downey, Thomas Downing, Sam Gilliam, Jacob Kainen, Rockne Krebs, Blaine Larson, Morris Louis, Ed McGowin, Howard Mehring, Robert Newman, Kenneth Noland, Alma Thomas and Anne Truitt. By 1970, art in Washington reflected the impact of a group of emerging younger artists, whose importance was suggested by Arlene Corkery, in the catalogue for "Washington: Twenty Years." "The emergence of spatial concern marks a second major stage in the development of Washington art. Along with a new interest in space is a concurrent and equal fascination with light. This concern also came out of the original body of the concepts of the Washington Color School but is extended to treat light in a larger context than that of its identification with color." [42] Stackhouse had two works featured in this exhibition, *Section of Blades*, and *Watchings*.

As Renato G. Danese, Curator of Contemporary Art at the Corcoran Gallery of Art, explained in the catalogue *New Sculpture: Baltimore, Washington, Richmond*, the twenty four contemporary artists featured in this exhibition were not as well known as many of the more established area artists. "They remain generally unknown both here and in Baltimore and Richmond and, for the most part, the quality of their work has yet to be recognized. Most of these artists are relatively young and almost without exception have never been seen in a Washington museum." And, based upon the quality and the diversity of their work, he suggested that the activities of these artists signaled the emergence of a new type of Washington School. "Among the area's emerging artists there seems to be a growing preference for sculpture. If an interest in sculpture is truly in the ascendency we may be witnessing the establishment of a permanent sculpture tradition in Washington—a region dominated for almost two decades by painting." [43] The evolution of the arts in the Washington area during these years, prior to the group Danese had identified for the Corcoran exhibition, was concisely summarized by Walter Hopps and Nina Osnos, in an article published at that time in *Art International.*

> *The development of contemporary art in Washington during the past fifteen years has been marked by three successive waves of activity. The work of Morris Louis and Kenneth Noland represents the first, and that of Gene Davis, Howard Mehring, Thomas Downing and Paul Reed the second. Around 1964, a third, and still current, period of activity began to solidify. It is within this wave, which constitutes a major portion of work now being done in the area, that Sam Gilliam, Rockne Krebs and Ed McGowin occupy forefront positions.* [44]

Stackhouse presented two of his newest works in the "New Sculpture: Washington, Baltimore and Richmond" exhibition, the *Great Rain Snake* and *Watchings* (Figure 3.17). This work was directly related to the processes involved in the creation of both the *Great Rain Snake* and *Sky Song*. Using heavy crossed wooden beams, inspired in part by Ronald Bladen's *The X* created for the Corcoran Gallery as well as by his own continuing interest in Minimalist forms, he built a massive sculptural piece designed to be shown either outside or inside a large gallery setting. Because he had encountered structural problems when he first assembled *Watchings* for the Baltimore exhibition, he worked to reinforce the massive piece with metal joints, carriage bolts and supporting posts for an extended period of time. Then, exhausted, he fell asleep and dreamed about this sculpture. In his dream, the sculpture possessed one large eye, placed in its center where the beams crossed, that gazed directly at Stackhouse for a time, and then winked at him. When he woke up, with this striking image still fresh in his mind, he decided to fabricate a sculptural eye, and then placed it on the sculpture at the same place he had seen it, in his dream. A second version of his dream eye, created in Mylar, was attached to the drawing in *Sky Song*.

During the years from 1969 to 1972 changes in Robert's life affected his work and his outlook on his future development. One year after his 1970 divorce from Dolores, he learned that his grandmother, Inez Holland, who had always seemed like a second mother to him, especially after their years spent together at Lundy's fish camp, had died in Tampa. It was a great loss for the artist and his family, signaling the end of a matriarch's era in the Holland-Stackhouse family. In 1972, his parents sold their Tampa house and moved to a condominium overlooking the bay in Gulfport, Florida, the home where his mother still lives. By the time of his parents' move to Gulfport, Robert had met and was living with the artist Mary Beth Edelson in her house located in Washington's Cleveland Park area (Figure 3.18). The studio he created in the basement of this house served as the center of production for his first one-man exhibition at a Washington area gallery, the "Journeys" exhibition presented at Henri Gallery in 1972.

During these same years, changes at the Corcoran Gallery's art school brought about a new, less formally structured approach to teaching art at the Corcoran. This began in 1970, when George Washington University, which had been associated with the Corcoran art school for many years, disaffiliated itself from the Corcoran's program and restructured its art department to become a B.A. degree granting program (moving away from the B.F.A. program model at the Corcoran). Under Roy Slade's direction, the Corcoran's art school designed a controversial new foundations and core art program, one based upon a team teaching approach. The new program was designed as an independent four year B.F.A. course of study, one that was conceived as a creatively oriented approach to the study of art. Robert played a central role in this transition in teaching philosophies. Then, in 1972, when the school's art students went on strike, refusing to study with teachers and rejecting the school's system of grading, Robert worked with the protesting students to develop revised new approaches to the class structures at the school's main campus and its Dupont Circle program.

The more student-driven program that resulted mirrored, in many ways, the structure of the program Stackhouse had known and appreciated from his studies with Harrison Covington in the USF art department. Changes in his teaching philosophy centered on the development of more interactive learning processes, ones that moved away from the traditional academic methodology that was well established at the Corcoran, one of the nation's oldest art schools. This transition in his teaching methods also caused him to rethink aspects of his approach to creating and exhibiting art. In the five year period, extending from 1972 to 1977, this philosophical and aesthetic evolution led to the creation of distinctive new art forms, including Stackhouse's signature A-frame structures. These new works challenged viewers to become more actively involved with his works, calling for them to move through and around these works in an architectural sense, resulting in a personal experience of exploration and discovery that was intended to transcend the normally more intellectual process of viewing a sculpture or sculptural exhibition.

The course of his evolutionary path was evident to those who attended the opening of his first exhibition at the Henri 2 Gallery exhibition. While the city's Jefferson Place Gallery was more closely allied with the masters of the Washington Color School during this era, the Henri Gallery was considered to be more experimental and more open to the visions of talented new artists, an appropriate venue for artists like Stackhouse, Christenberry, Mary Beth Edelson, Martin Puryear and others associated with the next generation of emerging artists in Washington. The exhibition was centered on the presentation of his "Journeys Series," featuring the larger horizontal floor scale pieces, mounted on pipe frames, and large vertical wall pieces, as well as a series of smaller works designed to fit the more intimate scale of

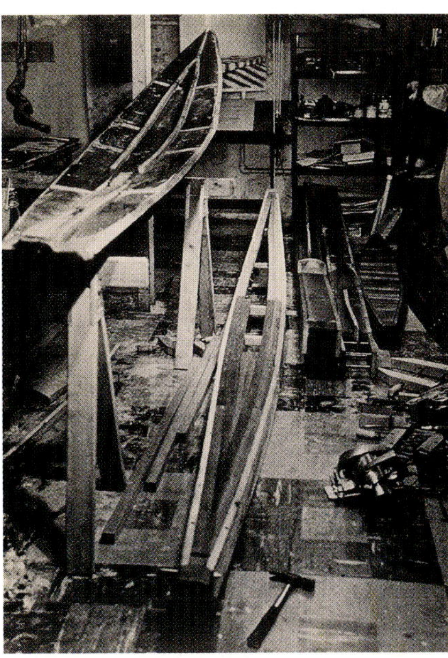

3.19

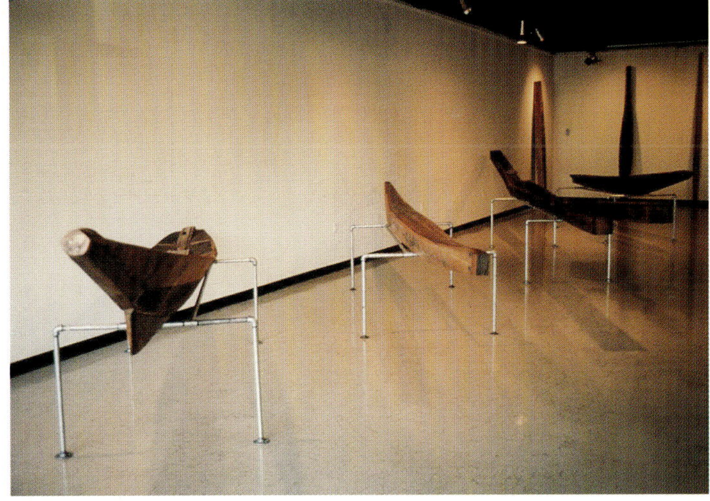

3.20

Invitation to Robert Stackhouse's first exhibition at the Henri Gallery in Washington. (Photograph of his studio by Mary Beth Edelson).

Journeys, 1972,
installation at Henri Gallery.
(Photograph by Mary Beth Edelson).

Boat shape from *Journeys* series.

Eye Shape/Boat Shape from *Journeys Series.* (sculpture) 1972

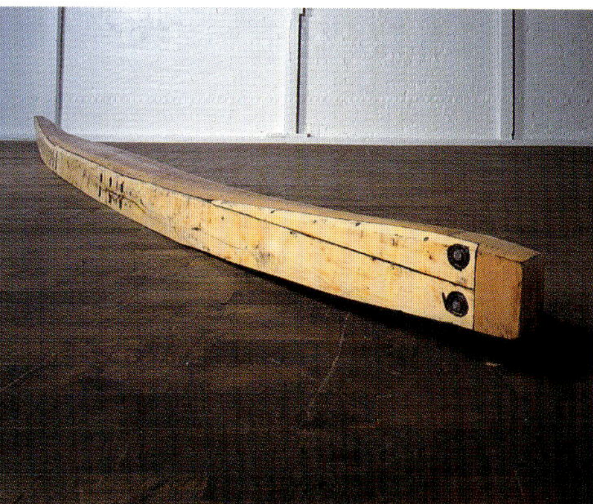

3.21

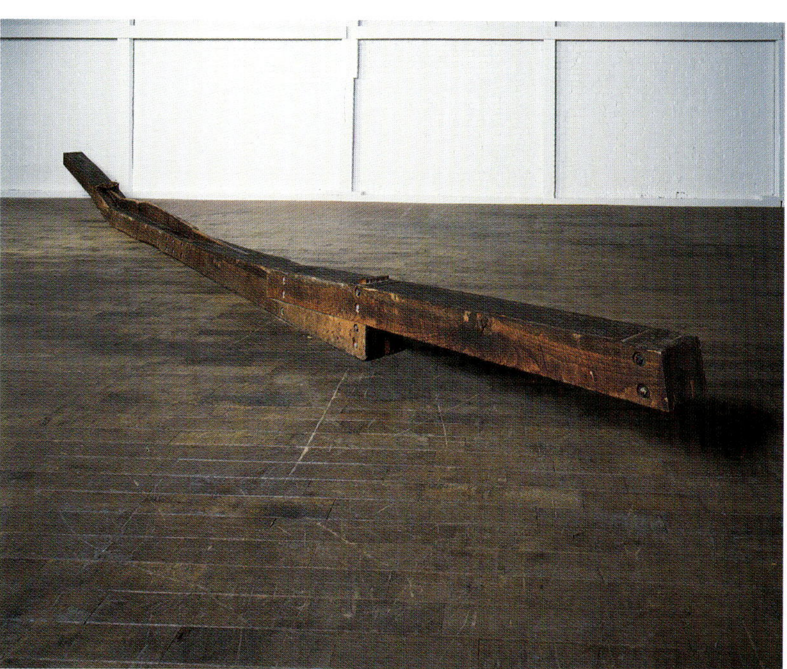

3.22

Washington area homes. The exhibition invitation used a photograph, taken by Mary Beth Edelson, that showed Robert's modestly scaled basement studio in her house, the space he used to create the majority of works in the exhibition (Figure 3.19).

In this exhibition, Stackhouse's continuing interest in Minimal forms merged with his exploration of boat forms (Figure 3.20), resulting in suggestive wooden sculptural forms that elicited a wide range of responses from viewers, collectors and critics. Paul Richard, for example, wrote in the *Washington Post*, that this exhibition was "a kind of spiritual journey, an intuitive exploration of the subtle evocations, some sexual, some nautical, that the wooden form suggests." Richard noted that "the act of making sculpture is for Stackhouse a sort of summoning of spirits," and suggested that there "is a Jungian sensibility apparent in his work, but his primitivism is not precious." The complexity of Stackhouse's wooden boat forms, including their influences and allusions, was also described, along with a reference to his experiences in Florida. "Stackhouse sees that form as phallic in its longness, but softly curved and vaginal as well, and its presence brought to mind memories of West Coast whaling canoes and of his boyhood explorations of the swamps of Florida, and it reminded him as well of the sarcophagi of Egypt." [45]

Benjamin Forgey, writing in the *Washington Star*, described the Henri Gallery installation as the "Robert Stackhouse ethnological museum," adding that "the 10 handcrafted wooden sculptures on view are resonant with the spirits of ancient or 'primitive' cultures." Regarding the "strange, timeless, haunting quality" the writer discovered in the show, Stackhouse responded to Forgey, "Anytime I can get anything to look like a dream, I'm very happy." And, considering the artist's allusions to boats Forgey offered the following analysis. "These pieces of sawed, carved, sanded, riveted and bolted oak, cedar, black walnut and redwood would float, but that's about all. They aren't boats any more than they are the residue of any specific tribe or any specific set of historical experiences. They are art artifacts without practical function; they illustrate nothing. Their purpose is to invoke the spirit of magical ages past" (Figure 3.21). In conclusion, he added, "These are strong, strange pieces, lovingly crafted with a kind of purposeful awkwardness." [46] The following year, Susan Sollins, writing in *Arts* magazine, referred back to this show and these works, suggesting the complex duality of Stackhouse's own response to these works. "He thought of his last show, almost a year ago, as a simple exploration of horizontal and vertical sculptural forms, but in retrospect views these works as almost archetypal in form....Their archetypal quality stemmed from a dreamlike feeling that they stimulated: the boat form moves one back and forth through history—the Egyptian boat of the dead, the Eskimo kayak, the American Indian canoe." [47]

From childhood, Stackhouse had loved water and had grown up in a series of his own small wooden boats, including "Bobby," most without motorized power. From Peach Lake to Lake Julianna, these boats symbolized mobility and independence, serving as the vessels of his youthful explorations and discoveries. At Lundy's fish camp, where he was often left to entertain himself in a community of aging adults, he loved to escape on the water, drifting in his small wooden boat on the lake under the bright and sometimes highly animated cloud patterns of the Florida skies, allowing his imagination and dreams to float freely. At other times, his boat was the vessel of focused adventure and discovery as when he stalked the rogue bull alligator he knew so well from his days on the lake. In this exhibition, Stackhouse used Minimalist techniques and his deep knowledge of boats and boating to create metaphorical vessels that reflected his own earlier experiences and his inner voyages and journeys during these critical years of evolution and transition. His earlier dream of the eye/boat form clearly informed the creation of some of these works, as in the piece he titled *Eye Shape/Boat Shape* (Figure 3.22). The emerging vision and importance of the serpent form was also reflected in the works of this period, as in his two part work, #5, which seems to present a portion of one of his abstract wooden boats forms, in both watercolor and carved wooden sculptural forms (Figure 3.23). However, upon closer examination of the watercolor's surface, ostensibly a highly detailed depiction of the grains and patterns of the wooden piece, the viewer sees suggestions of scales as well as the subtle hint of eyes and the blunt edge of a predator's snout.

During this same time, Mary Beth Edelson, who started to teach classes at the Corcoran in 1971, was becoming increasingly recognized for her leadership role in the feminist art movement. During their last years in Washington from 1972 to 1975, Stackhouse and Edelson both became immersed in a study of shamanistic practices and spiritual rituals, including Edelson's research into images of the earth goddess and asso-

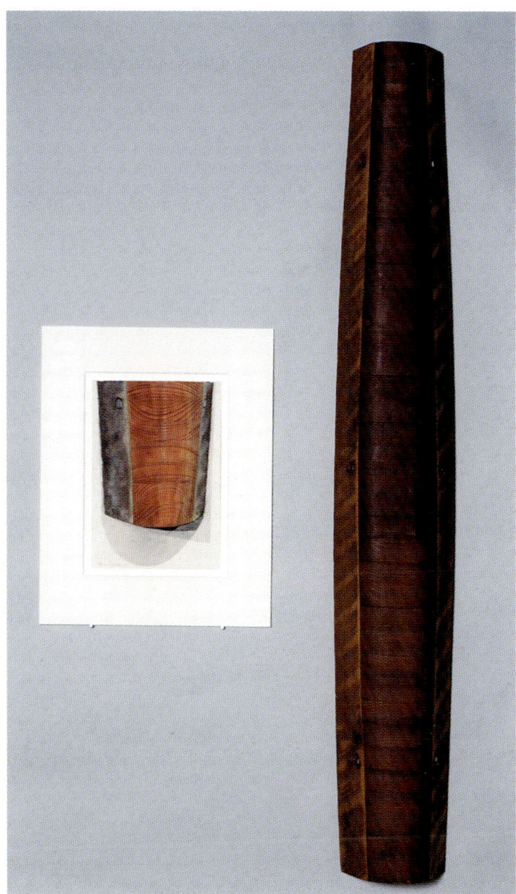

#5 (Sculptural Element)
#5 (Drawing Element)

3.23

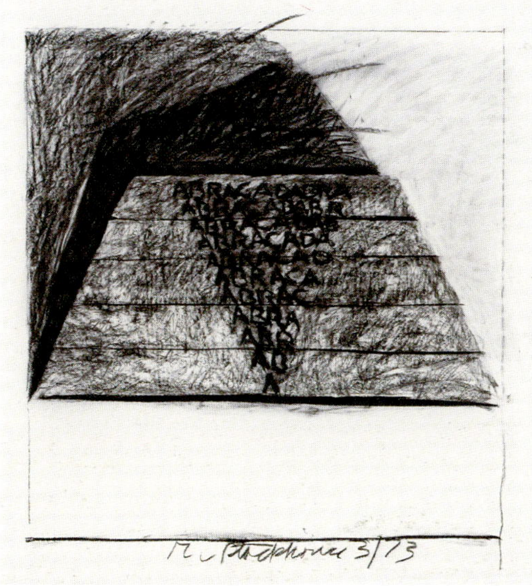

Abracadabra, 1973

3.24

ciated rituals which inspired her own performance pieces. The 1972 conference she helped organize in Washington, the First National Conference on Women in the Visual Arts, served as a milestone feminist event, one that contributed to the rediscovery of artists like Alice Neel. Her well-known poster, *Some Living American Women Artists/Last Supper*, quickly became a feminist icon after this conference. [48] The next year, she presented an exhibition at the Henri Gallery, titled "22 Others," that grew from suggestions and comments submitted by Washington area artists regarding a range of challenging possible art projects. After this exhibition, she became more focused on incorporating rituals and performance pieces into her work. Regarding these pieces she said, "In using my own body as a sacred being, I broke the stereotype that the male gender is the only gender that can identify in a first-hand way with the body and, by extension, the mind and spirit of a primary sacred being." [49] In the early 1970s, as Stackhouse recalls, she participated in an advanced Jungian philosophy seminar at Georgetown University, then returned home to review her notes with him, leading to intense discussions and a resulting expansion of their explorations of these issues. This proved to be a critically important influence for him. She was a significant influence on him and his work at this time, he recalls, including her determination and her work ethic, more disciplined than his own.

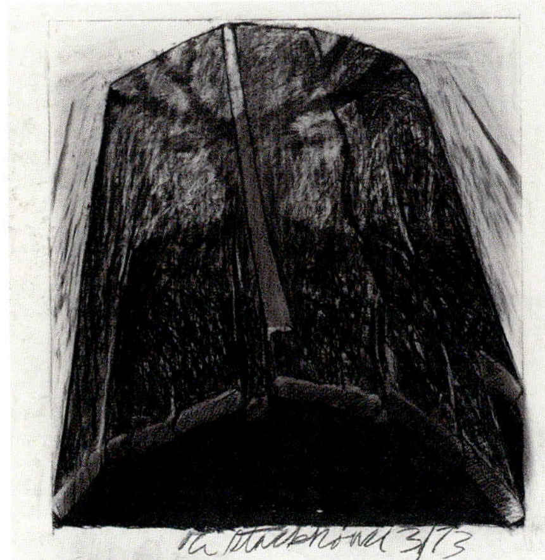

3.25

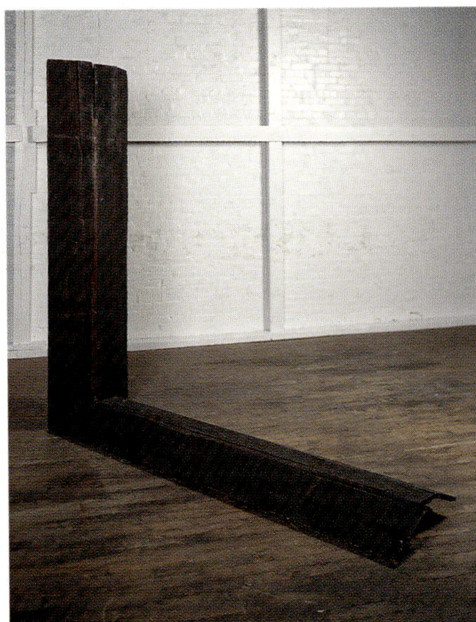

3.26

Sleeping King with Shadow (charcoal) 1973

Sleeping King (sculpture) 1973

The works he created from 1973 to 1975 show the diversity of his artistic concerns, as well as the consistency of his focus on more transcendental issues. In 1973, the work *Abracadabra*, inspired by political life in Washington, created from the wood used in the platform constructed for Richard Nixon's 1972 inaugural ceremonies, continued his wooden Minimalist forms, yet introduced a witty element of word play into the work (Figure 3.24). Responding to this work in a New York exhibition that year, Susan Sollins noted that "the letters form a magic symbol, the triangle, and must also be read or spoken. Word equals energy." [50] His primary focus in these years, and the subject of related exhibitions at both the Corcoran Gallery and the Henri Gallery in 1973, was the large, diverse range of works included in the project he called "The Sleeping King." An early charcoal drawing in the series, *Sleeping King With Shadow*, presents a rounded wooden form (Figure 3.25), that was based upon a wooden sculptural piece, *Sleeping King*, that he had completed that same year (Figure 3.26). A 1974 lithograph, *Winged Goddess* served as a means to expand and continue his interest in the two earlier works (Figure 3.27).

The major work in this series is titled *Sleeping King Ascending*, a title that may refer to the artist's own increasing self-awakening, as well as his growing aesthetic self-confidence and expanding vision (Figure 3.28). Partially inspired, as earlier indicated, by Ronald Bladen's massive black *The X* sculpture built for the atrium of the Corcoran Gallery, and informed by Giacometti's thinly profiled sculptural compositions, this constructed piece took the form of a thin, two-sided pyramid, stretching from the mezzanine level of the atrium up to the ceiling and the skylight areas of the building. Built of approximately 2000 strips of wood lathing, it was completed over an extended period of time, resulting from the repetitive acts of labor required to attach and assemble a piece of this magnitude using basic construction techniques and tools. The two major art critics of the city immediately recognized *Sleeping King Ascending* as a significant work, one that built upon recent traditions in the city and also extended them into new levels of possibility. Paul Richard, writing in *The Washington Post*, compared this work to Ronald Bladen's *The X*, Tony Smith's *Smoke*, and Rockne Krebs' *Ra*, all monumental, and temporary, works designed and constructed for the Corcoran Gallery's central atrium. "Another first rate work, monumental and impermanent, is on view there now. It's a kind of painting made of the cheapest lumber. It's enormous, fragile and translucent." Continuing, he describes the importance of the process and the relationship of the piece to its context.

> *His materials all were alive, and the process that produced the work, all that humble nailing and sawing, seems like a kind of ritual. Stackhouse makes his*

viewers think of homage paid to nameless gods, of spirits conjured up....Other sculptures shown there made the museum's fluted columns seem touchingly old-fashioned. But by reaching backward toward the timeless, by evoking hints of sunworship, burial mounds and totems, Stackhouse has made those columns seem a forest of branchless, artificial trees. [51]

Benjamin Forgey, writing in the *Washington Star-News*, pointed to the "delicacy, refinement and restraint" of *Sleeping King Ascending*, and observed that "the piece has an almost intimate feeling—something you want to go up close to and touch. This is because even when building a pyramid Stackhouse chose to concentrate on surface qualities, such as the texture of the untreated lathing and the linear effect of stacking them one upon the other." Most notably, Forgey suggests that, despite its scale, this work relates to Stackhouse's other artistic abilities. "The piece is 20 feet high but no more than six inches wide, and it can be described—not unkindly—as a sort of drawing in space" (Figure 3.29). And, in this context, he described the "excellent charcoal and graphite drawings in the same spirit as the sculptures," acknowledging Stackhouse's total vision for the work, a multiple piece project based upon interrelated parts comprising a greater unified vision.[52] In 1975, after the work had been disassembled, Stackhouse completed a watercolor and charcoal composition that recreated, in a different medium, his temporary sculptural project (Figure 3.30). This two-dimensional work, an independent painting that builds upon and extends his design and experience of the earlier sculpture, allowed him to "possess" the temporary sculpture, and to improve upon it or create variations on the central theme, a creative response that offered tremendous opportunities for the future of his development as a painter and printmaker.

In 1974, working at the Henri Gallery, he created another milestone work, *Ghost Dance*, a self-supporting piece that continued and expanded the issues first addressed in *Sleeping King Ascending* (Figure 3.31). In fact, these two works seem to have ended one stage of his career, which concluded more formally when he moved to New York in 1975, and opened the portals to the next stage in his evolution, beginning with the A-frame structures he initiated in his 1976 exhibition at the Max Hutchinson Gallery, works that commonly broke free of the constraints of the gallery and museum environment. In fact, as he recently indicated to the author, he realized, while he worked on the construction of both *Sleeping King Ascending* and *Ghost Dance*, that a next logical step in the evolution of his work would be the creation of something like the A-frame structures, even though he did not complete the first of these works until 1976, following his move to New York. In this same context, as he recently recalled, he engaged in conversations with members of the staff at the Phillips Collection, before he decided to move to New York, regarding a possible double walled sculpture commission that, he now admits, would have become the first of his A-frame structures. Because those discussions ended without a commission, the first A-frame, which he titled *Running Animals/Reindeer Way*, was created and exhibited in New York, rather than in Washington, where it was received with significant critical recognition by the art press of the period.

Both *Sleeping King Ascending* and *Ghost Dance* also appear to have evolved, at least in part, from the structural image he had included in the drawing for *Sky Song*, an image that presented this constructed form out of doors, in a seemingly limitless environment. The critically important transi-

Winged Goddess (lithograph) 1974

Sleeping King Ascending installation

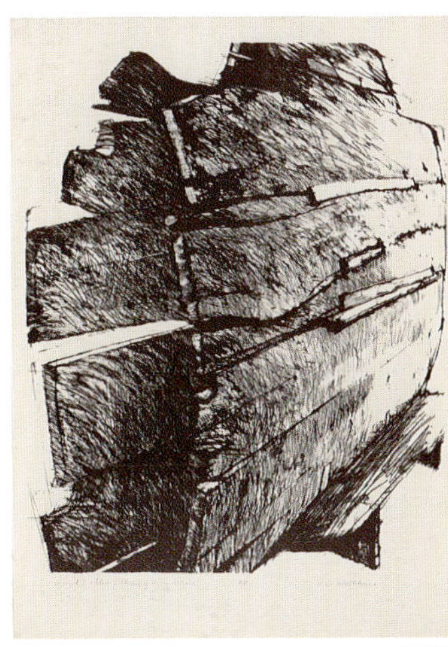

3.27

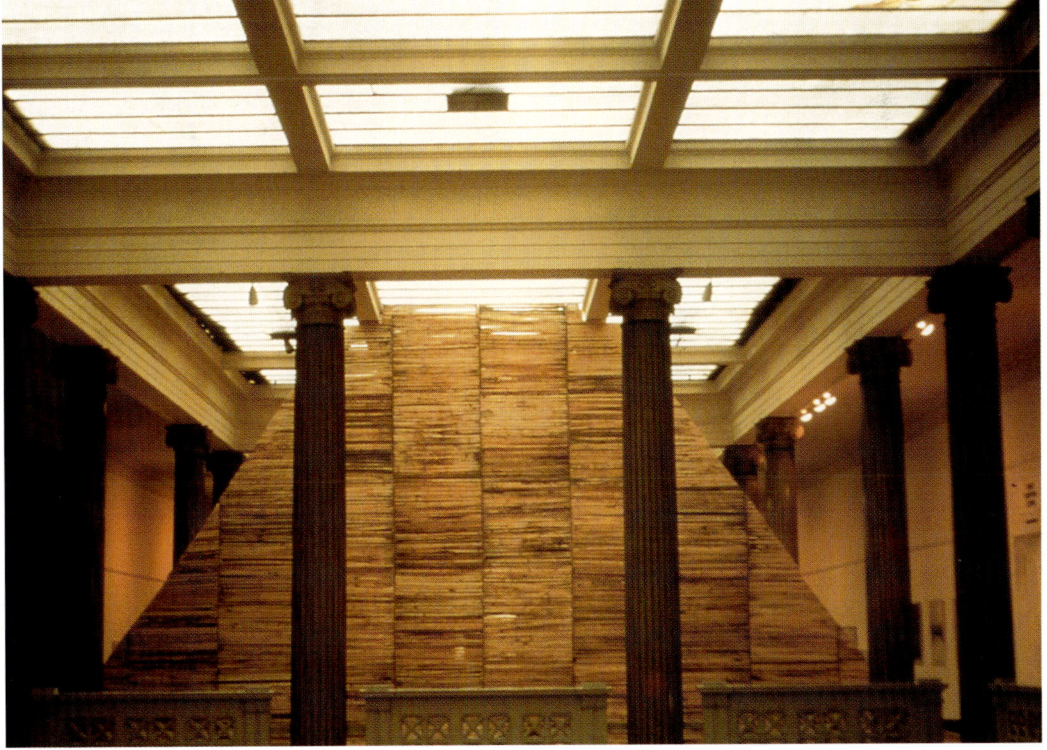

3.28

tional nature of *Ghost Dance* was recognized and described by Carter Ratcliff in 1991.

> *The Minimalists showed him how the shape of a room can clarify the form of a right-angled sculpture. Inverted, this is a lesson in how to generate ambiguity: substitute complex curves for the simplicities of right angles, as in* Ghost Dance, *and, no matter how wall-like the object looks, it will make no formal allegiance with a gallery's interior architecture. It will seem out of place. Only by providing themselves with their own environment would Stackhouse's sculptures be at home. This meant that they would have to enclose space, which they did by doubling themselves. The wall-like singularity of* Ghost Dance *became the two walls of A-frame works like* Running Animals/Reindeer Way *(1976),* Niagara Dance *(1977), and* Dance at Cranbrook *(1978).* [53]

Sleeping King Ascending, side view

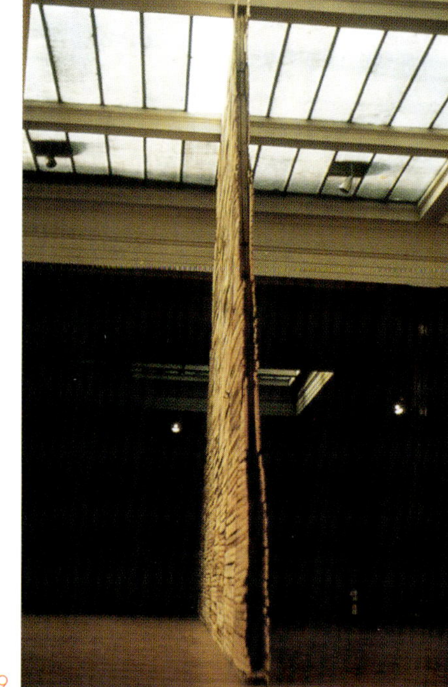

3.29

Sleeping King Ascending (watercolor) 1975

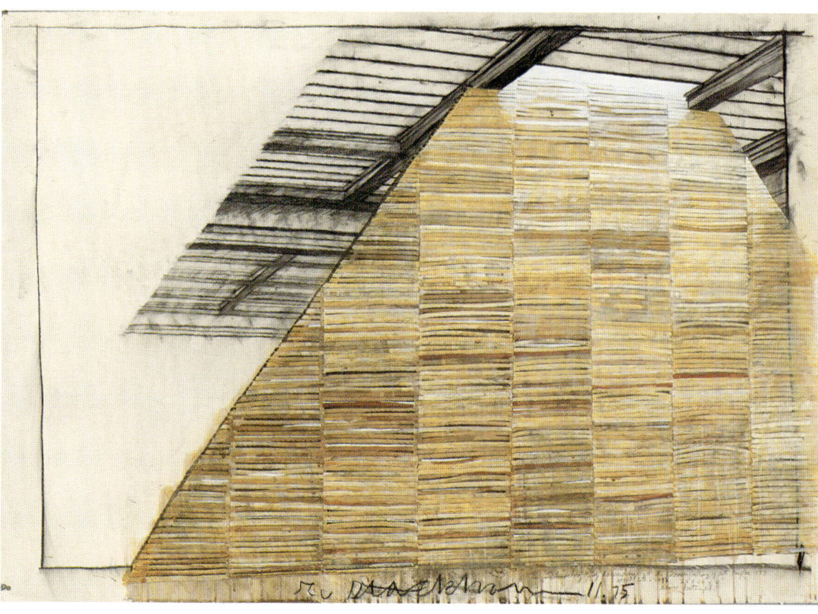

3.30

The title of *Ghost Dance* refers to his interest at that time in the Native American mystical ritual, the Ghost Dance, associated with the tribes of the Great Plains region. He was fascinated by the transformative spiritual powers inherent in the performance of the Ghost Dance, a power he hoped to somehow understand and apply, in a modified manner, in his own approach to working with the creative forces of the unconscious mind. Martin Friedman, writing at the time the Walker Art Center presented Stackhouse's 1977 A-frame construction, *Shiphall (A Passage Structure Borrowing Some Lines from the Oseburg Burial Ship)*, in its galleries, referred back to Stackhouse's extensive research and his associations with the Ghost Dance rituals that had helped to inspire the earlier work.

> *The finished sculpture consisted of concentric half circles that, according to Stackhouse, echoed the patterns of the dancers. He wanted visitors to experience this mystical association. "As you walked around the piece," he says, "you were doing the* Ghost Dance.*" Inside the work, on one of its laths, he penciled the name "Jack Wilson," the Anglo name of the religious leader, Wovoka, who brought the ceremony to prominence in the 1890s. He then overpainted the name so that it became absorbed within the work.* [54]

Stackhouse was also intrigued with the accompanying sense of desperation that nurtured the dance, a desperation born of the recognition that Native American tribal cultures were threatened with the distinct possibility of annihilation, or, at the least, removal to reservations, as an advancing white culture claimed the territories of the West. He shared, in a very different way, a sense of creative desperation, another reason for the selection of this title, because he had assured the director of the Henri Gallery that he would be able to prepare, from inception to completion, a major gallery exhibition in a period of only two months. And, adding to his sense of desperation and urgency, he also announced that he would employ a new approach to his manner of planning such an exhibition, by using two dimensional drawings, inspired by his ability to tap into the creative unconscious mind, as a way to derive, in a reversal of his usual manner of working, the actual concept and design for the structural work he would then build for the gallery space. He discovered this creative process during the making of *Sleeping King Ascending* and he hoped to affirm the success of the process by using it to create the work that eventually became *Ghost Dance*. Intrigued by this notion and by the artist's enthusiasm for such an experimental approach, Henri agreed, granting him an exhibition at her gallery in two months. Then she waited.

Three drawings featured in that 1974 exhibition at Henri Gallery illustrate the specific nature of this experimental working process. "I did the *Ghost Dance* drawings conscious of the fact that I was going to create a sculpture out of doing the busy work. This was an experiment. I had not done this before. I had to complete the drawings and come up with a sculpture to validate this process to myself." And, in affirming the possibilities of his process, he recognized that he had established an approach that was filled with tremendous potential for the development of his future paintings and projects. "That was when I really believed that whole strategy of doing a sculpture, of letting it be destroyed if it had to be, then doing a painting of it. And, while I was doing a painting of it, I could revisit that sculpture and continue to deal with that sculpture in other forms to a point where it regenerated itself into a new piece, into a series of new ideas."

In his *Drawing for Ghost Dance #1*, (Figure 3.32), he documented his studio process of shifting from his conscious, rational mind to the unconscious, spontaneous mind that contributed to his creative process. "I was trying to educate myself to the process of doing a lot of busy work. In that busy work there is a kind of ritualization, which frees you from your consciousness and leads you into that different state of unconsciousness. I started by doing a drawing of myself, basically copying a photograph Mary Beth took of me in my mask (Figure 3.33). And I thought that it would be busy enough that I would start thinking of sculptures to do, perhaps even scribbling on the borders of the drawing and come up with the idea for the sculpture." When that was not successful, he added another element. "As I got into the drawing, somehow, as I stood over the paper, my shadow came into the drawing, so I decided to allow the shadow to enter the work. And, at some later point, I decided to allow the antlers into the work." He had been using the antlers recently as a subject for drawings in his studio. He initially discovered and photographed these antlers on the Outer Banks of North Carolina, as he rode his motorcycle along the beaches, searching for historic shipwrecks that he had seen featured in an issue of *National Geographic*. As he moved close to the deer skull with his camera, his shadow covered the skull, merging his image, and in a ritualistic sense, his spirit, with that of the deer (Figure 3.34). This fascination with the transforming power of the photographic shadow may have informed the drawing, consciously or unconsciously, and would be reflected in his later works.

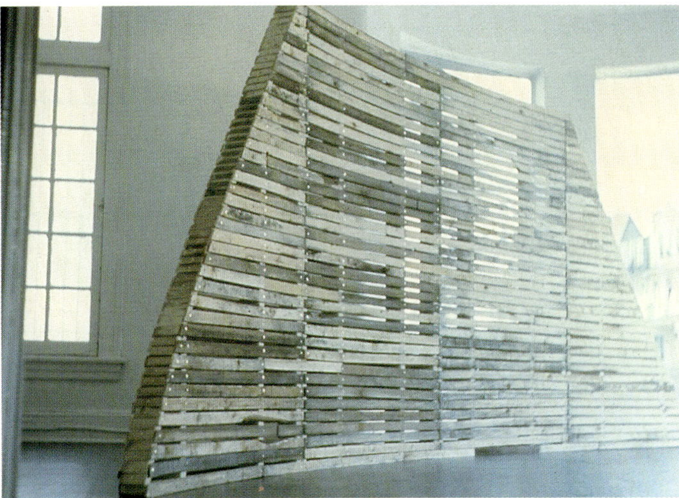

3.31

Ghost Dance, 1974.

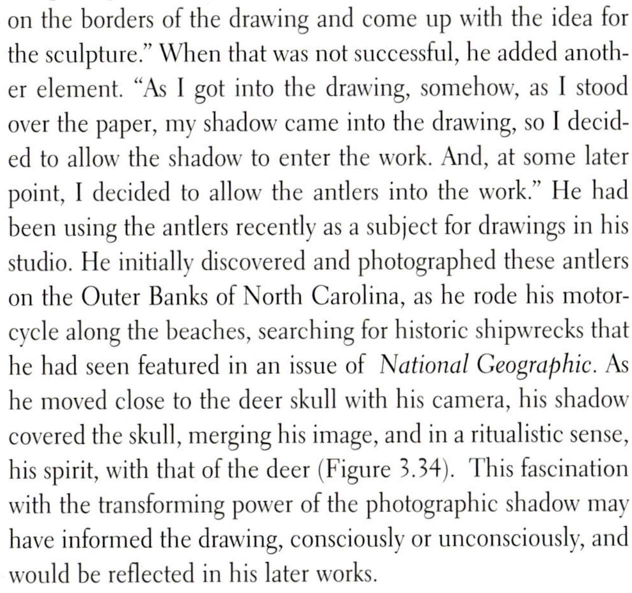

Realizing that the experiment had not yielded a sculptural concept, he moved on to another drawing. And, in *Drawing for Ghost Dance #2*, he focused as has been suggested earlier, on recreating the painstaking details of a deer's head, taken from a magazine illustration, that he associated with the watercolors of Don Ray, the artist who had been so close to his family at Peach Lake (Figure 3.35). In this second drawing, he presented, in the background, walls and architectural details suggesting the gallery space at Henri's that he intended to utilize in his exhibition. "Again, I was staring at this thing, and I was becoming too conscious of it, so I realized I had to trick myself one more time. As I got into the drawing, I realized that it was not releasing me. I selected this deer's head and decided to paint it, one hair at a time, and that rendering was all about seeking that release by allowing my conscience mind to drift off course. What came out of it was the suggestion of all these curves." This led to the final of the three drawings, *Drawing for Ghost Dance #3* (Figure 3.36). In that work, he showed the deer again, this time as a skull, suggesting, as he recently noted, "that the deer had been used, and there was this transforming process of the deer living its life." Here, in the third and final drawing, he discovered the form and the concept for his sculpture. "That curved shape informed *Ghost Dance*, which is a curved form, a curved wall. *Ghost Dance*, which is a sculpture that the Corcoran Gallery now owns, is a essentially a curved A-frame. So that is why I did this, and did it on purpose."

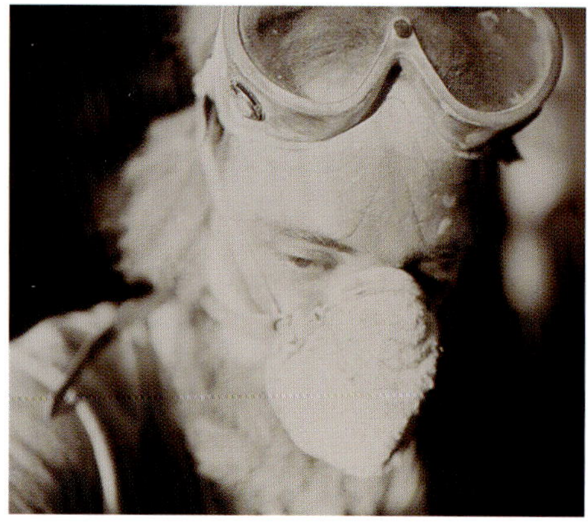

3.33

Robert Stackhouse, wearing goggles and face mask in studio. Photograph by Mary Beth Edelson.

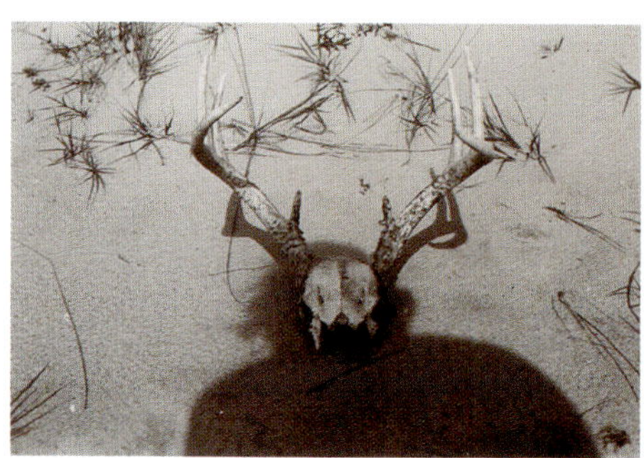

3.34

Robert Stackhouse shadow with deer skull, on the Outer Banks of North Carolina, 1974.

Stackhouse went to the Outer Banks with Edelson in the summer of 1974, spending a month at a house they rented at Nag's Head. He remembers spending much of his time riding on his BMW motorcycle, searching the beaches for the ruins of the wrecked, ghost-like ships that he discovered scattered along the water. One morning, feeling the need to catch up on the news, he went out on the motorcycle and stopped to pick up a newspaper. The headlines reported that, on the preceding day, August 8, 1974, Richard Nixon had resigned his presidency. This event added to the mood and the tone of the month at Nag's head, a time of intensive activity and reflection for both of them. This was certainly true for Edelson, who produced one of her most famous series of work that August on the island. Using her body as a surrogate form for the Goddess, she performed a series of private rituals, related to her research on the Goddess, and photographed herself performing these rituals. She then applied color and imagery to these works, creating the series known as "Woman Rising," which was featured in an article devoted to her work, written by Jack Burnham, published in *Arts* magazine in the fall of 1975, not long after their move to New York. In that article, she explained the nature of the "Woman Rising" series.

> *Having found a spot on an isolated beach where I would not be stumbled upon, it was my intention to try to communicate with the ancient goddesses. Using body paint to set me apart, as well as ritual position, I hoped to move toward a physical and psychological state of receptiveness. Once I did, I concentrated on communication....The markings on the photographs enabled me to put down my feelings of spiritual energy, the forces that I felt rising from my body and mind, as extensions beyond myself.* [55]

By the end of 1974, both Robert and Mary Beth realized that they were beginning to outgrow the range of possibilities that Washington could offer them. Despite the successes both of them had enjoyed in Washington, with the museum and gallery responses to their work, and in the related positive and supportive critical response to their exhibitions and diverse projects, as well as in their teaching careers at the Corcoran, they felt that it was time to move beyond Washington, to New York. In New York, they thought, they would be closer to the major museums and galleries, to the curators and dealers of the greatest consequence, and to the most advanced artists who were commonly directing the next trends and directions in the course of the art world. Mary Beth was particularly eager to get to New York, the unquestioned center of the expanding feminist art world, where she was certain of a greater degree of involvement and participation in unfolding national events. In 1975, she began traveling to the city more often, searching for a loft in the city's art district, one suitable for both of their living and working studio needs. When she discovered a large loft space priced within her budget at 110 Mercer Street, in the heart of the SoHo area, they decided that it was indeed time to leave Washington and to move to New York. Robert, who felt strongly connected to the faculty, the students and programs of the Corcoran, decided that he would retain his position on the faculty and would commute back to Washington and the Corcoran on his teaching days. The shift to New York, back to the city of his birth, began.

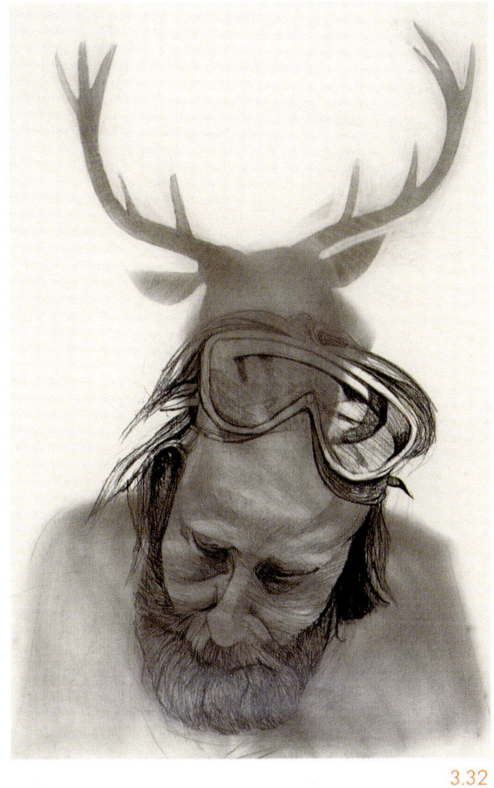

3.32

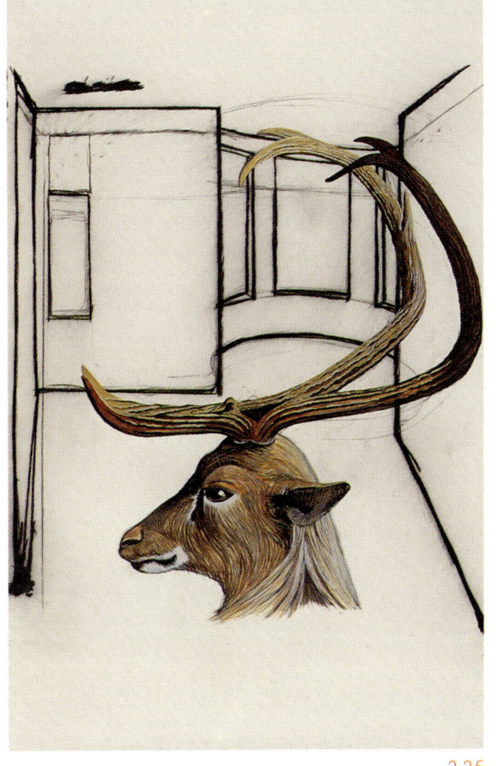

3.35

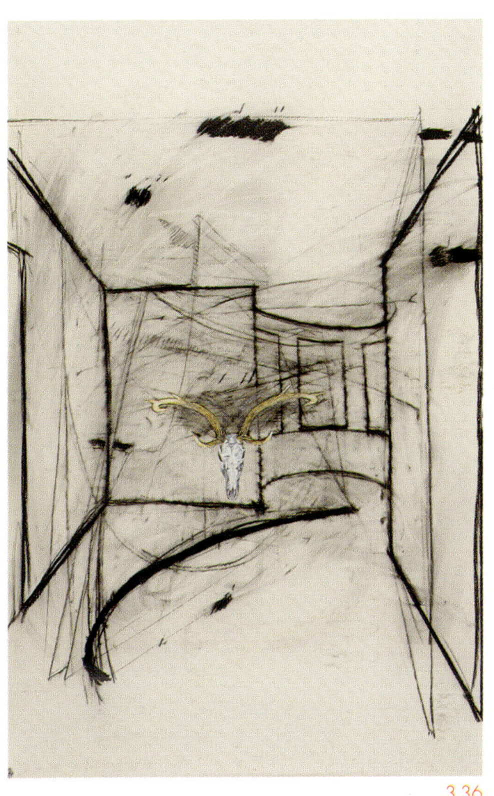

3.36

Drawing for Ghost Dance #1
(1974)

Drawing for Ghost Dance #2
(1974)

Drawing for Ghost Dance #3
(1974)

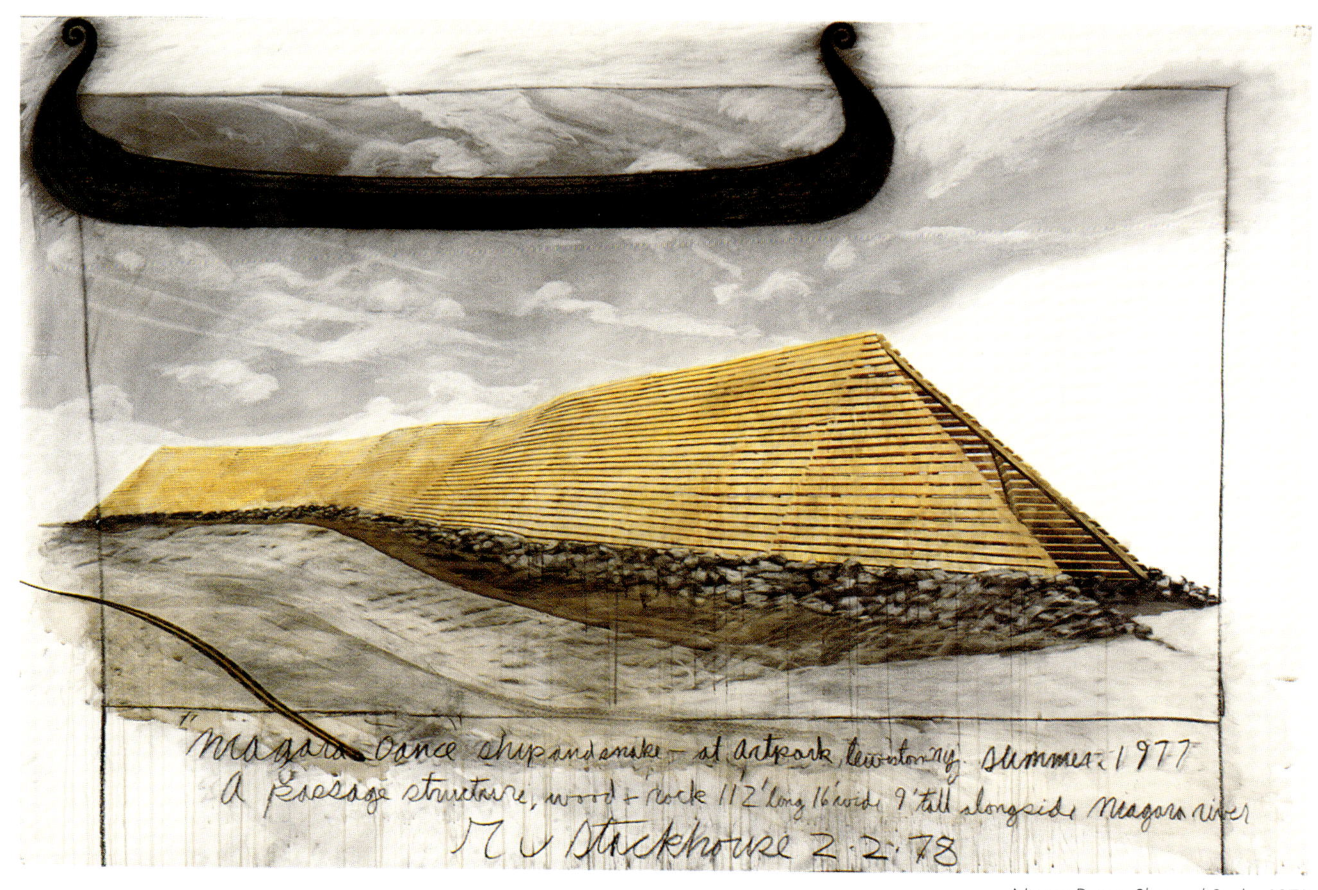

Niagra Dance Ship and Snake, 1978

CHAPTER FOUR

New York and Washington

Robert Stackhouse and Mary Beth Edelson moved to New York during a time when dominant movements and styles in the art world were breaking down, during a "post-modern" era, which resulted in a complex and often contradictory art environment in the nation's art capital and elsewhere across the nation. In 1977, Martin Friedman described the conditions at that time. "In its social and economic aspects, the 1970s is an era of contradiction, consolidation and introspection. Why should its arts be an exception?" Continuing, he compared this period to the preceding decade. "The atmosphere today is considerably different from the heady, open-ended 60s whose protests, peace marches and other manifestations of social concern now seem light years away." [56] Changing attitudes toward the importance of the gallery and museum environment caused a number of artists to create projects and exhibitions too large for galleries or museums, reflecting the continuing influence of Robert Smithson, Michael Heizer, Walter De Maria, and other artists associated with earth art and environmental art issues. Feminist artists continued to play an increasingly influential role in national art issues during this period while protests and marches at major national museums, led by African-American artists, called for equal rights in the institutional collecting and exhibiting of artists, regardless of race or sex. [57]

By the time they arrived in SoHo, the area was recognized as a center for artists and contemporary art galleries. Paula Cooper opened her gallery there, as she has indicated, because of its distance from the uptown art scene. "My gallery was the only one in SoHo when I opened in 1968. The reason I came downtown in the first place was to get away from the old pattern of the uptown galleries: It was moribund, too set in its ways. I wanted to be independent." [58] Ivan Karp opened his gallery in SoHo soon after Cooper's arrival because, as he has explained, "many of my visits to artists' studios within the previous two or three years had been downtown in what is now SoHo. I lived in the area myself, along with forty or fifty artists, many of them not legally in residence. Within a week I found an enormous space on West Broadway, an abandoned warehouse with seven thousand square feet....I opened O.K. Harris in October 1969." [59] By 1971, the city of New York contributed to the growth of SoHo as an arts center when it finally legalized the use of area lofts by artists. Two years later, SoHo became the first commercial neighborhood in New York to be designated an historic district by the Landmarks Preservation Committee. SoHo's arts district had become so popular with New Yorkers and tourists, who crowded into the area's fashionable galleries, boutiques and restaurants in ever increasing numbers, that a national magazine could devote a cover article to the question, "Has Success Spoiled SoHo?"[60]

By this time a growing number of artists, including many who had been trained as painters, began to recognize that sculpture was rising to a level of professional stature previously accorded only to painting in America. Museum and institutional acceptance of American sculpture was evident in the proliferation of sculptural exhibitions that were being presented across the country. One of the most important of these was "200 Years of American Sculpture," presented by the Whitney Museum of American Art, with major support from the National Endowment for the Arts and Chase Manhattan Bank, as its major 1976 American Bicentennial exhibition. With this extensive survey of the history of American sculpture, presented in an installation designed by architect Robert Venturi, the Whitney Museum, known for its support of American painting, validated the medium of sculpture and the wide range of artists associated with it. In the exhibition's catalogue, Tom Armstrong, the director of the museum, explained that the Whitney's decision "was made after consideration that such an endeavor, commemorating this historic occasion, should provide new scholarship in a subject not fully surveyed previously. American sculpture was chosen as our topic because it has been overlooked in the study of American art." [61] Whitney curator Barbara Haskell, in this same catalogue, explained that by "the early sixties...American sculpture became as prominent and vital as painting. This emergence of sculpture as a primary force in the evolution and redefinition of art has been one of the critical changes in American art during the last two decades." [62] The evolution of this process was also described by Martin Friedman.

> *The issue of scale became crucial in American sculpture during the 1960s. Bigness in art was pioneered by the ambitious Abstract Expressionist generation in paintings that covered entire walls. That excitement was contagious and heroic scale soon spread to sculpture. As a result of the public art boom that began in the mid-1960s, abetted by federal grants and corporate patronage, large scale sculpture gained prominence and respectability. This new opportunity to work on an ambitious scale, utilizing industrial materials and processes, was a key factor in the dramatic development of recent American sculpture.* [63]

Naturally, as Martin Friedman knew, and as Stackhouse and many of his colleagues working with sculpture in the Baltimore and Washington area had demonstrated before the Bicentennial, not all contemporary artists were interested in "utilizing industrial materials and processes." In fact, many, including Stackhouse, were more interested in the use of natural materials and more traditional techniques of construction and fabrication. Commuting to Washington on a regular weekly basis, Stackhouse maintained his significant relationship with the leaders of that city's arts scene while he continued to teach in the core program at the Corcoran Gallery's School of Art. During his first year in New York, the 1975-76 academic year, Stackhouse remained actively involved in the renovation of their SoHo loft, completing much of the major carpentry and electrical work himself. During that summer, before they were able to move into their new space, they stayed in a loft belonging to Enid Sanford Cafritz, an acquaintance from Washington, who had purchased her converted studio loft from Kenneth Noland. Stackhouse enjoyed the use of this space, in part because of its associations with Noland, and even more so because it was located in the same building as the studio of David Haxton, his good friend and colleague from the USF art department. Haxton, working in the city as an artist as well, was by that time associated with two prominent galleries, the Castelli and Sonnabend galleries, both located in SoHo.

Soon after moving to New York, Stackhouse set about the process of contacting galleries, seeking a venue for his first New York gallery exhibition. Not long after his arrival, in the fall of 1975, he established contact with Max Hutchinson, who promised to visit the artist's studio. Stackhouse immediately planned and constructed a studio sculptural installation, to demonstrate his abilities to Hutchinson. The work was not an A-frame or passageway piece, it was instead built of two walls that crisscrossed each other. However, as Stackhouse recalls, Hutchinson did not come to the gallery for many months, not until the late spring. The sculpture remained there, undisturbed, for this entire period while Stackhouse commuted to Washington and worked on their loft when he returned to New York. When, finally, Hutchinson came to the studio in June, he said little, looking quietly at the art, asking only the dates and the chronology of the works. As Stackhouse later learned, Hutchinson's silence was not caused by the art, he had just come from a dentist's appointment and was in pain. As he left, almost as an afterthought it seemed to Stackhouse, Hutchinson turned and asked if Stackhouse could be ready in

September. Remembering one of Harrison Covington's cardinal rules about the art world, to never say no, he replied in the affirmative. Then, he remembers, he asked "Ready for what?" Hutchinson explained that he was offering him a show in September, only three months later, if he could be prepared for it. Once again, Stackhouse agreed, assuring the dealer that he would be ready on time.

Without doubt, he recalled the challenge that he had set himself in his 1974 exhibition at the Henri Gallery. By 1976, he had proven his ability to perform under tight schedules and to apply his distinctive working methodology to this process. He was confident that, somehow, he would be able to mount his first major New York exhibition by that fall. In the interim, he continued to read and to explore issues of importance to his research at that time. After settling in New York, Stackhouse's reading took a much more serious turn as he began to focus and complete research on a range of specific subjects. In Washington, from 1969 to 1975, as he now recalls, he read many books including *Forms of Japan* by Yuichiro Kojiro, Black Elk's *Black Elk Speaks*, Carl Jung's *Man and his Symbols*, Jack Burnham's *Beyond Modern Sculpture* and *The Structure of Art* as well as a wide range of books and articles on herpetology. In New York, he expanded his reading to include books such as Mircea Eliade's *The Sacred and the Profane: The Nature of Religion and Shamanism*, James Moody's *The Ghost-dance Religion* and *Wounded Knee*, Jerome Rothenberg's *Shaking the Pumpkin*, Gunter Grass's *The Flounder*, Frank Herbert's *Dune*, Carlos Castenada's books on Don Juan and Guy Underwood's *The Pattern of the Past*. From 1976 to 1978 he read Julius Caesar's *The Conquest of Gaul*, *Beowulf*, *The Mabinogion* and numerous Penguin classic books devoted to Nordics, including Egill Skallagrimsson and *Naal's Tale*. From 1978 to 1980 he read almost every available book on Vikings. Beginning in 1976, he regularly studied books on naval architecture and history, as well as books devoted to archeological boats including Sutton Hoo, Gokstaad, the Cheops ship, the Titanic and publications on discovered shipwrecks. In many different ways, these readings affected the evolution of his work in these years and to the present.

That summer he also had agreed to teach for one month at the Corcoran's summer art program in Tenant's Harbor, Maine. During his month in Maine, he would discover, in a most significant fashion, the continuing power of one of his most potent symbols and subjects, the snake. Quite unexpectedly, during the middle of this summer workshop, far away from New York, his studio and the pressure he felt to complete a work for his fall exhibition, a most unusual event took place. As a result of this event, which he describes, a specific work, *Snake Story* (1976) (Figure 4.1), was created as a form of documentation of the process. Then, when he returned to the studio, he produced a large body of works, including the drawings that would lead to his sculptural piece, inspired by this event.

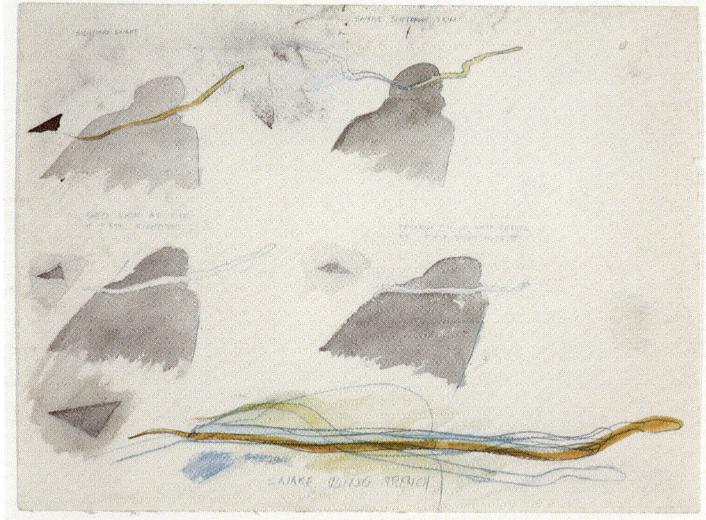

4.1

Snake Story, 1976

> *I was planning my very first New York show. I was at a workshop. And a group of students were making fun of me because I had this little thing going with a little garter snake who lived under a sidewalk outside of the farm we were staying on in Maine. And I tried to photograph it every day. One day at breakfast a student said, your snake is out there. So I grabbed the camera and ran out to a bunch of student giggles. When I came out my little garter snake was shedding its skin. And I was standing, watching, with my shadow overlapping it. So I watched the snake literally turn itself inside out. It chewed some grass, got its jaw attached, and it just split right out of it. And that V shape appeared, as in the drawing, with my shadow over it. I went back, dug a trench, where this event had happened, got some white crushed oyster shell and filled it in, and went back out there every day for a couple of weeks. I waited for the snake to come back to complete the circle, and it did. It came back to the trench, and I photographed it. And, I kept the snake skin as well. The snake at that time gave me a gift. The serpent gave me this impulsive information. This work and the process it reflects is not about the snake as much as it is about the impulse. The snake is only an*

indicator of that. I am afraid of snakes. And, I am afraid of that impulse as well.

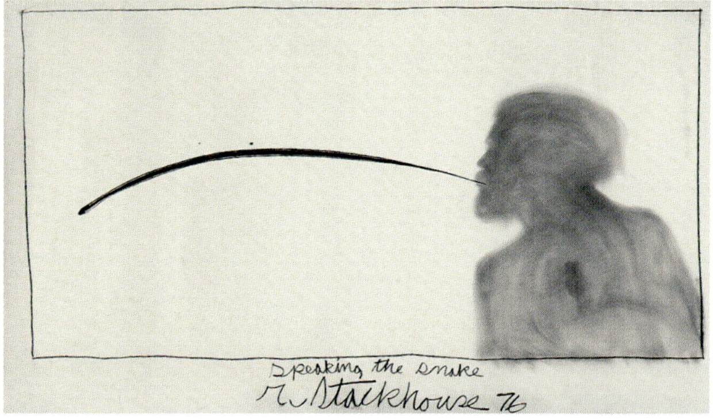

4.2 Speaking the Snake, 1976

He was especially taken by this process because, at the same time, he had been reading a book about dowsing, *The Pattern of the Past*, by Guy Underwood, about Stonehenge and English stone monuments. The book explored issues related to geomagnetic lines and how the force of these lines had influenced a broad range of cultural and historical developments. Of particular interest to him was the information describing how animals followed these lines, the geomagnetic lines, instinctively. He also became aware that animals often migrated by reading these currents in the earth. As he absorbed this information, he continued to think about the process of planning and constructing the sculpture for his show. His experiences with the snake and with the absorption of this information had a significant influence on the development of *Running Animals/Reindeer Way*.

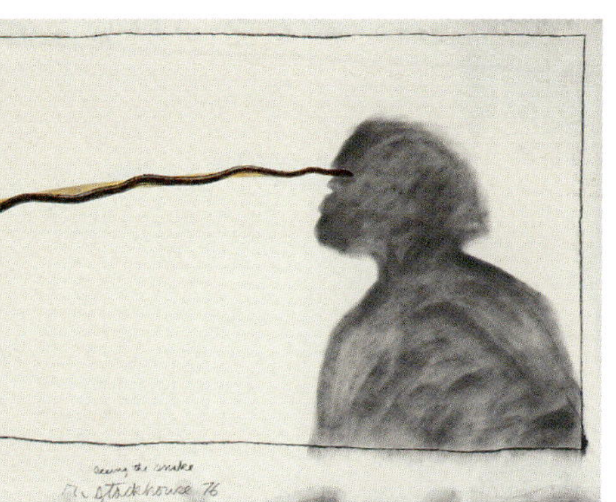

4.3 Seeing the Snake, 1976

When he returned to his studio, he did a tracing of his shadow, still thinking of his experience with the snake in Maine. This resulted in the work titled *Speaking the Snake* (Figure 4.2) He was involved in a process of experimentation and exploration, and, because of this, he was not reluctant to leave a trail of his actions upon the surface. As a result, there are erasures, rubbings and markings that reflect the intuitive processes at work in this piece. A related piece, also completed at this time, was called *Seeing the Snake*. (Figure 4.3). The process of seeing and watching the snake in Maine reminded him, no doubt, of some of his earlier experiences with snakes at Peach Lake and in Florida at Lundy's fish camp. This process, combined with his extensive reading in related issues, expanded his fascination with the use of overlaying shadows, self-portraiture and the process of merging his shadow self with these snake and deer forms. While studying the ways and the rituals of earlier civilizations, he actually began to experience some of earlier man's connections to the mysteries of the natural world. Similar activities had guided Mary Beth Edelson in her art and performance pieces, including performance and ritual on the beaches of the Outer Banks in 1974. From the forms in *Speaking the Snake*, specifically the curving line of the snake, he derived a curving line in drawings, one that was informed by the pattern of the walls in his earlier work, *Ghost Dance*, and one that would inform his next major piece, *Running Animals/Reindeer Way*.

During the summer, in Maine and in New York, his experiences, his readings and his creative processes all combined to bring him back to one of his most important continuing subjects, the snake, updating and expanding the direction he had pursued in the past. He had arrived in New York, as previously indicated, with a clear understanding of the inherent possibilities for the A-frame structure derived from his work on both *Sleeping King Ascending* and *Ghost Dance*. This knowledge and the immersion in the snake experiences in Maine that summer contributed, once again, to proving the viability of his creative drawing system. One impressive large drawing from this year, *Recollection of a Great Snake #3* (1976) (Figure 4.4), reflects both his readings about ancient cultures and his training as an Abstract Expressionist painter. In this work, with this subject in mind and charcoal in hand, he began to produce the work through a series of large sweeping gestures, not unlike the gestures he knew Jackson Pollock made over his most famous canvases, gestures filled with energy and creative expression. Like many of Pollock's abstract compositions, this work by Stackhouse serves as more than a completed art work with a specific image, it also serves as a record of the artist's creative process, including his gestures and motions before the paper.

In addition to the series of snake images, he produced a series of related drawings, also associated with the Max Hutchinson Gallery project. Using a dense and interrelated series of images and ideas—the lines and patterns he had derived from the serpent images in Maine, his research on the geomagnetic attraction of animals and their migration patterns, his understanding of the relationship of animals' tracks and trails to the patterns used in neolithic stone monuments—he began to sketch possible patterns (trails) for his New York sculptural project, as in *A Working Drawing For Running Animals #1* (Figure 4.5). And, once again, returning to the shadow of the deer form, he layered the sculptural patterns with the form and spirit of the deer, in the work titled, *Two Studies for Running Animals* (Figure 4.6). Another stage of this drawing process, evident in *Running Tracks-Sculpture Study*, (Figure 4.7) produced perspective studies, an analysis of lath systems and probable light patterns within the sculptural form, as the artist has suggested. "I was interested in the curvilinear aspect of these drawings and the forms. I was reading a great deal about shamanism, about comparative religion. I was interested in the ritualization and how in ritual the unconscious is unlocked. That was something I was desperate to learn. The serpent is all about impulse. It is dangerous. It is scary." Continuing, he explained how his other major symbol and working subject, the ship, was becoming increasingly important in this process. "And I think the ship is a vehicle, literally, to get from here to there. And the combination of those two things, a reinforcement of movement, is like the old saying about 'working yourself through it.' It was very important to prove to myself that by working on certain subjects in the studio it would unlock my unconscious, or at least distract my consciousness enough so that I could receive certain things. My imagery is the result of a specific creative process."

The completed installation for *Running Animals/Reindeer Way* reflected these issues and also had to relate to the spatial configuration and limitations of the interior spaces of Max Hutchinson's Sculpture Now gallery. Informed by his earlier experiences in theater and stage design, including his studies of stage lighting in Florida, Stackhouse presented the piece in a dramatic installation that invited the viewer to enter the work and to explore the path it created. Moving through the work, visitors experienced the interior spaces, the shifting light patterns, the different available perspectives on the surrounding gallery and varying movements as the sculpture snaked its way through the environment (Figure 4.8). Even before he had completed his first New York installation, David Bourdon, writing in the *Village Voice*, reported on the powerful presence of the work. "For the past several days, a huge, walk-through construction has been rising in the lower gallery of Sculpture Now....The walls are nearly 12 feet high and about 66 feet

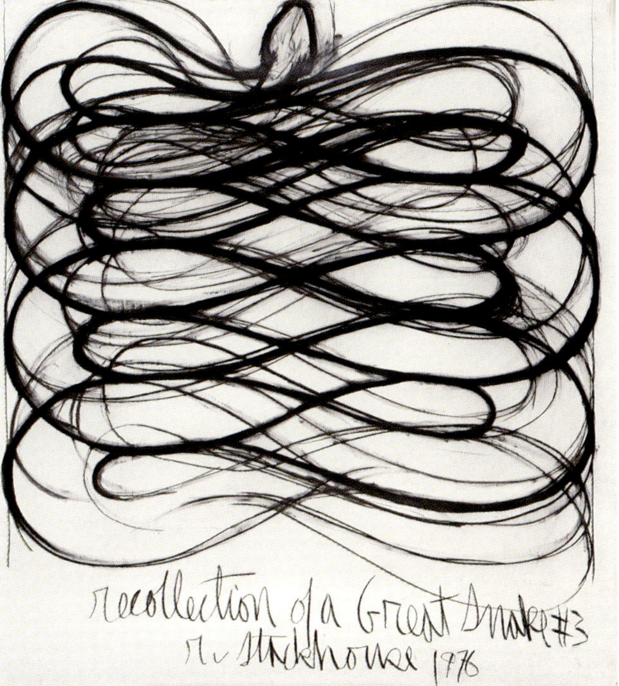

4.4

Recollection of a Great Rain Snake #3, 1976

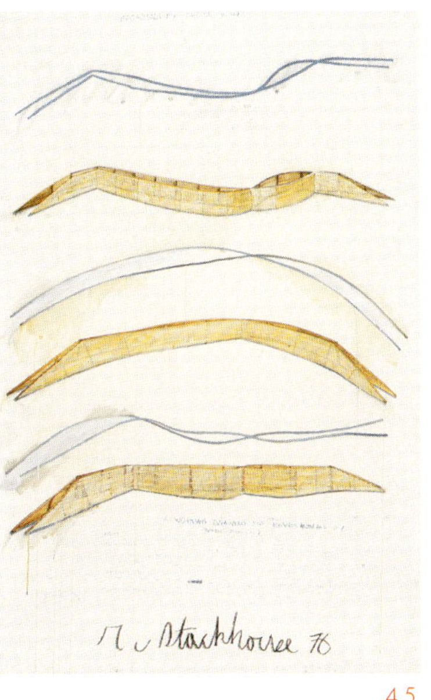

4.5

A Working Drawing for Running Animals #1, 1976

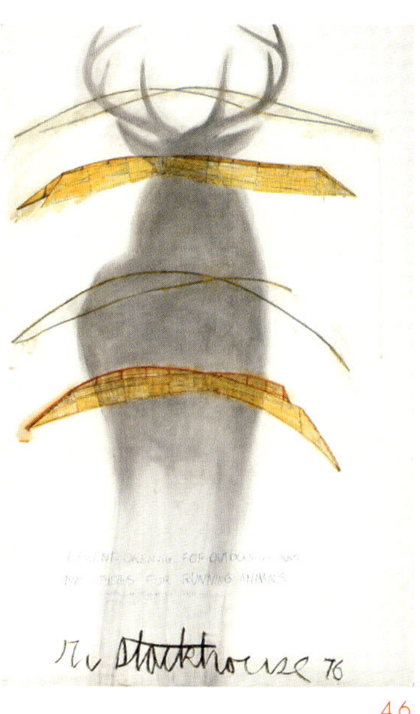

4.6

Two Studies for Running Animals, 1976

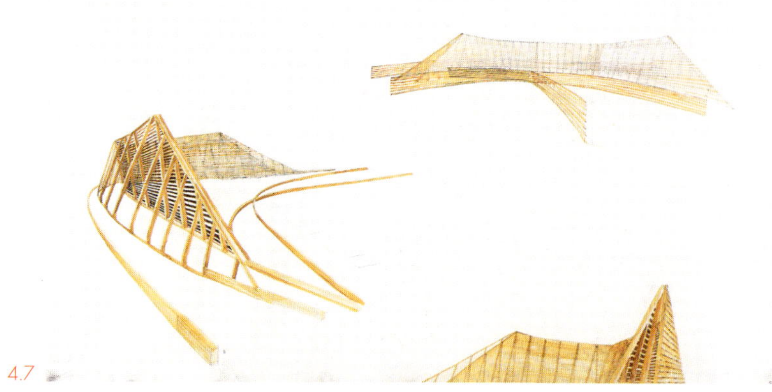

4.7

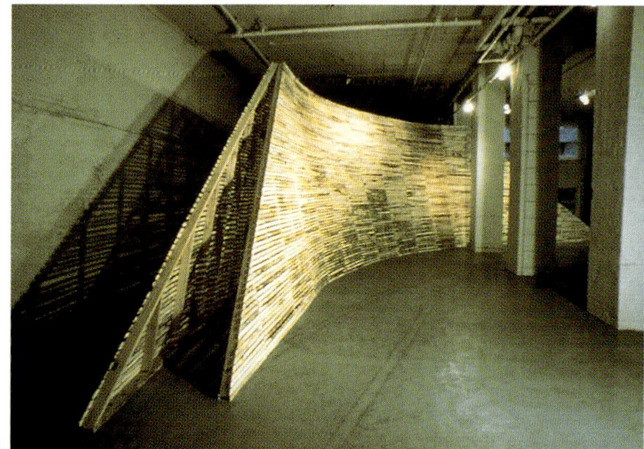

4.8

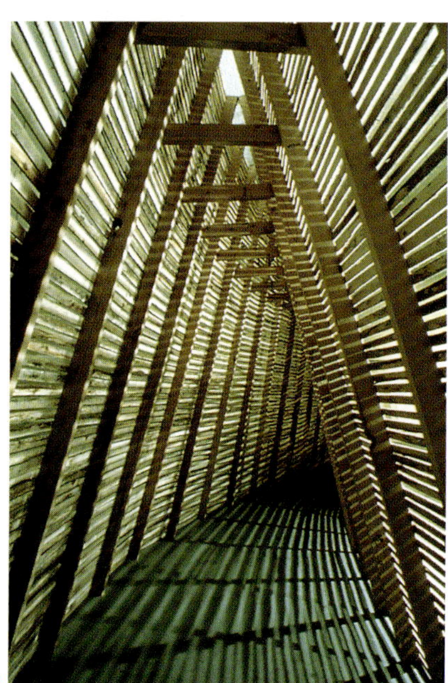

4.9

Running Tracks - Sculpture Study, 1976

Running Animals/Reindeer Way, 1976

Running Animals/Reindeer Way, 1976, Inside Veiw

long. The construction consists mainly of some 2400 laths screwed together horizontally into 2 x 4 supports." After describing the exterior, he moved to the inside, the central space of the project (Figure 4.9), and the center of Stackhouse's intended focus for the viewer/participant.

> *While the exterior of the piece is somewhat forbidding, the arched interior becomes a soothing, protective, cathedral-like space. The corridor is filled with the criss-crossing shadows of the laths, and the spectator feels concealed, while still able to look out. Acute observers will have no difficulty spotting two sets of deer antlers, symmetrically located on overhead latticed ledges several feet inside each end of the corridor—concrete evidence that* Running Animals *is not just another Minimalist construction....Initially, he intended to make* Running Animals *more complex, with a secondary structure—signifying the running tracks of the reindeer—placed alongside the walls.* [64]

Bourdon examined this exhibition, and the artist's related philosophies, more thoroughly in an influential and widely-read article, "Robert Stackhouse: On the Trail of Legend," published in the December 1976 issue of *Arts* magazine. To avoid confusion on his intent in regard to his incorporation of animal references, Stackhouse offered the following statement to Bourdon. "I'm not making art about animals. They are just a reference, a symbolic element of my art. The creation of legend and myth is what I'm interested in." Bourdon referred to Stackhouse's recurring use of the deer, his "other" self, and printed the artist's explanation of its importance. "The horned being is my shadow self." In Bourdon's article, Stackhouse suggested a much larger context for this project, and, in so doing, indicated the direction that would become clear in the following A-frame projects of the next two years.

> *Animals possess instincts greater than ours, close in harmony with seasonal changes. An animal's ability to make and follow migratory tracks remains in large part a mystery, explainable perhaps by the rhythms of the world. The animals, their "power," became objects of human ritual, the beginnings of religion. Sites*

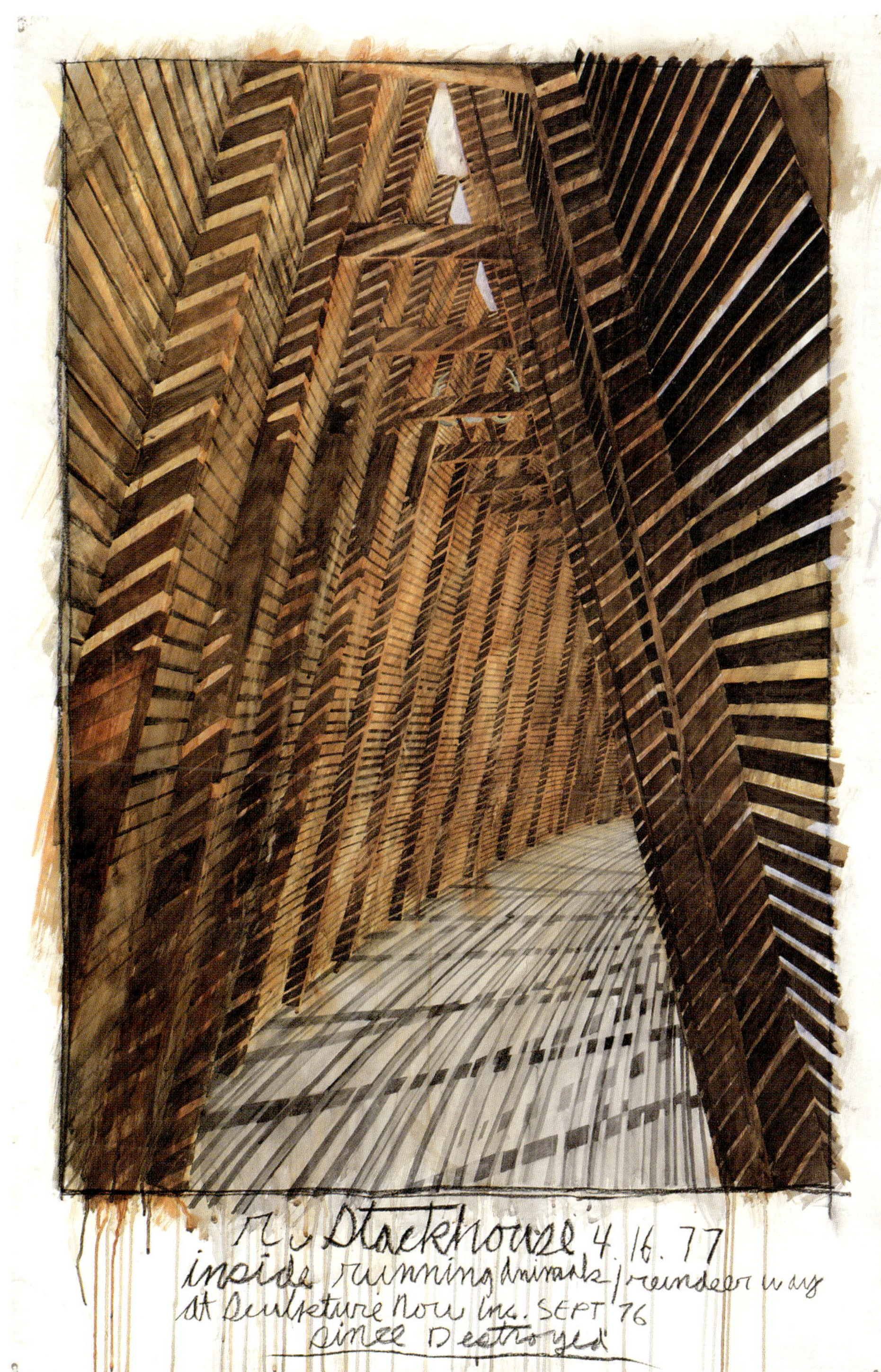

4.10

Inside Running Animals/Reindeer Way 1977

along the migration routes that were inhabited by hunters, first sparingly, then repeatedly, picked up more spiritual significance in each successive visit, by generation after generation. As a site became more "hallowed," temporary shelters gave way to more permanent structures, some endowed with sacred connotations, which in turn changed the site from temporary to permanent, the beginnings of towns. Running Animal/Reindeer Way *suggests the rhythmic span of social setting, growing out of natural order that links one time to another.* [65]

In this project, Stackhouse fused his wide ranging interests and diverse personal experiences—ranging from his childhood memories of the rafters in the Peach Lake house to his experiences in theater, dance and performance in Tampa and Washington—to create a work that marked his entry into New York's art world and opened opportunities on a broader level, as he has indicated. "After the *Village Voice* and *Arts* magazine articles, other national magazines picked up on the piece, giving it good reviews. Out of that show—which included vertical drawings of reindeer dance images—those drawings brought me other projects, including Artpark, the Walker Art Center and the Ship at St. Agnes, in Cleveland. All three of those came after the show with Max. It gave me a New York presence. It was the perfect time for the exhibition." Along with Mary Beth's successes, this quickly proved the importance of their move to New York. A large watercolor and charcoal composition, *Inside Running Animal/Reindeer Way*, completed in 1977 after the work was destroyed, conveyed the architectural experiences (and scale) of the piece (Figure 4.10). Like the skull of the deer, this served as part of a seemingly natural process, the cycle of death and rebirth, in nature and in art. Additionally, reviews in art magazines discussed this piece into 1977, extending its life in other ways. Describing it as "an enormous force," Jean-Louis Bourgeois wrote in *Art in America* that "there is no question that in a most unlikely place, a cavernous SoHo gallery, Stackhouse evoked an animal's experience in the woods—a swift, hide-and-seek, dappled world." [66]

4.11

During the spring of 1977, he traveled to Cleveland, where he built *Ship at St. Agnes*, using vacant land adjoining the base of the twelve story bell tower of St. Agnes Parish (Figure 4.11). The site had formerly served as the location of St. Agnes Church, until structural problems with the church caused it to be razed. To serve as a complement to the remaining bell tower, Stackhouse constructed a horizontal wooden form, measuring approximately 110 feet in length, built of about one thousand 2 x 4 and 4 x 4 construction grade wooden components. Unlike working alone in his studio or in a gallery space, for the first time Stackhouse had to recruit assistants on this project, as he would on many of his future outdoor projects. These consisted of an art professor, Jim Osher, and some of his art students from Cleveland State University as well as several Job Corps trainees, who worked during part of the day. On this project, unlike many future public projects, there was little help from volunteers in the adjoining neighborhood or the parish members, most of whom were elderly, except for a surprisingly supportive group of neighborhood children. As described by James Osher and Marjorie Talalay, these children, who nicknamed Stackhouse's project "Noah's Ark," played an important role in the project.

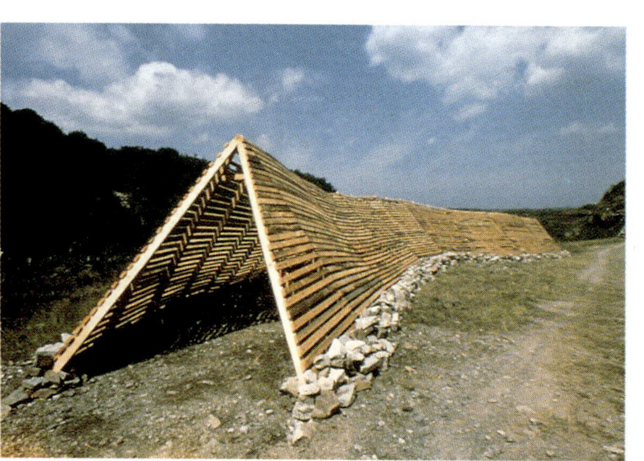

4.12

It was in these youngsters, many of teen age, that Stackhouse discovered a marvelous resource: they quickly learned to handle the drill and the socket wrench, and thus were able to take on much of the time-consuming task of drilling and bolting the structure. Every day after school between five and nine youngsters appeared, ready and eager to work....In the evening the entire work crew resembled an extended family group, working and joking and getting to know one another. The experience of working on the site was in marked contrast to the youngsters' daily encounters with alcoholism, fights, prostitution, crime and drug addiction, and these young people seemed to respond. [67]

In his project drawing for this work, Stackhouse explored the relationship between a curving linear depiction of a snake shedding its skin, the long curving wall of the Cleveland project and a Viking ship, the Gokstad Grave-ship. Unlike *Running Animal/Reindeer Way*, this project did not offer visitors an internal passage. Rather, it was more like a closed version of that work, hugging the ground, then rising up to two narrow vertical openings at either end. As he indicated in Cleveland, "I did not want to compete with the belltower in any way. I wanted [the tower] to reign supreme. I work, however, with it and I am building a piece that is hopefully as horizontal as the tower is vertical." [68] When a writer for the *Cleveland Plain Dealer* visited the site, she described the civic nature of this project, noting that this "project proposes to spur community spirit in distressed areas by engaging neighborhood participation in the transformation of eyesore lots into concrete evidence that someone walks there, cares, has rearranged things in some way to his liking aand has seen a glimmer of hope in the process." Turning to Stackhouse's work, she referred to his successful involvement of the children in this mostly poor black neighborhood in the creation of his sculpture. "Though environmental in concept, Stackhouse's work is the City Project's single preconceived truly sculptural piece. In his case the helpers have been mostly neighborhood children, who have crowded around after school....The work will require a total of nearly 1,500 large bolts to lock it in place; at peak hours, I was told, the kids stand in line for socket-wrench duty." [69]

From this project on a lot in Cleveland's inner city area, Stackhouse next moved to a very different location, Niagara Falls (Figure 4.12). He was one of a group of significant artists—including Laurie Anderson, Alice Aycock, Sam Gilliam and Martin Puryear—invited to work at Artpark, in Lewiston, New York, during the summer of 1977, the fourth summer of the program's existence. Inspired by Robert Smithson's approach to the use of sites that had been "disrupted by industry, reckless urbanization, or nature's own devastation," Artpark was created in a complicated natural environment, one described by Nancy Rosen as "two hundred acres of

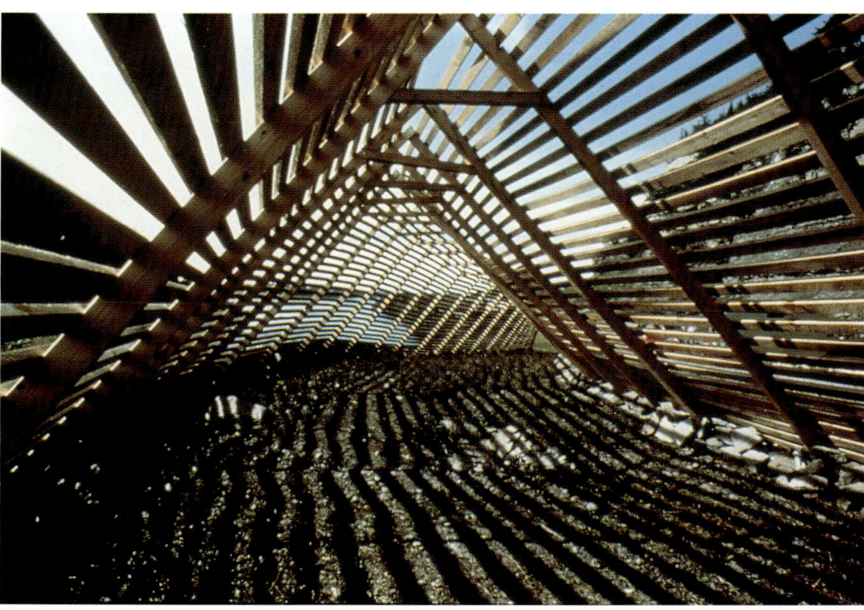

4.13 *Niagara Dance*, inside view.

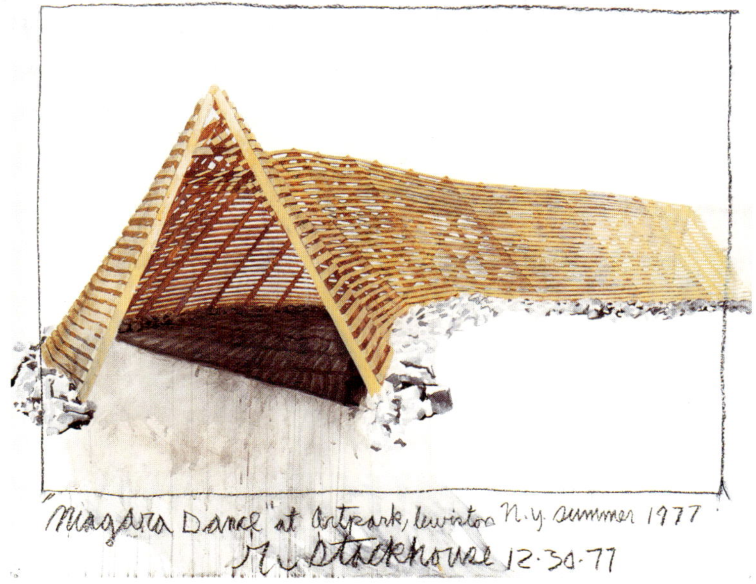

4.14 *Niagara Dance*, 1977

Shiphall (actual installation image)

Inside *Shiphall*, 1977

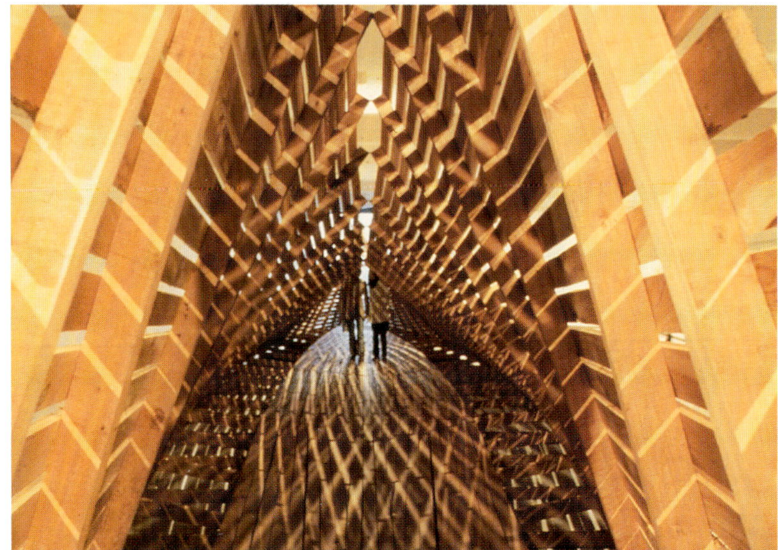

4.15

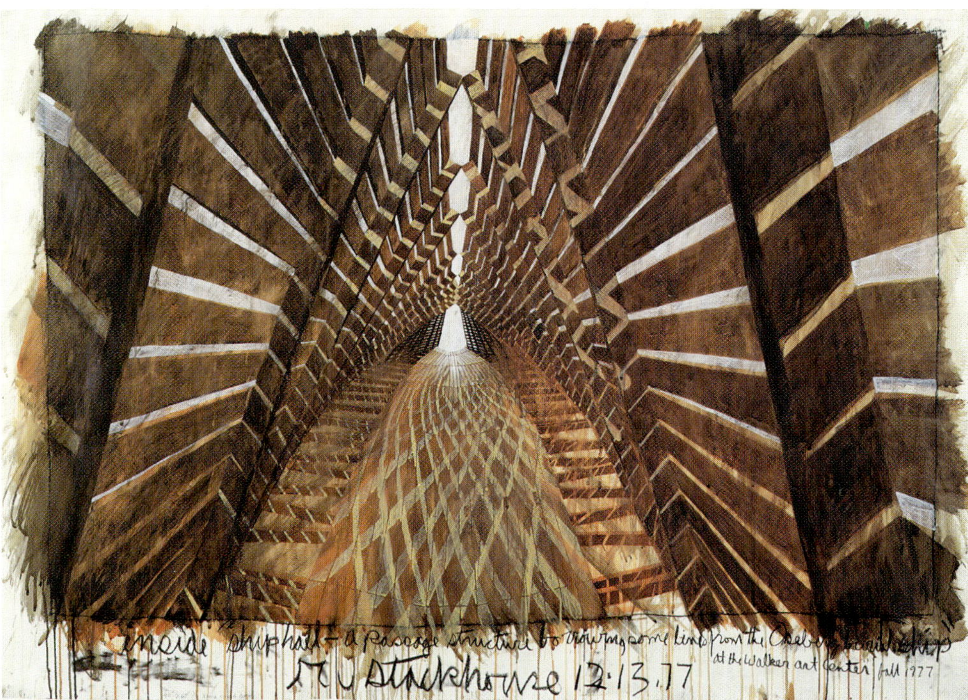

4.16

land, approached along highways that are wrought with industry and hydro-electric technology, two hundred acres that sprawl along the dramatic gorge of the Niagara River, land that is embedded with evidence of remote millennia and twentieth century debris." Working on land located along a gorge shaped by Niagara Falls, and by man's often destructive hand as well, artists were brought to Artpark, according to Rosen, to "explore and expose the terrain and its unique resources—both material and human." In a location far from the world of the museum, the city and the art market, artists were challenged, according to Rosen, to become actively involved in the process of making art in a highly public fashion. "The artist is no longer anonymous or absentee; he is visible and accessible to the visiting public as he goes through the stages of realizing an idea." [70]

Stackhouse regarded this as a significant opportunity, both to create sculpture and to advance his specific method of working on public projects. "*Niagara Dance* was important because it was a major outdoor piece, one of my very first. It was *Running Animasl/Reindeer Way*, but outdoors." In addition to its being based directly upon his earlier gallery installation in New York, it also served as an extension, as had the preceding Cleveland project, of his growing philosophical conviction regarding the importance of public art in this country. An artist with a deeply introspective approach to searching for the universal sources of his art, Stackhouse nevertheless quickly developed a distinctive public persona for the physically demanding and often highly political process of creating these projects. "With public art I was more interested in the universal. I wanted audiences to get into the structure I built. And I wanted that structure to function in a general way, to be more readable by the viewer, whether they knew much about art or not. In public art that is a major concern of mine, that it be readable, that it be accepted as such. I try to avoid the hierarchal language of art-speak. That alienates the viewer."

Here, once again, he created a long (112') winding "dance" composition, responding to the curves and changing elevations that were unique to this outdoor site, quite in contrast to the more controlled environment he encountered at Max Hutchinson's gallery. This location offered an opportunity to adapt that earlier design to fit a more natural setting overlooking one of the world's most famous natural wonders. The area around the falls had attracted the attention of countless artists, including many masters of the earlier Hudson River School, who commonly focused on the sublime power and grandeur of the falls. In contrast, Stackhouse, recognizing the obvious power of the falls as a subject, responded to the spirit of the place in a different way, by creating one of his lath covered A-frame structures intended to offer the viewer/participant an opportunity to experience this location in a unique new way.

Because of the winds and the distinctive weather patterns at the falls, he adapted his earlier design by incorporating large stones from the area, using them as weights and bracing support, and as an integral part of the aesthetic concept, anchoring the work quite literally to its site, as he explained during the time he worked on the project.

> *Its structural elements are typical of my previous work (A-frames connected with horizontal laths), but the unique character of the piece is derived from the repeated curves of the river, the curve of the old Portage Road, and the curve of the cliff, which the piece rests on. The lathing echoes the horizontal strata of the cliffs. And the serpentine stone wall that anchors the piece and contours the unlevel ground comes from fossilized rock of the cliffs that are constantly falling. This work then, is made for and from the Niagara Gorge itself, millions of years of continuous erosion that have helped to create Niagara Dance, a temporary structure.* [71]

The serpentine nature of the site, and the constantly changing environment that hosted his temporary installation, perfectly suited Stackhouse and his approach to the creation of works such as this one. If ancient rituals were to be evoked, including movement through such a constructed wooden passageway, few sites could offer greater natural power and palpable energy. The temporary nature of the Artpark projects, designed to exist for only one summer season before being destroyed for the next year's projects, also suited his philosophy about public works of this type. Six months after he completed *Niagara Dance*, and after it had been disassembled, he created a watercolor, charcoal and graphite version of the piece, one that stressed the curving, serpent-like form and the open, seemingly inviting interior spaces that challenged the viewer to enter and experience the perspectives presented from within (Figure 4.14). As placed on the plane of the paper, and even as framed by the thin outline that serves as a border, the entry and passage area seems to inevitably draw the viewer inside, into the heart of the intended experience.

By the time he completed his painted version of *Niagara Dance*, he had returned from Minneapolis and the creation of another major work, his gallery installation project for the Walker Art Center, titled *Shiphall (A Passage Structure Borrowing Some Lines from the Osberg Burial Ship)*. As this longer, and more detailed, title suggested, this A-frame, lath passage piece was inspired, in part, by the curving lines and horizontal forms of a very specific Viking ship, a ninth century Norwegian burial ship contained in a museum located in Oslo. Yet, as specific as these references might be, this construction, like all of these projects, was intended to be filled with more universal qualities, as suggested by Martin Friedman (Figure 4.15). "A passage through one of Stackhouse's wooden corridors is a walk in an abstract wilderness. Dappled light and cast shadows on their lath surfaces enhance the spatial ambiguity of these enclosures, dematerializing them. These enclosures are as much about light as they are about form....They evoke such diverse associations as American Indian longhouses, Gothic vaulting and Viking ships."

This work was featured in a major exhibition at the Walker titled "Scale and Environment: 10 Sculptors," that included the works of Siah Armajani, Michael Hall, George Trakis, Donna Dennis, Also Moroni, Thomas Rose, Harry Roseman, Joel Shapiro and Charles Simonds (who had recently worked in Cleveland with Stackhouse). Stackhouse's piece, which once again utilized the dramatic effects of a controlled gallery lighting environment, was intended to be experienced from inside, passing through and looking out. As the title suggested, this work was intended to evoke, in part, the experience of an ancient ship, and the sense of passage or journey associated with such a vessel. As he suggested in proposing this project, "It will have a V-shaped floor and a keel right down the center. It will be like walking through the hull of a ship instead of through a passenger's compartment." [72] The inclusion of the floor or decking was an important transitional step in the evolution of his public sculptural forms, one that would have immediate implications for his future pieces, especially one like *Sailings*, created in the following year. And, as suggested in his large painted version of this piece, titled *Inside Shiphall*, completed at the end of 1977 (Figure 4.16), this addition of floor decking could be used to enhance the illusion, especially with the patterns of light and shadow shown by the artist, of scales and an internal environment, like being swallowed by a serpent or other sea creature, an experience associated with the voyages and mythic adventure of the Vikings who served as inspiration for this work.

The completion of these three projects, and the resulting publicity and art world recognition that accompanied them, quickly led to new projects and a period of intensive activity, in a wide range of natural settings in diverse regions of the country. One of the major projects of this period offered Stackhouse the opportunity to work with Michael Hall as well as with Roy Slade, who had left the Corcoran to assume the presidency of the Cranbrook Academy of Art, in Bloomfield Hills, Michigan. From its inception, the grounds at Cranbrook had been devoted to the integration of sculpture and landscape design, most notably with the works of Carl Milles. In the period from 1978 to 1980, beginning with Stackhouse's project there, Cranbrook invited several important sculptors to create site specific works for these grounds. The other artists were Alice Aycock, Siah Armajani and Michael Hall (who was also head of the sculpture department at Cranbrook). Stackhouse's piece, *Cranbrook Dance*, (Figure 4.17) was described by Roy Slade. "The first installation was Robert Stackhouse's *Cranbrook Dance*, a long wooden structure placed along the hill overlooking Kingswood Lake. *Cranbrook Dance* is intended to be viewed both from a distance and from within. The sculpture can be viewed from across the lake or can be walked through, giving us changing experiences of the landscape and the sculpture." [73]

After working out-of-doors at Niagara Falls and in Cleveland, and having refined the A-frame in gallery spaces in New York and in Minneapolis, Stackhouse was confident in his abilities to adapt his structural forms to diverse variations in climate and environment. At Cranbrook, he discovered that there was little natural sense of pathway or passage available to him, so he created a pathway and a related area of passage when he constructed his work. Once again, he welcomed the opportunity for a chance encounter, for nature to have a hand in the outcome of his piece. "I could see the topography—the ground was uneven—would present a lot of peculiarities to the piece—would control it more than I could imagine, so whatever I did would be different than I could visualize." Asked during his time at Cranbrook about his architectural influences, he replied: "I do derive these passage structures from longhouses, cathedrals, forests and certain agricultural buildings. I have the idea of it as a meeting house, enhanced by the light patterns of the architecture and the quality of the rafters." However, it was, he emphasized, the interior that was the focus of these works. "I do not think too much from the outside. That's just the residue. The experience is on the inside. It's totally an inside-outside experience." And, summarizing the importance of animals and animal spirits for his work, he explained that animal forms served "as images of transition and rebirth. The shedding snake, antlered deer, the antlered shadow of myself, these three images along with the Viking ship, are images of passing. They reflect my own growth, always going forward and trusting my instincts." [74]

In a complex and image-laden work created in response to his experiences with the Cranbrook project, *Cranbrook Dance*, completed in May of 1978 (Figure 4.18), the artist seems to

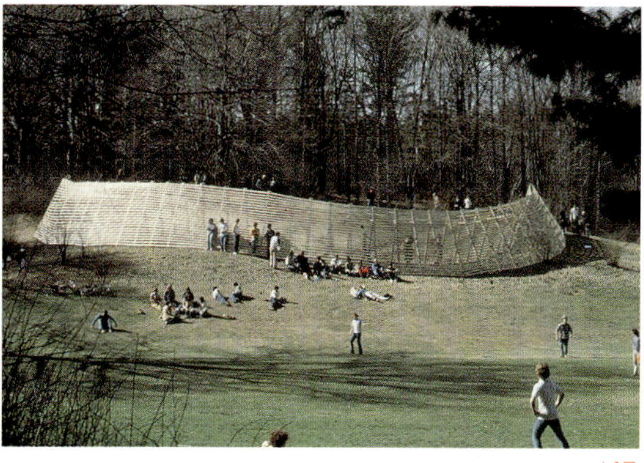
4.17 *Cranbrook Dance* (1984 Installation image)

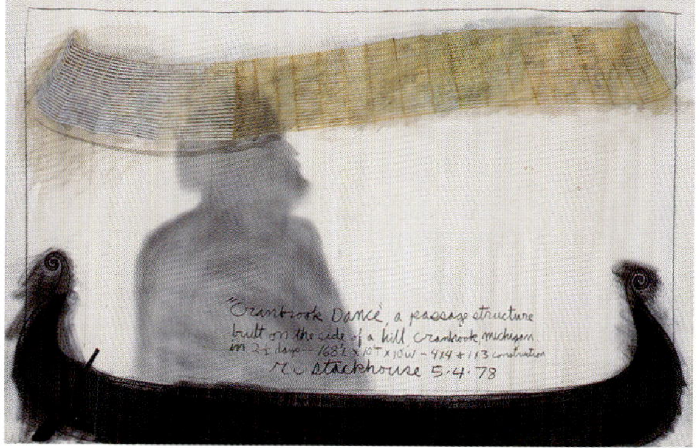

4.18 *Cranbrook Dance*, 1978

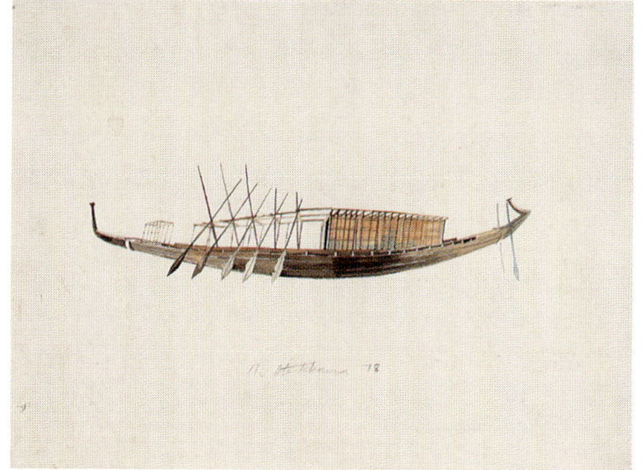
4.19 *Cheops Ship*, 1978

suggest the beginning of a period of intensive transition, marked by a metamorphosis from his A-frames to the ship forms. In this painted work he juxtaposed his shadow figure self, a long Viking ship, the *Cranbrook Dance* installation and a serpent running on the ground along the bottom edge of the sculpture, echoing its curves and swells, one that intersects with his eyes, passing through the back of his head. The head of the snake merges, in fact, with the profile view of his eye socket, suggesting that, once again, he may be "seeing the snake." This work is both a document of the piece as completed, "built on the side of a hill...in 2 1/2 days" with the dimensions and construction technique indicated, as well as a projection of future possibilities and reflections on other matters, essentially the shadow self and the form of the Viking burial ship (and its implied passages, its implied journey). Notably, the artist's shadow is caught between the two major forms, with his head literally "in" his recent project, *Cranbrook Dance*, while his body seems to emerge from the Viking burial ship. Like the placement of his shadow over the transforming snake in Maine, depicted in *Snake Story*, we are presented with a figure in between, balancing itself between new and old skins as it begins the process of regeneration from one form to another.

In fact, Stackhouse entered a period of significant transition, extending from mid-1978 through to early 1980, a period when the A-frame seems to have served its initial purpose for the artist, then, like the shedding skin of the snake or the antlers of the deer, it was transformed into a series of new, related forms based upon the structure of the A-frame that would set the stage for much of his best-known work of the 1980s. His study of the architecture of ships during these years, and his related interest in the archaeology of ships seems to have fueled this process, supplying him with images including the Oseberg burial ship, the Cheops ship from Egyptian history (Figure 4.19), diverse clipper ships, vernacular boats including ordinary rowboats as well as a working oyster schooner, the L.A. Jeffrey (Figure 4.20). These ship forms served, both literally and metaphorically, as the vehicles (or vessels) of his latest artistic transformation.

The importance and relationship of his three most powerful subjects, the serpent, the A-frame and the ship are clearly illustrated in a work from 1978, *Niagara Dance Ship and Snake*, which depicts *Niagara Dance* as the central image, the Viking burial ship floating above, over the A-frame at Niagara Falls (a loaded image that he would soon begin to utilize) and the serpent, seen moving from out of the border (from off stage?) into the composition, along the lower border and down, merging into the handwritten title of "Niagara Dance" (Figure 4.21). By the end of 1978, he had initiated the last of the early A-frame projects in Philadelphia, *Dance at Tyler*. This work, completed on the campus of Tyler University, was intended to have a direct relationship to the Cranbrook project, in both scale and design. However, as he discovered soon after he arrived in Philadelphia, the materials budget, similar to that at Cranbrook, was not adequate because of the vast disparity in the cost of wood and materials in the two cities. As a result, this piece was created on a reduced scale. And because of other problems, including the severity of the winter weather in Philadelphia, the piece was completed in a manner that he found less than totally satisfactory. By that time, however, he had become increasingly more interested in the possibilities of the ship forms.

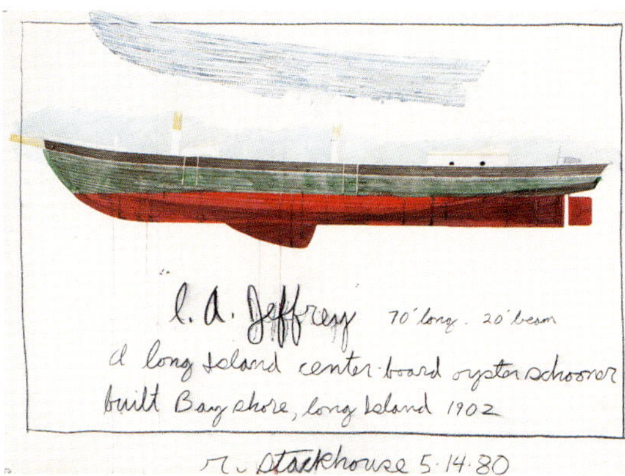

4.20

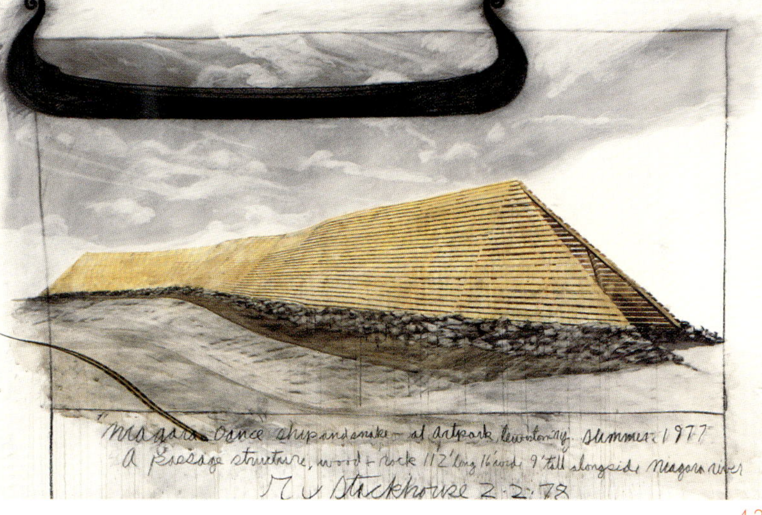

4.21

Stackhouse's process of evolution toward the ship forms is well documented throughout his drawings and paintings of this period, perhaps nowhere so well as in two working drawings he completed in October of 1978. In *Working Drawing For Sailings #1* (Figure 4.22), the artist positioned a floating Viking burial ship, the model for the two A-frames *Shiphall* and *Ship at St.Agnes*, over the ruined remains of another ship's deck, suggesting the design of his next major piece, *Sailings*, completed at the Hudson River Museum. As the artist has indicated, the placement of one ship above another in this drawing suggested another future work, *Sailors*, presented in 1979 at his Max Hutchinson Gallery show. And, from conversations with Max Hutchinson in the gallery during

L.A. Jeffrey, 1980

"Niagra Dance" Ship and Snake, 1978

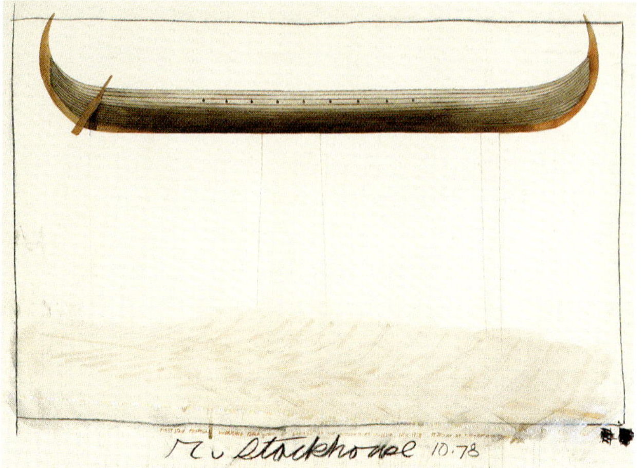

4.22

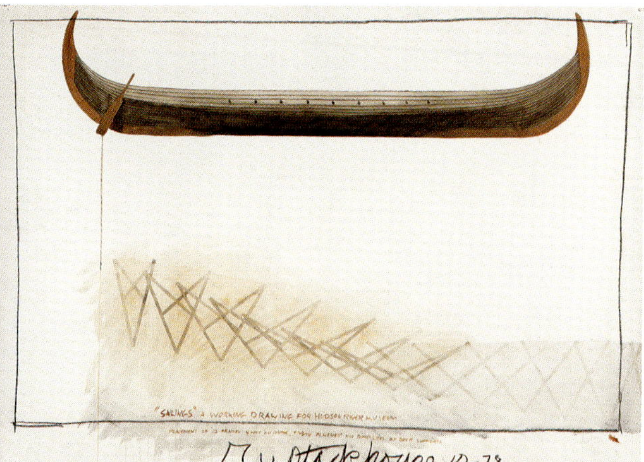

4.23

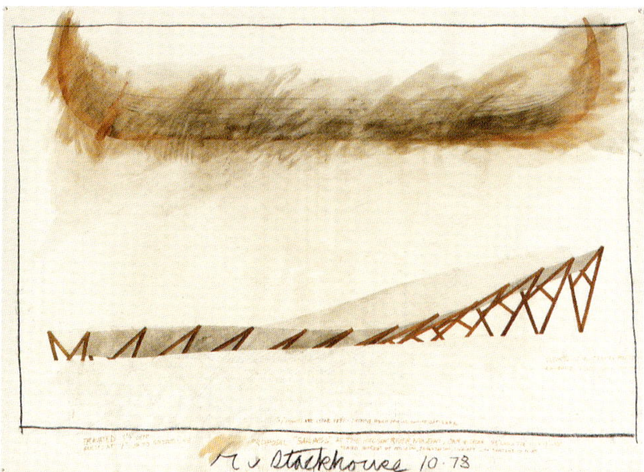

4.24

Working Drawing for Sailings #1, 1978

Working Drawing for Sailings#2, 1978

Working Drawing for Sailings #5, 1978

that exhibition, a conversation that took place while they stood before this work, Stackhouse derived the concept of building a ship on floating supports, a notion that evolved into the *Eau Claire Sailings* project of 1979. Notably, he followed through this process with a series of drawings for *Sailings* that documented the transformation from one form to another. In *Working Drawing For Sailings #2* (Figure 4.23) he explored the inversion of the A-frame, making it a supporting element for the evolving deck shape, derived from the deck created for *Shiphall*. And, in a final stage, shown in *Working Drawing For Sailings #5* (Figure 4.24), he literally rubbed out the Viking ship and presented its new evolved form below it, the design for *Sailings*. He recently commented upon this process and its relationship to his own continuing interests.

> *The Gokstad ship is rubbed out in the drawing; it had served its purpose. It was a vehicle, a vessel in the process. So I no longer need that. In this drawing you see the source on top, the result below, the Viking ship above and the inverted A-frame below. This was a product, in part of my readings on the history of ship architecture at the time. It also reflected my other readings, including* Beowulf, Caesar's Conquest of Rome, *and a wide range of other materials devoted to Nordic, Celtic and Viking cultures. I was intrigued by the sense of movement associated with the ships, the raids, and their constant cycle of exploration and discovery. And, as I have recognized for some time, I never go, or need to go, to those actual places—to North England, or Ireland, or Scotland, or Norway. It is not about those places, it is about me. I am Anglo-Saxon, a person from that past. My family can be traced back to England and to where before that, no one knows. My ancestors may have been involved in these diverse Nordic rituals. I am not borrowing or stealing from anyone else's culture. This is, I believe, my own heritage. And, as you see in the drawings and completed works, all of the curves and the meandering forms I have used are derived from those same cultures.*

In working on *Sailings*, he would provide another demonstration of his ability to work with diverse public audiences, in this case, at the Hudson River Museum, not far from where he had grown up in Yonkers, overlooking the Hudson River. This was almost his own old backyard, an area filled with great personal and family history, reflecting his days in Yonkers as well as his many journeys from Yonkers out to Peach Lake, along and through the Hudson River Valley. The site given to him for his sculpture also overlooked the Hudson River, the same river that had inspired so many artists and painters of the past, some of whom, like Frederic Edwin Church, had even built their homes and studios in nearby locations, looking over the river valley. *Sailings* (Figure 4.25), offered an interesting departure from the earlier A-frame forms for Stackhouse. Although the supporting element is derived from the A-frame form, the most visible element of *Sailings* is its deck, its projecting surface area that is unlike any of his earlier outdoor pieces. The deck was derived from the flooring or decking he created in *Shiphall*, in the preceding year, at the Walker Art Center. One again, Stackhouse demonstrated the evolutionary process of creativity, and he demonstrated his ability to adapt his designs and ideas to the fit the reality of specific sites and conditions.

As he completed this project in Yonkers another of his loves, baseball, entered into the picture. "I worked on the sculpture in October, during the World Series. The Yanks were down 0-2 to the Dodgers as they came back to Yankee stadium." Back in his old childhood neighborhoods of Yonkers, following the progressive of the World Series with the home town Yankees playing nearby and building his forms overlooking the Hudson River Valley after two years of growing national stature, Stackhouse brought great confidence and energy to the creation of this piece. And, as he indicated in his renderings of the completed work, as in 2 *Views of Sailings*, the scale and the perspectives presented from the deck opened up a new realm of structural possibilities, just as his earlier creation of the A-frame form had done (Figure 4.26). In this work on paper and in *Sailings* at The Hudson River Museum the artist also became, the first time, quite interested in depicting the architecture of the site around one of his completed works (Figure 4.27). Both of these works, in fact, present sensitively rendered images of the museum and the tower of its older main structure, a surprising inclusion for a former Minimalist sculptor. It seemed that the artist had suddenly begun to embrace the traditional Beaux-Arts approach to architectural renderings, using bold watercolor compositions on large scale sheets of paper. When asked, he recently recalled seeing exhibitions during this period filled with grand architectural drawings and watercolor renderings, works that exerted a surprising influence upon him. With this developing interest, he would have been prepared for the Beaux-Arts revelations included in "The American Renaissance, 1876-1917," a milestone exhibition organized by the Brooklyn Museum, and presented at that institution later that year, from October 13-December 30, 1979, prior to its national tour to Washington, San Francisco and Denver.

In 1979, he pursued issues inherent in his 1978 drawings in the exhibition "Sailors," presented at Max Hutchinson's Sculpture Now gallery in New York. Returning to the space that had given him his first New York triumph with *Running Animals/Reindeer Way*, he constructed a supported deck, floating over the floor in a manner first attempted in *Sailings*, only more horizontally positioned, then he created the exposed skeletal form (not unlike the dinosaurs he had enjoyed as a child at the nearby Museum of Natural History) which he then suspended from the ceiling (Figure 4.28).

Sailings
(actual installation image with children/workers overlooking Hudson River)

Two Views of Sailings 1979

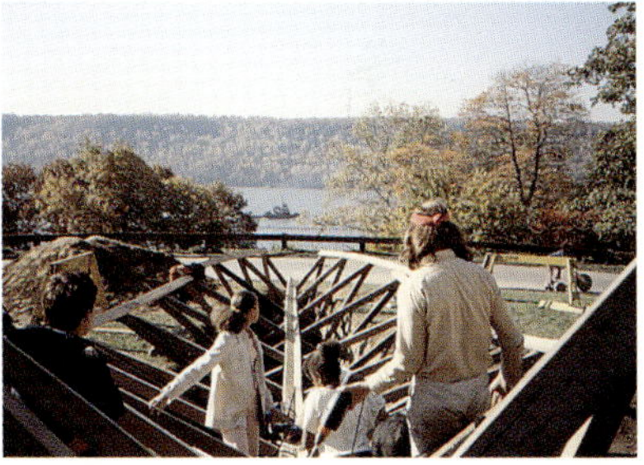

4.25

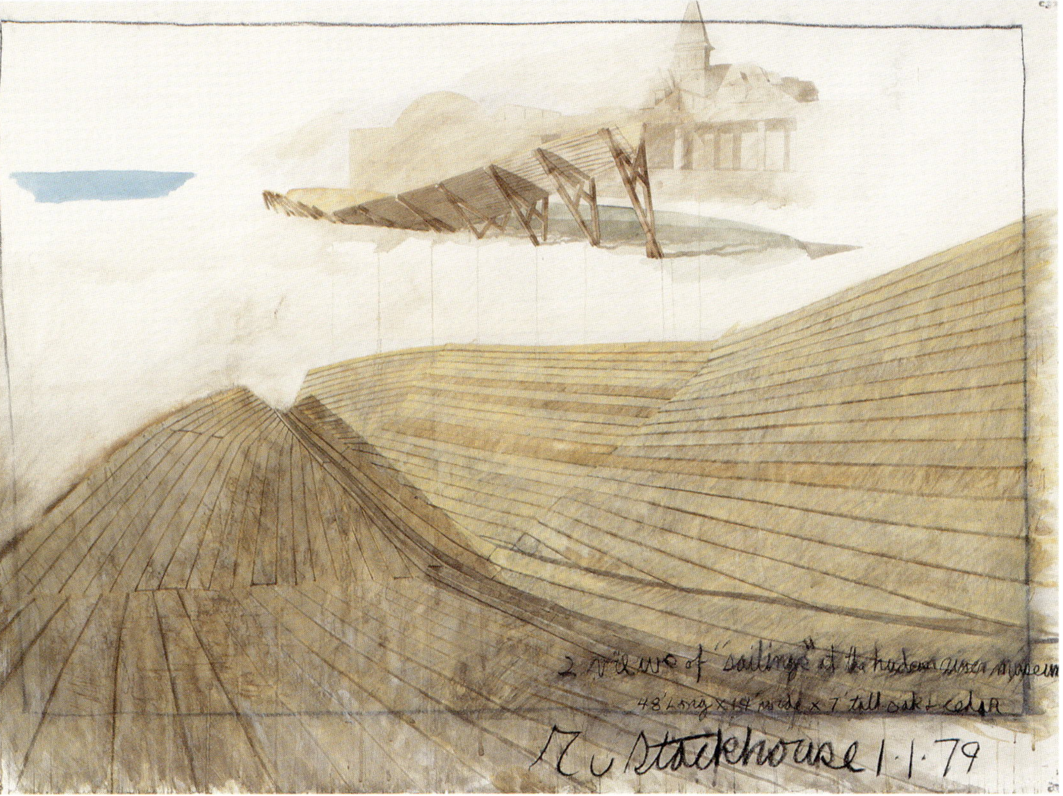

4.26

Sailings at the Hudson River Museum, 1979

Sailors, 1979 (Installation image)

4.27

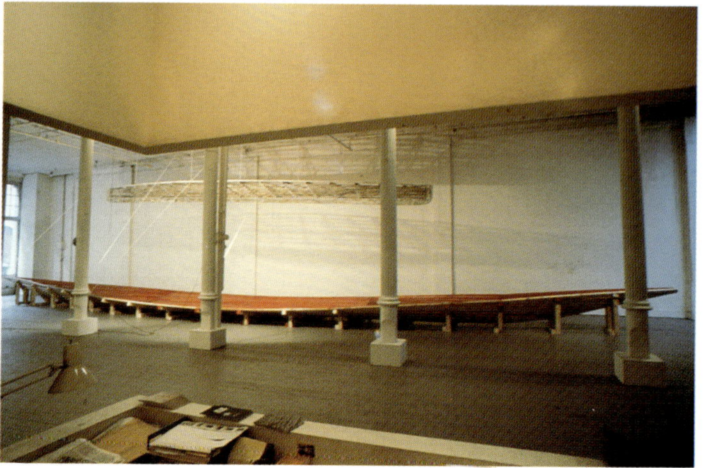

4.28

Initially suggested in *Working Drawing For Sailings #1*, this concept of a ship suspended in air had intrigued him for some time. He explored additional possibilities for these forms in *Working Drawing for Sailors #1* (Figure 4.29), which combined a number of Stackhouse's iconic images—the Viking ship, the A-frame, and the eye/boat form, first seen in *Watchings* and *Sky Song*, that now began to suggest endless new possibilities for these decks configurations. For the first time, he also applied paint to one of his vessels, introducing the element of color to the Hutchinson gallery installation, another new element filled with possibilities for his future projects. The use of color, the sweeping scale and the relationship of the grounded and aerial ships is suggested in his later painting of these works, *Sailors At Sculpture Now, Installation* (Figure 4.30).

From this exhibition, and the drawings and paintings he exhibited along with the completed sculptural forms, Stackhouse received a series of later projects, just as he had done with his first showing at Hutchinson's gallery. One day, he stood with Hutchinson, looking at the suspended sculptural form of *Sailors*, and studying his earlier drawings. Stackhouse was contemplating the possibilities for his next outdoor sculptural project, which became the piece known as *Eau Claire Sailings*, completed for the University of Wisconsin at Eau Claire, Wisconsin, later in 1979. He still recalls how the idea for the work materialized.

> *I had just done the show at Max's, and I was looking at a drawing. And Max said, in his Australian accent, "How are you going to get that up in the air? Are you going to hang it from a tree?" And I did not have an answer. And I looked at the first drawing of* Sailors, *the one with the erased ship, and I looked at the drips, and I said, after looking at the drips, "I will put posts under it." The idea just came to me. That is the way it goes. I did not know how to make it stand up, out of doors. Then I saw the drips and it was the answer. My engineering goes that way. I have had to teach myself that I have an intuitive sense of how to make something stand up. That is a very creative part of what I do. I enjoy it immensely.*

From this working idea, he developed the working plans for *Eau Claire Sailings*, (Figure 4.31) a work constructed with a team of workers on the campus site, using 2 x 2s as supports for the raised ship form. When completed, he painted the ship, adding another element to his exterior projects, one suggested by his earlier Hutchinson gallery exhibition that year. The following year, in the work he called *Passings*, created at the Nassau County Museum of Art, in Roslyn, New York, he took the concept of applied color to a new level and he also used telephone poles as structural elements in a new fashion, as seen in his *Passings*,

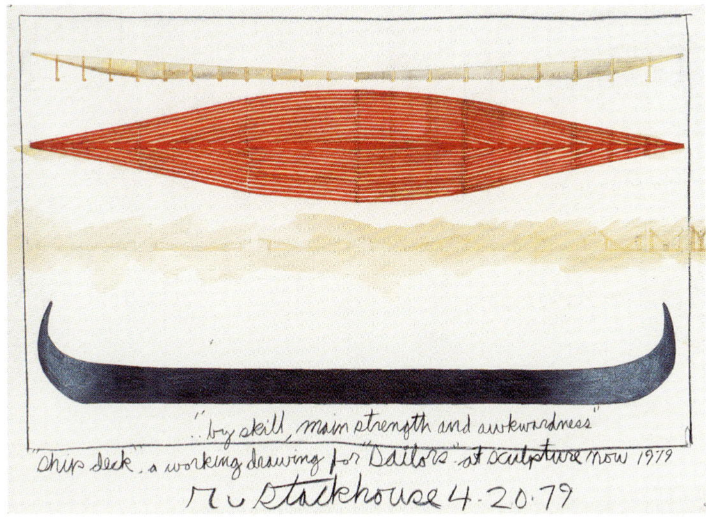

4.29

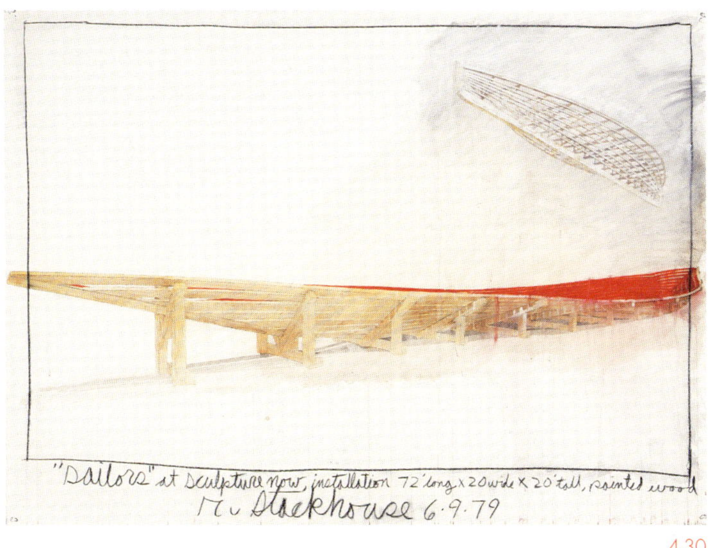

4.30

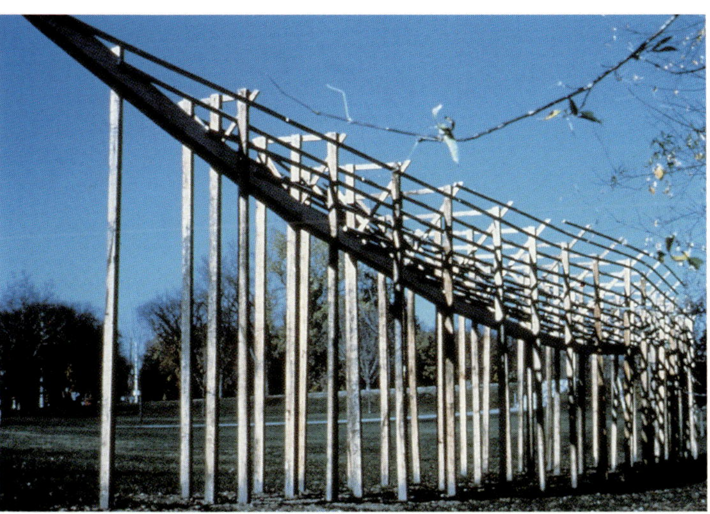

4.31

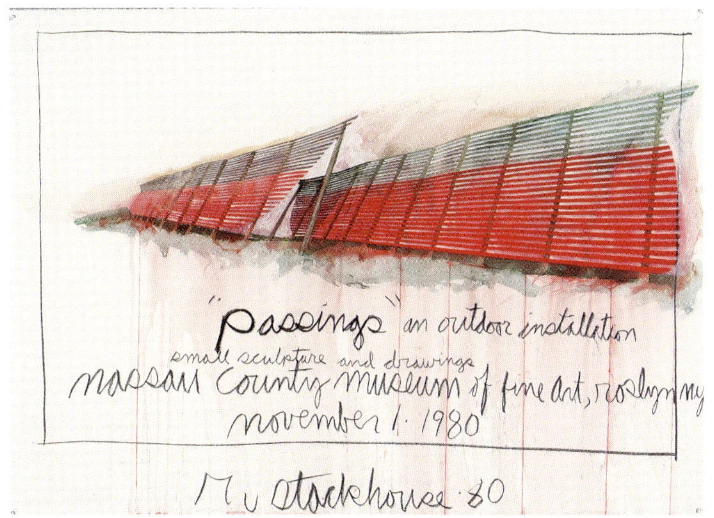

4.32

Working Drawing for Sailers #1, 1979

Sailers at Sculpture Now, Installation, 1979

Eau Claire Sailings, (actual Installation)

Passing, (an outdoor installation), 1980

An Outdoor Installation (Figure 4.32). April Kinsley has described her impression of this piece. "One thinks of ships passing in the night; unfulfilled longings for contact; and white, swollen-sheeted clipper ships scudding past one another, propelled by the trade winds as they bring tea to England or woven cloth to Malaysia." After referring to the design, which invited people to climb on it, "becoming like sailors in the rigging," she offered a description of the completed work.

> Passings *is composed of two dozen telephone poles and a number of unpainted 1" x 6" boards arranged in two billboardlike configurations that are tilted back and canted laterally to enhance the illusion of movement through a play of diagonals. One "ship" is painted red below the "waterline" and brown above. The other is all white. They overlap and are set 10 or so feet apart, creating an illusion of depth despite their obvious two dimensionality, which viewers mentally expand when they "fill-in" the width that would exist across two ships' beams and the space needed to pass one another.* [75]

Continuing to explore the concept of floating ships suspended over one another, and increasingly fascinated by the viewer's perceptions of these ship forms from below, he created an exposed skeletal form, again reminiscent of those he had known as a child at the Museum of Natural History, and suspended it over a staircase for his *Prudential Installation* in 1980. The ship design was derived from the pattern of a specific ship form, that of the "Clipper City," a Great Lakes board schooner built in Wisconsin in the 1850s. The color red was used, continuing his exploration of color on sculptural surfaces in this period. Notably, and again drawing on his past experiences as a stage lighting designer, he projected light through the work, making the looming shadow on the concrete lobby wall below the work a central part of the composition. With light and shadow, central concerns since his first exhibition at the Hutchinson Gallery, he suggested the presence of another ship, a shadow ship, just as he often used a shadow version of himself in his drawings and paintings during these years. The relationship of the two forms was reconsidered in this later version of the work, *Prudential Installation*, painted in 1981 (Figure 4.33).

Prudential Installation, 1981.

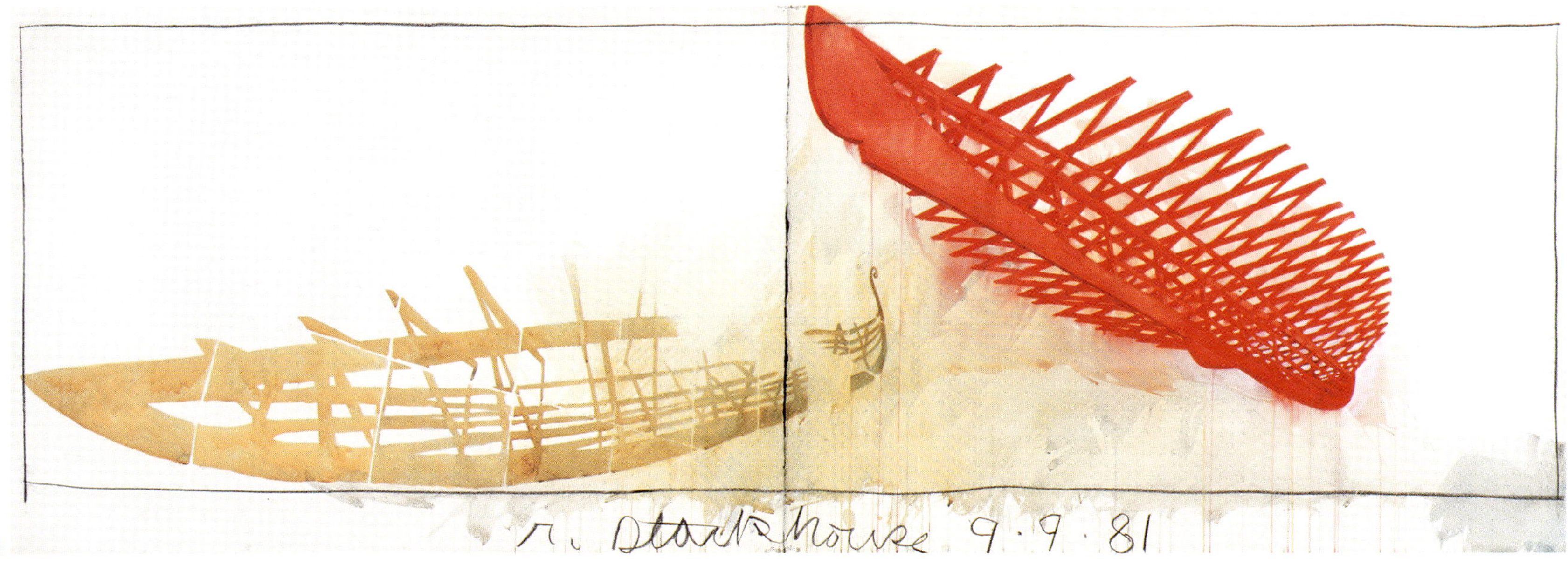

4.33

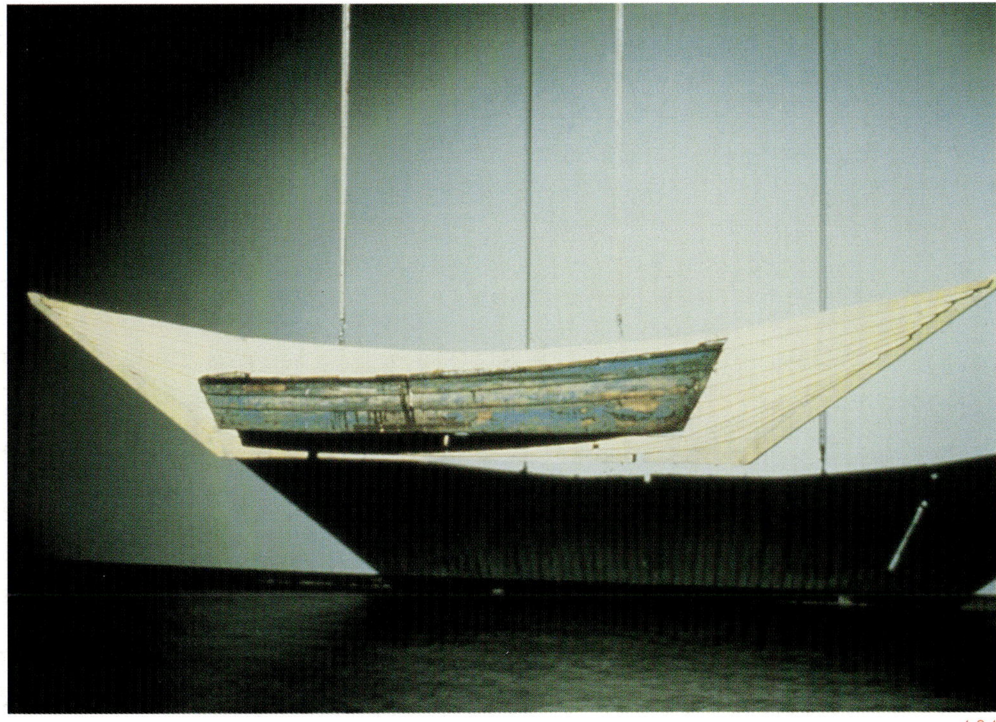

Dreamers, 1978.
(actual installation image)

4.34

The Prudential project was complete in 1980, and preserved in its painted form in 1981. In 1980, at his exhibition at the Hutchinson Gallery, he explored another approach to the use of boat imagery when he used a real boat in the work titled *Dreamers*. (Figure 4.34). In 1981, he and David Haxton were featured in a two-man exhibition at the University of South Florida in Tampa. This was an important exhibition for him, not only because it gave the two friends an opportunity to exhibit together, but also because it forced Stackhouse to reconsider his relationship to Florida and to the USF program. When he left Florida he had become engrossed in his activities in Washington and New York. Suddenly, back on the campus and involved with the faculty and staff again, he realized just how vital and important the program and the department had become. He and Haxton returned as honored alumni, both with professional careers and growing reputations in the New York art world. From this time on, Stackhouse rebuilt and maintained the strong affiliations he has maintained with the school, its art department, its Contemporary Art Museum and the Graphic Studio program to the present date. This year also concluded another period of his development. Beginning in 1982, when he created his first large format watercolor paintings, Stackhouse began to inventory his past accomplishments and his development of iconic imagery, preparing for another period of evolution, including the beginning of his period of international sculptural projects, that would continue for ten years, until 1992.

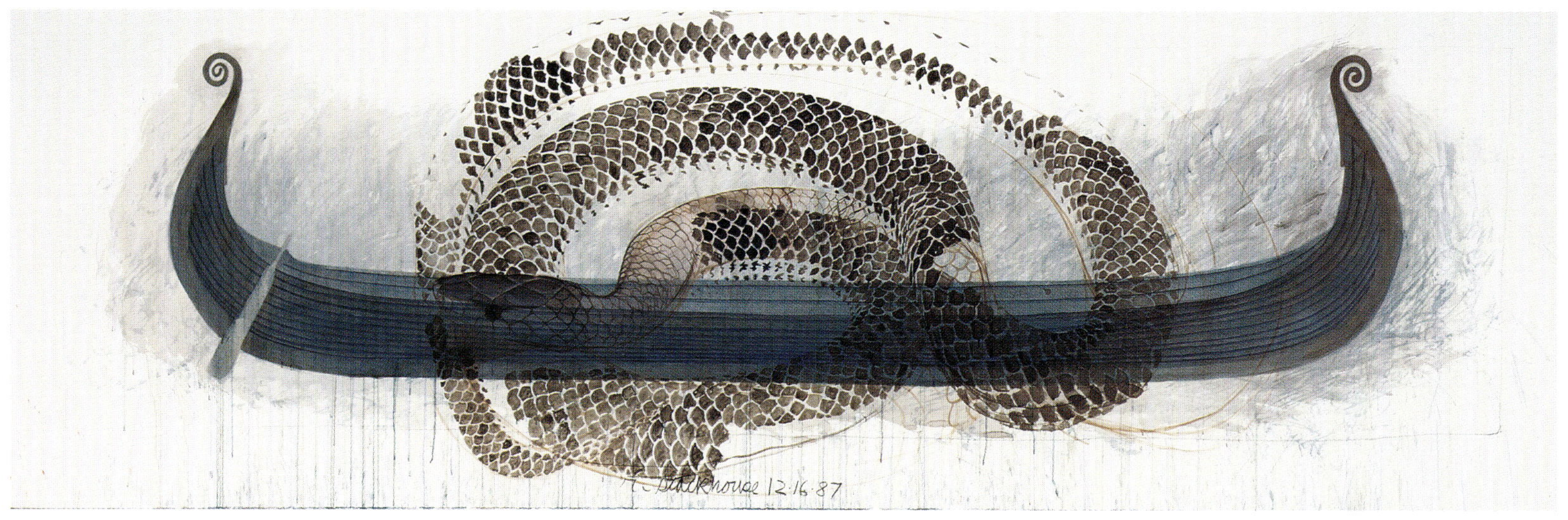

Dragon Fight, 1987

CHAPTER FIVE

New York and Washington

In 1982, as Robert Stackhouse prepared to return to his studio to begin an important new series of large scale watercolors, significant changes were developing in the art and gallery environment of SoHo, evident not far from the doors of his Mercer Street studio. After he and Mary Beth Edelson arrived in SoHo, in 1975, the area had experienced an unprecedented period of renovation and rejuvenation, one driven to a significant degree by the artists and art dealers who increasingly populated the district. Little more than a decade earlier, Paula Cooper and Ivan Karp were considered to be art world pioneers when they opened galleries in SoHo. By 1982, a wide range of important dealers, including many with galleries in other major cities, had established gallery spaces in the area. In addition to Paula Cooper and Ivan Karp, prominent art dealers operating SoHo galleries by this time included Leo Castelli, Andre Emmerich, Nancy Hoffman, Holly Solomon, Ileana Sonnabend, John Weber, Alexander Milliken, Phyllis Kind, Ruth Braunstein, Carl Solway, Edward Thorpe and Louis Meisel. Max Hutchinson, Stackhouse's dealer, operated two galleries in the area, the Max Hutchinson Gallery at 138 Greene Street and Sculpture Now, which had opened in 1974, at 142 Greene Street. Both were located just a short walk, literally around the corner, from Stackhouse's studio. On Saturdays, after he had returned to New York from teaching at the Corcoran, Robert and Mary Beth regularly toured the galleries of the area, studying the current exhibitions and watching as a new group of emerging artists rose to prominence.

During the preceding decade many artists had rejected the perceived constraints of the established gallery and museum systems. While certain artists maintained that earlier independence even into the 1980s, they became an increasing minority as the gallery world flourished in response to a new wave of collecting and collectors, both institutional and private. For example, in the late 1970s, art identified as "Graffiti Painting," which first emerged in the Lower East Side of New York, then became associated with the city's subway system, moved into the galleries, including those of SoHo. Jean-Michel Basquiat, Keith Haring and Kenny Scharf, who all rose to different levels of prominence during this decade, were associated at one point with graffiti art.[76] Emerging artists, including Robert Longo, Cindy Sherman and Jack Goldstein, were shown at Metro Pictures, a new SoHo gallery opened in 1980 by Helene Winer and Janelle Reiring, which became one of the most high profile galleries of this era.[77] A group of these young artists, including Julian Schnabel and David Salle, were commonly referred to by the art press of the 1980s as the Neo-Expressionists. Schnabel, known for incorporating broken plates and velvet backgrounds into his large compositions, was often described on a grand scale in

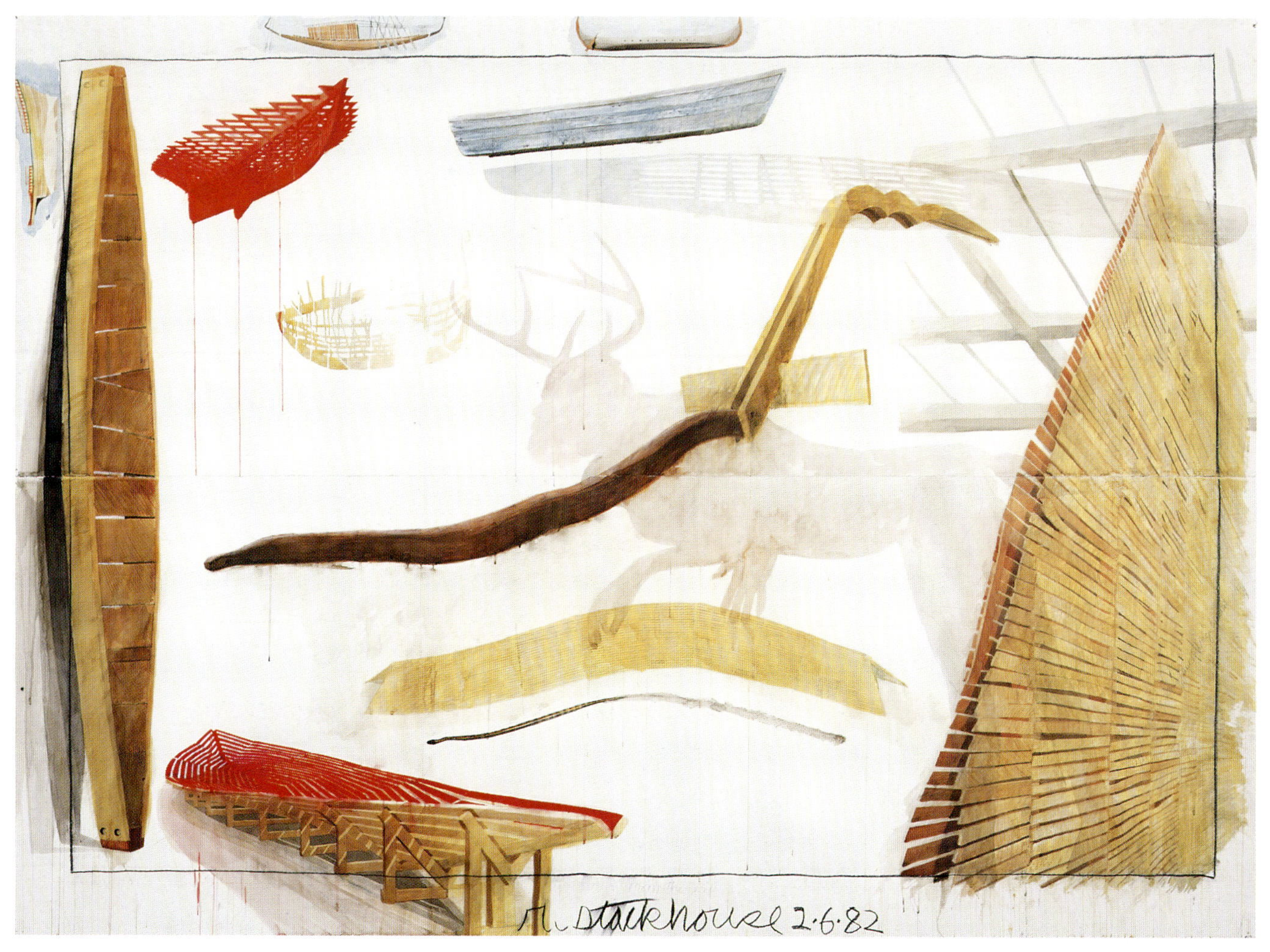

5.1

From the Deep, 1982

this era, as evident in a selection from a 1984 museum catalogue featuring his art. "Schnabel is reminiscent of the fifties and sixties artists who are perceived as heroic figures; like de Kooning and Rauschenberg who are able to put aside differences between themselves, their lives and their art, Schnabel achieves an art which is more heroic than its maker's myth." [78]

As the 1980s unfolded, many younger artists achieved a level of public recognition and financial success that was unprecedented, often seemingly at the expense of more mature and more serious artists. Not everyone in the art world greeted these developments uncritically, as suggested by Robert Hughes's recent reassessment of the era.

> *Never before had star artists been so bathed in adulation. In the 1970s it had been movie actors, in the 1990s it would be supermodels, but in the 1980s it was hot young postmodernists and their dealers. The doings of collectors, the gyrations of the market, the increasingly passive promotional role of museums, the whole social circus attached to the art world, supplied limitless fodder for breathless journalists. Art magazines devolved into sycophantic praise-bulletins...95 percent of the writing published in them was the merest puffery, garnished with opaque Derridian and Lacanian jargon....The "art world," in its older form, had now become Artworld, a theme park you could visit, full of temporarily interesting rides.* [79]

Robert Stackhouse moved from Washington to New York during the 1970s, found a SoHo dealer, presented a well received and widely reviewed first New York gallery exhibition, then created a diverse range of museum, public and private sculptural projects and exhibitions that built his growing reputation in the art world. At Artpark, Cranbrook, the Walker Art Center and elsewhere, his work was featured along with projects by Alice Aycock, Siah Armajani and others who worked in an architectural and environmental manner. By 1982, he was a respected teacher at the Corcoran and had achieved recognition as a New York artist. In essence, he had accomplished much of what he had set out to do.

When he entered his studio in 1982, aware of events in the art world around him, conscious of his own recent achievements, he paused, taking time to analyze his development to that point. After moving to Washington he had been featured in major shows at prominent museums in Washington and Baltimore. His first one-man gallery exhibition, at the Henri Gallery, had taken place ten years earlier, featuring the "Journeys" series. Then, beginning with *Sleeping King Ascending* and *Ghost Dance*, both presented at the Corcoran Gallery, he developed the forms that evolved into his A-frame constructions, first shown at the Hutchinson Gallery in 1976, leading to projects including *Niagara Dance*, *Dance at Cranbrook* and *Shiphall*. And, by 1982, two new developments in his sculpture—the deck form and the suspended ship form—were well established.

So, when Stackhouse turned to the creation of his series of four expansive watercolors in 1982, works which, he soon realized, served as a summation of his activities during the preceding years, he had much to consider. On February 2, 1982, as clearly indicated near his signature on the work, he completed *From the Deep*, incorporating many of the most important images and projects he created from 1969 to 1982 (Figure 5.1). "I tried to present some of the haphazard work, things that came to me on a purely intuitive level. I was like a shaman, like the snake shedding its skin. I was painting like an Abstract Expressionist again, and yet, at the same time, it felt like I was painting on a cave wall." When he completed this work, he decided to call it *From the Deep*, because, as he recently explained, "it meant that this was all intuitive, it was impulsive. These things happened accidently, spontaneously, through the creative process I developed in those years." Appropriately, the center of the composition focused on *Great Rain Snake*, the sculptural form that signaled the beginning of his period of original art making in 1969, the beginning of allowing his intuitions and feelings to direct him in the development of his art. Behind the serpent, his shadow figure (with the profile of his face and beard), presented as a deer with antlers, reproducing the famous cave image of the *Sorcerer of Trois Freres*, floats over *Running Animals/Reindeer Way*, positioned just over a serpent shedding its skin, the inspiration for this first A-frame. To the right, he featured the image of *Sleeping King Ascending* at the Corcoran in 1973, and, to the left, from his "Journeys" exhibition at the Henri Gallery in 1972, he included one of the boat forms that had marked the beginning of his solo gallery exhibition career.

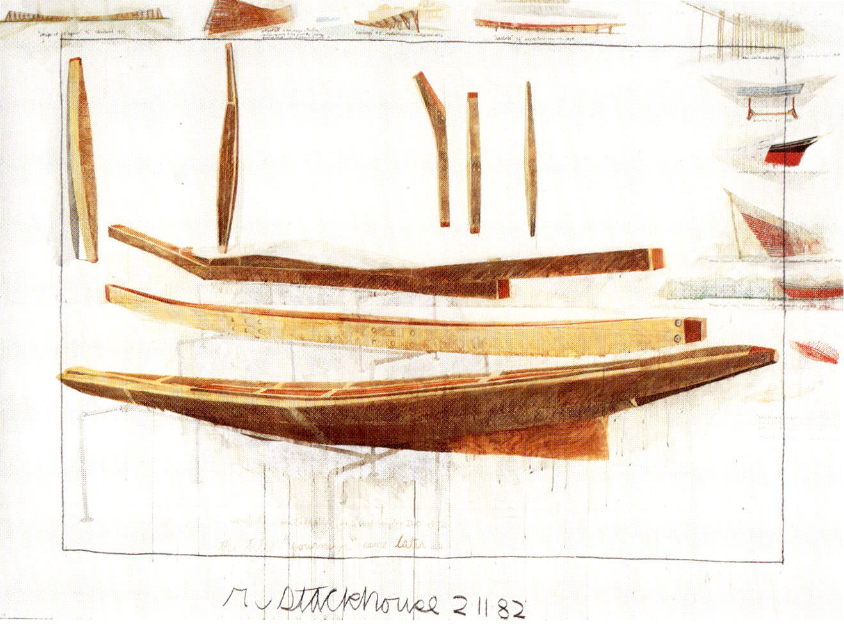

5.2

Major Projects, 1982

Below these central images, he placed *Sailings*, his first painted wooden boat form, originally shown in the installation at the Hutchinson Gallery. Above, as if floating in space, he placed the skeletal form of the ship in the Prudential installation complete with its painted shadow form. And, next to that is the rowboat he used in *Dreamers*. Inspired by Friedel Dzubas's admonitions to him about the power of the border, and reminiscent of Don Ray's earlier use of animal imagery in the borders of his sporting art watercolors, Stackhouse loaded the edges of his composition with allusions. Several of the central forms also break the borders, those thinly drawn lines that he used to enclose and demarcate the central space of the work, spilling out into the edge. Outside of the border, as if literally in the margins, or as if part of his own working process (which it was, just like the rubbing out of the Viking burial ship image in the *Sailings* drawing), one sees several important forms that influenced the evolution of the works in the central plane of the composition. These are the Clipper ship, the Cheops and the Gokstad burial ship of the Vikings, ship forms that would continue to influence the future development of his work.

Recently, looking at this work and considering the creation of this series, he described the importance of watercolor as a medium in his larger body of works, alluding to the significance of these compositions in a technical sense. "My skills in sculpture are based upon my intuitive engineering abilities. Much of the writing on my art has been about this. However, I think my real skill lies in painting, and I am most proud of my skills in watercolor. No one else works in watercolor like me. I think that I can get more out of color at times, and that I can push watercolor far beyond what most people can do with it. That is what I am most proud of, what I have been able to achieve in watercolor." His first watercolors were completed on a vacation trip to the beach, with Mary Beth Edelson and a group of friends in the 1970s, when he purchased a watercolor kit and tried to paint, as accurately as possible, the details of wood included in one of his works. This experience convinced him of the possibilities of the medium, and, as he later noted, showed that he could teach himself watercolor painting without an instructor. "I never really learned how to do watercolor. I made it my own process, in my way. As a trained painter, I had learned to look at something and then paint it. I did the same with watercolor, and with the possibilities of color in this medium."

In so doing, he discovered that he was able to develop another way to create work during the periods between his major intuitive sculptural endeavors, the projects that, until the 1990s, he regarded as his most important activity. "After the intensity and the creativity of the sculptural process, I tried to complete charcoal drawings of my works. But they never had the same feeling, the same immediacy. This feeling finally came, however, in the watercolors. It was doing the watercolor painting that brought painting back into it, that gave me the feeling that, in between the impulsive nature of these sculptural forms and projects, I could return to being a painter again." And, he admitted, he welcomed this opportunity to find a way back to his roots as a painter.

> *Doing these early watercolors is what brought painting back. Watercolor gave me a way to create a body of work in between the sculptural projects. I think, at heart, that I am a two dimensional artist. I think primarily in two dimensions. One of my greatest skills is now in color. I don't owe that to the Washington Color School, I owe it to watercolor. I*

build up so many layers and trap the light and sometimes I simply want the intensity of a color—the blue or the red. And, to get it, I use the negative space, the white, and the light coming through. Watercolor has made this possible for me....I was taught how to paint well at the University of South Florida, but I just did not paint my own subjects. Then, finally, I discovered that I could paint my own works, using watercolor. And, because my works were temporary, I started by doing a painting of one of the sculptures. It gives me ideas for other forms, creating a powerful regenerative energy that I am able to utilize.

Next, on February 11, 1982, he completed *Major Projects* (Figure 5.2). The entire central space is filled with works that were featured in the Henri Gallery "Journeys" installation, with the boats shown floating on the metal pipe frames he had fabricated. The long horizontal planes of these sculptural forms dominate the central space of the composition, contained by the thin lines of the boundaries, while above them, as they had in the original gallery installation, the wall sculptures lean vertically, as if propped against a wall or supporting element. Around these forms, in and out of the borders, works are placed surrounding this central set of images, as the artist has noted.

"In this watercolor, *Journeys*, the depiction of an actual show is featured, and around it are all the diverse works that came from it later." These later resulting works included, along the top border, *Ship at St. Agnes*, *Shiphall*, *Sailings*, *Sailors*, *Eau Claire Sailings*, and then, along the right border, *Dreamers*, *China Clippers*, *Passings* and the Prudential project, completed with its painted shadow. Once again, the artist has not only supplied the viewer his iconography, he has also illustrated the chronology and the process of his working methodology, a notable achievement in a single watercolor.

The third watercolor in the series, sold through one of his galleries (to the Hunter Museum in Chattanooga), featured an inventory of ships with his face superimposed over a stylized ocean. "That work was where I claimed the color blue—deep dark blue—as ocean, as universe, as the unconscious." And, using the potential of watercolor painting to depict this ideal blue color, he realized the continuing power of blue for his future work, something that continues to the present date. "The blue became important for me from that point on. *Blue Diviners*, later, was primarily about walking into blue. It was about walking into a blue grotto-like space. It was simply just about that blue." Then, on February 24, 1982, he completed *Inside Four Structures* (Figure 5.3), in part because he was seeking a way to possess one of his temporary architectural constructions on a more permanent basis. "I did not have an A-frame that I could go visit. I wanted to have one that I could visit. So, instead, I created this painting of an A-frame that I can visit, anytime I want. The scale of it is large enough to allow you to walk into it and the four corners represent the four pieces that you could walk into. Once again, it was like Friedel Dzubas, working out on the edge. However, it also has that sense of push and pull, all of those things I originally absorbed reading Hans Hofmann and the writings and theories of the Abstract Expressionists." Around the large dominant A-frame structure he placed, both inside and outside the border, at left, *Running Animals/Reindeer Way* and *Niagara Dance*, and to the right, he placed *Dance at Cranbrook* and *Shiphall*.

Inside Four Structures, 1982

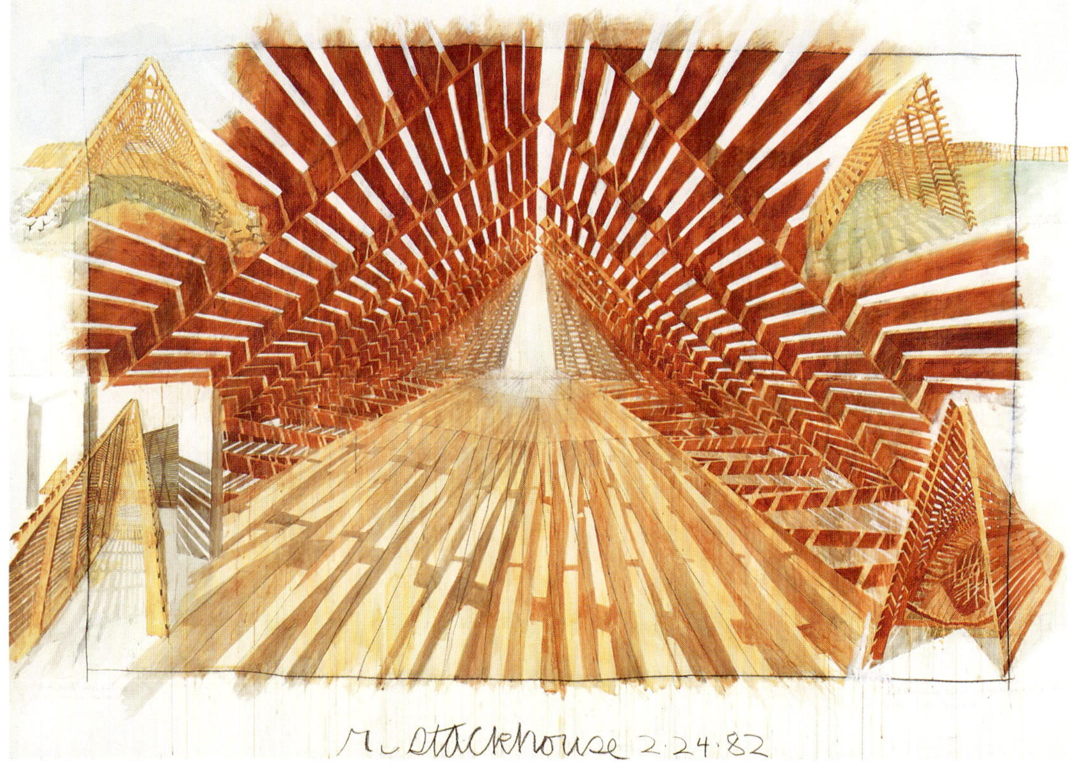

5.3

Mountain Climbers installation, 1984, Sculpture Now, New York.

Working Drawing for Mountain Climbers, 1982

Bones Installation (actual installation)

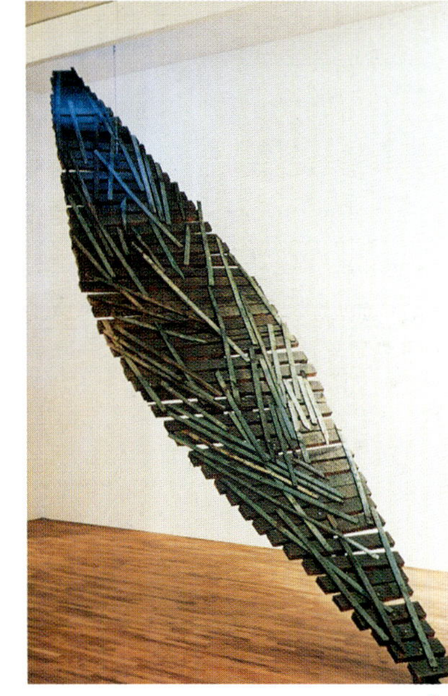

5.4

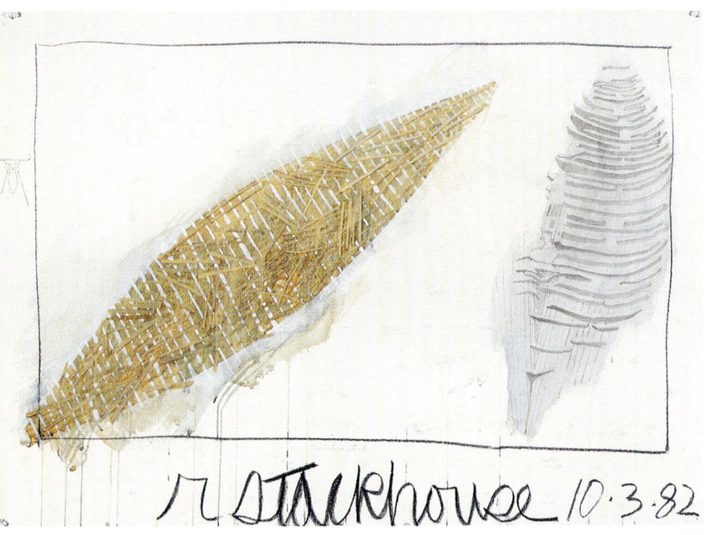

5.5

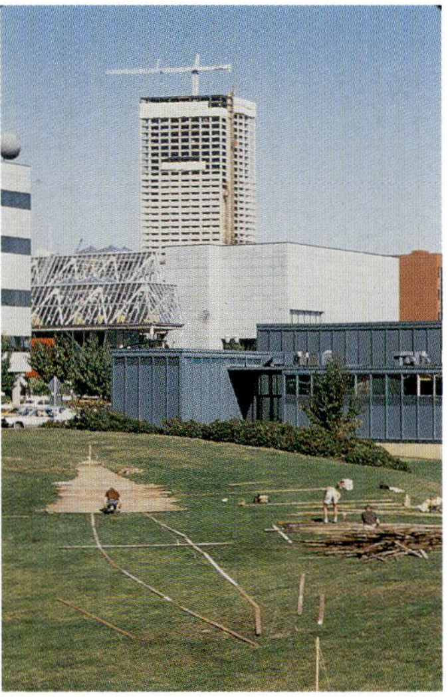

5.6

The large format watercolor of the last piece, more than the other works in the series, sought to convey a sense of the actual scale of the works as well as the experiences encountered in the passages, including the light, the pattern and the way each A-frame adapted to the earth and land forms around it. After he completed the fourth work he paused once again, reflecting on these watercolors. "When I completed these four I felt for sure that I had crossed an important point, I felt very good about them. These four paintings were featured in the gallery show with *Dreamers* and, as a result, I don't think their importance hit me until somewhat later. I did them to see if I could do a really large watercolor. I had never done anything on that scale and welcomed the challenge." As indicated, he exhibited these works at Max Hutchinson's gallery, in his 1982 exhibition. Later, he showed them at the Portland Center for the Visual Arts. "For Portland, I rolled them up, placed them in a large tube, took them out with me on the airplane, and then just tacked them up, directly to the wall."

After completing the series, he decided to submit slides of them to the NEA for a grant. In part, he was curious to see the results of the review process and the resulting official level of classification, according to their categories. He learned, from Renato Danese, that he had been awarded an NEA grant. "I had received an NEA grant. And I assumed it was for painting, had been told it was for painting, so I went around telling everyone that these works were paintings. Then I watched for the announcement of the category in *Art in America*, where it was first posted to the art world. I looked and I wasn't listed as a painter. Then, confused, I looked under the graphics category and there was my name. They must have decided that I had applied in the wrong category. So they did not disqualify me, they just put me in another category." He would have to wait, it seemed, until a later date to verify that he was actually a painter.

After completing these watercolors at the beginning of the year, reviewing and reconsidering the evolution of his career to that point, he entered a period of intensive activity devoted largely to a range of sculptural projects. As he had happened when he left Washington for New York, with the knowledge of his next aesthetic step in mind—the development of the A-frame which directed so much of his art through the late 1970s—he entered this new period with another set of new sculptural forms in mind, forms that had evolved during his preceding period. These forms, the deck derived from *Shiphall* and refined in *Sailings*, both in 1978, and the raised or suspended ship form, initiated with his "Sailors" show at Sculpture Now and refined in the *Eau Claire Sailings*, both in 1979, exerted tremendous influence upon the evolution of his sculptural and painted forms during the 1980s, continuing in many ways to the present date. Like his serpents, eye/boat shapes and A-frames, these newer elements, the deck—whether suspended or supported above ground, or placed directly on the ground—and the elevated ship form—whether raised alone on poles or wooden supports, or integrated into more complete structural forms—became standard parts of the Stackhouse iconography, forms that have remained essential parts of his art until the present time.

The first application of this form in 1982 came with the installation of *Mountain Climbers* in his 1983 Sculpture Now exhibition for Max Hutchinson (Figure 5.4). Beginning with the earlier profile of the type of deck he had created for *Sailings*, and modifying it to reflect his continuing studies of ship wrecks and undersea explorations of ship remains, he designed a form that could be installed by hanging it, using a simple suspension system he devised. The horizontal cross timber pattern of the boat form, with a series of seemingly random scattered wooden planks attached to this surface, became a basic sculptural form for his works of this period. For the Sculpture Now installation, he suspended it from the gallery's ceiling, adding a slightly twisted angle to give the piece a more dynamic presence. In the *Working Drawing For Mountain Climbers*, completed in October of 1982, he presented a detailed view of this basic form and juxtaposed it with an image of the type of ship ruins that had initially inspired it (Figure 5.5). It was exhibited at the Museum of Modern Art the following year.

That year he also created another use for this sculptural form, applying it directly to the ground, when he encountered a series of budgetary and materials complications during the initial stage of creating a proposed project in Portland, Oregon. Initially planning a piece that was more structural, Stackhouse modified his first concept to reflect both the budget and materials constraints as well as his immersion in the study of shipwrecks and the patterns of ship ruins discovered in important archeological sites including the site of the Cheops ship in Egypt. This completed piece was titled *Bones* and was constructed at the Portland Center of the Visual Arts (Figure 5.6). Once again, as the artist recently recounted, the use of intuitive approach to these sculptural projects offered him a resolution to a most challenging dilemma, one he almost refused to accept.

> *This became an important piece because of its engineering and the organic nature of its design and installation. It was not as literal as some of the pieces I had been doing. Its ultimate success was a result of my research and investigation. The artist before me went over budget and I did not have any money for the project I had proposed. At first, I told them to leave me alone, at least long enough to decide if I was still going to try to do the piece. Then they found me some old hotel floor boards, 16' long tongue-and-groove oak floor boards. We even had to pull the nails out. Because there was no money for an armature or a foundation under it, I just glued the boards together and screwed them onto a track made of the same boards. Initially, it was going to be a more elaborate deck, a construction. Next to it, I placed a second piece, a 135 foot long sculpture, this made from siding taken from the same house, painted a sort of faded blue white. There was a hollow in the ground and when it rained it filled up with water. We just nailed the boards into the ground, with long aluminum spikes. When you walked on the one that was glued together it moved in a very special way. Many people asked how I had designed and engineered this. It was a gift, it was intuition. When I go out on these projects, I am very aware of what can happen versus what I think will happen.*

In addition to the budget problems caused by the preceding artist, Stackhouse had arrived in Portland shortly after the eruption of Mt. St. Helens, a catastrophic natural event and one that severely crippled the usually thriving lumber business of the Pacific Northwest. He arrived at a time when there was a major crisis in the lumber industry, and, at the same time, there was a severe economic recession underway. Even though many of the board members of the Portland Arts

P.C.V.A. Project, 1982

Bones Installation, 1983

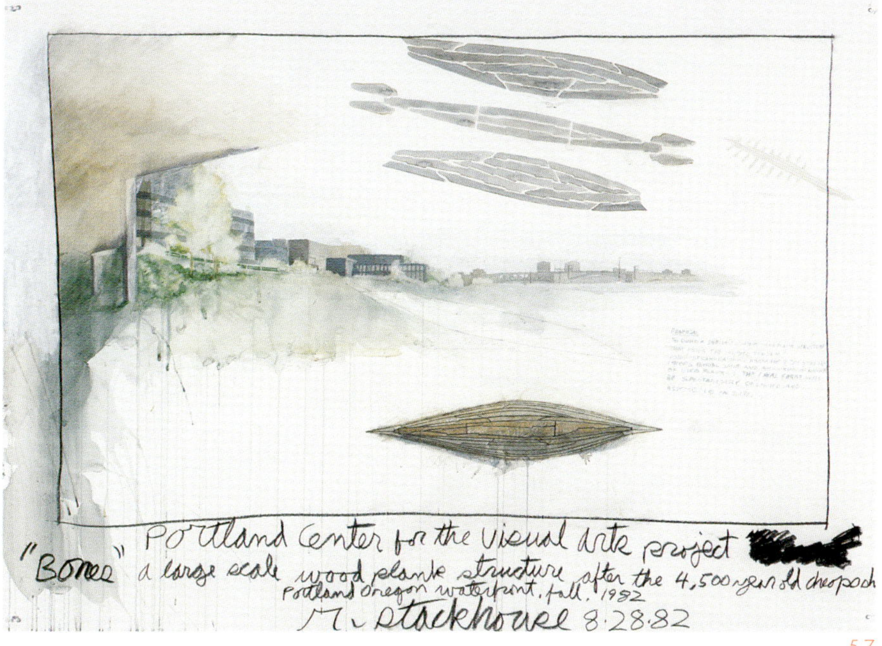

5.7

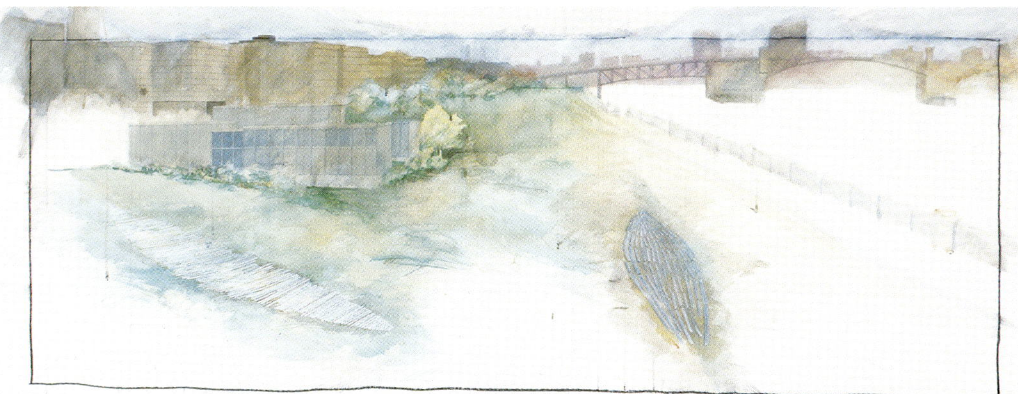

5.8

Center were in the lumber industry they could not get him lumber either. As had happened in the past, in the process of using the recycled wooden materials he developed a new application for his sculptural form, this one no doubt influenced by the suspension version of the piece he had created for his Sculpture Now installation. The evolution of his thinking on this project, and his related study of Norse burial ships and the Cheops ship, were evident in a drawing titled *P.C.V.A. Project*, that he completed in August of that year. (Figure 5.7) As the handwritten text on this drawing explains, *Bones* was designed as a "large scale wood plank structure after the 4500 year old Cheops ship." In a series of stacked design studies for the work, he featured, most prominently, a form that clearly revisited his earlier eye/boat iconographic imagery.

In this watercolor and in a later watercolor drawing, *Bones Installation*, completed in March of 1983, (Figure 5.8) he showed the scale of the larger site. In the later version he also included the second work he designed and built, the architectural setting of the arts center, the waterfront and the bridge area, amplifying the context and the relationship of the works to the nearby water. As seen in these two watercolor images, both reflecting his continuing interest in the Beaux-Arts tradition of classical watercolor architectural renderings, the viewer can clearly see the "bones" form and its implications for his future use of the form. And, as evidence of his continued study of the Cheops ship during this period, he completed *Cheops Ship In Its Burial Pit* on January 30, 1983, well before he painted *Bones Installation*. (Figure 5.9) Recently he talked about his interest in the Cheops ship, and the reasoning behind his creation of this large, labor intensive watercolor image. "This was a source drawing which taught me new types of abstraction. I had a great deal of trouble with this painting, even creating holes in the painting, but it remains one of my favorite pieces." His interest was visual, historical, nautical and technological, as he noted. "What intrigued me about it was that it was 4500 years old. It was big—180 to 190 feet long—and it was designed and built to be taken apart. I was interested in its history—it is made of wood and it is still here, reflecting a superior level of technology. What fascinates me about the Cheops ship is the ingenuity that went into it, including the fact that it was sewn together."

Another work created in this year, *Toronto Passages* constructed in the old part of Toronto, served as his first interna-

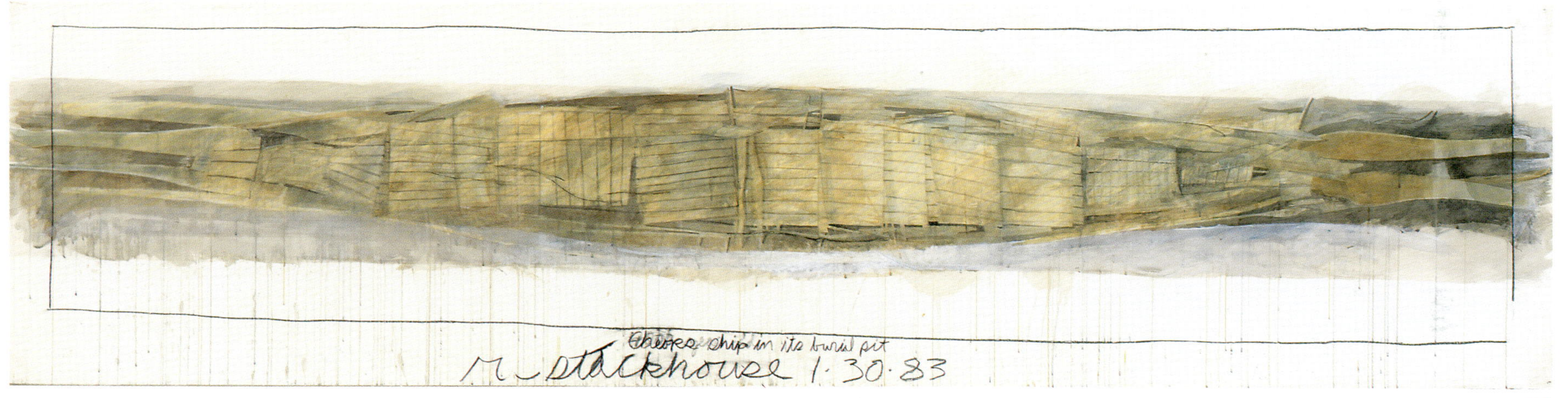

5.9

Cheops Ship In Its Burial Pit, 1983

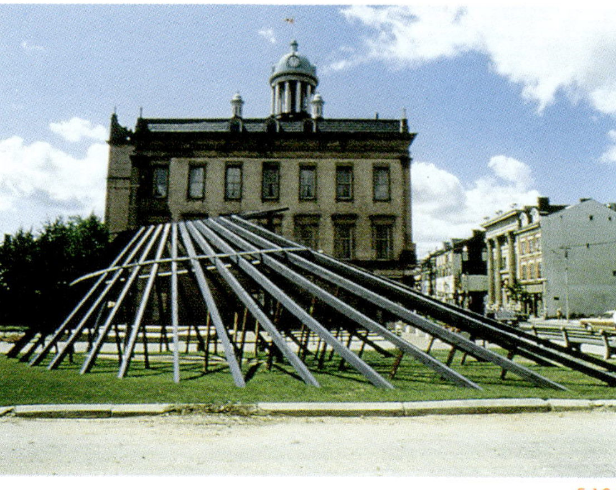

5.10

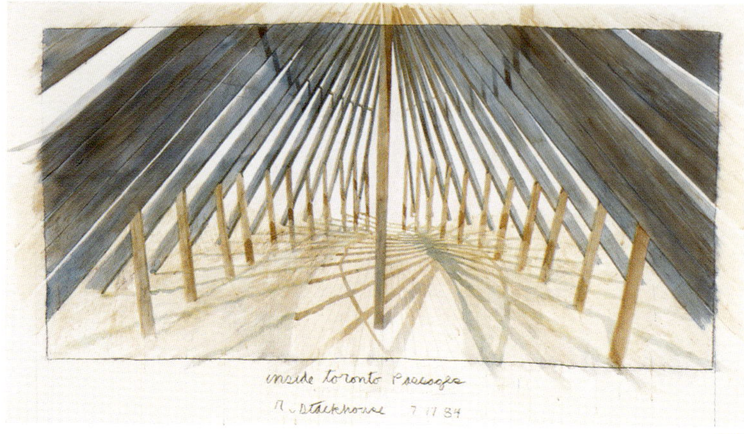

5.11

Toronto Passage, 1982
(actual installation image)

Inside Toronto Passage

tional sculptural installation, the first of several in this period (Figure 5.10). The tilted wooden form of this work was designed to relate to the slope of the site and the historic character of the architecture of the surrounding neighborhood. Painted wood, by now an increasingly common element for Stackhouse, added to the visual impact of this piece. As *Inside Toronto Passages*, a watercolor version of this work suggests (Figure 5.11), this wooden form continued and updated the range of design possibilities for his earlier wooden A-frame passage pieces. The expanded circular pattern enclosed space in a different fashion, opening up the A-frame pattern to new applications, and created opportunities for plays of light and shadow across the interior spaces. And, as suggested in the shadow painted in this watercolor image, this shape offered new ways to reference his growing knowledge of ship architecture, specifically his studies of hull designs.

During the spring of 1983, a variation of his ongoing exploration of the possible range of applications for the deck pattern was presented in Chicago, in his *Red Deck*, a temporary painted wooden platform piece, one built at an angle twisting slightly up from the floor, and tilting upward toward the exposed trusses of the exhibition building that housed it (Figure 5.12). The space suggested by the angles of these trusses may well have reminded him, consciously or unconsciously, of those wooden support trusses at the Peach Lake house that had made such an impression upon him as a child. And, as in the past, a wooden deck, whether painted or unpainted, was reminiscent of the docks, floating platforms, and wooden boats he had also known during his childhood on Peach Lake and Lake Julianna, in Florida. This image, painted as a watercolor (Figure 5.13), served as the cover for the guide to the Chicago Sculpture International, presented at the Chicago Navy Pier, May 19-24, 1983.

Another, very different location for the application of his wooden deck sculptures was presented in New York, not far from his SoHo studio, when he was invited to design a sculptural installation for Creative Time's Art In The Anchorage project, billed as "A visual and performing arts program celebrating the Centennial of the Brooklyn Bridge," presented from May 19-October 10, 1983. The installation space in the anchorage, originally visited in 1982, was described as "dark, cold, wet, full of city surplus tires, and absolutely beautiful." Other artists included in the installation projects were R. M. Fischer, Ned Smyth, Bruce Dow, Jane Greengold, Suzan Pitt, Sal Romano, Taro Suzuki, Warner Wada and Thomas Weaver with over a dozen performance groups involved as well.[80] For Stackhouse, a major point of interest was his admiration of the use of advanced technology by Roebling, the designer of the bridge, and his application of suspension cable systems to support the weight of the bridge (Figure 5.14). "Roebling actually designed an interior mall in the anchorage area of the bridge, complete with notches inside for floor joists. He planned it, on two levels, for a number of stores in there but the city was using it for storage. The inte-

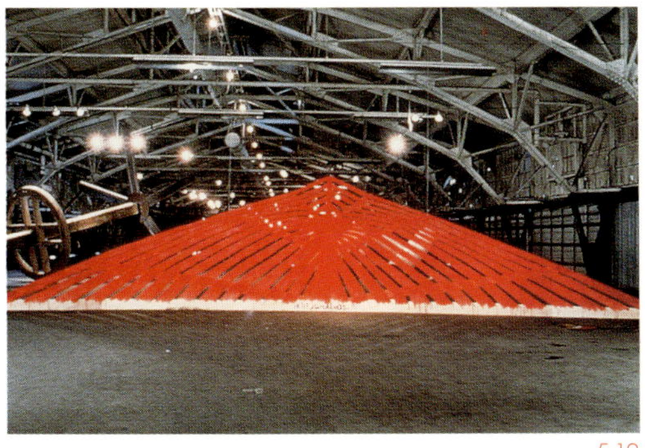
5.12

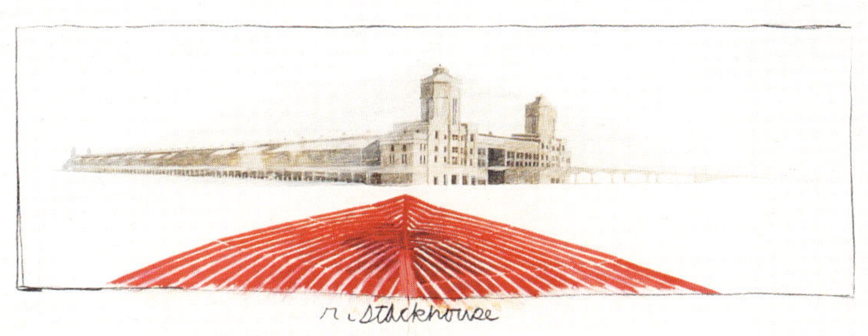

5.13

Red Deck 1983
(actual installation image)

Chicago Sculpture International/Mile 2, 1983

rior space was about 45' tall. The sculpture I designed was horizontal lath that was wing-bolted onto a chain, a chain hanging from two points in the ceiling, and connected to a big block of the bridge that had fallen below. So it was, by design, a suspension bridge that hung from the ceiling."

As evident in the submission drawing for this project (Figure 5.15), Stackhouse went to great lengths to design an appropriate work to fit the architectural and engineering spirit of the location. And, as equally evident from the watercolor proposal he used as his model, this structure was another logical evolutionary application of earlier designs, most specifically the design of *Mountain Climbers*, shown the preceding year at Sculpture Now. This work also benefitted from his own ongoing technological experiments, commonly focusing on simple, sturdy approaches to the installation of temporary sculptural forms, a process that had been greatly advanced by his earlier experiences in stage and theatrical design work at USF. And, once again, he used and modified his eye/boat shapes to fit another environmental situation. "It was one of my lozenge shapes, but it had a curve, and the diagonals were added later. The whole thing rolls up like a snow fence. It is 45 feet long by 16 feet wide. I was able to roll it up, put it in my truck and drove over there with it. I really enjoy that type of engineering, it is fascinating. Once again, the engineering was intuitive and it was very economical. In certain ways, it was economical like the *Great Rain Snake*, touching on only three points. Both were the result of intuitive engineering and solving a specific problem."

Another application of this form, one combining the deck pattern with the raised ship design, was used in *Ohio Prospect*

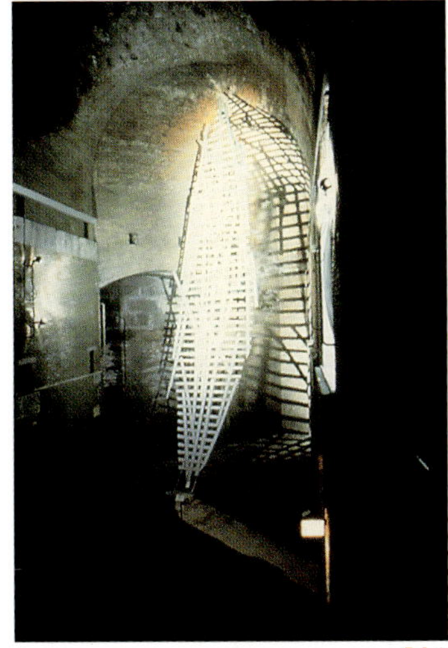
5.14

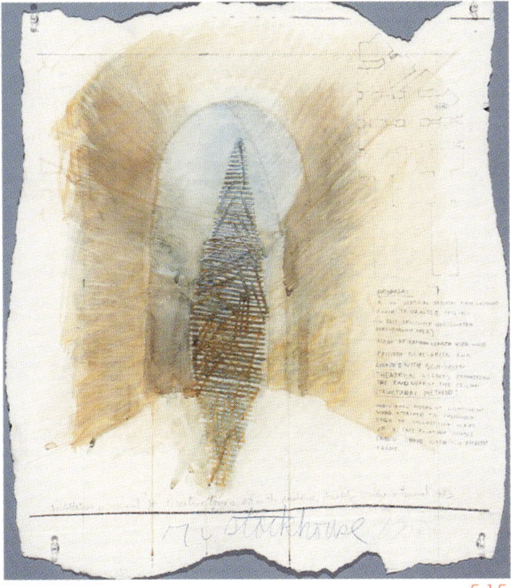
5.15

Brooklyn Bridge Project, 1983
(actual installation image)

Proposal for Brooklyn Bridge Centennial, 1983

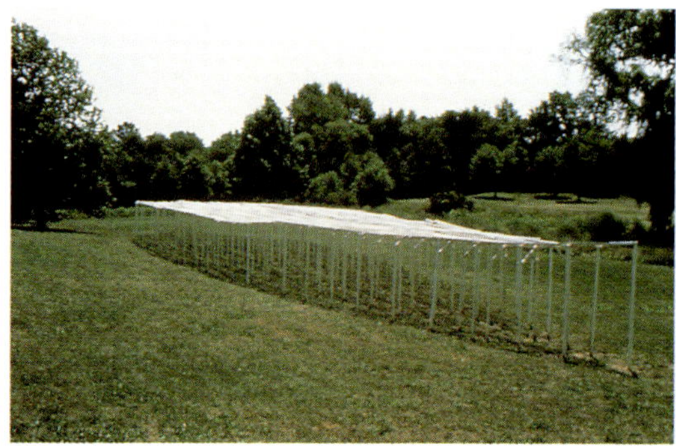
5.16

Ohio Prospect Bones, 1984
(actual installation image)

Bones, created for Crosby Gardens, in Toledo, Ohio (Figure 5.16). Stackhouse completed, as evident in an extended series of drawings, and a later scale model, a complex series of design concepts and final drawings to derive a suitable solution to this site and its distinctive qualities and variations (Figures 5.17, 5.18 and 5.19). These drawings show not only the modification of his concept for this site, they also show the continuing evolution of concepts that would be applied, in numerous ways, to other projects in the coming years. The three-dimensional model completed for this project served as a prototype for many of the installations he completed throughout the 1980s and into the 1990s. And, continuing the "bones" designs applied to a ground-level installation in Portland only two years earlier, he created an elevated and floating structure, one that presented a lively pattern of vertical poles and patterned shadows that also suggested future possibilities to the artist (Figure 5.20).

That same year he completed another international project, a major commissioned piece for the National Gallery of Australia, the same museum that had earlier paid a record price for Jackson Pollock's noted painting, *Blue Poles*. The design of this work (Figure 5.21) can be traced back to the development of his concepts for the Portland project, to the creation of a ground piece that seemed to merge with its environment, creating an organic synthesis with its site. He remained intrigued by the possibility of creating a sculptural form, one based upon his study of ship wrecks, that was a product of the fusion of the organic and the man-made, the constructed shape and form. And, it offered him an opportunity to develop, using more permanent materials, another step in the exploration of one of his most significant images. "For *On the Beach Again*, I used the lozenge shape, the eye/boat shape of my work, and it had this random, overlapping, serpentine element. At first, I did not know for sure if it was an object, or a being. In fact, I learned, it was both. I was able to pursue this for quite some time, through the *Deep Swimmers* period, creating a structure but one with this sense of an organic quality to it."

The planning of this project became an important event and process for Stackhouse, one that caused him to reflect upon the relationship of this form to his earlier works as well as to his own experiences in environments similar to this, specifically in Florida. He began by conducting extensive research on reptiles, on alligators and crocodiles. He began to remember the nature of his experiences at Lundy's fish camp, especially his experiences with the water snakes and the rogue alligator he had pursued in his little wooden boat, armed with his camera and his BB gun. He had, as he realized during his adult years, become very close to nature and the natural order during those years in Florida, years when he was forced as well to confront himself, his own nature, including his sense of isolation from his parents and the difficulties of his particular family situation. Thinking about Florida, about his direct connection to the natural orders he encountered around Lundy's fish camp, affected

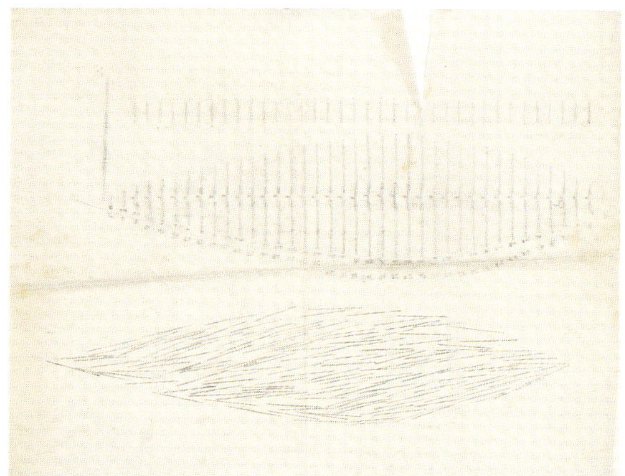
5.17

Plans for Crosby Gardens, 1984

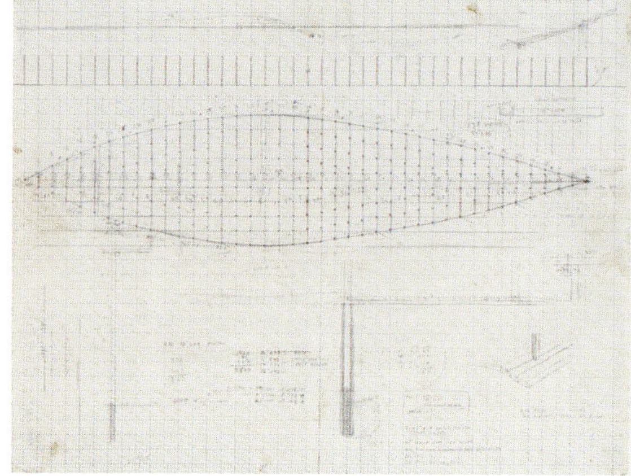
5.18

Plans for Crosby Gardens

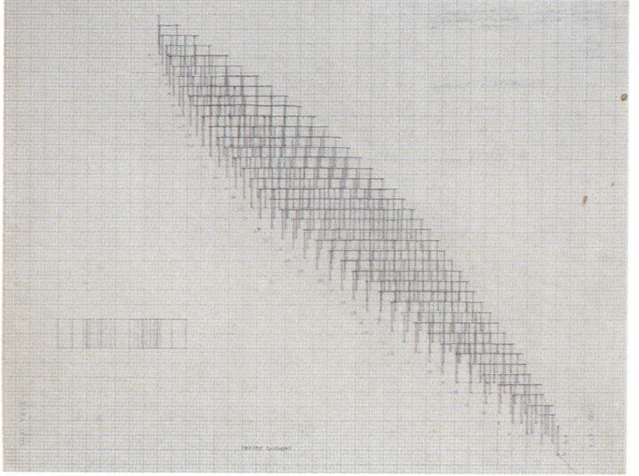
5.19

Working Drawing for Crosby Gardens, 1984

the creation of this piece, as he has recently affirmed.

> *Australia is so primal. It is like Florida, especially where I grew up. I have seen things like this in Florida—the way it is there, something lurking in a casual way there, something stealth-like, just waiting. And, like those memories and experiences of Florida, this work is meant to be encountered as a surprise. For example, I can't tell you how many times I have been in my little row boat and run up against that 14' bull alligator that they were trying to kill on the lake I lived on because it was a rogue. I used to fool around with my BB gun and my Hawkeye camera. I always got a shot of its nose, sticking up out of the water. So, here, with this project in Australia, you see that alligator. That to me was a central issue in this work, getting the form back down into the grass, into the earth, into the water.*

One of the few requirements of this commission from the museum was that he create a piece that could be located both in and out of the water, reflecting the centrality and importance of the water and garden designs features that had been integrated into the design of the museum and its grounds. Stackhouse welcomed the challenge. As his planning advanced, he realized that this also was related to his concept of the journey, symbolized in his own life by his solitary explorations in a wooden vessel, usually a small and fairly insubstantial one. Looking back to his more recent works, one also finds connections to *Mountain Climber* and his Brooklyn Bridge anchorage piece, especially in the use of seemingly flexible forms, ones that can float suspended in the air, or, in this case, be allowed to float, half in and half out of the water. Considering the importance of this commission, he explained his development of his final approach to the design of the project.

> *This is about ending a journey. It is where I try to deal with the architectural and the organic at the same time. Some might say that you have beached your boat. And I could say yes, but, on the other hand, maybe that form is an animal slipping into the water, to become a whale, an alligator, or some other crea-*

Ohio Prospect Bones, 1984

On the Beach Again (site)

Site for *On the Beach Again* at National Gallery of Austrailia.

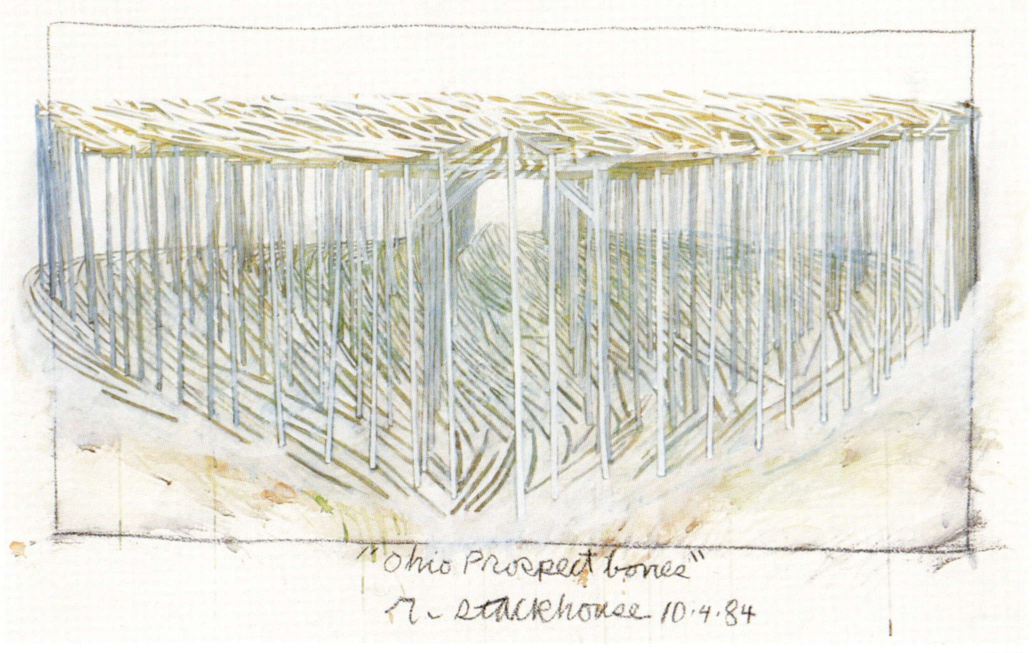

5.20

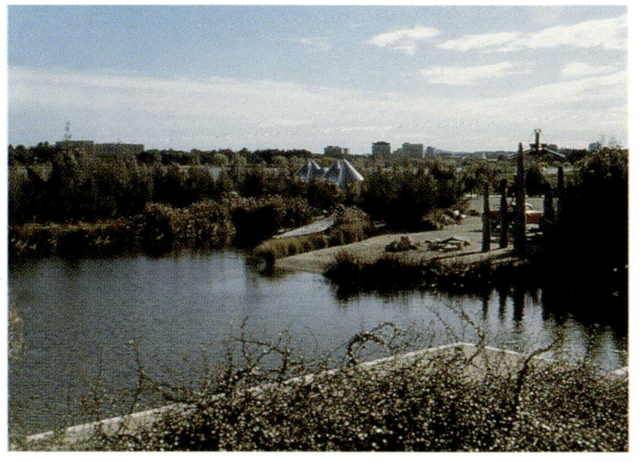

5.21

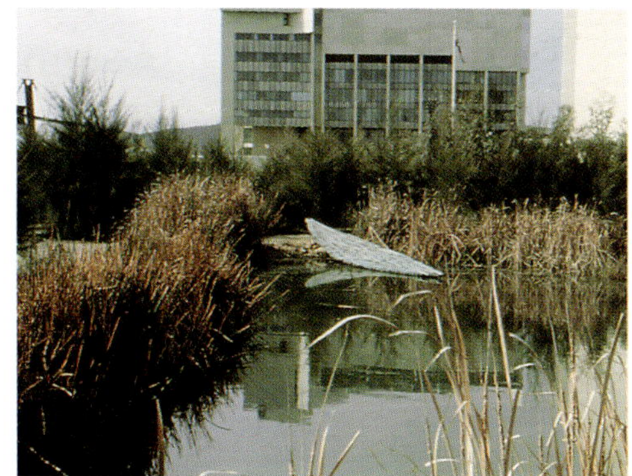

5.22

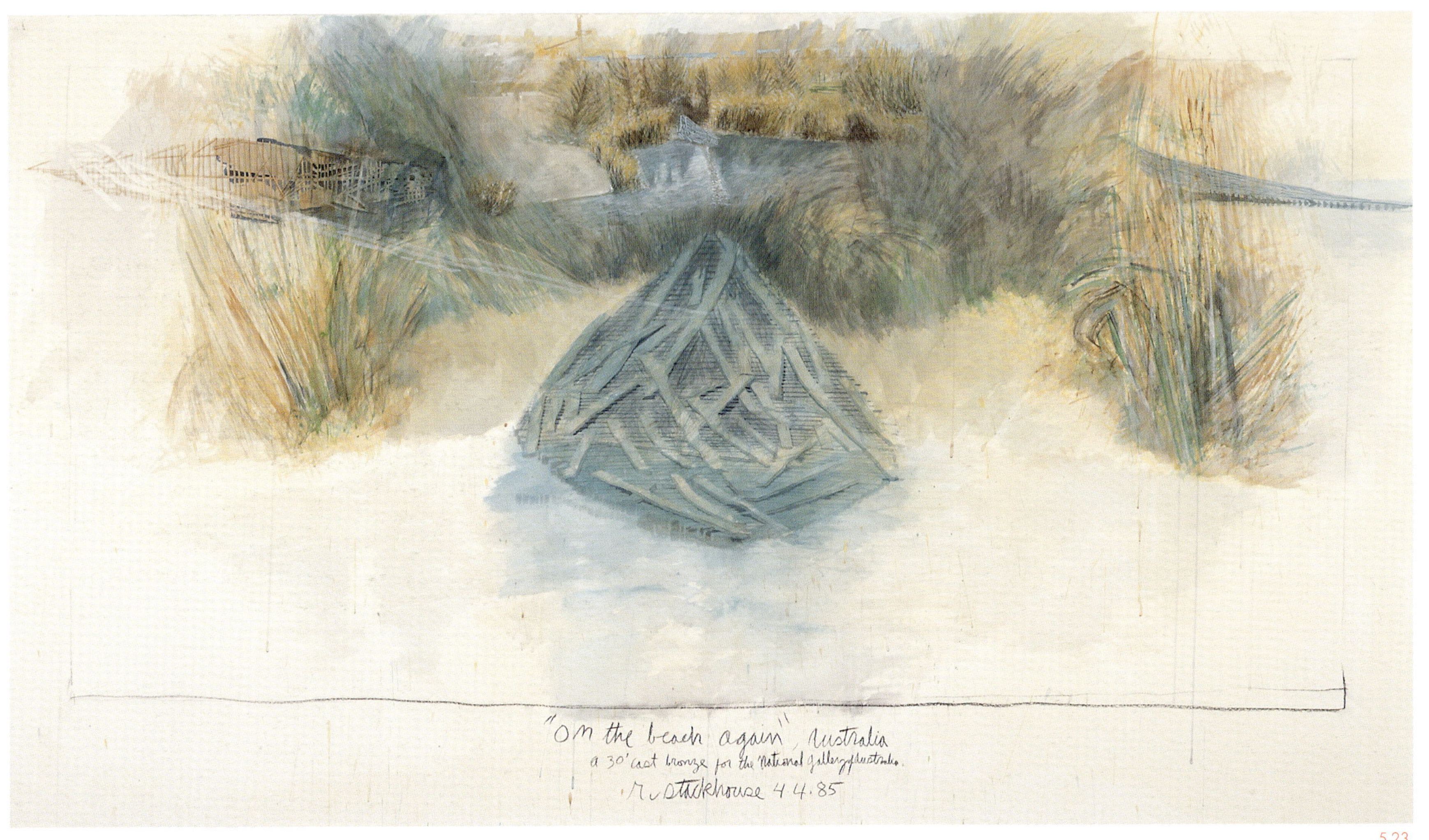

5.23

On the Beach Again Austrailia, 1985

ture. The title, On the Beach Again, *was an escape clause for me. Because, I recall, I was once asked by Jack Burnham if I ever thought about beaching my boat. And I replied that all my art was about the journey. There was no destination. If I ended the journey then I might not make art anymore. I was required to put one of my sculptures half on land and half in water. By calling it* On the Beach Again *I meant to suggest that it had already been there. I could resolve the issue for me, because it was not the end. It was like the ferry to nowhere; it can't be resolved. And, of course,* On the Beach Again *was the well-known book about the end of the world.*

His later watercolor painting of the sculpture located in its site, *On the Beach Again Australia*, completed in the spring of 1985, presented his vision and perception of the work and its relationship to the surrounding environment (Figure 5.23). The central cast bronze form, dominant in this composition, is shown in a manner suggesting that, like an alligator or similar creature, it could be slipping into or out of the water. To the right, he placed a structure in the tall grass like the lurking alligators he remembered from Florida. And, to the left, he created ship ruins, remnants from an earlier visit, perhaps, by an earlier culture who had sent explorers and colonists to this site. In the far distance, away from this suggestion of primordial activity, is faint evidence of modern civilization. Because of the location and the larger budget, he designed and fabricated the sculptural form in wood and then it was cast in bronze. When he visited the foundry, in Taiwan, he saw that the foundry workers had painted the wooden prototype white, making it easier to fit the parts of the work back together, like reassembling the parts of a puzzle (Figure 5.24).

He was intrigued by the evolution of his own piece, in its wooden and its bronze forms. In addition to the fabrication crew, the installation of the completed bronze sculpture required the use of a crane and a team of workers to properly set the work in its location, on the edge of the water and the grass (Figure 5.25).

He continued to explore some of the inherent possibilities he had discovered on his Australian project in his 1984 *Deep Swimmers* installation and exhibition at the University of Tennessee at Knoxville. A new natural form, the whale and its skeletal structure, had inspired this project, as evident in his watercolor, *For Deep Swimmers*, completed in November of 1984 (Figure 5.26). A second drawing for this work shows, on the borders, designs for *Toronto Passages*, *Eau Claire Sailings*, and *Bones* in Ohio, indicating that they were all prototypes for this piece, serving as parts of the evolutionary design of the work. After his interest in serpents and alligators, curiosity about the skeletal structure of whales was a natural evolutionary step for Stackhouse. And, for much of his life, he had been fascinated by the dinosaurs and by the whale skeletons he had seen hanging, often high over his head, in natural history museum installations. The form was quite familiar to him by that time, so he decided to explore the use of this concept for the traveling exhibition, titled "Deep Swimmers," organized by Sam Yates for the University of Tennessee Art and Architecture Gallery. In 1985 and 1986, that exhibition traveled through the South to locations including the Hunter Museum in Chattanooga, the Clemson University Gallery, the Greenville County Museum of Art, the Huntsville Museum of Art, and Cheekwood Fine Art Center, in Nashville. It also traveled to the Laumeier Sculpture Park in St. Louis, in connection with the planning for a sculptural installation of his on the grounds there.

Stackhouse planned and constructed a structure, an architectural form, an elevated version of his deck form, with long, evenly spaced wooden ribs rather than random wooden planks, as on the earlier shipwreck forms. He also designed the work to be part of the traveling exhibition, therefore it had to be

On the Beach Again
Fabrication image

Installation of
On the Beach Again

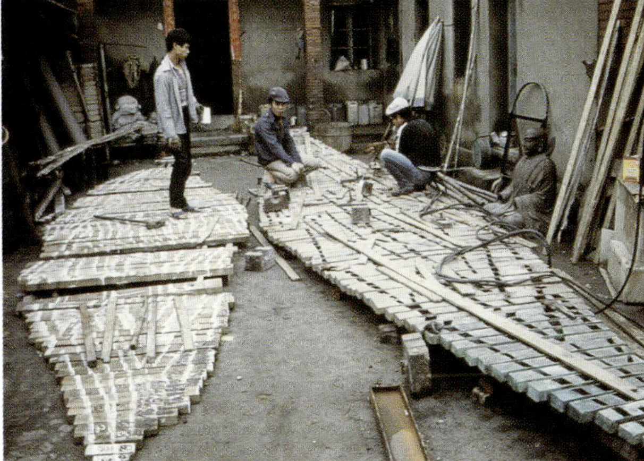

5.24

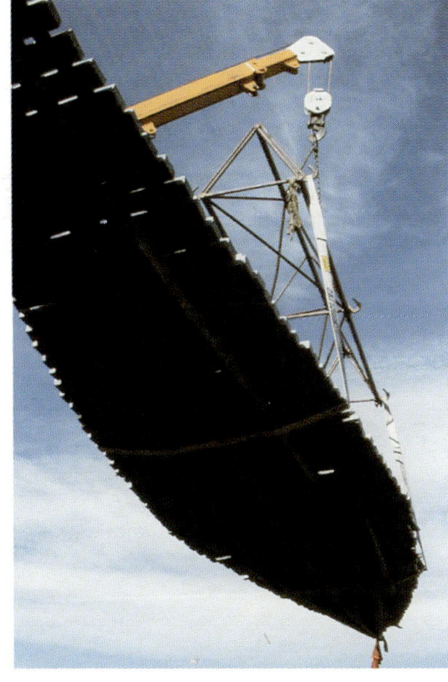

5.25

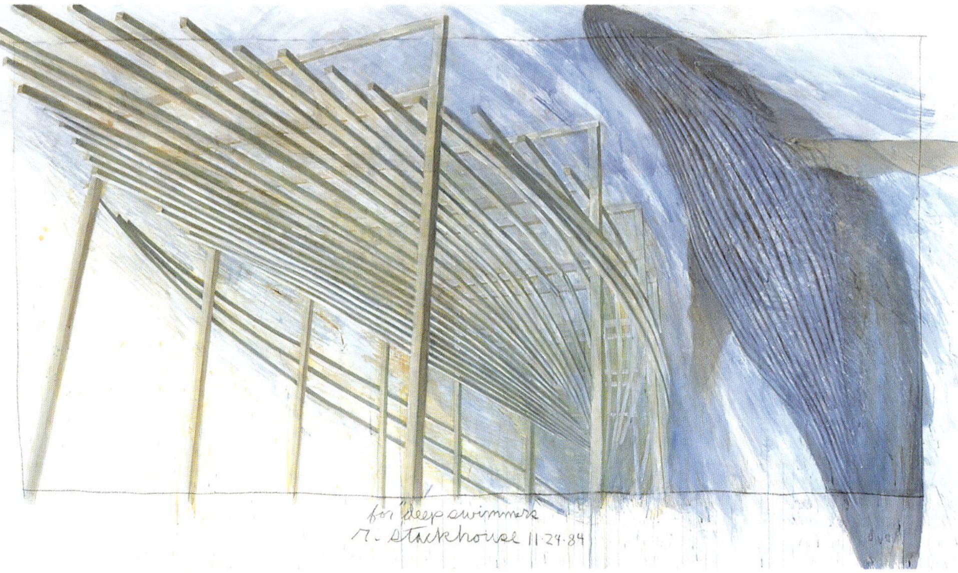

5.26

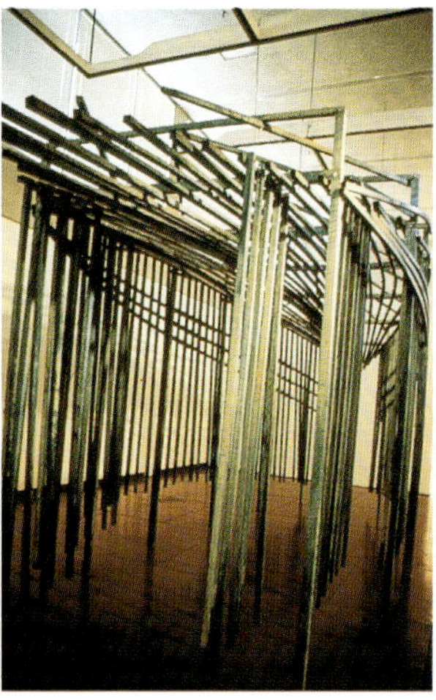

5.27

For Deep Swimmers, 1984

Deep Swimmers 1984
(actual installation image - Knoxville)

designed for ease of assembly and disassembly throughout the two-year traveling exhibition. It was, he noted in the exhibition's catalogue, a new form and a new experiment in sculptural design for him. "The sculpture *Deep Swimmers* is new to me. In a sense it is a temporary passage structure similar to what I would build outside for a short period of time....The scale is something new for me....It is 28 feet, my smallest passage structure yet. However, it does have enough interior that it gives you a sense of being inside." Once again, as he had intended with his A-frame structures, the artist designed the piece to create a sense of passage and discovery, as he went on to explain. "The title and the piece *Deep Swimmers*, imply that the image may look like a deep swimmer, but walking through it we become an even deeper swimmer because we are beneath the deep swimmer itself."[81] In his accompanying essay on Stackhouse and this work, Donald Kuspit pointed to the act of passage associated with this work and other works by the artist.

> *Stackhouse's primitive ghost ships evoke a primitive sense of ritual passage to buried archaic selfhood, a passage as transformative as archaeological in import. As much as Charon's ferry, Stackhouse's sculptures transport us to what we thought was dead in us, the archaic, primitive, ghostlike, natural, seemingly timeless self that we had forgotten...The environmental pieces—and all Stackhouse's sculptures are implicitly designed for a natural site—are ghost dances through which we recover our archaic self-identity. The ship has the archaic shape of the snake—is the snake of the self in its form as passage ("ghost dance") through life. The ship of the archaic self retains its shape whatever cargo it carries. It is as though we cannot know how well our sense of self has survived—how flexible it is—until we have undergone the rigors of psychic passage suggested in Stackhouse's shipshape structures.*[82]

Stackhouse recently indicated that the use of the whale form was something that he logically developed, based upon his readings and research, and his personal experiences with the whale skeletal structures he had encountered during his research and in his childhood experiences. It was not, as had been the case with his earlier major forms, something that came directly through his unconscious mind and related sense of creativity. As such, it was a conscious leap, one of the first he had developed to that point in the selection of his subjects. "None of the leaps have been conscious leaps. The closest you can come to seeing a conscious leap in my work was the whales." And, after experimenting with the form for some time, creating two large works and four or five other related works, he decided that its possibilities were too limited for him.

That same year, Stackhouse had examples of his works featured in two important exhibitions, in "An International Survey of Painting and Sculpture," presented at the Museum of Modern Art and in "Drawing Since 1974," at the Hirschhorn Museum and Sculpture Gardens in Washington. At the Hirschhorn, located not far from the Corcoran Gallery, where he still taught at that time, Stackhouse's painted versions of *Inside Running Animals/ Reindeer Way*, *Shiphall*, and *Niagara Dance* were featured in the exhibition installation. Notably, in the catalogue for this exhibition, Stackhouse emphasized, once again, his primary role as a trained painter, not a sculptor. "Drawing is an integral part of my work; source drawings, plans for sculptural projects, and documentations of finished installations fill the majority of my studio time. Because I originally studied painting, I conceive of my sculpture two-dimensionally rather that in three dimensions. I see them as pictures, not volumetric structures."

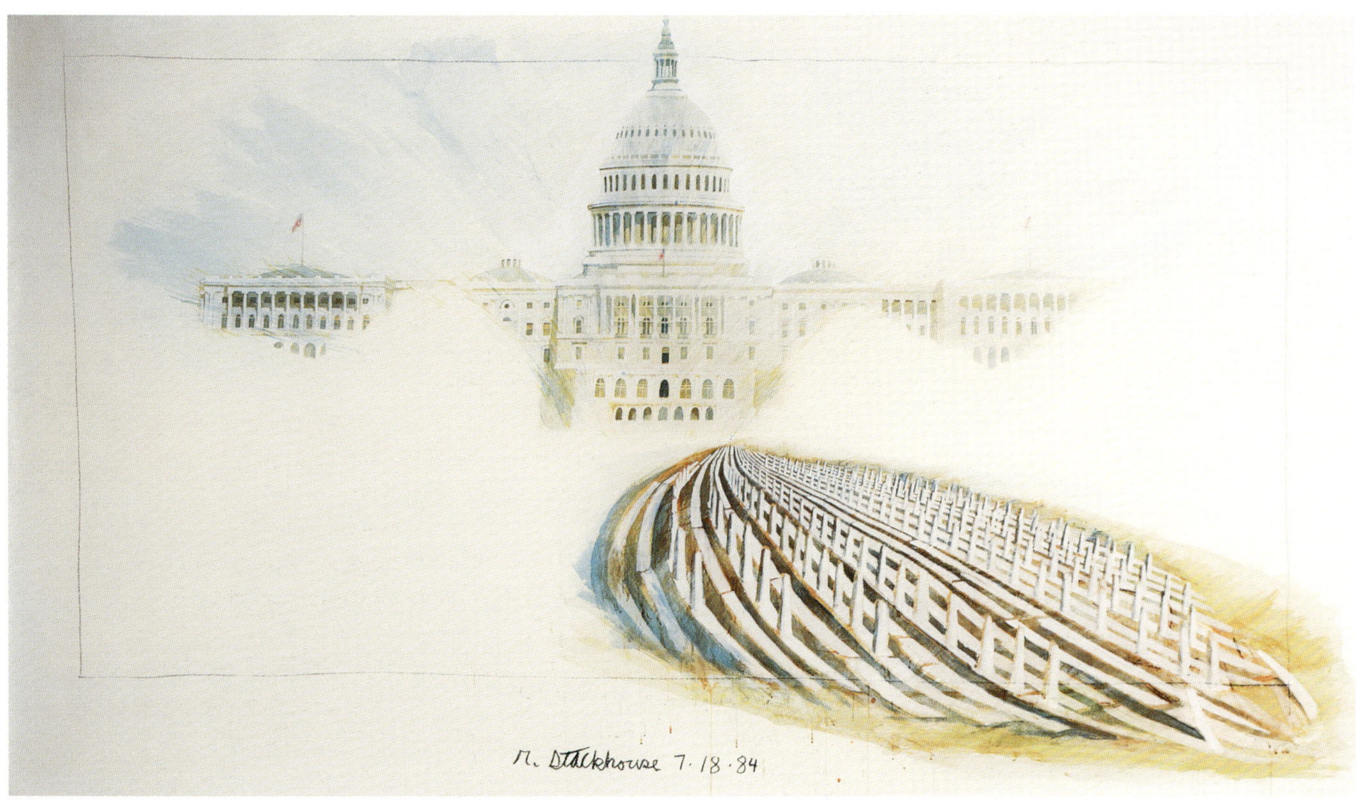

5.28

Continuing, he explained the source of his imagery and concluded with a clear statement regarding the primacy of drawing in his work. "The source of my imagery is change—change as in growth, life and death, journeys, knowledge, and transformation. The sources I draw are ships and serpents and shadows. These source images can appear at any time on my project plans or documentation drawings....My drawing chronicles my method. Making my sculpture is an experience; drawing is my skill." [83]

The opportunity to work again on the Hudson River arose when he was invited to participate in the exhibition and environmental art project, "Land Marks, New site proposals by twenty-two original pioneers of environmental art," curated by Linda Weintraub for the Edith C. Blum Institute at Bard College, located at Annandale-on-Hudson, New York. Each of the participating artists—including Alice Aycock, Jackie Ferrara, Nancy Holt, Mary Miss, Robert Morris and Dennis Oppenheim—was invited to design a project, with no cost or budgetary limitations, for a proposed site located along the Hudson River. Stackhouse's watercolor painting, *Hudson Prospect/River Bones*, continued his ongoing "bones" projects, focusing, as he explained at the time, on the possibilities of working without budget constraints. "I had no idea how difficult an unlimited project could be. Could it be bronze? Or as large as I wanted it to be? I had to give myself a lower budget and settled on cast aluminum and a smaller scale. What I ended up with is a structure related to ships; abandoned, wrecked, a graveyard of Hudson River history." [84]

The "bones" project he painted in June 1, 1984, for this exhibition proposal, inspired by the ships and the extensive ship graveyards he had known from the time of his childhood growing up along the Hudson River Valley, was directly related to one of his most exquisite large-scale architectural watercolor paintings, *U.S. Capitol Bones Not A Likely Prospect*

U.S. Capitol Bones Not A Likely Prospect, 1984

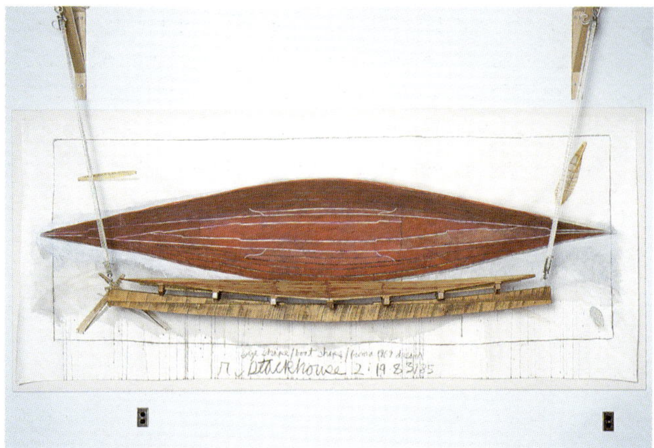

Eye Shape/ Boat Shape/ From a 1969 Dream 1983-85

5.29

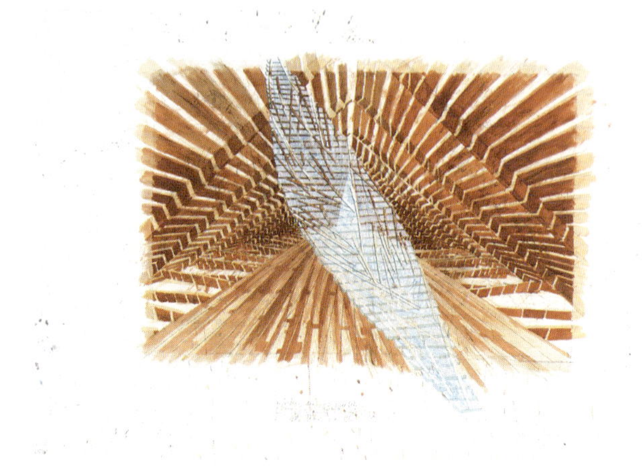

Working Drawing for Pace Litho, 1986

5.30

(Figure 5.28). Completed on July 18, 1984, only two weeks after the Fourth of July celebrations in the nation's capital, this work proposed a monumental version of one of his "bones" project for the grounds overlooked by the capitol, the seat of congressional power for the nation. The use of a highly refined and highly accomplished Beaux-Arts architectural style gave a distinctive finish and edge to his proposal. It also demonstrated his accomplished mastery of large scale watercolor painting as well as offering a knowing artistic nod of respect to the styles and traditions of the great Beaux-Arts master architects who had shaped the vision of the nation's capital and its public plazas and parks, including the Washington Mall connecting the Capitol to the Lincoln Memorial. This was also a tribute to the architecture and the man-made environment that he knew so well from his years of living and teaching in Washington, including the years he had lived near this site, in the Capitol Hill area.

As the range and complexity of his national and international projects of 1984 demonstrated, and as his inclusion in major museum and institutional exhibitions and projects that year proved, Robert Stackhouse had become increasingly recognized as an important American artist. As these events took place in the art world, another event, a less positive one, took place elsewhere. That year his father, Jerry Stackhouse, died of a heart attack in a hospital outside of Gulfport, Florida, just two days after his 71st birthday. In the years after his parents moved to their Town Shores waterfront condominium in Gulfport, in 1972, living on their own for the first time in their married lives, Robert saw changes in his father that helped bring the two of them closer together. For much of his childhood, he had lived away from his father, especially during the years he spent at Lundy's fish camp with his grandparents, when his grandfather, Hoyt Holland, had served more as a father than his own father. After 1972, Robert and Jerry Stackhouse had become closer, addressing issues that had long affected their relationship. During this time, his father, who had never risen to the stature and levels of success associated with his wife's family, the Hollands, was able to witness with growing pride Robert's accomplishments including his growing stature and recognition as a professional artist. The death of his father was a great loss for Robert, a loss he mourned for an extended period. Phyllis Stackhouse decided to remain at Town Shores after her husband's death. It was a location where they had been very happy together, and she has continued to live there to the present date.

As the events of that year transpired, Robert remained busy with his diverse art projects and with his commuting to Washington and his teaching at the Corcoran School of Art. By this time, he had become active as an administrator as well as a teacher, having been appointed to the position of director of the Core Program, the undergraduate B.F.A. program, at the school. In this capacity, he had assumed responsibility for maintaining academic standards and programs in the school and also took an active role in planning new programs and outreach activities for the future of the school. By this time, however, he was becoming increasingly disenchanted with teaching and commuting on a regular basis, activities that were causing an increasing drain on energies that he might have devoted to a full-time art career. At the end of the 1980s, after he left his position at the Corcoran in 1987, Stackhouse commented on his experiences at the school in a published interview.

> *I could use my teaching as an excuse not to push myself. I was getting very comfortable. I was very good at it, and I liked to invent all these new things. Luckily I had a faculty who would follow, and a dean who would listen and a fairly flexible school. I had visions for the Corcoran to be the greatest art school in the world. But I don't care about any of that now, that was an escape from the reality that I had to face. Here I am, I have everything at my feet in New York, and all I have to do is do it; but that frightened me. I finally realized this after fifteen years. Being in the thick of it, I was showing all the time. I had sort of hidden myself in New York.* [85]

One of his continuing archetypal images, the eye/boat shape, contributed to the construction of a piece he created over a two year period, from 1983 to 1985, a work titled *Eye Shape/Boat Shape/ From a 1969 Dream* (Figure 5.29). As in his earlier *Sky Song*, where an eye shape (now a more clearly defined eye and boat shape), was positioned on a work on paper, over a wooden construction, in this work a boat was suspended, like a lifeboat hanging from ropes and pulleys. As the patterning of the eye indicates, the sculptural deck forms and the shipwreck forms that had influenced them contributed notably to the evolution of this form, and it, in turn, had underpinned the evolution of many of the artist's most recent projects. This continuing use and regeneration of his own archetypal images could also be seen in this period as he developed studies for a print series he was producing for Pace Prints, in New York. In *Working Drawing For Pace Litho* (Figure 5.30), he juxtaposed the image of the eye/boat shape used in *Mountain Climber*, *On the Beach Again*, the Brooklyn Bridge piece and his diverse "Bones" projects over the A-frame structure, merging his dominant sculptural project form of the 1980s with the dominant form of the 1970s, melding these two types of passages, showing as well the diverse uses of wooden materials and the resulting patterns of light, color and shadow. And, as in all of his print projects, he struggled with the challenge of recreating the qualities of light and color that so strongly attracted him to watercolor.

And, in 1986, he began an association with the Morgan Gallery in Kansas City that would lead to the next major period in his career, beginning in 1993. Through the success of a major gallery exhibition in Kansas City, he began to work on a number of projects in Missouri and the Middle West, and began as well his affiliations with the Belger Family Foundation in Kansas City.

That same year he also painted an important work, *Indigo Way*, that marked the return of the serpent image on a large scale, juxtaposing it with an A-frame structure, not unlike his approach that year to the juxtaposition of the eye/boat shape and the A-frame in the Pace lithographic study (Figure 5.31). As he had shown previously in his 1982 watercolor, *Inside Four Structures*, it was possible to create a work on a large enough scale to actually suggest the experience of entering one of his A-frame structures, even after that work had been destroyed. In this enormous new watercolor, he painted both the serpent and the A-frame on a large, full frontal scale, using the resulting tension and balance between the two to create a sense of the continuing power and mystery of these two archetypal images. As a result, he introduced a level of direct experience into the viewer's domain, breaking down the traditional established barriers between viewer and painting, just as he had earlier done the same with his sculptural forms. This painting continues to intrigue the artist, as he recently indicated while viewing it in a retrospective exhibition of his work at the Albrecht-Kemper Museum of Art.

> *First, it begins with the simple fact that there is a snake and an A-frame and they are alone. One side of the painting pushes you back, the other side pulls you in. It is like a revolving door. There is a strong dynamic energy. It is large enough to give you a sense of actually being in the space. I don't really know if it is a painting of a sculpture or a sculpture*

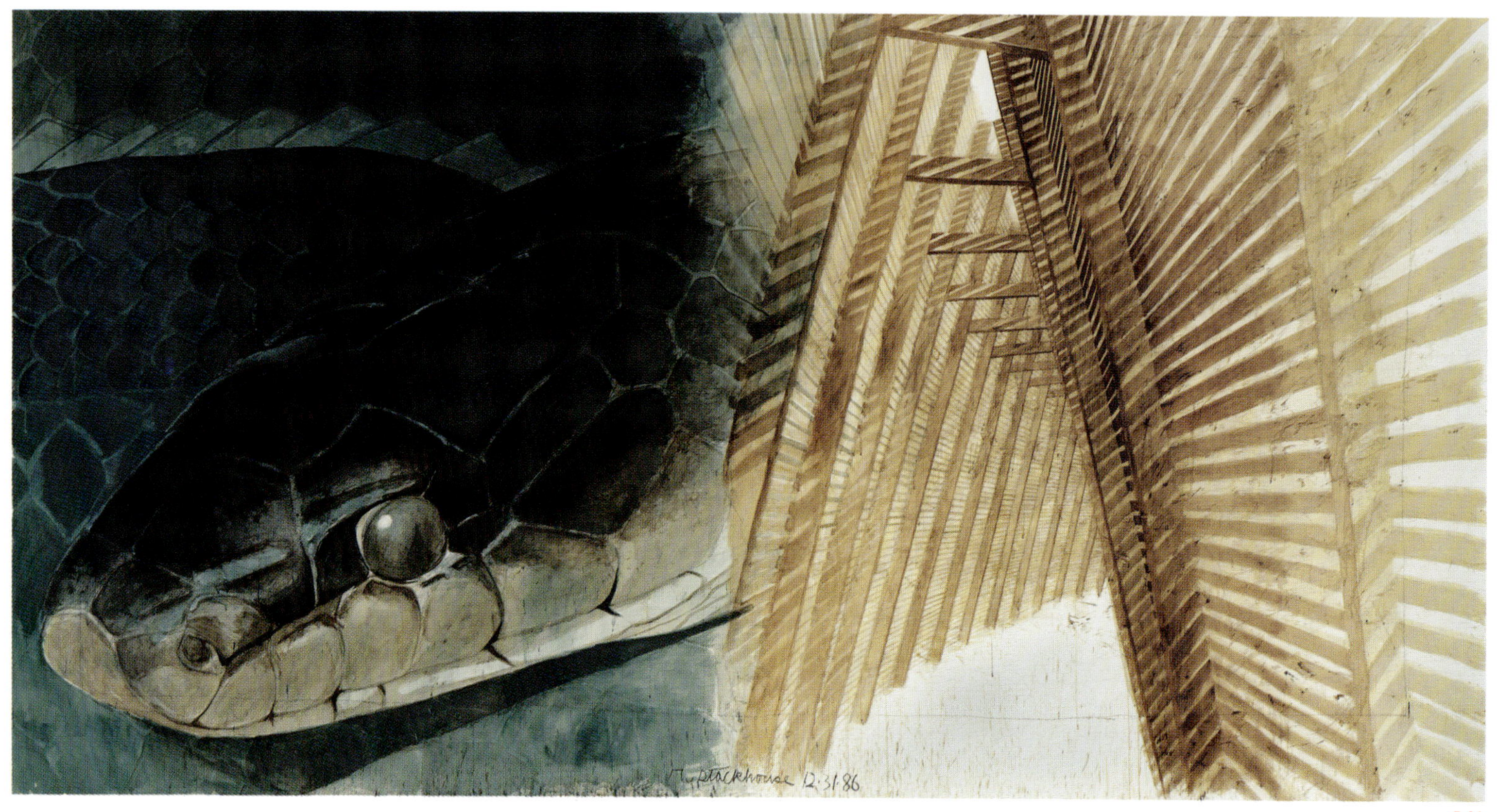

5.31

Indigo Way, 1986

of a painting. This piece remains so important to me. The snake is very menacing. And yet it is not quite a snake. There is also a duality, the cool on one side and the warm on the other. The dynamic can be traced, at least in part, back to the push and pull of the Abstract Expressionist era, back to Hans Hoffman. There is a sense of a corner to be turned in the A-frame and you don't know what is waiting around that corner. It is blue. It is dark. It is mysterious. You don't know the answer. And, as a result, it is very much like life, isn't it?

An even larger format serpent and wooden structure was shown in the project proposal for his entry in the 19th Sao Paolo Bienal, held in 1987 (Figure 5.32). The other American artists featured in this exhibition were Stephen Antonakis, Michael Singer and Pat Steir. Here, on an enormous scale, he proposed merging the form of a painted red A-frame with an equally large and menacing red mamba snake, coiled, with the head and eye leering out over the top of the wooden structure. This form repeated, in a certain way, the compositional elements he had presented in the drawing of his 1969 work, *Sky Song*, featuring an eye floating over the curving wooden roof form, suggestive of his future A-frames and the skeletal frame work shown in this proposal. As actually built and installed at Sao Paolo (Figure 5.33), the work greeted visitors, unavoidably, as the intense red focal point of an entry ramp that led directly to the piece. About this work, he noted at the time: "Seen from a distance, because of the open latticework, the viewer sees the two pieces as one.... When the viewer stands between the drawing and the structure...the viewer sees both as separate entities. Each of these physical processes stands for a personal journey from the past to a hopeful future. A future we can only dream may be utopian." [86] That year he also created a smaller version of this work, *Ruby Brazil*, built of a painted red serpent and a red lattice boat, designed and installed in a fashion similar to his 1983-85 work, *Eye Shape/Boat Shape/ From a 1969 Dream* (Figure 5.34).

As projects of this scale and international magnitude continued to be presented to Stackhouse, he decided to resign from his teaching position at the Corcoran Gallery School of Art. Although still somewhat ambivalent about a departure from the academic world after all of his years of association with it, he realized that teaching, administrative duties and the time spent commuting were interfering with the challenges and demands he faced in his professional art career. So he decided to become a full-time artist, based in New York, ending his regular connection to the academic world and the teaching profession. However, he would maintain his teaching activities on a more limited and selective basis over the next eleven years as a visiting artist in numerous positions around the country. In gratitude and as a tribute to his service to the Corcoran Gallery's Art School, on May 16, 1987, he was appointed Professor Emeritus at the Corcoran, "in recognition of outstanding teaching and his academic leadership for the past twenty years."

At the end of that year, and perhaps in a most symbolic fashion, he initiated but could not complete a major painting combining two of his favorite archetypal images. *Dragon Fight*, depicting an intense battle scene involving an enormous serpent, suggestive of a mythic sea serpent, and a Viking burial ship was signed, uncompleted on December 16, 1987 (Figure 5.35). Part of the reason for his inability to complete the work was technical, based on properties of the paper used for the composition. "I had trouble with the paper. The right hand side had no sizing on it. So it was like painting with watercolor on plaster. But the left had sizing, so it took all the washes. I kept working on it." His difficulties with the piece, in part a reflection of his ambiguous attitude toward the importance of his own paintings, especially those created independently of sculptural forms, was a key element in this, his own "Dragon Fight." His ambiguity even affected his willingness to show it to others. "This, I now know, is an important piece. However, I was embarrassed when I did it. I would not show it to people, like the more recent painting, *Drifters*. At the time, I thought it was insignificant work." This large, forceful work also suggests the battles he faced, leaving the securities of his position at the Corcoran, setting off, not unlike a Viking explorer, on unchartered waters, where both new opportunities and mythic dragons and sea serpents awaited him.

Opportunities to explore new possibilities for the application and evolution of the eye/boat shape, and the more recent deck and elevated ship forms, came from several different directions beginning in the year he decided to leave his posi-

Sao Paolo Bienal Proposal, 1987

Ruby Birth, Sao Paolo Bienal, Brazil, 1987 (installation photo)

Ruby Brazil, 1987

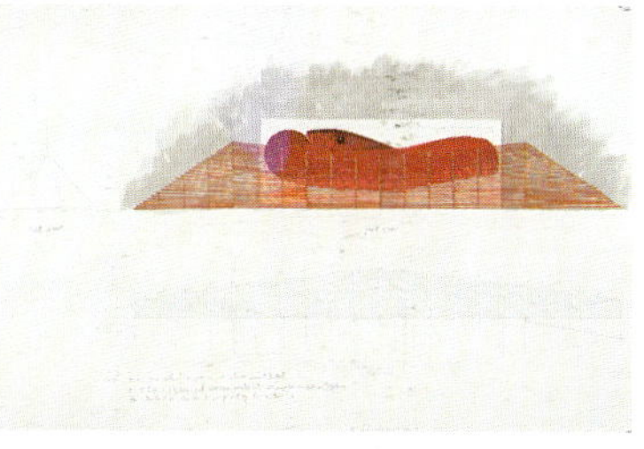
5.32

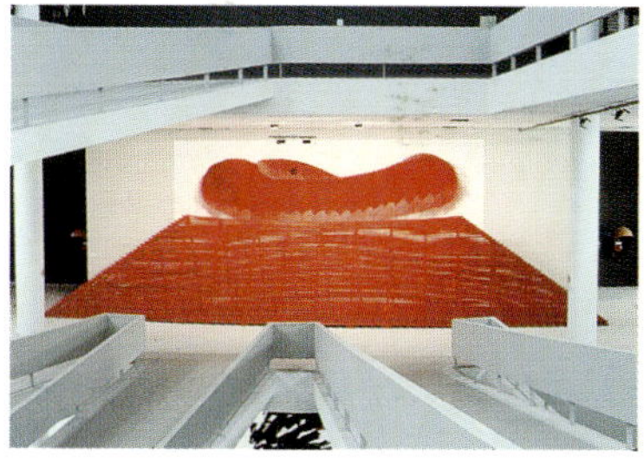
5.33

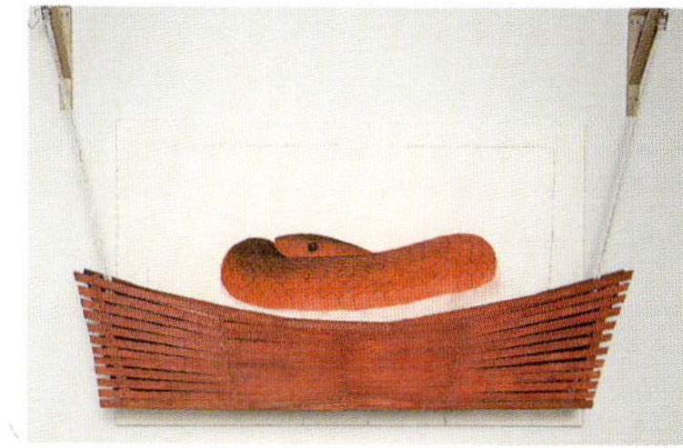
5.34

Dragon Fight, 1987

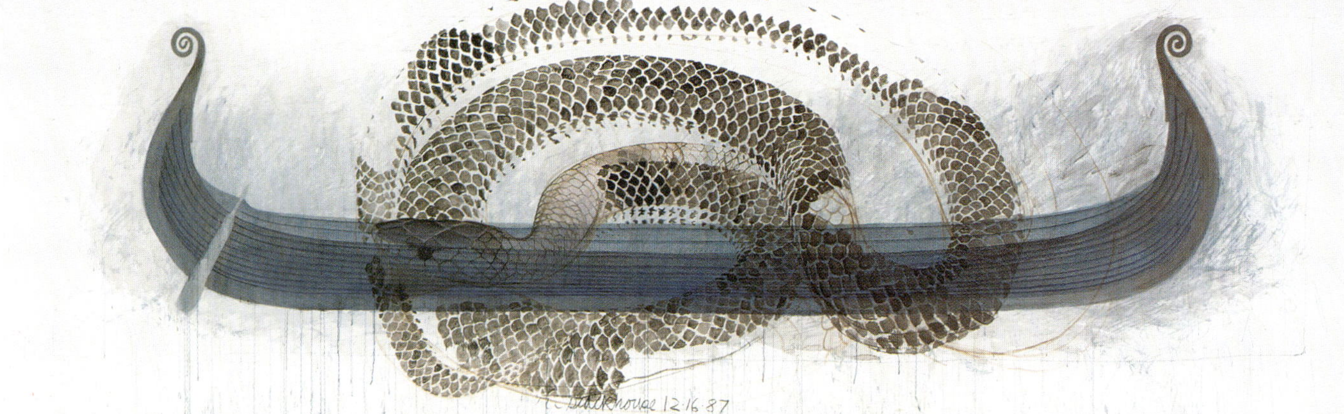

5.35

tion with the Corcoran and continued through 1989. Four projects completed in these years document his exploration of the possibilities associated with these forms, setting the stage for new projects and shifting directions in 1990 and 1991. These projects were *East River Bones* (1987), *St. Louie Bones* (1988), *Les Os du Quebec* (1989) and *Oliver Ranch Bones* (1989). He built *East River Bones* for the second Socrates Sculpture Park project, presented from May 17 to September 15, 1987, on a Long Island City site along the East River—a transformed garbage dump that had become the largest sculpture park in New York City—overlooking Manhattan's skyline. Continuing his earlier exploration of possibilities for elevated versions of the "bones" form, he reflected his understanding of New York's history as a harbor and port city, including his own childhood memories of ships in the docks along the Hudson River and the daily passing of the cruise ships and the working harbor boats. He offered a concise description of the work for the exhibition catalogue. "A reference to the river, its history and many uses. Double-ended, the structure not only looks to the past, but suggests journeys and new beginnings." [87] His concept of a canted wooden deck form is presented in *Model of East River Bones*, completed in 1987 (Figure 5.36). The completed piece, painted white, presented a striking image along the banks of the East River (Figure 5.37). And, continuing the photographic and painted explorations of the form that he had initiated in *Sailings*, built overlooking the Hudson River in Yonkers, he created a floating deck that seems to suggest flight as well as floating, movement into space as well as movement across water (Figure 5.38). This interpretation of his eye/boat shape and the related deck shape became influential upon the evolution of his imagery through the 1990s, serving, for example, as direct inspiration for the painting, *Flex Flyer*, completed almost a decade later, in 1995, as well as numerous other works completed in the past eleven years.

The following year, he traveled to St. Louis to complete *St. Louie Bones*, a permanent installation for Laumeier Sculpture Park (Figure 5.39). This wooden outdoor sculptural piece was commissioned for the St. Louis sculptural park following the presentation of the "Robert Stackhouse: Deep Swimmers" exhibition and temporary sculptural installation there from March 23 to May 11, 1986. Stackhouse became one of a distinguished series of artists to be commissioned for works at Laumeier, including Jackie Ferrara (1981), Mary Miss (1983-85), Alice Aycock (1985), Ursula von Rydinsvard (1988-89), Vito Acconci (1988), Richard Fleischner (1989), Dan Graham (1990), Beverly Pepper (1985-1990) and Jene Highstein (1990). Working on a rolling hillside located about eight miles from the Mississippi River, Stackhouse created a work, as described by Susan Waller, that reflected the river history of St. Louis and the region. "The boat-shaped deck of *St. Louie Bones* inevitably recalls those who lived and trav-

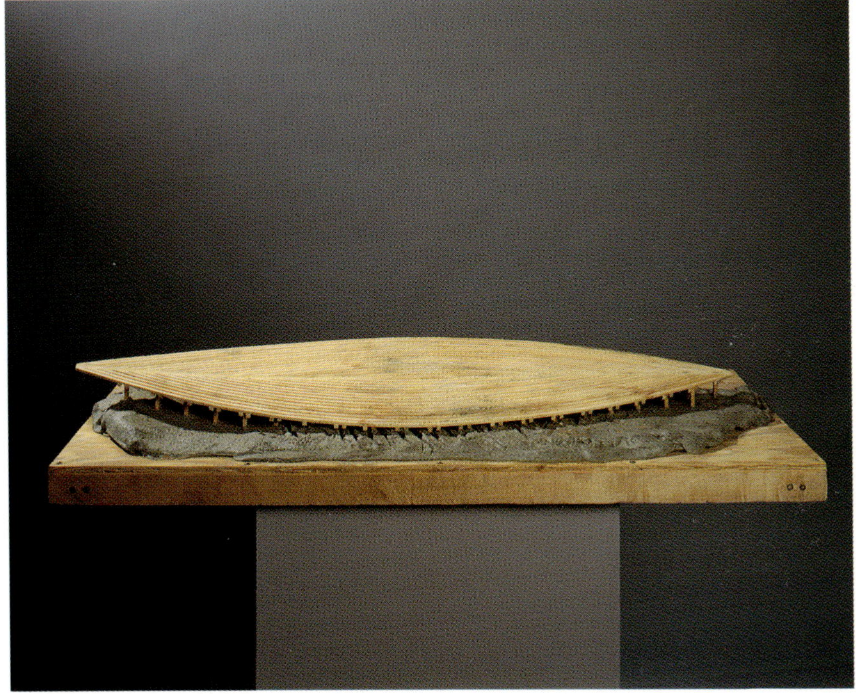

5.36

Model of East River Bones, 1987

East River Bones, installation on Long Island City, New York, 1987.

East River Bones, 1987

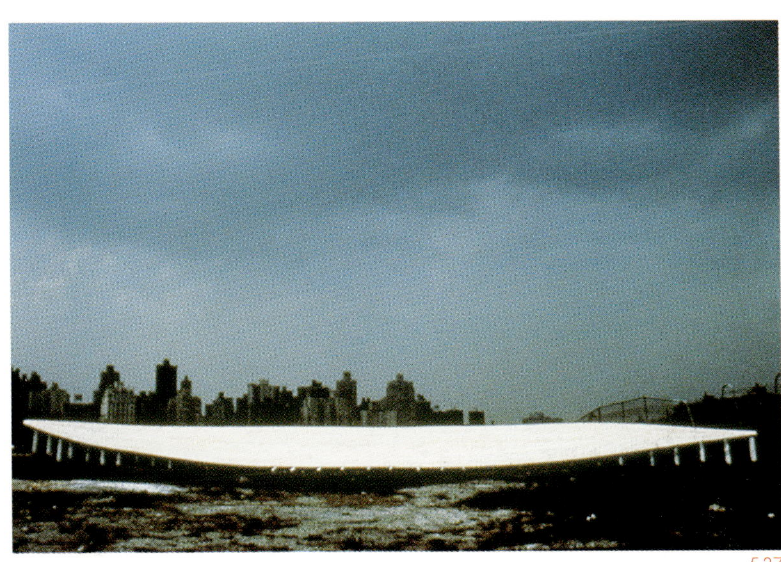

5.37

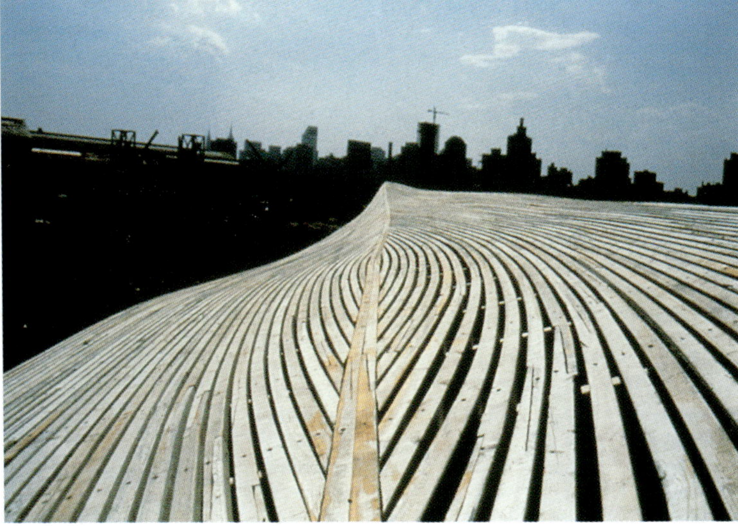

5.38

eled by the neighboring river: from the Missouri tribes— 'the people of the wooden canoes'—to the German and Italian immigrants who arrived on the steamboats." And, seemingly in anticipation of his approach to a different sloping hillside site in Quebec the following year, he created a piece that, from one direction, seemed to blend into the environment, as described by Waller.

> *The low structure is initially hidden from pedestrians who trace a path across the grounds. As they mount the curve of the hill, it appears suddenly at their feet. Seen from the slope above, the swelling plane of the white ribbed deck flattens against the ground; a slight bulge distinguishes "bow" from "stern" or "head" from "tail"....The curves of the ribs waver, there are deviations in the narrow gaps between the ribs and warps in the pattern of the lap joints across the surface. These subtle distortions seem to record strains from use in times past. The white-painted structure seems not new-made, but the bleached deposit of history.* [88]

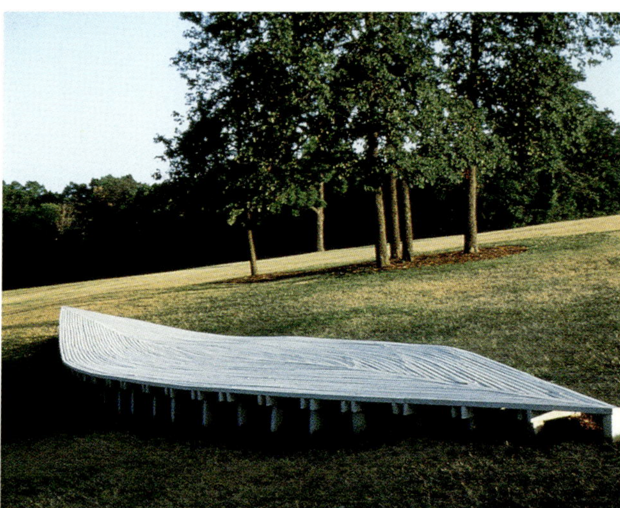

5.39

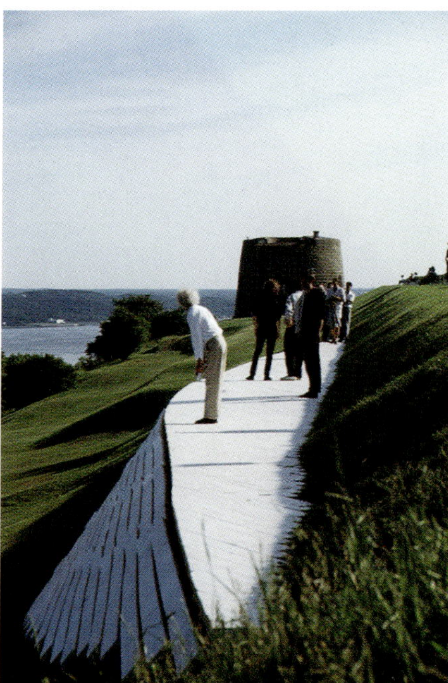

5.40

St. Louie Bones, Installation, 1987.

Les Os du Quebec, 1989

His explorations of creating deck structures that were both organic and architectural reached a new level of scale and ingenuity in Quebec in 1989, with the installation of *Les Os du Quebec* at Quebec City (Figure 5.40). Located on a hillside site, overlooking the St. Lawrence Seaway, the painted wood sculpture he created, measuring approximately 200' long, was designed to take maximum advantage of the site, as he has explained. "*The Bones of Quebec*, a play on the term, was built along the St. Lawrence Seaway, on the side of an underground reservoir located on the Plains of Abraham. If you walk along the pathway near it, the sculpture doesn't exist, it seems to be invisible. Then, if you move around, you can suddenly see it, this large piece. I have never completed a drawing of this work because it doesn't draw attention to itself. It is not there unless you look for it." Like *On the Beach Again* and *St. Louie Bones*, this work focuses on a form that seems to be there, and not there, visible, yet hidden, waiting—almost like one of Stackhouse's Florida alligators waiting for its prey—for the observant viewer to find it. Others, less perceptive, will miss the work, and the experience it offers.

Oliver Ranch Bones, a permanent installation completed at

the Oliver Ranch, in Geyersville, California, in 1989, took a very different approach to relating to its landscape setting, raising the deck well off the ground, and in the process, creating a strongly articulated architectural space (Figure 5.41). The owner, whose site served as both an art park and a sheep ranch, requested a raised deck structure capable of holding forty to fifty people during a wine tasting party and practical enough to offer some shelter and protection for his sheep. As the artist describes, he looked back to earlier works, including the Crosby Gardens project, for inspiration. "I looked back to organic forms as well as architectural ones. And, what I designed for Oliver Ranch was organic but became a more architectural object. There was more architecture, carrying over from the past, from earlier structural works. The owner requested a deck where he could have wine tastings, so I built it, then added a ladder so his guests could climb onto it." Carter Ratcliff has suggested connections to other specific earlier works. "*Oliver Ranch Bones* is a deck that grew legs. Its bulk raised off the ground, this piece has a resemblance to the house-like *Deep Swimmers*. With the help of the interior view given by a painting of *Oliver Ranch Bones*, one sees that this sculpture is not only a long-legged deck but an A-frame. Each of Stackhouse's works is a variant of others. Each launches the imagination on the stream of Stackhousian narrative at more than one point."

5.41

Oliver Ranch Bones, 1989, Geyersville, California.

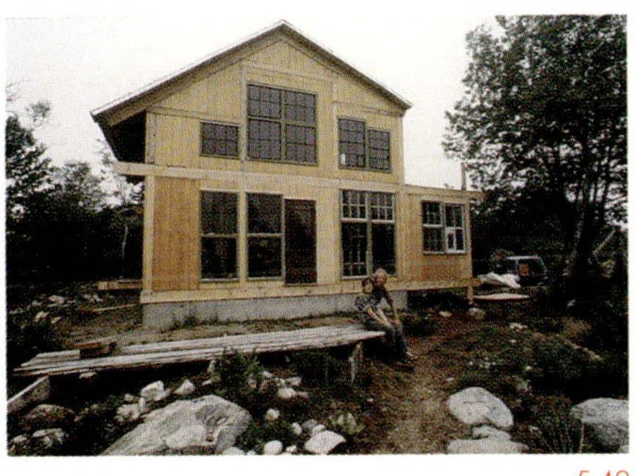

5.42

Maine house, construction, Photograph by Mary Beth Edelson

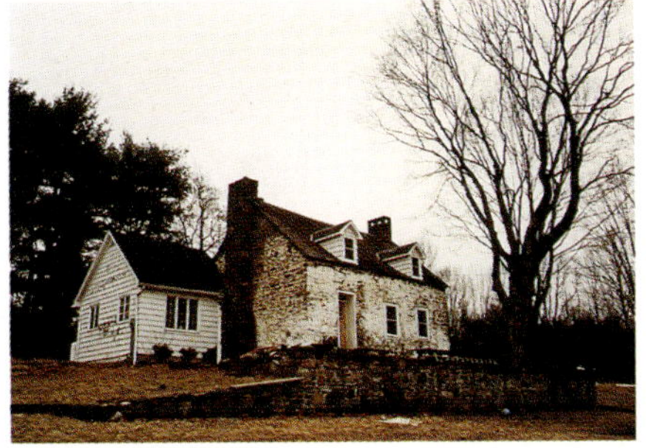

5.43

Stone House at Stone Ridge, New York, Winter, 1990, Photograph by Mary Beth Edelson

One year after his departure from his Corcoran faculty position, Stackhouse returned to Washington, and the Corcoran, to participate in that museum's Spectrum series of contemporary artists' exhibitions. This exhibition, "Mary Beth Edelson, Martin Puryear, Italo Scanga, Robert Stackhouse," was presented at the Corcoran from October 13-December 31, 1988. These artists shared a connection, as explained by Christopher French, to the city and its art world. "Edelson, Puryear, Scanga and Stackhouse are also related by circumstances and environment. They met in the early 1970s, as they began their careers in Washington at the Henri Gallery, and are perhaps the best known of a group of younger artists whose work displayed a deep ambivalence towards the Color Field school of painting that dominated the thinking of Washington's artistic community at that time." [89] In a published interview in *Washington Review* following the presentation of this exhibition, Robert explained part of his reasoning for leaving Washington. "Washington would have been safe for me, I could have developed a career here and enjoyed myself. One show every other year and a group show in the off year. In New York I multiply that by ten. I think that might be the difference between people staying here or going to New York. It can be trouble, you can get too good in a way and the pressures to meet deadlines are incredible." [90]

As the 1980s came to a close, Stackhouse and Edelson decided to sell the house they built together in Maine, a retreat that had offered great release and the opportunity to return to the world of nature each summer for Robert, in a sense reestablishing his familiar childhood routine of spending the school years (later, the art year) in the city of New York and the summers at Peach Lake (later, Maine). They had originally purchased property at Port Clyde, Maine, in 1978. By 1980, they had started the ongoing task of hand building their house (Figure 5.42). This wooden structure, using a modified form of traditional timber

From *Sources and Structures*, 1988-1989

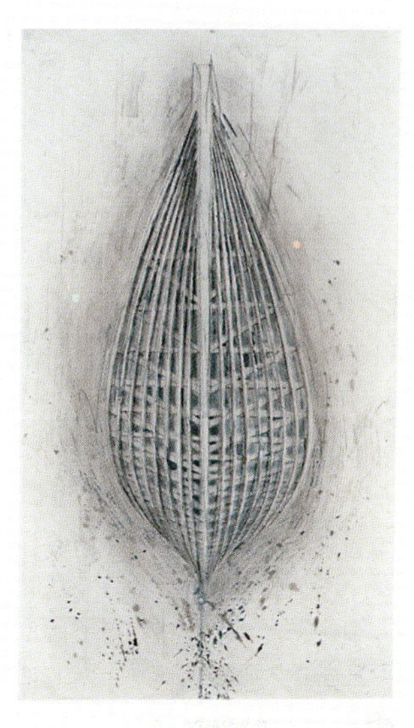

5.44

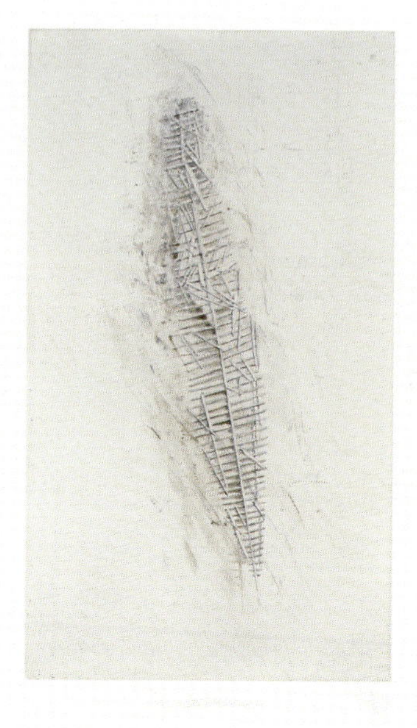

5.45

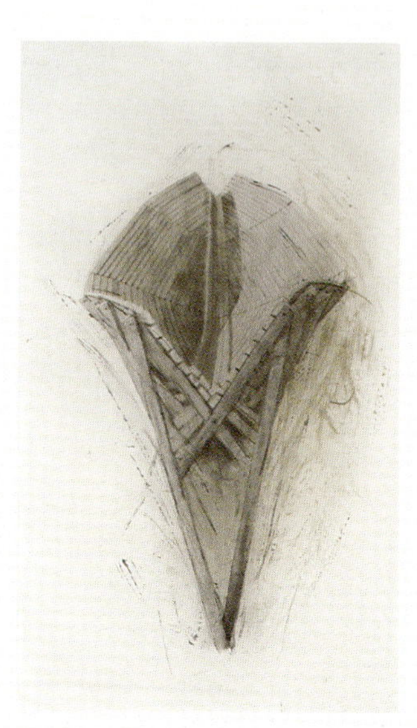

5.46

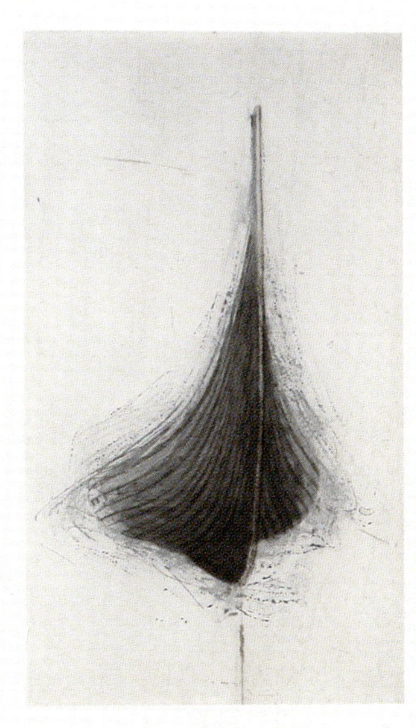

5.47

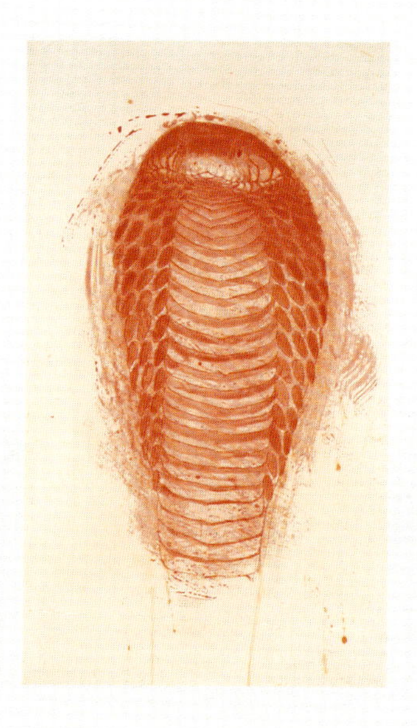

5.48

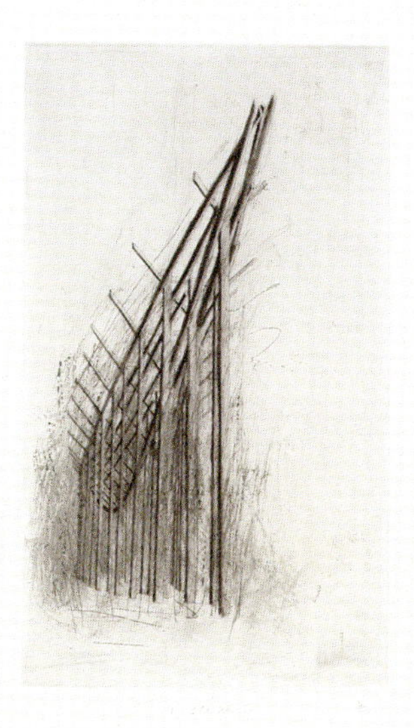

5.49

beam, open hall construction, was designed by Mary Beth and built by Robert, Mary Beth, and her children, Nick Edelson and Lynn Strauss. It served as a living sculptural environment, one that reflected Robert's attitudes toward the use of wood in sculpture. Over the years, he had looked forward to the annual retreat from SoHo and the New York art world at the beginning of the summers, repeating a pattern that he had learned from his grandfather, Hoyt Holland. Like his successful grandfather, who made his fortune in New York's business world and spent much of his summer on Peach Lake with his family, Robert had become successful enough in the art world, in his own way, to afford to do much the same thing, leaving the city during the summer with his family, then returning when the art year began in the fall. Not long after they sold the Maine house, they acquired a 250-year-old stone house on property located in Stone Ridge, New York (Figure 5.43).

Exploring new options for the creation of his art forms, and, once again, pausing to take stock of his iconography and professional development as the decade came to an end, in 1988 and 1989 Stackhouse created a set of significant etchings for Pace Prints in New York, titled *Sources and Structures*. As the title implied, these prints traced the evolution of many of his most important recent and older images, serving, as had his large watercolors of 1982, including *From the Deep*, as a lexicon of his continuing symbols and forms. Using spit bite etching, he created prints depicting the prow of the Gokstad ship, *Eau Claire Sailings*, a hooded cobra's head, a ship ruin similar to the boat deck forms he had used in his projects of this era and other related forms, each depicted in a manner showing the similarities in these forms (Figures 5.44, 5.45, 5.46, 5.47, 5.48 and 5.49). And, just as as he had done in 1982, when he summarized the forms he had used to that point, he also set the foundations for the possible use and expansion of these forms in new works during the 1990s. The creation of these familiar images as an extended suite of prints, making them available to broader collecting audiences than his larger and more expensive paintings and sculptural forms, was more than an astute marketing strategy. It also demonstrated how he had learned to use the power of the print medium to add a new level of regenerative life to his art forms.

From this process emerged a new form, one based upon this evolutionary activity, featured in a series of exhibitions in 1989 and 1990. In 1989, he created *Blue Diviner*, a painted structural form that was created and reinstalled several times in this period, at the Dolan/Maxwell Gallery in New York, out of doors as a sculptural installation in Philadephia and inside in Washington, at the Kornblatt Gallery (Figure 5.50). As indicated earlier, he created this image of a red serpent (one evolved from the Ruby images created in Brazil) and its related structural form because of his increasing love of the symbolically charged color blue, seeking a way to create a blue field that could literally become an environment that

Blue Diviner, 1989

Two Diviners, 1989

Untitled, 1990

5.50

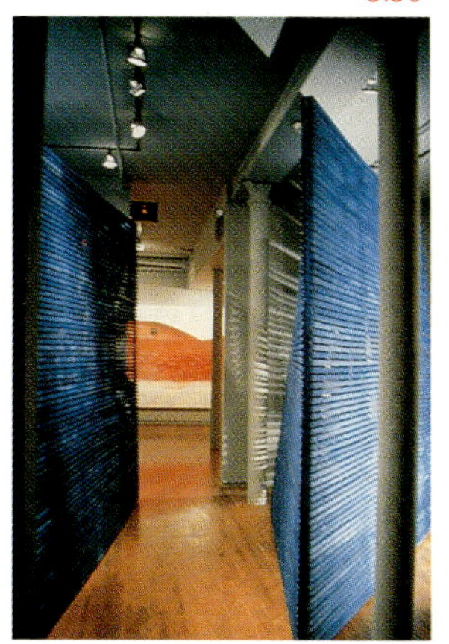

5.51

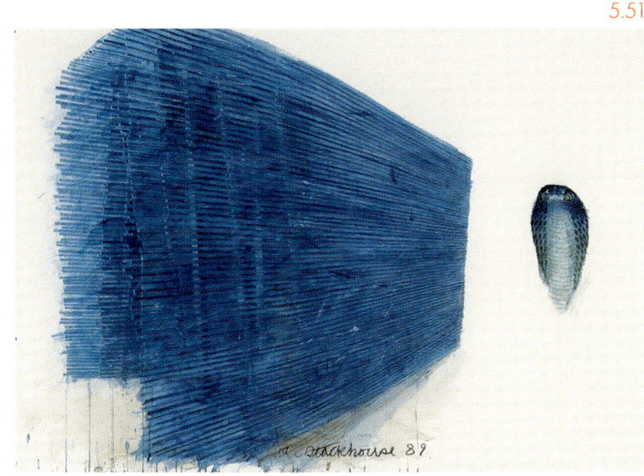

5.52

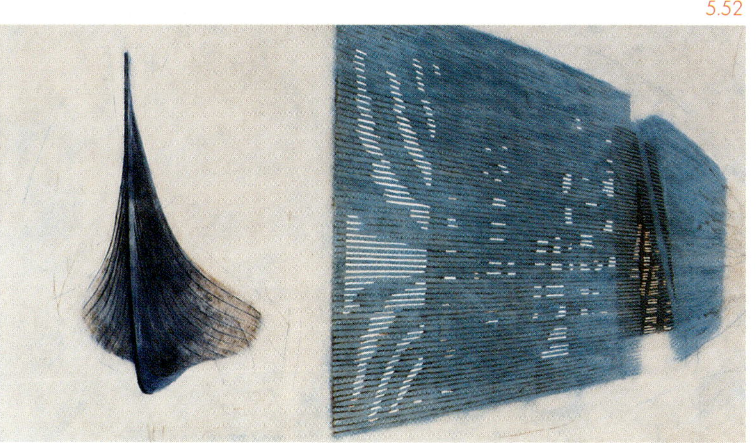

would surround a viewer. Using wood lath and the construction principles he had developed for the A-frame form in the 1970s, he developed a new type of structural element, one suggesting his growing interest in architectural forms. In 1989, he documented his vision of this form in *Two Diviners*, a watercolor image that juxtaposed the structural form with a floating raised cobra head (Figure 5.51). The following year, he created another spit-bite etching using the prow of the Gokstad burial ship—as he had in the "Sources and Structures" print series—and juxtaposed that image with the open, light filled form of the *Blue Diviner* structure, suggesting the nautical relationship of the two forms (Figure 5.52). In 1990, he constructed a temporary wooden form of *Blue Diviners* at the Honolulu Academy of Arts.

The wooden structural form leading to a serpent's head, a continuing evolution of the *Ruby* construction created in Brazil in 1987, and a logical evolution of the serpentine form of the A-frames he had created during the 1970s, took a direction he titled *Encounterings*, when he presented these works in galleries and museums in 1990. *Encounterings* (Figure 5.53), based upon a broadened variation of the A-frame structure leading to the lurking head of a serpent, positioned at eye level, directly facing the viewer/participant, was created in indoor installations at the Virginia Museum of Fine Arts in Richmond, at the Dolan/Maxwell Gallery in New York and at the Kornblatt Gallery in Washington (Figure 5.54). This form quickly evolved into another variant that year, which he titled *Delaware Passage*, when he constructed it for an extensive exhibition of his works, "Common Places, Painting and Sculpture by Robert Stackhouse," presented at the Delaware Museum of Art in Wilmington (Figure 5.55). In another variation of his painted wooden architectural form, Stackhouse juxtaposed the serpent and the passageway, leading the viewer once again, it seemed, on the inevitable journey to the snake and the process of death and regeneration. Carter Ratcliff, in his essay for this exhibition's catalogue, suggested that the course of the artist's ceaseless explorations had a specific intended effect for art audiences.

> *Though he has never said so, I believe that he intends these spectacular struggles to be exemplary. He wants us to follow him to the place they occur, and to understand that this place is unimaginable,*

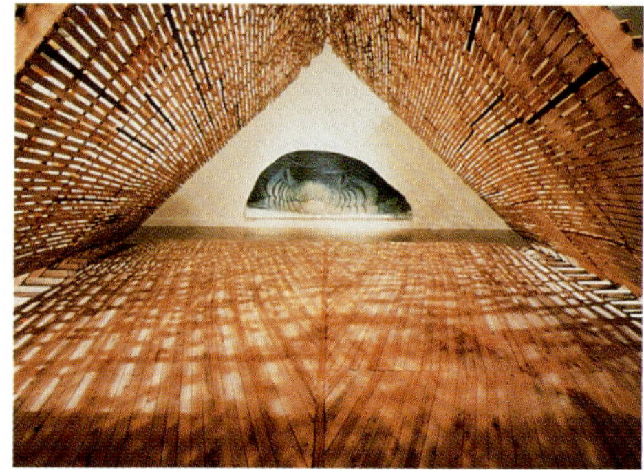

5.53

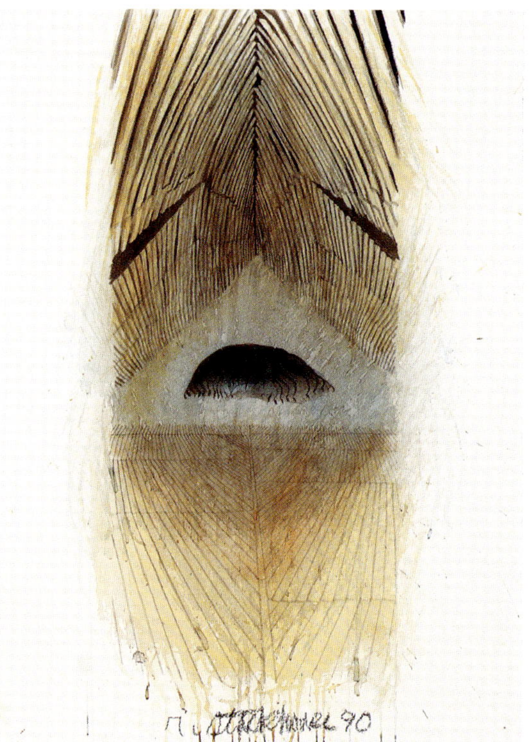

5.54

Encounterings, Installation, 1990.

Inside *Encounterings*, 1990

for it is the site of the imagination itself. Stackhouse encourages us to see how we arrived at this site, this unmappable place. His art prompts us to imagine ourselves imagining our way to the reconciliation of disparities, and to see how this process gives meaning to what we have reconciled. He wants us to see how we can see, and he offers himself as the model of a seer. [91]

While these constructions were designed and created in these museum and gallery environments, he continued to explore the possibilities of the deck form in *Divers*, a work he created in 1991 at the Marine Science Building at the University of Hawaii. He built it from extruded brass tubing, experimenting with materials after it was learned that he would not be able to create it as originally envisioned, as a thirty foot cast bronze sculpture. "With budget cuts and drastic changes in the economy, this was my solution for the piece. I used extruded brass square tubing that I could bolt together. My assistant and I were able to build this with no special equipment. It weighed about two tons. We built it, took it apart, and packed and shipped it in its original crates to Hawaii. Then we put it back together, placed it on a cart and two dollies, rolled it to the site, then dropped it in place with a car jack. As a result, I discovered a way to build a permanent bronze sculpture at a low cost." This work was placed in a subtle fashion, like other examples of his outdoor installations in the 1980s, so that it was visible from only certain angles, including from the adjoining office windows (Figure 5.56).

As this period came to a close in 1991, he was given the opportunity to return to Tampa and the USF campus, where he completed the work *Soundless* in their new Contemporary Art Museum. Utilizing the contemporary shape of the new structure, a trapezoidal form that defined the gallery, he created a painted structural form that continued his ongoing architectural interests in a work that carried the implications of *Encounterings* and *Delaware Passage* into a new direction (Figure 5.57). With a painted white structure, an ethereal and seemingly weightless form, he projected and painted a white related image on the wall of the gallery. This image, taken from the last known photograph of the Titanic sailing at sea, was presented in a ghost-like fashion, like a white shadow, there, and not there. Like his own shadow, used throughout his earlier imagery, the shadow of the Titanic suggested transitions in his work, elements emerging from the unconscious that would direct the next shift in his own aesthetic course. He later real-

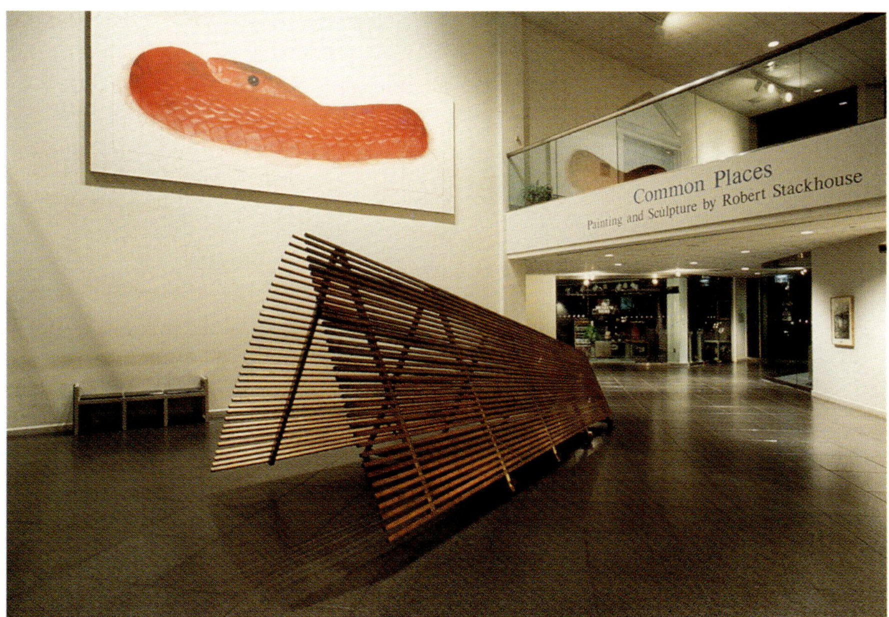

5.55

Delaware Passage,
Installation at Delaware Art Museum, 1991

Divers, installation at the University of Hawaii, 1991.

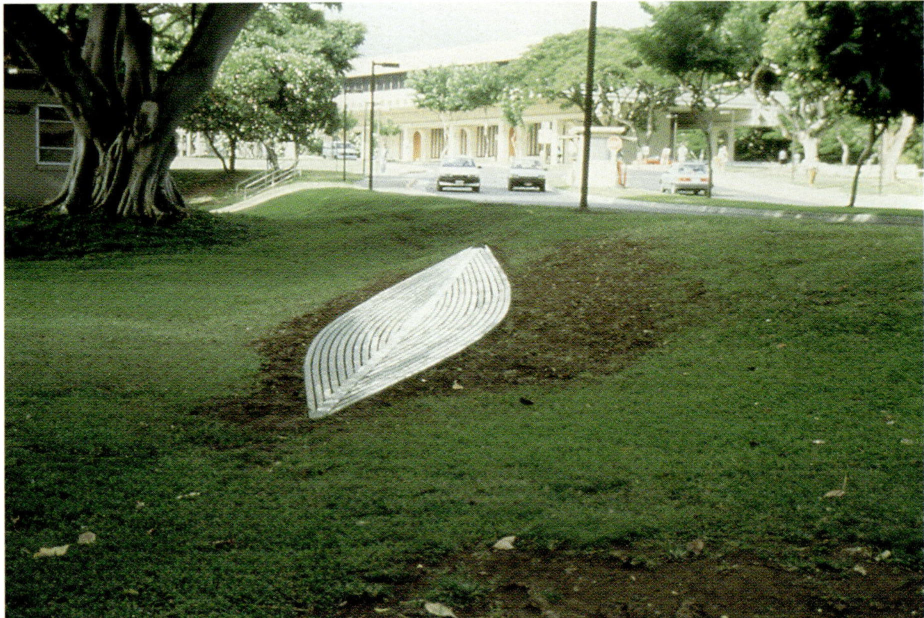

5.56

ized that he was moving increasingly at this time toward the creation of architectural places, what he has described as "a place rather than an object," anticipating, in many respects, the structural forms he would create during the late 1990s, including works such as *K.C. Way*, built in Kansas City in 1996. In the 1990s, architecture and a sense of place became increasingly important to Stackhouse, as he recently explained. "I am most interested in my sculptures that evoke a place, a sense of a place. Barnett Newman said that a painting is a place. That is what I began to seek in these works." Then, following the direction this work offered, he completed a related print, *Soundless* (Figure 5.58), exploring possibilities in forms, color and light, which was issued in 1992 by Tandem Press.

As this period in his career ended, he welcomed the opportunity to return to Florida, where he had spent such an important part of his life. Throughout the 1980s, he had continued to expand and build upon his relationship to the art department at USF that Harrison Covington had established, the department that, like the serpent, was growing and regenerating, taking on a new level of meaning and importance for Stackhouse. In this time back in Florida, he also was able to spend time with his mother at Gulfport. Together, they had time to continue to mourn the loss of Kurt, her son and his older brother, who had died in 1990, the victim of a heart attack, like his father. Stackhouse lost his father and his only brother in a six year period, leaving only himself and his mother in his immediate family. Fortunately, he still had his cousins and the other members of his extended family who offered an ongoing sense of structure. He entered the next phase of his career with a sense of loss, and a sense of a new direction developing. That direction would center on painting, and on the introduction of a new series of nautical themes in his work, themes suggested by *Soundless*, created at his alma mater, in Tampa. His course, it seemed, was also being steered increasingly away from New York.

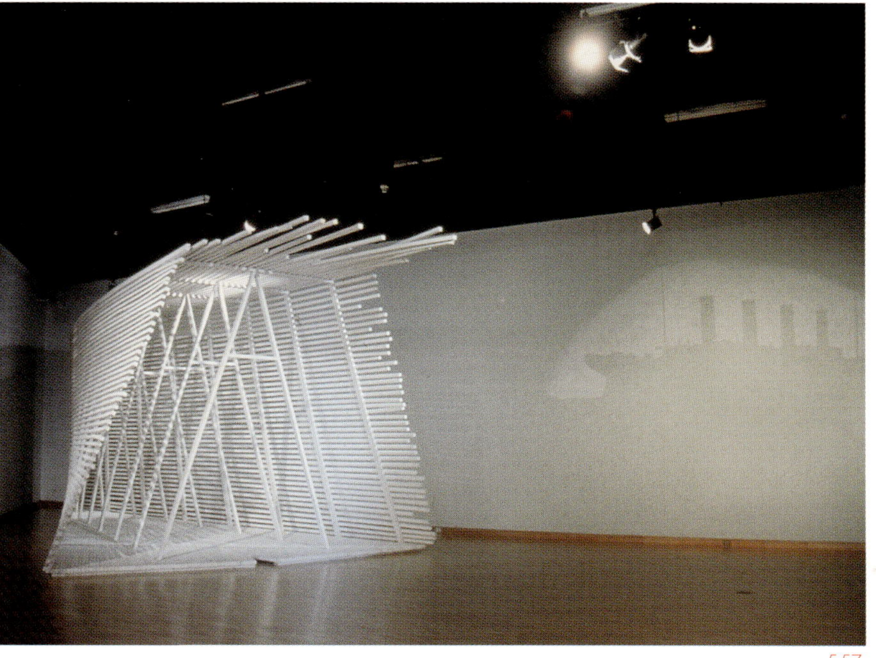

5.57

Soundless, installation at the Contemporary Art Museum, University of South Florida, 1991.

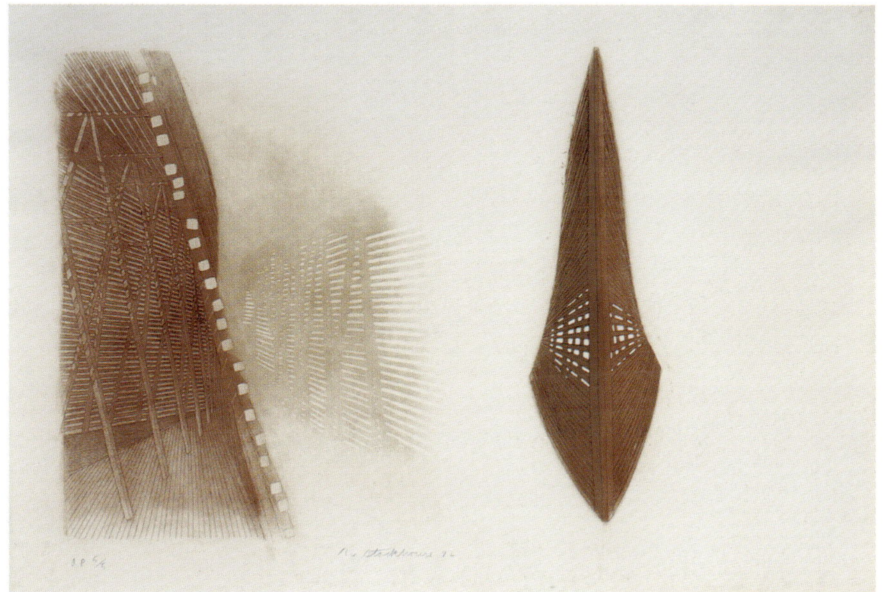

5.58

Soundless, 1992.

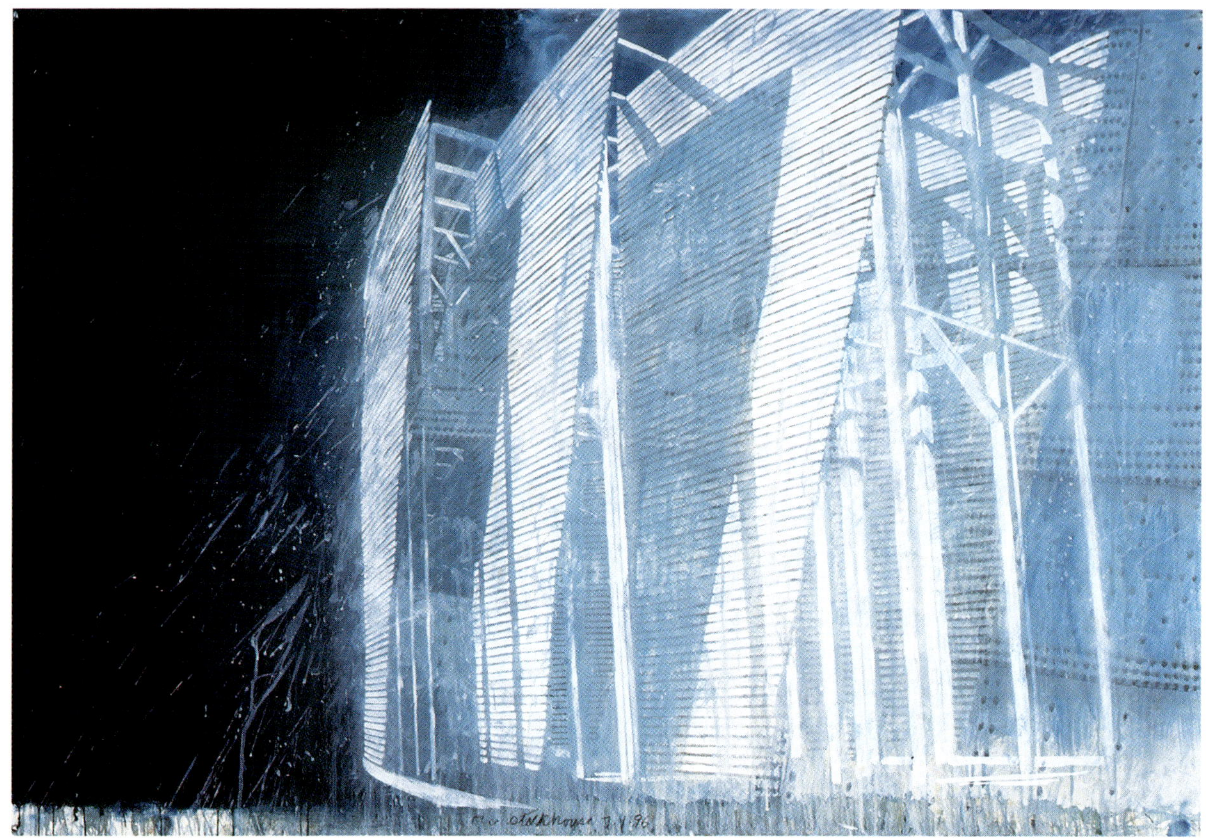

Dick's "K.C. Way", 1996

CHAPTER SIX

Kansas City and New York

Robert Stackhouse returned to New York following the opening of his exhibition at the University of South Florida, still intrigued by the strength of the public response to this show as he returned to work in his studio. As he had done in the past, the artist began to develop new ideas for projects by using his working images to plot his course and his alternative paths, incorporating these into the drawings as documentation of his unfolding aesthetic explorations. Sometimes, new ideas emerged from the images he created in the margins—the zone Friedel Dzubas had encouraged Stackhouse to use during his tenure at USF. These spontaneous images often generated drawings and watercolors that served as the foundations for his next experimentations with form and subject. Looking back to the University of South Florida installation, the first public exhibition of his Titanic imagery, he considered new possibilities for the use of the Titanic, including the shadow ship he painted directly onto the gallery wall—not unlike his painting of a shadow on the wall of the Prudential installation—and of the white *Soundless* structure he had built in the gallery. These forms and images carried great resonance for him because, reacting to critics and writers who consistently classified his work as "archaeological," he had been searching for new subjects, more modern subjects that were less focused on the wooden ships and archaeological ruins he had explored for years. With the Titanic, he seemed to have discovered that new subject.

In a published review of the *Soundless* exhibition in the *St. Petersburg Times*, Mary Ann Marger described two large watercolors from the show. One, *Stella*, a coiled snake image measuring ten by ten feet in size, served as an increasingly potent form for Stackhouse, as suggested by Marger. "Consider her name, which means star. Her coiled configuration relates to a spiral nebula, such as you might find in deep space, which refers back to *Soundless*." Another major work in that installation, *Drawing For Soundless*, suggested important new possibilities for Stackhouse as he worked in his SoHo studio in 1992. A distinctive horizontal watercolor that measured 40 inches by 25 feet, it was described in Marger's article. "The other work, *Drawing for Soundless*, is a long black panel with a pale white skeleton at one end. The reference is to the Titanic. It evokes the idea of a deep ocean, which again refers back to the show's title." [92] In this work, a skeleton, floating in a suspended state, appeared to be contained, coffin-like, by a large dark form, a ship form. The ship was the Titanic, at rest on the ocean's floor, silent like a steel coffin, a sarcophagus. He had long been fascinated by the wooden remains of ritual burial ships, especially the Egyptian Cheops ship and the Viking Gokstad ship. Now, as the 1990s unfolded, he became increasingly interested in the Titanic, which he came to regard as a modern burial ship, one resting on the ocean's floor, silent, in the "soundless" depths, a cold steel monument to the many passengers who were killed when the "unsinkable" Titanic was stopped, tragically, by a lurking force of the natural world, an iceberg. Man's desire for the extremes of what a luxury liner could offer in an age of elegance and great wealth, and the accompanying human arrogance associated with the claims surrounding this "unsinkable" ship, seemed to defy the orders of the natural world. Using the form of an iceberg—a form not unlike one of the alligators or serpents that Stackhouse knew well, predators capable of waiting patiently in water for prey—nature seemed to have answered man's challenge, sending the ship to the bottom of the sea on its maiden voyage.

Stackhouse's interest in the Titanic evolved during a time when undersea exploration teams revealed major new discoveries about the Titanic and other lost luxury liners from earlier in the twentieth century. After decades of speculation about the location of the lost Titanic, it was first discovered, in September of 1985, by Dr. Robert Ballard and a crew from the Woods Hole Oceanographic Institute in Massachusetts. On July 14, 1986, using a three-man submersible vessel, the Alvin, Ballard and his crew were able to maneuver around the ship. Advances in technology, including the creation of this submersible and recently developed underwater cameras and recording devices, made it possible for them to navigate around the Titanic, once a proud symbol of man's technological prowess. News of the original discovery had spread rapidly around the world, and from this second expedition images of the ship, broken and rusting, became available and were widely reproduced. A third expedition in 1987, and a fourth in 1991 maintained interest not only in the Titanic but also in the archaeological process of discovery that was taking place. In June of 1991, as Stackhouse prepared for his USF exhibition, Soviet and Canadian film crews, using two submersibles, the Mir 1 and the Mir 2, spent several weeks recording footage of the Titanic for an IMAX documentary, one released to the public in 1992.[93] For Stackhouse, it seemed that the historic and the mythic had merged with advanced science and technology, to present breaking new evidence about one of the most mysterious subjects of the twentieth century. Once again, it seemed, a new subject—and a new archetype—was emerging, literally and figuratively, from the shadows, from the deep.

Inside his SoHo studio, Stackhouse studied these developments, reading and following the course of events related to the Titanic and other underwater explorations, while he also experimented with new subjects, plotting the direction of his work in preparation for future exhibitions. Outside his SoHo studio, he witnessed the dramatic changes that had taken place in the city of New York since 1982. Because of the crash of the economic markets, and the ensuing crash of the art and auction markets, the art world environment was radically different from what it had been in 1982. America's explosive economic growth during the 1980s came to a staggering halt, as if the economic ship of state had hit an iceberg. By the early 1990s, New York had one of the most depressed economic environments in the country. Reflecting this grim reality, some art galleries began to close while others struggled to survive by cutting back staff, exhibitions, publications and support of all but the most bankable artists. As Robert Hughes has suggested, the years from the early 1980s to the early 1990s constituted one of the most dramatic cycles of change in the history of the nation's art world.

> *The 1980s utterly transformed the American art world; it became the beneficiary—and ultimately, the victim—of speculative mania. Ronald Reagan...had enormous indirect effects on the art world...[because] in the course of tripling America's national deficit to a trillion dollars and filling the country with oceans of borrowed money, his financial policies helped create the art-market boom of the 1980s. This bubble burst in 1990, never to reinflate, but it had blinding iridescence while it lasted....Indeed, it was the art market itself—rather than any individual work of art—that became the chief cultural artifact of the 1980s.*[94]

During this same cycle of growth, the nation's museums, art galleries, community art centers, public sculpture gardens and public art projects boomed at an equally remarkable rate. At the same time, imposing new corporate office buildings appeared across the country, often filled with new and expanding corporate art collections and featuring outdoor sculptural installations. Regions of the country that had been no more than minor players in the world of art and culture were transformed into major powers during these years, bringing art world realignments as emerging cities sought cultural status equal to their new economic and civic stature. New museums or major additions to museums appeared across the country in these years, including the Dallas Museum of Art, the High Museum of Art, the Museum of Contemporary Art in Los Angeles, the Museum of Modern Art, the Metropolitan Museum of Art, the Seattle Art Museum and the Getty Museum in Los Angeles. More dramatic, in many respects, was the activity in medium and smaller sized cities in the South and the West, where museums, symphony halls and cultural facilities arose, often where none had existed before, reflecting the rapid ascension of these cities, and their regions, to more serious levels of cultural status[95] For many artists, including Robert Stackhouse, these changes would have profound implications, beginning in the 1980s with numerous regional projects and commissions. During the 1990s, as New York became increasingly inhospitable, and an ever more expensive working and living environment for artists, many decided to leave New York to relocate to these emerging regional art centers. Robert Stackhouse became one of them in 1997, when he moved from New York to Kansas City, where he had established an increasing presence after 1992.

Working in his SoHo studio in 1992 and 1993, Stackhouse discovered, often to his own surprise, that his primary creative impulse was toward painting, not sculpture. New subjects and images, many building upon his earlier iconography, began to emerge, increasingly focused upon early luxury liners, especially the Titanic. Reluctant at first to trust these new images, he followed his instincts and, encouraged by key advisors, friends and patrons, he painted watercolors of these ships, working on a scale similar to that advanced by the Abstract Expressionists who had influenced his development as a painter. In 1965, when he arrived in the Washington area, advanced artists commonly believed that painting had lost its primacy, turning instead to sculpture and multi-media art forms. Though Stackhouse had become recognized as an important sculptor during the 1970s and 1980s, he consistently indicated in interviews and catalogue essays in that period that he considered himself, above all, to be a painter. Often he referred to Barnett Newman's desire to create a "place" in his painting. Carter Ratcliff, who wrote the essay for Stackhouse's Delaware Art Museum exhibition catalogue in 1991, also wrote about Barnett Newman for *Art in America* in September of that same year, referring, as did Stackhouse, to Newman's desire that his paintings "give a man a sense of place: that he knows he's there, so he's aware of himself. In that sense he relates to me when I made the painting because in that sense I was there....I hope that my painting has the impact of giving someone, as it did me, the feeling of his own totality, of his own separateness, of his own individuality, and at the same time of his connection to others, who are also separate." [96]

Returning to the imagery of his Soundless installation in the months after the exhibition closed in Florida, he created a range of works that reflected his continuing interest in the possibilities of this subject. One of these, *Soundless Installation*, preserved, as he had done earlier with his demolished A-frame structures, his response to the work and its energy (Figure 6.1). In 1992, he also produced *Encountering*, a ten color spit bite etching that explored the form featured in his Virginia Museum exhibition, as well as *Delaware Art Museum Sculpture*, a watercolor based upon the A-frame derived structure he had constructed for the Delaware Art Museum (Figure 6.2). New variations on his spiral serpent image also appeared this year, as evident in *Spiral Stella*, a watercolor mounted on four panels in a manner suggesting the dynamism of a pin-

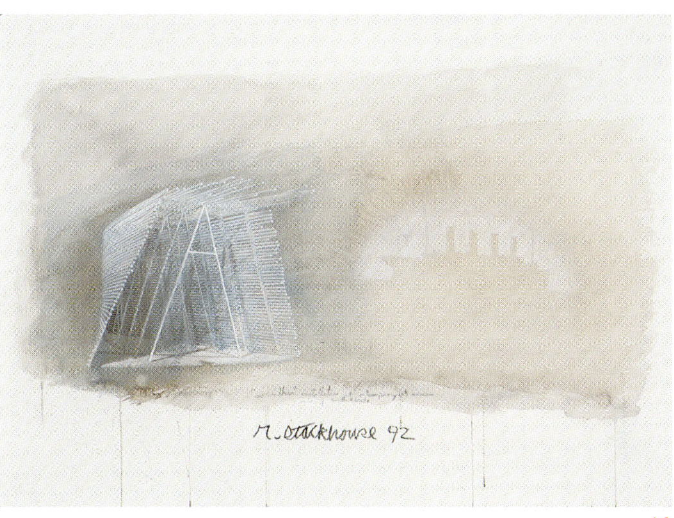

6.1

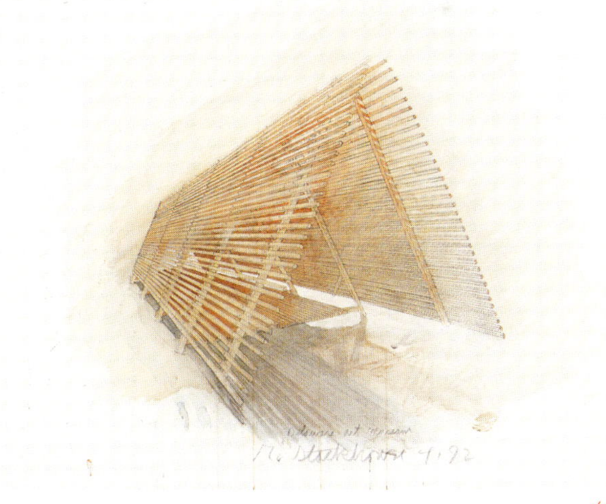

6.2

Soundless Installation 1992

Delaware Art Museum Sculpture, 1992

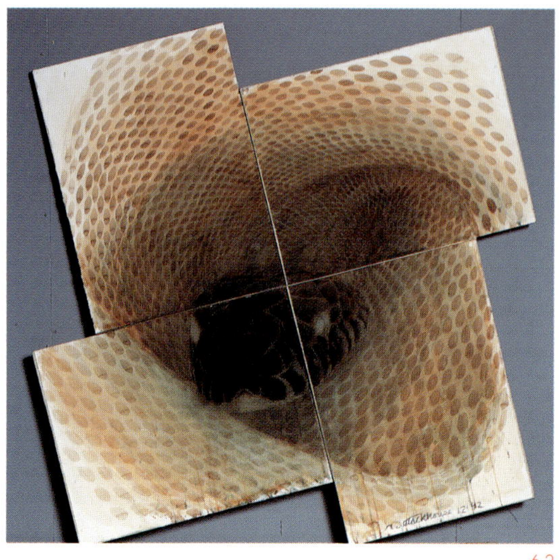

6.3

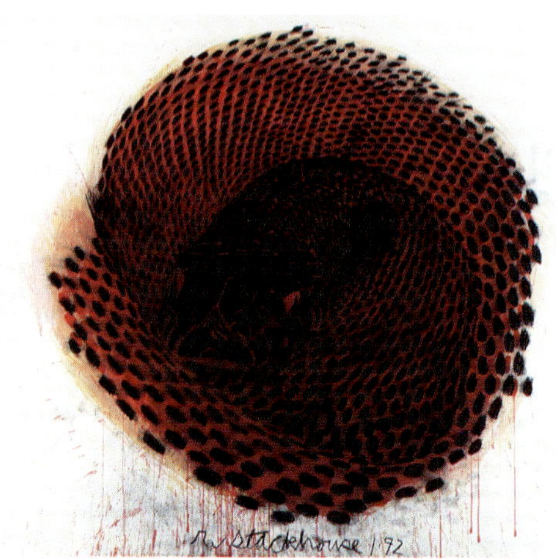

6.4

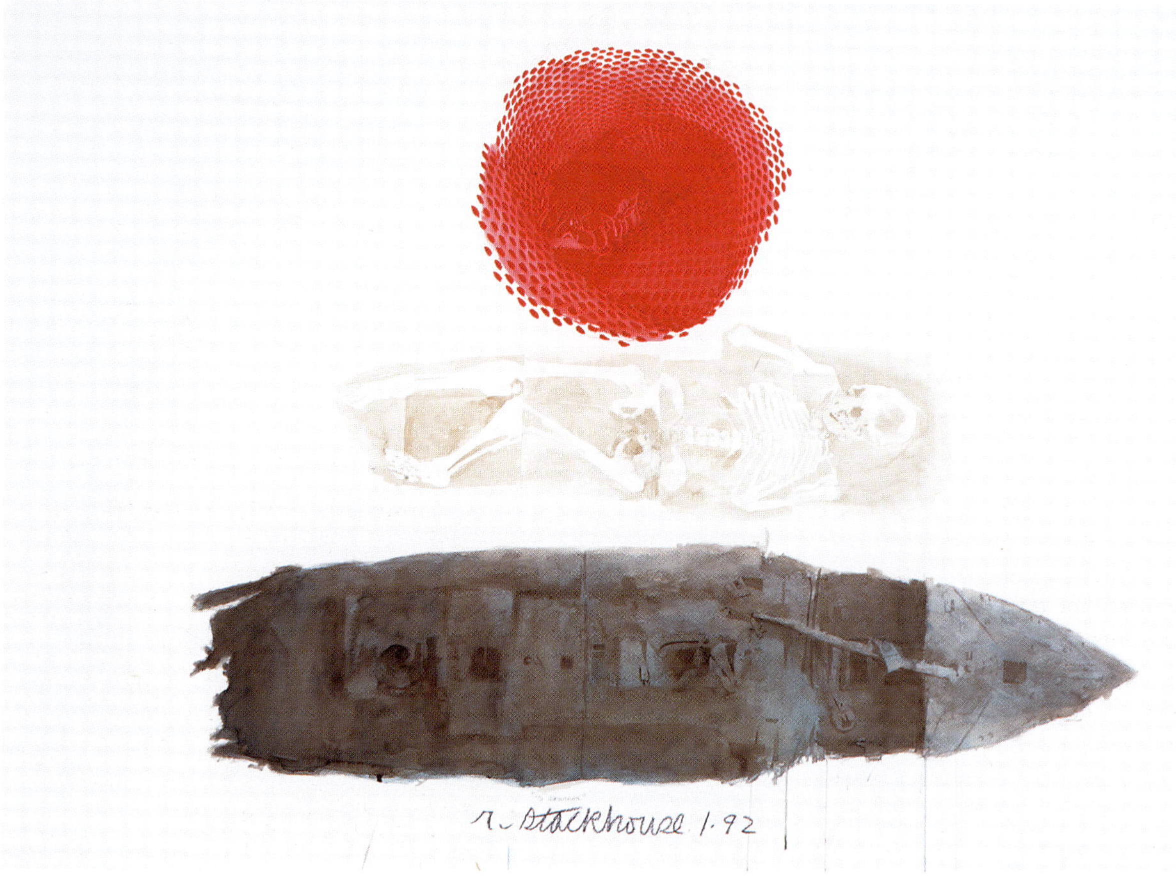

6.5

Spiral Stella, 1992

Hot Stella, 1992

Three Sources, 1992

wheel (Figure 6.3). Another, and equally suggestive variation on this approach to the serpent image, appeared in the work titled *Hot Stella*, in which the intense eyes of a serpent glare out at the viewer, camouflaged in the tightly woven red and black spiral pattern of the composition (Figure 6.4).

In *Three Sources*, a significant watercolor completed in January of 1992 (Figure 6.5), Stackhouse incorporated images from the USF exhibition and layered three separate images horizontally, including one of his red *Spiral Stella* forms, a ghostly skeletal figure and a view looking down at the Titanic resting on the ocean's floor. These forms served as major components in the works he created over the next year for his exhibition at the Morgan Gallery in Kansas City. A variation of this skeletal figure—*Aster*, which he derived from a published *National Geographic* photograph documenting an unearthed 17-year-old woman's skeleton in Alaska—floating mysteriously and ominously in a dark, seemingly limitless void was presented in *Descend #3* (Figure 6.6). Located in a similar dark, inky environment, a profile of a coiled serpent, the familiar Ruby from his Brazil series of 1987, is shown in a coiled position, its head turned slightly toward the viewer, and its one dark eye mirroring the background color and atmosphere (Figure 6.7). A ship's deck in a dark void-like space, shown glowing red with crisply rendered white points of light—rivet holes across its surface—may suggest a detail from the Titanic or another sunken vessel, yet it clearly carries forward the familiar deck form seen in numerous paintings and sculptural works, beginning with *Sailings* (Figure 6.8).

Reconsidering the possibilities he had established in his enormous 1991 *Drawing for Soundless*, Stackhouse decided to divide this work into its two component elements. The skeletal form, originally painted as a horizontal image, as reflected in the fluid lines of his watercolors, was turned vertically, becoming the work named *Aster's Leap* (Figure 6.9). Then he reworked the remaining image of the Titanic to create one of his most important works of the 1990s, which he titled *Transtitanic*, a composition which resulted from a notable fusion of Stackhouse's skills as a painter and a sculptor (Figure 6.9). Looking through a heavy riveted copper frame, suggestive of a weathered or sunken ship's hull, or perhaps the windows of the submersible that discovered the Titanic, the viewer is presented with an image of the forward section of the Titanic at rest on the ocean's floor. While the divisions of the frame might suggest a triptych format, alluding to altarpieces and traditional religious imagery, the consistent iconography of Stackhouse's career, especially evident in this perspective of the clearly identifiable Titanic, links it to earlier burial ship remains, extending from the Cheops ship to traditional Viking burial vessels. As in *Soundless*, there is a sense of distance, of removal, suggestive perhaps of a dream-like or surreal state. His perspective is not that of the powerful and "unsinkable" Titanic in its glory, rather it is a view of a ghostly sarcophagus, a burial vault, permanently anchored to the ocean's floor. The work also suggests something unearthly, perhaps even a vessel or wreckage in outer space.

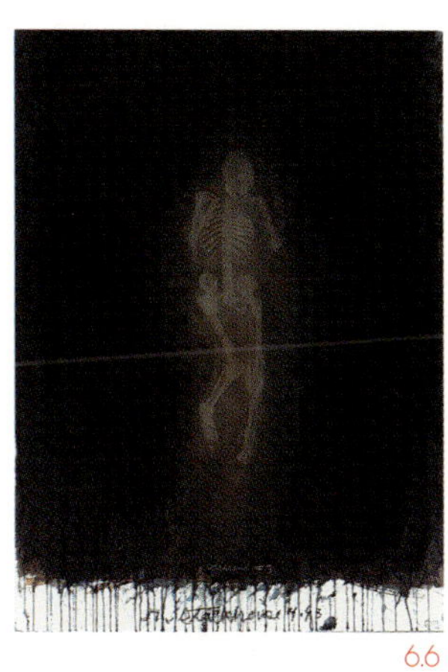

6.6

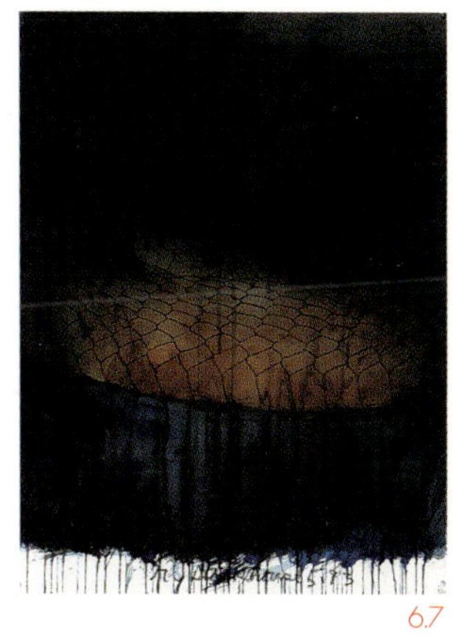

6.7

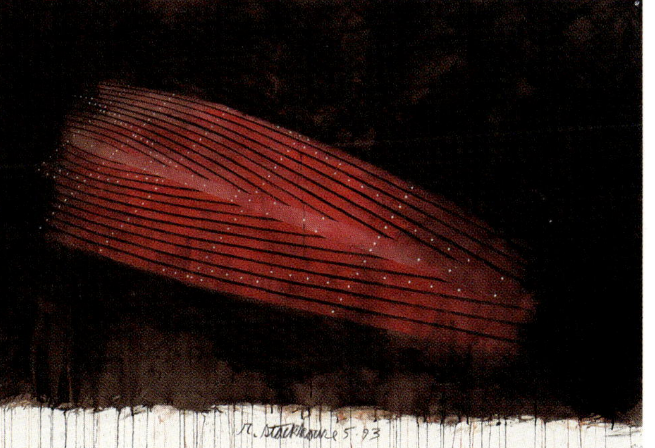

6.8

Descend #3, 1993

Night Ruby, 1993

Fire Deck, 1993

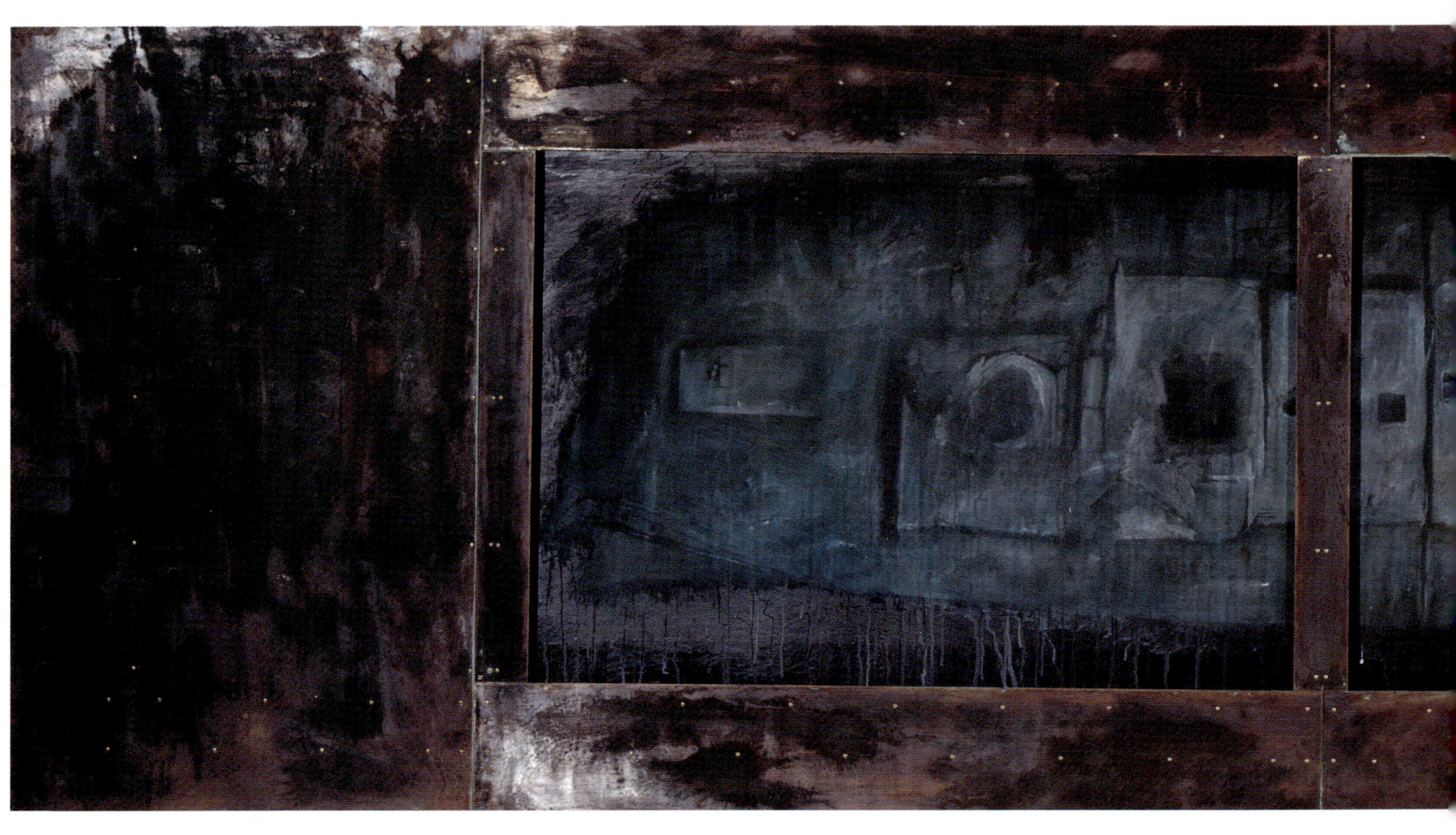

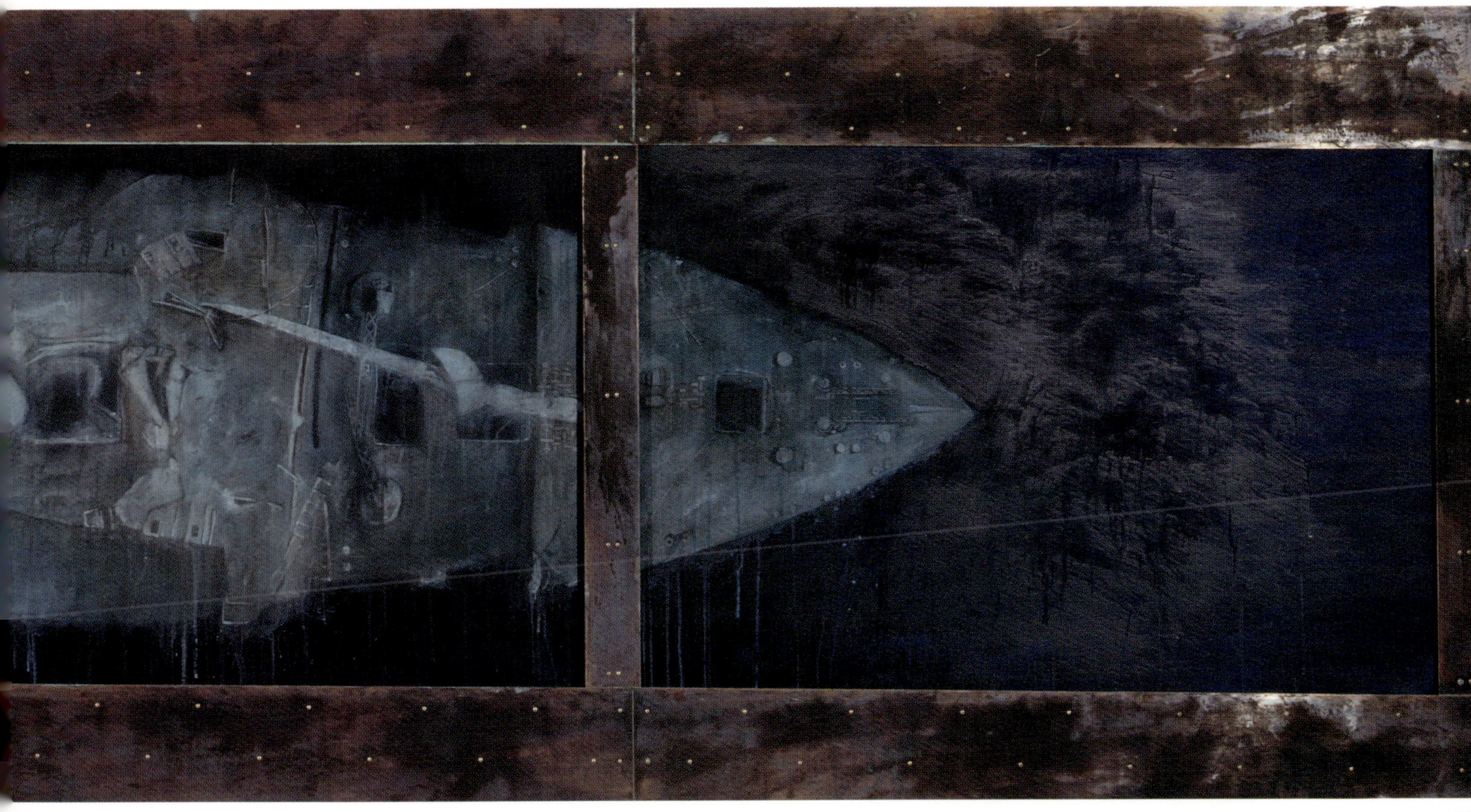

6.10

Transtitanic, 1991-1993

Aster's Leap

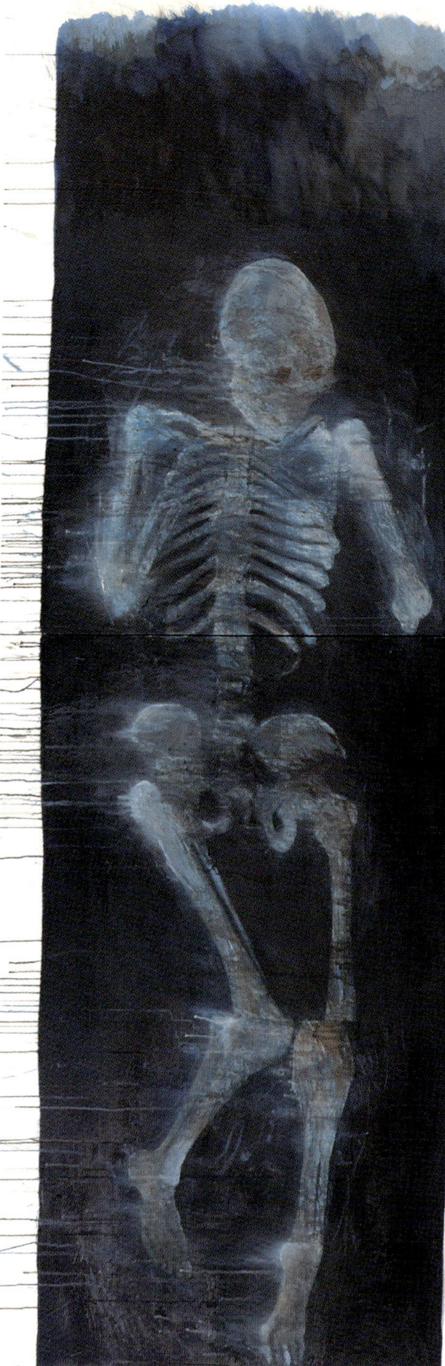

6.9

The creation of the metal frame significantly transformed this work, adding an even greater sense of depth and distance, at once encasing the image and projecting it even further into the void. He had never created a metal framing device like this before. "It was a way to work with the subject matter, the metal of the ship. I wanted to convey that I am able to work in materials other than wood, including bronze and other metals and it also gave me the opportunity to work again with chemical patinas. Putting that plate on it offered the opportunity to incorporate the sense of a sculpture in front of a painting, as I had done in the past. It created a window revealing the Titanic, and on another level, it suggested a type of vehicle that takes you down, into the blackness of the unconsciousness." As he had aspired to do in his earlier sculptural installations, Stackhouse wanted to present more than an image. He wanted to convey an experience to the viewer, including the mystery and the sense of overwhelming loss embodied in the broken form of the Titanic.

With the subject of the Titanic, Stackhouse discovered a modern archetype, one that had called forth associations throughout the twentieth century. For example, the conditions found in the wreckage were suggested in Thomas Hardy's 1912 meditation upon the Titanic, *The Convergence of the Twain*, which included these lines." In a solitude of the sea/Deep from human vanity,/And the Pride of Life that planned her, stilly couches she./ Steel chambers, late the pyres/Of her salamandrine fires,/Cold currents thrid and turn to ryhthmic tidal lyres./Over the mirrors meant/To glass the opulent,/The sea-worms crawl—grotesque, slimed, dumb, indifferent." [97] William Jennings Bryan, in a speech delivered in April of 1912, looked beyond his own time. "As to the future, nothing that we can say can bring back the dead. These occasions are for the future more than for now, for others more than for ourselves." [98] And, in that future, interest in the Titanic seldom waned, reinforced by books, poems, speeches, songs and a series of movies, many released during Stackhouse's life, including *Titanic* (1953), *A Night to Remember* (1958) and *The Unsinkable Molly Brown* (1960). More recently, more than five years after Stackhouse first introduced this subject in his USF exhibition, a Broadway musical, *Titanic*, and a major hit movie, James Cameron's *Titanic*, both appearing in 1997, affirmed the continuing public fascination with this topic and the deeper issues it suggests.

Stackhouse introduced these new works in his 1993 exhibition, "Recent Works," presented at the Morgan Gallery in Kansas City. The show, which was an immediate success in terms of both sales and critical response, served as a way to reunite Stackhouse's artistic activities with those of his friend and former colleague from Washington, William Christenberry. Christenberry had a related exhibition, equally successful, at the Morgan Gallery at this same time. Both artists, who had survived the economic hardships that had affected their galleries in New York and Washington, were surprised at the success they enjoyed in Kansas City. Equally important, these two exhibitions brought the artists' most recent work to the attention of Richard Belger, the director of the Belger Family Foundation in Kansas City and a collector of contemporary art who already owned significant examples of the work of both artists. "These were," Richard Belger recently stated, "two of the most incredible exhibitions I had ever seen in my life. Although I had known and collected their work for years, I was deeply impressed by the quality and range of the shows, including the way they demonstrated how much an artist could evolve in a career. It was a revelation to me." In addition to buying major works from both exhibitions for the Belger Foundation collection, the power of the exhibitions "planted an unconscious seed in me," Belger has explained, one that soon led to a significant reordering of the Foundation's collecting and outreach priorities. [99] By 1998, five years after his experiences at these exhibitions, working with Myra and Dennis Morgan at the Morgan Gallery, the Belger Foundation owned the largest comprehensive collection of works by both artists, and had supported numerous exhibitions, publications and research projects in the Middle West, in the South, and in Washington related to the evolution of their careers.

For both Stackhouse and Christenberry these developments brought major changes to their professional careers. As the Foundation acquired work from all phases of their careers, other collectors in the Middle West also increasingly supported their exhibitions and related art activities. Beginning in 1993, Kansas City, not New York, became the major center for gallery sales and exhibitions for both artists. Over the next four years, Stackhouse shipped work from his studio collection in New York to Kansas City. By the fall of 1997, the Belger Foundation had devoted almost an entire floor of its corporate office and warehouse building to the collecting and display of Stackhouse's works, including many of his massive remaining sculptural projects, providing an environment that allowed the artist and those working with him the opportunity to study the evolution of his entire career. This was the direct result of that "unconscious seed" Richard Belger had sensed in 1993, a developing focus for his family's foundation dedicated to the collecting and studying of works from all phases of the careers of a number of select artists, beginning with Robert Stackhouse and William Christenberry.

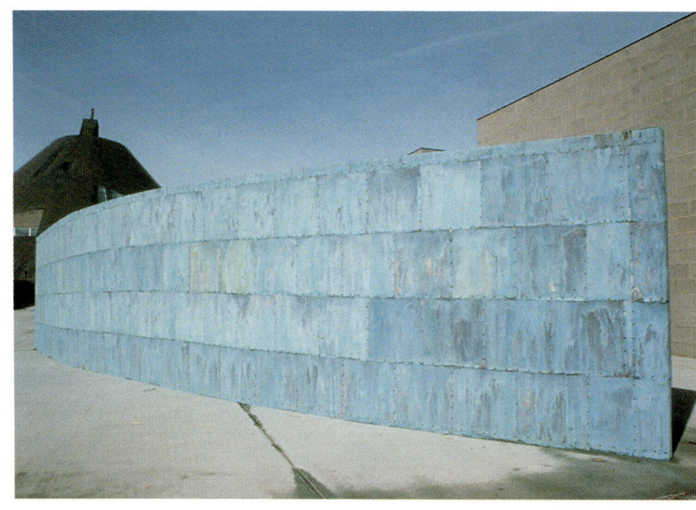

6.11

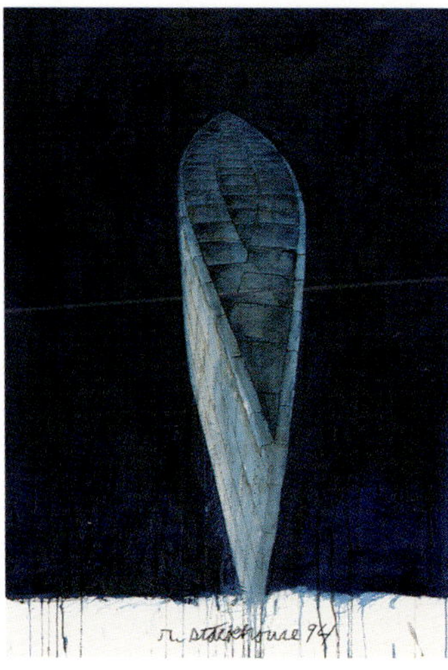

6.12

Wyoming Emersed, Laramie, Wyoming, 1993.

Vertical Wyoming, 1994

The growing interest and support of the Belger Foundation, as well as related collecting activities and sculptural commissions arranged through the Morgan Gallery, made Kansas City a major new base of operations for Stackhouse. It also opened up, in increasingly significant ways, a number of sculptural commissions in the Middle West and the West. When he returned to his New York studio to paint and to plan his next series of works, including several new print series, he also continued to plan for one of these sculptural commissions, a temporary sculpture to be installed at the new University of Wyoming Art Museum, in Laramie, Wyoming. This work, *Wyoming Emersed*, constructed of wood and copper with an applied patina (Figure 6.11), directly extended the concerns he had explored in the Kansas City exhibition, including his interest in the Titanic, focusing on a type of mysterious ship hull that had roots in his earlier works. This was suggested in a publication that accompanied his 1994 exhibition at the University of Wyoming Museum of Art.

> Wyoming Emersed, *an outdoor, temporary sculptural installation on the Lucile Wright Sculpture Terrace...at once appears displaced and yet completely at ease. The work, a 30' x 6' x 8' wood and*

copper nautical form, the manipulated patina reminiscent of a sunken ship, sits firmly atop the high plains of Wyoming amidst extinct sea beds unexpectedly and comfortably as the Ark rests perched upon Mt. Ararat. Wyoming Emersed *initially appeared as an untitled sculpture in 1972, and then was depicted in the two dimensional work* From the Deep *(1982).* [100]

The relationship of this sculpture to his continuing eye shape/boat shape form is most readily apparent in his 1994 painting of the completed work, which also suggests its relationship, despite its more solid form, to his evolving deck and "Bones" projects (Figure 6.12). A related vertical sculptural form, *Copper Naja*, fabricated of wood and patinaed copper in 1994, reminiscent of the wooden forms he featured in his 1972 "Journeys" exhibition, extends this sculptural concept while it also reflected its roots in his earlier works. That same year he also completed a series of studies for projected sculptural projects, titled "Icebergs," suggesting his continuing fascination with the Titanic saga, that were painted with vibrant, light filled colors, as in *Red Iceberg* (Figure 6.13). He also explored the possibility of creating "Iceberg" type forms, fabricated in red or cobalt blue glass blocks, as evident in *Blue Glass Study* (Figure 6.14). These works also illustrate his continuing desire to create total environments of intense color, usually red or blue, that extends back to earlier works like *Blue Diviners*. By using colored glass blocks he hoped to be able to obtain the best qualities of color and light he recognized from his understanding of watercolor techniques and combine that with the solid form and light filtering capabilities of structural glass blocks.

6.13 *Red Iceberg*, 1994

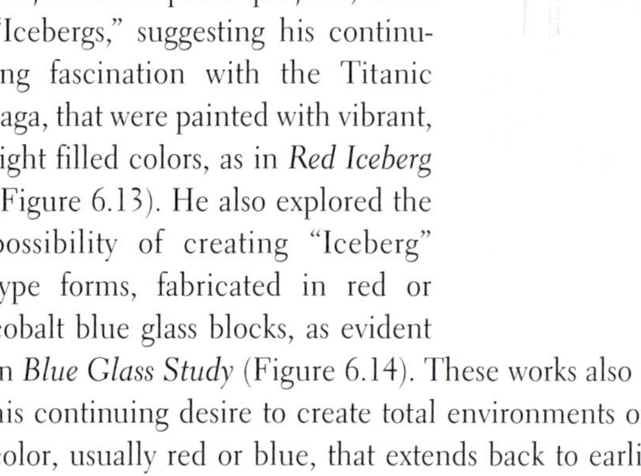

6.14 *Blue Glass Study*, 1994

In 1994, he also returned to serve an extended residency as a visiting artist at the University of South Florida, the first in a series of visiting artist positions across the country that have occupied him over the past four years. Driving the Porsche 944 Turbo that he purchased with the proceeds from his 1993 exhibition, with a kayak strapped to the car's roof, he returned to Florida to spend an extended period in the region he had known during his high school and college years. Staying in Gulfport, he regularly explored the bays and waters of the Gulf Coast in his kayak, recalling, in certain ways, his earlier explorations in the wooden boats at Lundy's fish camp. Commuting to the USF campus in Tampa, he reacquainted himself with the region around Tampa and St. Petersburg, which had grown dramatically since his undergraduate days in Tampa. While at USF, he spent time at Graphic Studio, and also worked with Margaret Miller, Director of the USF Contemporary Art Museum, where he had established a permanent collection of all of his printed works. He also renewed his acquaintances with Harrison Covington, Robert Gelinas, and other faculty members of the art department and reacquainted himself with senior members of the university administration, who remained supportive of him and encouraged his activities with his alma mater. During this period in Florida, he was reminded of how comfortable he felt there, on the water and in this distinctive landscape, where he had spent such an important part of his formative life. The city and the region had grown in significant ways by this time, as was reflected in the professionalism of the museum community evident at USF, at the Tampa Art Museum, the St. Petersburg Museum of Fine Arts, and other institu-

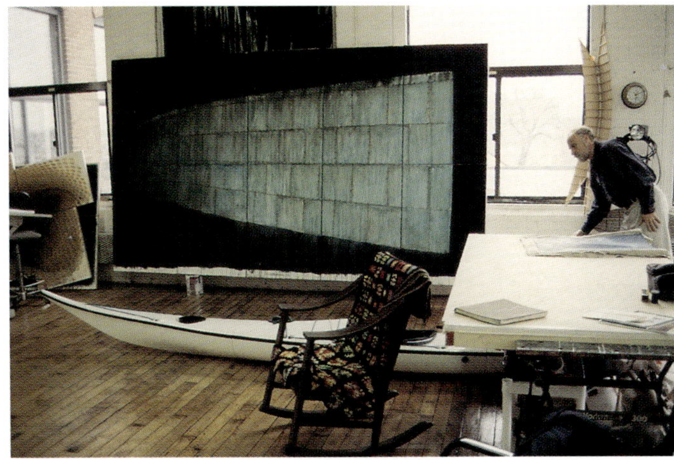

6.15

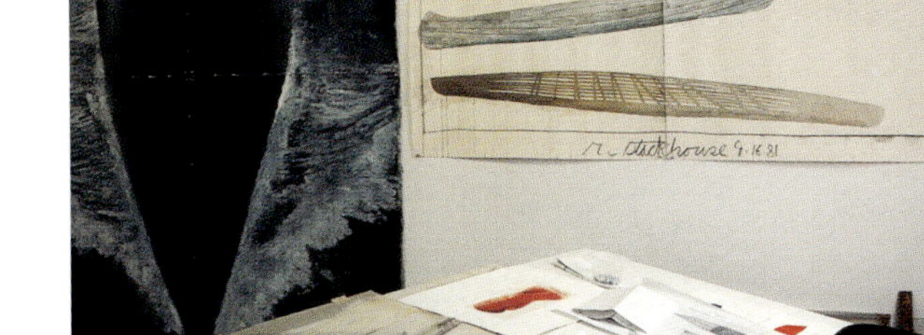

6.16

6.17

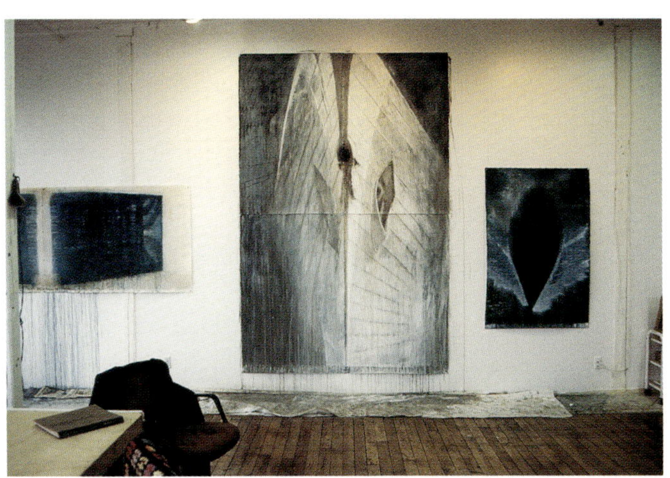

6.18

Four views of the artist's studio, Port Chester, New York, 1996.

tions and galleries in the area. While there, he also reflected on the growing number of national artists who lived and worked along the Gulf Coast, artists once affiliated with the New York art world, including Robert Rauschenberg and James Rosenquist.

Upon returning to New York, Stackhouse decided to move his studio out of SoHo, and out of the city. He relocated to a refurbished artists' loft and studio building in Port Chester, New York, located not far from Yonkers and the area where he had spent his childhood years in New York.

After moving, he commuted from SoHo on a daily basis, working in Port Chester and living in the city. Every morning, he walked from the loft on Mercer Street he shared with Mary Beth Edelson to a garage complex located along the piers on the Hudson River, retrieved the Porsche, and then drove up Manhattan's West Side, out to Port Chester, passing along the way the old apartment building he had lived in as a child. From Port Chester, he recently explained, he often drove over to his old Yonkers neighborhoods, and occasionally drove up to Peach Lake, to revisit the site of the family's fondly remembered summer house, the house that had been, like the Florida fish camp, such an important part of his early life. During a visit with the artist in September of 1996, the author accompanied him on this daily journey, a ritual he had come to enjoy, especially the drive along the Hudson River. As we passed by the old, often crumbling, pier areas along the West Side Highway, he recalled specific ships he had seen here as a child and described the historic ships that had docked here, contributing to Manhattan's reputation as a major port city. Because of his specific painting interests at that time, he also pointed out the dock area where the Normandie had burned and capsized, in 1942, the year of his birth.

Arriving after the trip along the Hudson River at Port Chester, where he maintained his primary working studio from 1994 to 1997, the visitor could have mistaken the space as the office or workshop of a boat builder or designer. Paintings of boats, ship drawings and designs on graph paper, floating deck forms hanging from windows frames, a kayak under a drawing table, scores of books on the Lusitania and the Titanic all filled the studio (Figures 6.15, 6.16, 6.17 and 6.18). In this working space, he had created the paintings featured in his second major Kansas City exhibition, presented in 1995, titled "Where Are We and What is It to Be There." Here he also planned many of the sculptural commissions that occupied him in 1996 and 1997. Downstairs from the studio, he maintained a large secured storage area filled with his early works. From this area, he regularly brought out older works, studied them, sorted through them and prepared them for his periodic shipments to Kansas City. As he reviewed and shipped his works from this studio in 1996 and 1997, and as he traveled from this space to his diverse teaching positions and sculptural projects, all located in the Middle West, the axis of his life seemed to be slowly, but steadily, shifting. In this period, New York became less and less the focus of his career. Kansas City and other points in the Middle West assumed increasing importance (Figure 6.19).

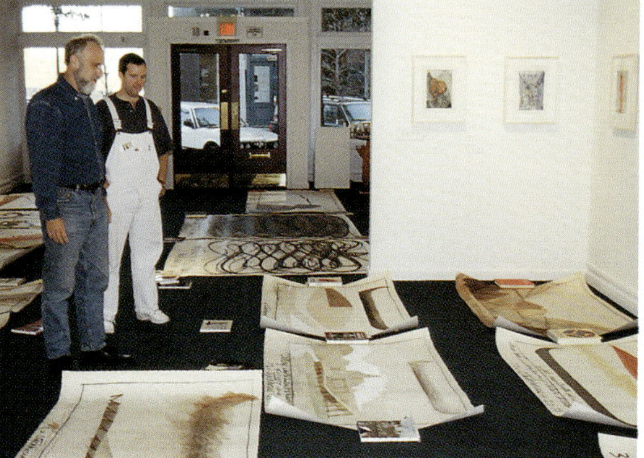

6.19

Robert Stackhouse and Dennis Morgan reviewing recent shipment of his works at the Morgan Gallery in Kansas City. 1996.

Continuing his interest in twentieth century ships, particularly those from the early part of the century, he became intrigued with famous liners including the Normandie and the Queen Mary. Widely recognized for her sleek bow, as well as her incredible speed, size, and luxury, the Normandie was, in many respects, an updated version of the Titanic. Known for her elegant array of passengers and her Art Deco interior furnishings, the Normandie was a grand symbol of her era. Sadly, after a tragic fire in New York harbor in 1942, the ship took on so much water that it listed, landing on its side in the harbor where it stayed, a haunting image, for eighteen months. After an enormous salvage enterprise, it was raised and towed to the Brooklyn navy yards, where it remained until after the war, when it was sold for scrap metal. [101] While he isn't certain, Stackhouse believes he saw the ship as a very young child, before it was destroyed.

Certainly, he could have seen it with his family, or heard stories and seen pictures that made it seem real to him. Unlike the Titanic, this ship had ties to his native city during his lifetime as did the Queen Mary, which operated out of New York harbor until its last voyage, in the fall of 1967. The Queen Mary had a much longer life than the Normandie, with a history of 1,000 ocean crossings covering over 3 million miles and service to two million passengers. Despite her history and her reputation, the Queen Mary could not continue to compete with modern jet service and she was sold to the city of Long Beach, California, which converted the ship into a tourist attraction. [102]

Among the range of significant works included in his 1995 exhibition in Kansas City, Stackhouse included a large painting, *Drifter*, that had been developing in his studio since 1993, along with his Titanic imagery (Figure 6.20). This composition, inspired by his studies of the Queen Mary, and explored in a variety of states over several years including a lithographic print created at the Lawrence Lithography Workshop in 1996, is dominated by its strong vertical orientation. In its original state, painted on a grand scale that looms over the viewer, it suggests the presence of a ghost ship, or a predator bearing down on the viewer. Here, rather than looking down upon the ruin of a ship, as in the Titanic images, the viewer is placed in a more threatened position, with this large ominous vessel bearing down, directly, on the viewer's space. This also may be viewed as a portrait type, one that continues to intrigue the artist, who still sees rich potential in the form. It is, above all, an evocative form, one that calls to mind a ghost ship or predator from a dream state, one that imparts a certain emotional state. And, like the abstract paintings of Jackson Pollock, this was originally completed on a large scale, with a running, gestural surface that suggests Stackhouse's early Abstract Expressionist training. In fact, the highly gestural and richly textured surface of this work seems to defy traditional notions of the limitations of watercolor, pushing the boundaries of the medium in both scale and execution. And, like Albert Pinkham Ryder's famous depiction of a Grim Reaper astride a horse on a racing track (*The Race Track, Death on a Pale Horse*), there is a sense of pressing mystery, and inevitability, to this work. Stackhouse, like Ryder in an earlier era, created an image that was directed to the unconscious mind, seeking to strike a universal note there.

Another image that evokes the memory of Ryder is *On the Deep #2*, one of several versions of this work, the largest being on a grand scale comparable to that of the original *Drifter* (Figure 6.21). Like Ryder's small painting, *The Toilers of the Sea*, contained in the collections of the Metropolitan Museum of Art, which depicts a small dark vessel surrounded by waves (or a wake) on a moonlit night, this work is more mysterious and suggestive than specific or detailed. Using dark blues, his color for the unconscious mind, Stackhouse presented a form creating a wake across a dark body of water. Many viewers see this as the view of a ship's hull seen from below, from the depths of a dark body of water. Stackhouse sees the work in a different way. "I see it from above. Everybody else seems to see it from below. It is interesting that way. If it is seen from below, it means the ship is actually there. If that is the case, then it is consistent with being under the whale, like being under the whale structure of the earlier work, *Deep Swimmers*. My intention, at least for me, was to create an image of a ship that was not there. I don't see a ship there, just a wake, like the invisible man, walking through the snow, leaving footprints, yet no one was able to see him." And, even though there is no ship to be seen, the artist did base this image upon his continuing research into naval architecture and nautical history. "This is a war ship. It is a guided missile cruiser. The wake is being made by a war ship. Even when it is there, it is more of an illusion. I acquired many books on military vessels, especially on submarines, because of my interest in the wakes. I am extremely interested in the form of a submarine but I haven't been able to paint one yet. This is the only image I have ever derived from one of those books."

A third major image from the 1995 exhibition is *Flexed Flyer*, another enigmatic image that seems, at first, to be another variation of the deck, *Bones*, or eye shape/ boat shape form, that informed this image and that in *From the Deep* (Figure 6.22, cover image). Reflecting the continuing evolution of this form over a period of more than two decades, and his constant regenerative approach to his essential iconography, this work appears both familiar and unidentifiable. Is this a sculpture, the deck of one of his constructed forms? Is it an underwater form now, transformed because of his intensive interests in the Titanic, the Normandie and similar ships? Or, is it an image from another dimension, another place, perhaps even from the depths of space? There is, it seems, a sug-

6.20

Drifter

1993

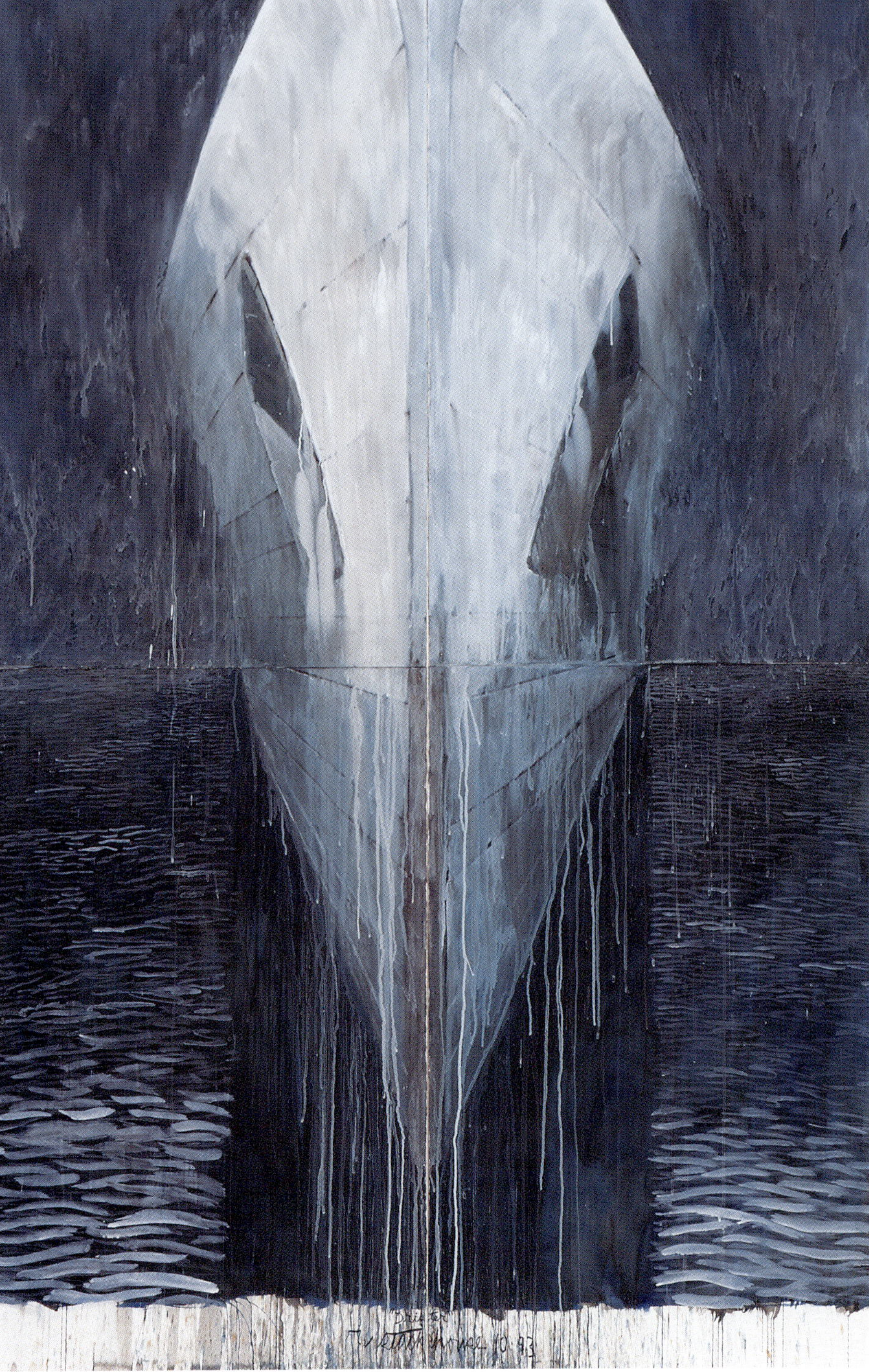

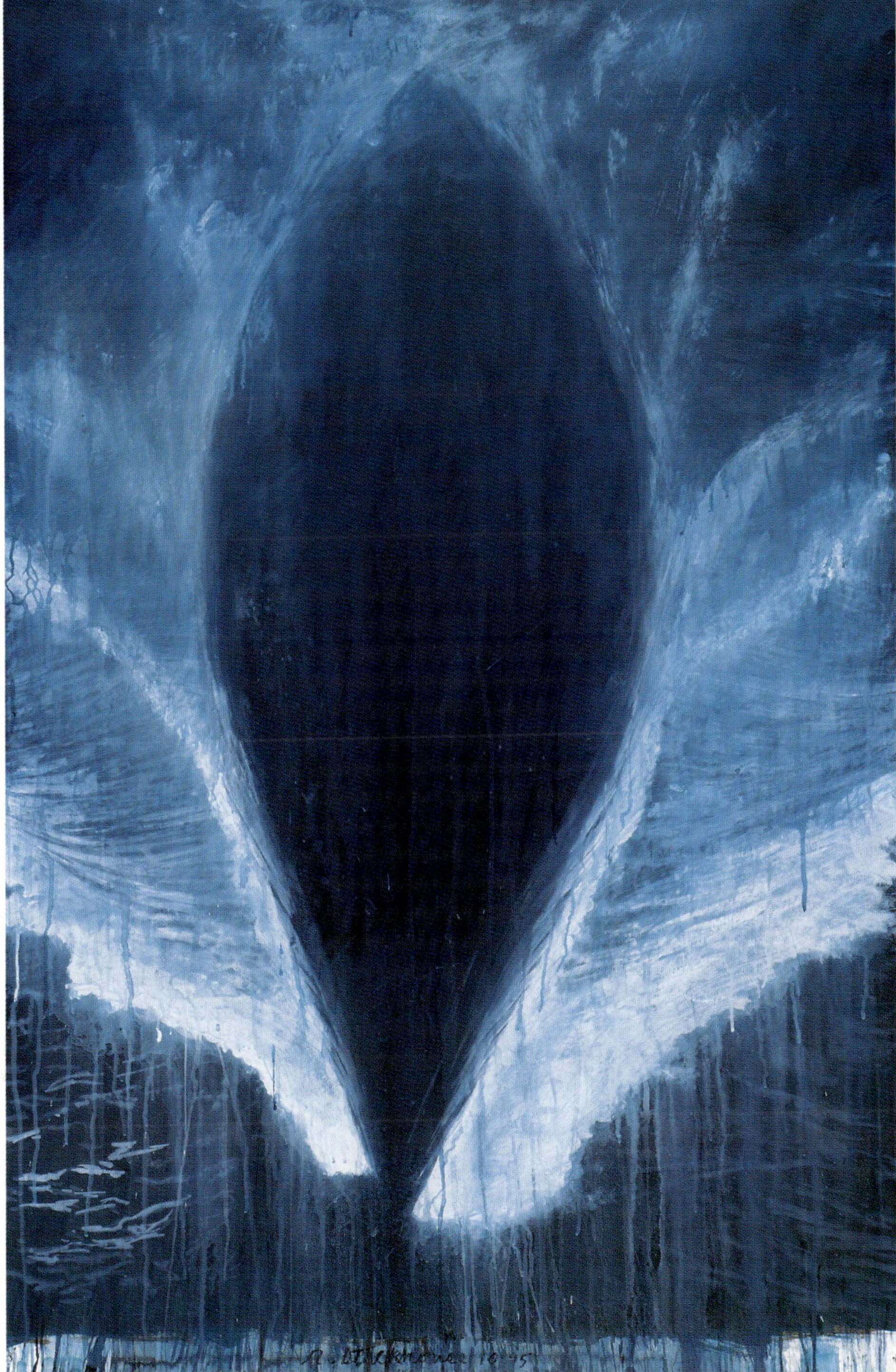

6.21

On the Deep #2, 1995

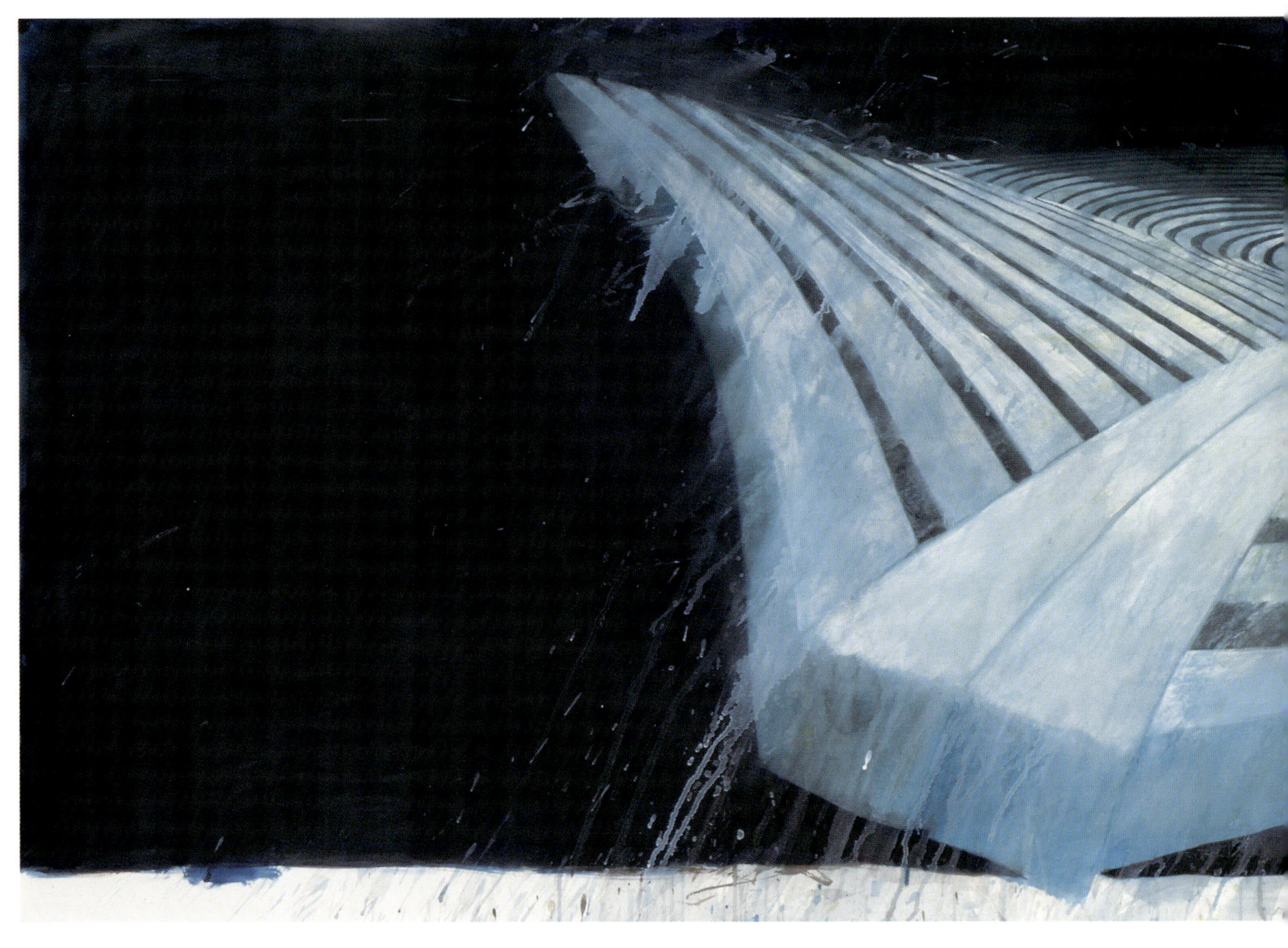

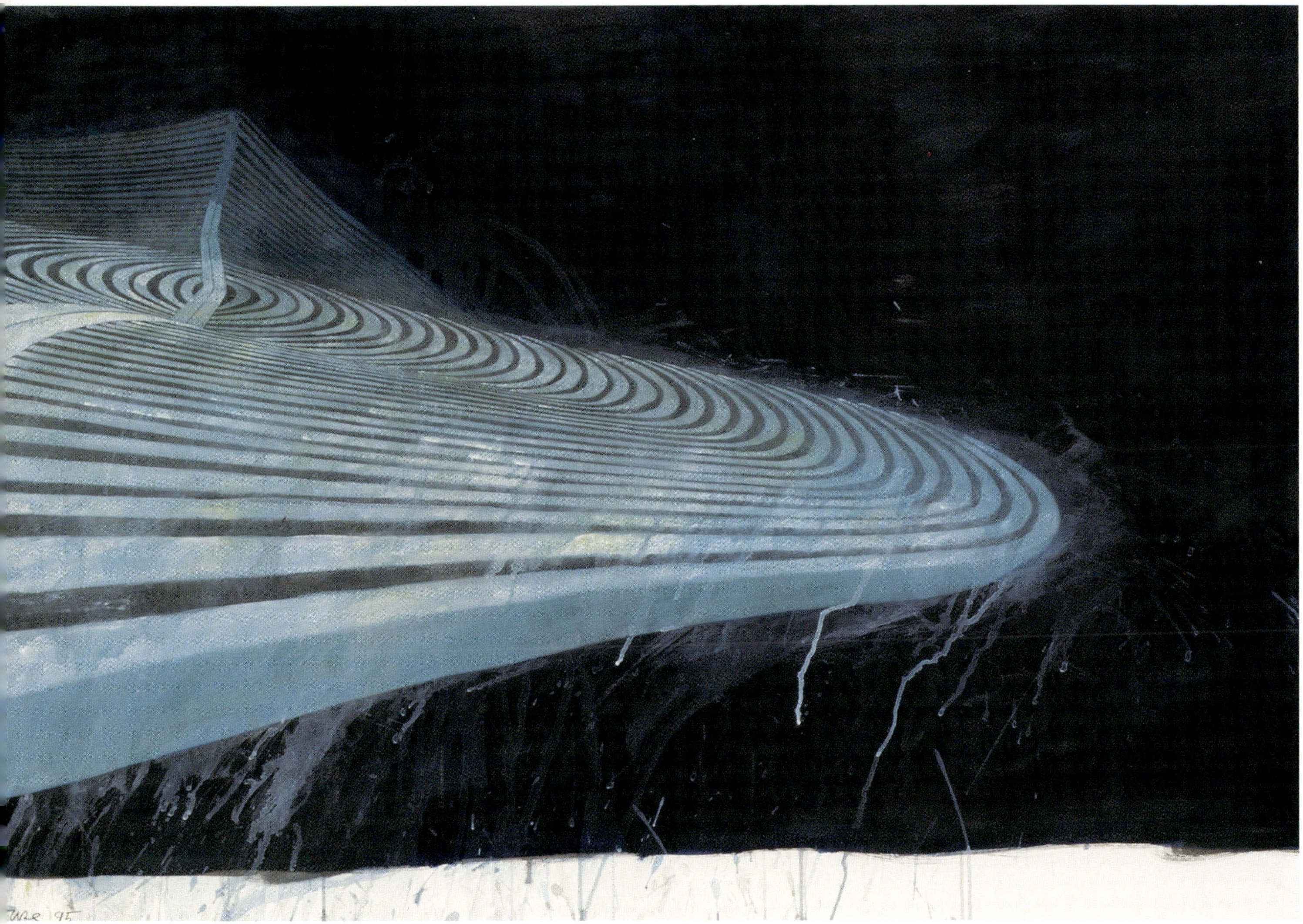

6.22

Flexed Flyer, 1995

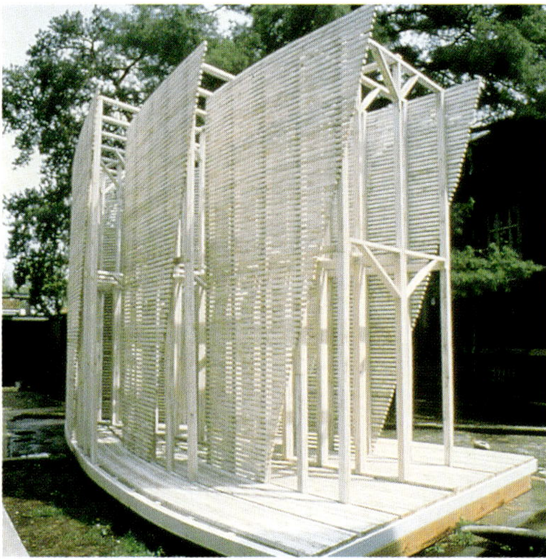

K.C. Way, installation at the Kansas City Art Institute, 1996

6.23

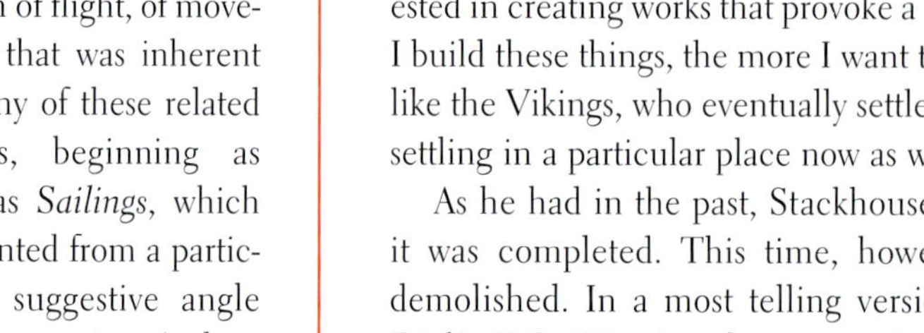

gestion of flight, of movement, that was inherent in many of these related images, beginning as early as *Sailings*, which he painted from a particularly suggestive angle and perspective. And, as the artist has recently indicated, he has become increasingly interested in other types of vessels, other types of ships. "During my research on twentieth century ships and their wakes, I have looked at many other books as well, including books on passenger planes, war planes, and space vehicles, studying them all as forms. I just haven't pulled the trigger with this material yet. However, I find these forms all absolutely seductive." Such an interest also continues his extensive earlier readings in science fiction, a subject complete with its own approaches to the use of myth and mythological imagery.

K.C. Way - Installation 1996 (Actual installation images)

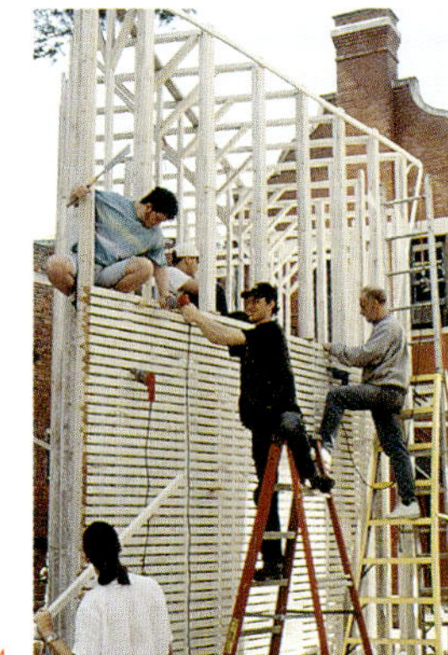

6.24

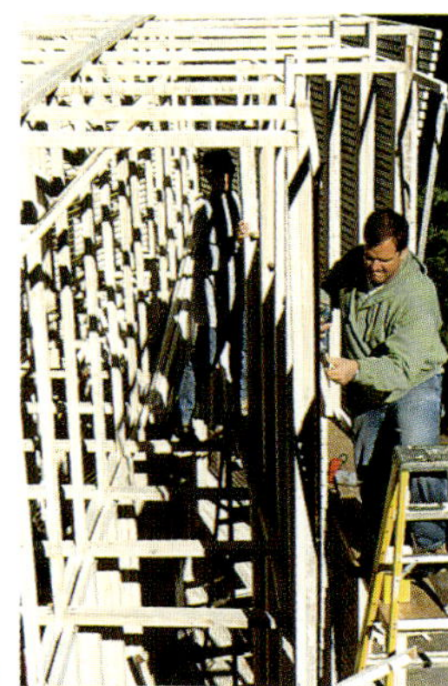

6.25

Over the past three years, Stackhouse's creative activities seem to have increased at an exponential level. In 1996, his associations with Kansas City were reinforced when he accepted a visiting artist position at the Kansas City Art Institute. During his tenure at the Art Institute, a school with a long and important history in the Middle West, he taught classes and planned the construction of a large, architectural public sculpture, titled *K.C. Way*, which he built on the school's campus, not far from the recently opened Kemper Museum of Contemporary Art and Design, initially planned to serve as part of the Art Institute (Figure 6.23). As part of the process of its creation, Stackhouse involved his students and other members of the Kansas City art community in the construction phase of the project (Figures 6.24 and 6.25), continuing his earlier philosophical approach to the nature of public art forms, extending back to his first public sculpture, created in Cleveland. And, as he has come to recognize in his most recent works, he is moving increasingly toward the creation of architectural forms and spaces. "I think that architecture is inevitable. I am less interested in objects now. I am more interested in creating works that provoke a sense of place. The more I build these things, the more I want to build a place. Perhaps, like the Vikings, who eventually settled, I may be interested in settling in a particular place now as well."

As he had in the past, Stackhouse painted this work after it was completed. This time, however, the work was not demolished. In a most telling version of this image, titled *Dick's K.C. Way* (a reference to Richard Belger), the artist overlaid the image of a steel hulled ship, covered with plates and rivets, moving under (or across?) the form of the recently completed *K.C. Way*. The dark blue ground of this work reflects his continuing fascination with the use of this color as a reflection of the unconscious mind, and also suggests either the depths of the ocean, or some other, equally mysterious space or environment (Figure 6.26). Another version, painted in 1997, titled *Close K.C. Way*, reverses the type of imagery and color usage associated with earlier works like *Blue Diviners*, floating the white forms of the structure over a deep, dark background, again suggesting the presence of a mysterious form emerging from (or disappearing into) the void. In her short essay, "A Dream Boat at KCAI," Roberta Lord referred to the importance of the ship image for Stackhouse, specifically as reflected in this work.

> *The allusion to ships has come to dominate his work in recent years....Ships connote levitation, frictionless travel, silent passage through darkness. Though the ship is man's invention, its form is lodged in prehistoric memory. Perhaps because to stay afloat (alive), a ship must conform to organic construction principles: it must have a spine and ribs. It must be streamlined for speed and agility. To withstand buffeting seas, it must be strong yet flexible. Ships are kin to salmons and swans, and so are we. Ships—to take this analogy about as far as it will go–are among the "lost tribes." They bear a family resemblance. It is this welcome, but surprising, familiarity that Stackhouse's sculptures so effectively play upon.* [103]

Continuing his momentum, he also served as a visiting artist at Illinois Wesleyan University, in Bloomington, Illinois, in 1996. During his tenure there, he designed and constructed, in an interior gallery space, the sculpture known as *Transplace*. Using large plywood panels, painted with a patina-like surface suggesting the hull of a ship, and drilled with a uniform pattern of holes meant to suggest rivets, this work presented a somewhat foreboding exterior (Figure 6.27) to the gallery goer. Then, perhaps surprisingly, the visitor encountered a glowing pattern of lights in the interior, light filtering through from the gallery "outside" the hull of this ship form, creating a space meant to invite passage and discovery, just as the earlier A-frame structures had done (Figure 6.28). Continuing his exploration of the Normandie's suggestive prow, Stackhouse created a seven color lithographic version of *Drifter*, titled *Adrift*, (Figure 6.29), then extended this process of exploration and rediscovery within his own imagery by completing a wooden form of this image in *Recollecting Angel* (Figure 6.30). Constructed of painted wood and lath, this form suggested not only the Queen Mary's prow but also a predator's head, a portrait, and even a Greek helmet, suggesting another historical association for his imagery.

In 1997 and 1998, Stackhouse participated in a continuing series of artist-in-residence programs and constructed, during these programs and in unrelated projects, the largest number of sculptures he has ever constructed within a similar time frame. He believes this is the direct result of his associations with the Middle West. "I think all of these projects are the result of my close connection to Kansas City and Missouri. The influence of the Midwest is apparent in the availability of more sculptural opportunities. In New York City, sculptural opportunities were not there, so I spent more time in my studio making major paintings. It seems to me that Kansas City is only about two and one half hours from everywhere. It is the heartland. And, notably, I have completed six sculptures within the last year." These recently completed works are: *Missouri Shift* (1997), *Blue Ryders* (1997), *Missouri Bones* (1998), *Angel Way* (1998), *Incomplete Angel* (1998) and *Michigan Swell* (1998). One other work, *Chicago Structure*, was completed earlier in 1997.

His evolving interests in architecture were brought to a new level when, during the course of his term as a visiting artist at Drury College in Springfield, Missouri, he taught in a program designed for both art and architecture students. When he had first enrolled at the University of South Florida,

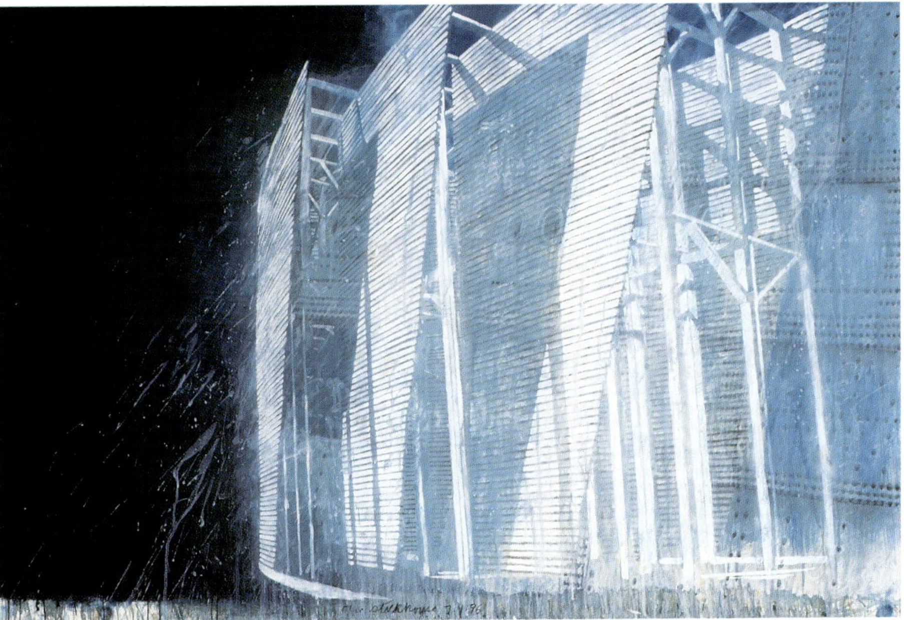

6.26

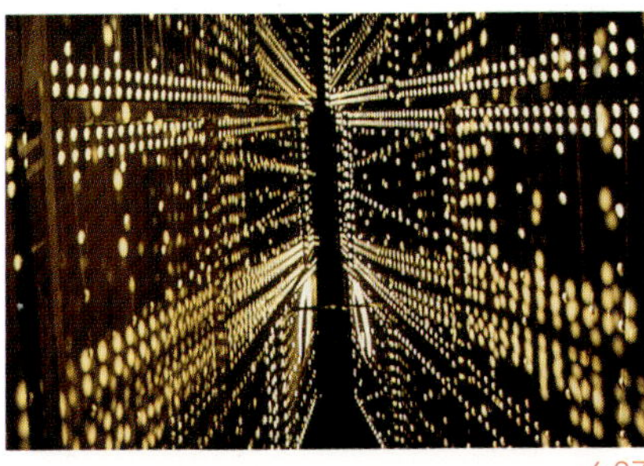

6.27

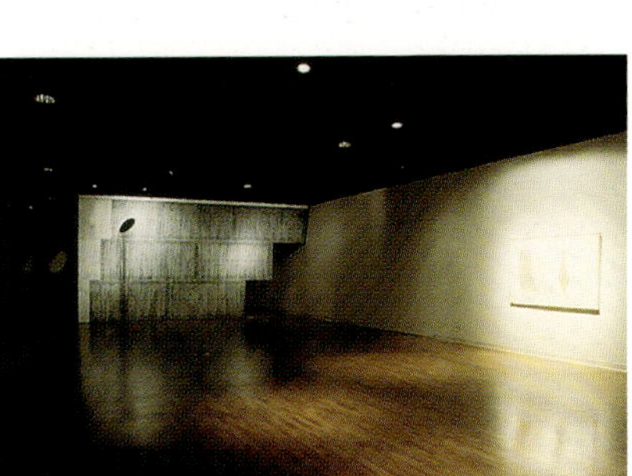

6.28

Dick's K.C. Way 1996

Transplace, exterior and interior views, Illinois Wesleyan University, 1996.

Adrift, 1996

Recollecting Angel, 1972-96

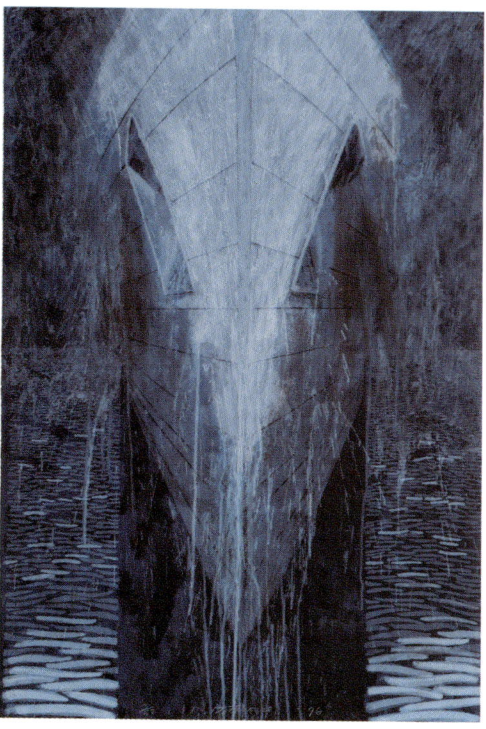

6.29

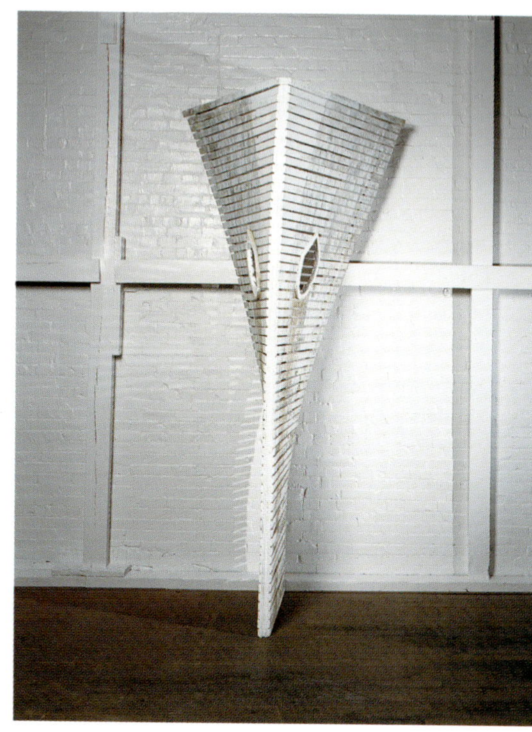

6.30

encouraged by his grandfather, Stackhouse tried to enroll in the architecture program at that new university. However, because of his poor math skills, he was denied enrollment in the program. In 1997, much to his satisfaction, and perhaps as a tribute to his grandfather, Stackhouse found himself teaching in an architectural program, as a distinguished visiting professor. The irony of this step in his career path was not wasted on him. During this time in Springfield, he constructed a large wooden sculpture, working with Drury students, titled *Missouri Shift* (Figure 6.31). Late last year, at Klein Art Works in Chicago, he constructed *Blue Ryders*, an indoor piece that was titled as a tribute to one of his favorite artists, Albert Pinkham Ryder (Figure 6.32). The completion of this piece was described by Kathleen Whitney, in a recent issue of *Sculpture* magazine.

> *The building process lasted four 16-hour days and culminated with Stackhouse painting the unprimed wood Dutch-Boy Blue. The final effect was anthropomorphic and mechanical. There is a distinct relationship to skeletal structure as well as to the elegance of Norse longboats. This extraordinary object was hung in front of a wall of windows over a highly polished floor, creating a multiple set of reflections which constantly shifted the viewer's perception. The choice of color—so shocking, deliberate, and unnatural—made any association with the object inherently unstable; nothing existed in nature that bears such an intense and unearthly coloration.* [104]

As 1997 ended, Stackhouse entered one of the most intensive periods of personal transition in his life. After 27 years, his relationship with Mary Beth Edelson, which began as both of them established their early careers in Washington, came to an end. While she remained in the SoHo loft they had moved to in 1975, he closed his Port Chester studio and moved, in December, to a new loft studio in the River Market area of Kansas City. After twenty-two years of living and working in the center of New York's art world, Stackhouse moved to the city that had increasingly replaced New York as the center of his artistic activity. Fifteen years earlier, in 1982, when Myra Morgan first contacted him regarding the possibility of showing his work at her Kansas City gallery, Stackhouse knew little about the city and its art environment. Increasingly, beginning in 1986, when the Morgan Gallery gave him his first one-man exhibition in the city, he developed ties to the city and its institutions and collectors. By the time of his 1993 exhibition at the Morgan Gallery and the beginning of his direct association with the Belger Family Foundation, the city had started to take on a much more serious level of meaning for him and his career. That continued to evolve as his exhibition, teaching, and foundation activity drew him increasingly to the city.

Not long after moving, he returned to his sculptural projects, beginning with *Missouri Bones,* an eye shape/boat shape deck form fabricated of aluminum for the grounds of the Albrecht-Kemper Museum, in St. Joseph, Missouri (Figure 6.33). Working with Mark Spencer, director of the Albrecht-Kemper, and Myra Morgan, representing the Belger Foundation, he participated in the planning of a selected career retrospective exhibition, the first Foundation sponsored exhibition of his works from that collection, which was presented at that museum over the summer of 1998, following the installation of his sculptural project on the museum's grounds. With the completion of this project, which has direct associations to the earlier *St. Louie Bones* project, the state of Missouri had more completed sculptural project by the artist than any other state. Later, he returned to Chicago and completed *Angel Way* for that city's annual sculptural exposition (Figure 6.34). Continuing his focus on an "angel" series, he constructed *Incomplete Angel* inside the Morgan Gallery as part of his 1998 exhibition there (Figures 6.35 and 6.36). With this work, Stackhouse seems to bear out the observations offered by Kathleen Whitney prior to its installation in Kansas City. "In all of Stackhouse's pieces, he uses power hand tools and a limited number of assistants, depending on the scale, but in every other way he forswears ambitious industrial construction techniques in favor of human parameters. The end results are physically modest and always in human proportion....The viewer moves through them, under them, and over them—causing an inescapable com-

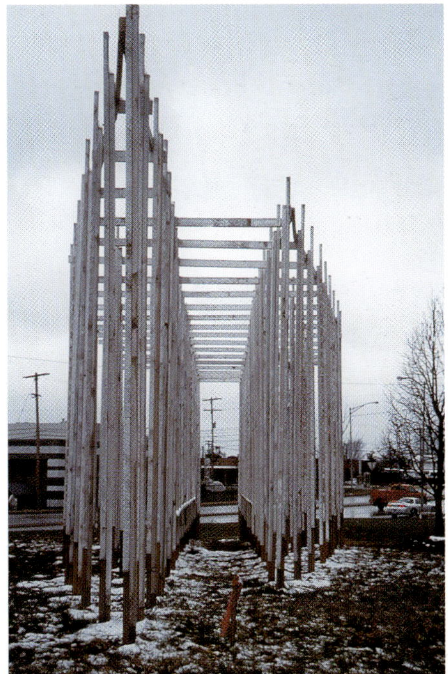
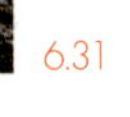
6.31

Missouri Shift, Drury College, Springfield, Missouri, 1997.

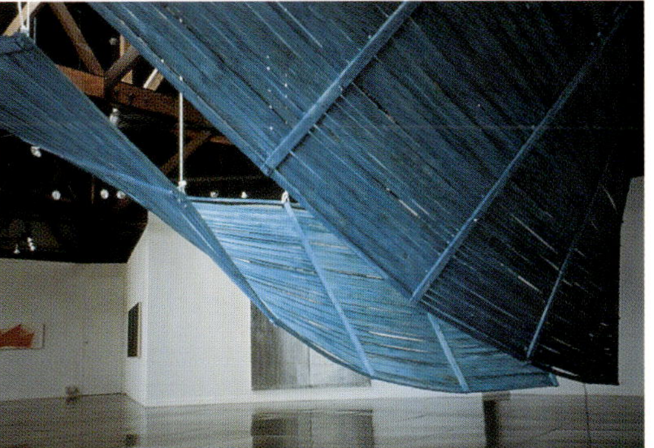
6.32

Blue Ryders, installation at Klein Art Works, Chicago, 1997.

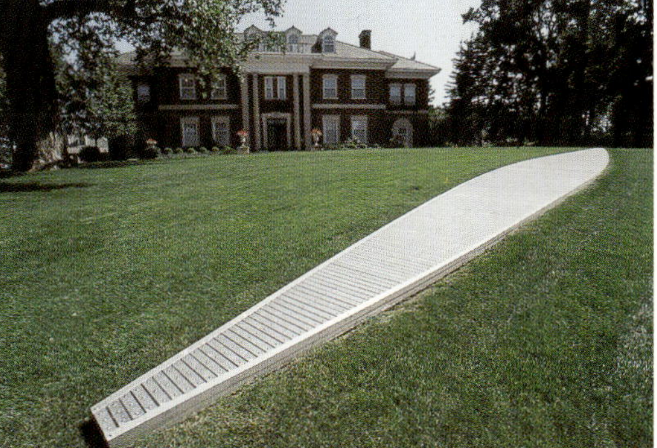
6.33

Missouri Bones, installation at the Albrecht-Kemper Museum of Art, St. Joseph, Missouri, 1998.

parison between the human body and the object itself." [105]

Inevitably, as one concludes an overview of the development of the artist's life and professional career to this point, in November of 1998, there is a tendency to speculate upon what comes next. There can be little doubt that the artist, whose career has developed intuitively, but quite logically in terms of evolving periods and stages of growth, has positioned himself for another stage in his evolution. This period may well have begun over the course of the past eighteen months, prior to his move to Kansas City. Because he has never been one to ignore his own past, as well as the evolution of his own forms and images, it can be anticipated that Stackhouse will continue to discover new meanings and new visual possibilities within the established iconography that has marked his mature career. And, based upon his prolific output of site specific sculptural projects during 1997 and 1998, it is logical to assume that he will continue in this direction, although he has expressed a growing desire to work in more permanent (and more expensive) materials, a factor which could reduce the quantity of works produced in the next phase of his career. New and emerging forms, like those evident in *Blue Ryders* and *Incomplete Angel*, may offer clues as to the future course of his sculptural development, but only time will tell if his intuition, his truest guide, will lead him in this direction. Over the past several years, he has expressed a growing interest in birds of prey and symbols of flight, including the structural elements of air "ships," as implied in works such as *Blue Ryders*, *Incomplete Angel* and *K.C. Way*.

There is, he admits, really no way to predict what will happen next. It is all only speculation, as he has learned over the course of his career. However, considering how significantly his life and his art have been shaped by his environment—from Yonkers and Peach Lake, to Lundy's fish camp, to Tampa and the University of South Florida, to Washington and the Corcoran Gallery, to Manhattan and the SoHo art world and to Port Chester—it may be presumed this his current location may contribute in some way to this next direction. It is certainly intriguing to hear what he sees, quite literally, when he looks out the window of his Kansas City loft, across the bend of the Missouri River, toward the old Kansas City Municipal Airport. "I love looking out my window. I look at an airport and a river and trains. While I don't know what effect this may have, I do know that I notice red-tail hawks, because of Dennis Morgan. And, I look at eagles soaring over the Missouri River, from my loft." Perhaps his view over the historic Missouri River will offer the next step in the cycle of discovery he once called "the beginning of the beginning to see."

Angel Way, Installation, Chicago, 1998

Incomplete Angel, installation at the Morgan Gallery, Kansas City, 1998

6.34

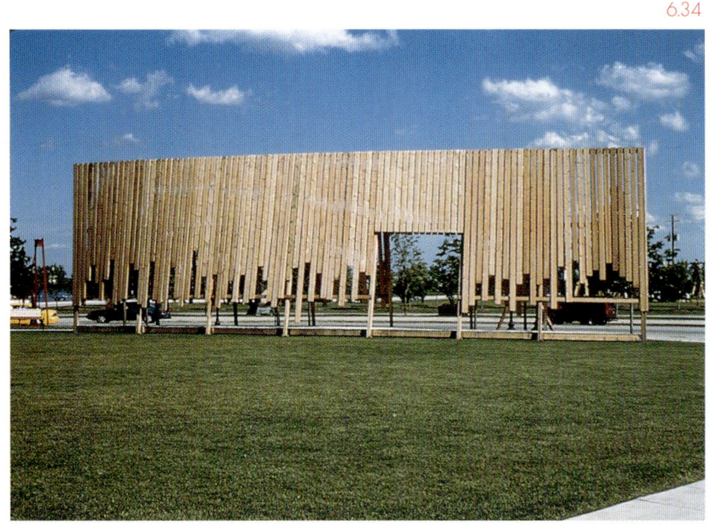

6.35

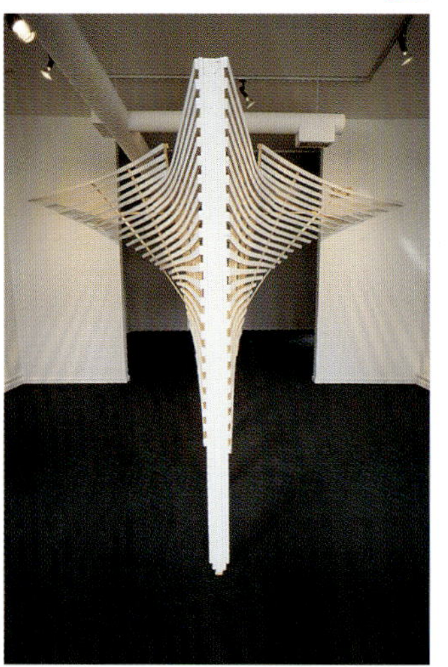

6.36

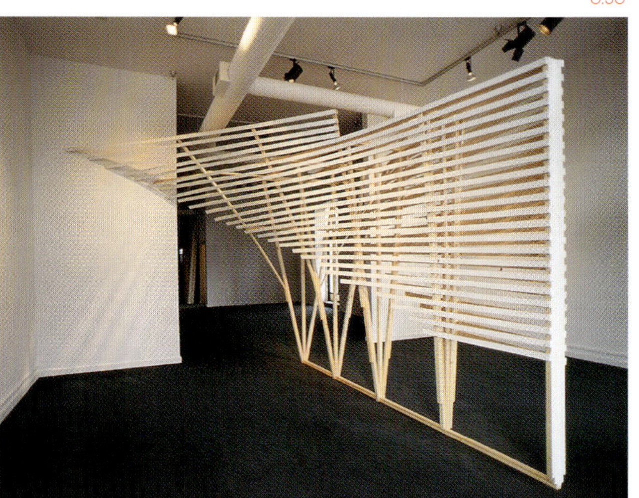

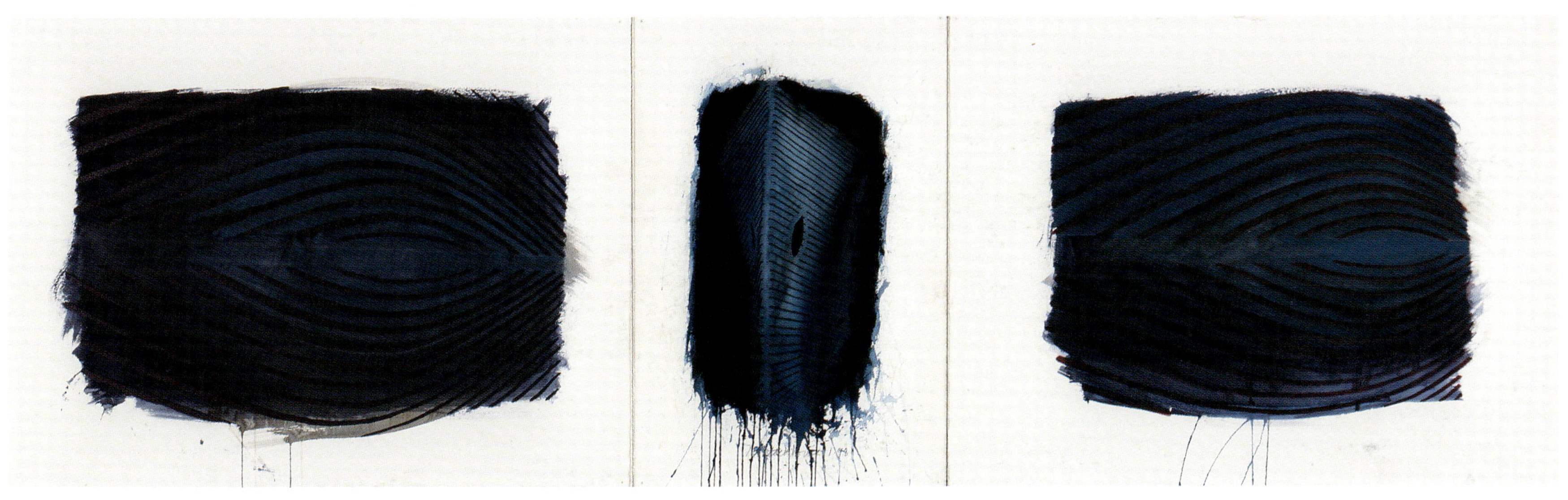

Blue Seeing, 1998

Endnotes

1. Interviews with Phyllis Stackhouse, in Kansas City, Missouri, in 1997, and in Tampa, Florida, in 1998. All references to the history of the Stackhouse and Holland families are based upon an extensive series of interviews with Phyllis and Robert Stackhouse and incorporate family historical materials contained in clippings files, scrapbooks, photographic albums and a brief typed family history written by Phyllis Stackhouse in June of 1994. All quotations by the artist, unless otherwise indicated, are taken from interviews and discussions, conducted from 1995 to 1998, with the artist in New York City and Port Chester, New York; Kansas City and St. Joseph, Missouri; Augusta, Georgia; and Tampa, Auburndale and Gulfport, Florida.
2. See David Gelernter, *1939, The Lost World of the Fair*, (New York: Avon Books, 1995); Barbara Cohen, Steven Heller and Seymour Chwast, *Trylon and Perisphere: The 1939 New York World's Fair*, (New York: Abrams, 1989); and, Helen A. Harrison, ed., *Dawn of a New Day: The New York World's Fair, 1939/40*, (New York: Queens Museum, New York University Press, 1980).
3. Holger Cahill, "American Art Today," in *American Art Today, New York World's Fair* (Poughkeepsie, NY: Apollo, 1987), 19-32.
4. See C. Edison Armi, *The Art of American Car Design: The Profession and Personalities* (University Park: The Pennsylvania State University Press, 1988), and Richard Guy Wilson, "Transportation Machine Design," in *The Machine Age in America, 1919-1941* (New York: Harry N. Abrams, Inc., 1986).
5. Quoted in Barbara Novak, *Nature and Culture: American Landscape and Painting, 1825-1875* (New York: Oxford University Press, Revised Edition, 1995), 10. Novak's influential study of American landscape painting and its broader cultural and philosophical context presents a significant survey of issues in 19th century American art that offers a background for understanding the aesthetic and historical context that consciously and unconsciously influenced Robert Stackhouse and other artists of his generation, including Robert Smithson.
6. See Ruth K. Beesch et. al. in *Florida Visionaries: 1870-1930* (Gainesville: University Presses of Florida, 1989). Other artists active in Florida include Louis Mignot, Xanthus R. Smith, John Mooney, Edward Moran, Alexander H. Wyant, George Herbert McCord, William Aiken Walker, Frank Shapleigh, William Lamb Picknell, Herman Herzog, Eliot Clark, Ernest H. Lawson, Anthony Thieme, William Glackens, George Catlin and Seth Eastman (many of whom are represented in the collections of the Morris Museum of Art). For a recent overview of artists in Florida see Gary R. Libby, editor, *Celebrating Florida, Works of Art from the Vickers Collection* (Gainesville: University Press of Florida, 1995).
7. See Estill C. Pennington, *A Southern Collection* (Augusta: Morris Communications Corporation, 1992), 76-77.
8. Federal Writers' Project of the Work Projects Administration for the State of Florida: *Florida, A Guide to the Southernmost State* (New York: Oxford University Press, Fifth Printing, 1947), 514-516.
9. Quoted in "Epcot Center," in *Fodor's 96 Walt Disney World, Universal Studios and Orlando* (New York: Fodor's Travel Publications, 1995), 53.
10. See "Walt Disney World," in *Insight Guides: Florida* (London: Insight Guides, 1998), 253-265.
11. Douglas Frantz, "Living in a Disney Town, With Big Brother at Bay," *The New York Times*, Sunday, October 4, 1998, AR 31.
12. See, for example, Ronald W. Haase, *Classic Cracker: Florida's*

Wood-Frame Vernacular Architecture (Sarasota: Pineapple Press, 1992).

13. This quote and all related materials based upon a telephone interview with Harrison Covington, October 19, 1998.
14. On Gelinas, see J. Richard Gruber, *William Christenberry: The Early Years, 1954-1968* (Augusta: Morris Museum of Art, 1996), 53-63.
15. All references taken from family files, newspaper clippings and scrapbooks devoted to the artist's undergraduate and graduate school years.
16. Hans Juergensen, "New Area Universities Emphasize the Fine Arts," *The Tampa Times*, April 14, 1965, contained in the artist's files.
17. Lurlene Gallagher, "Four More Weeks to Go on Mural," contained in the artist's files.
18. On the history and evolution of Ybor City, see Jose Rivero Muniz, *The Ybor City Story, 1885-1954* (Tampa: Jose Rivero Muniz, 1976).
19. Barbara Rose, "A B C Art," reprinted in Gregory Battcock, ed., *Minimal Art, A Critical Anthology* (New York: E.P. Dutton & Co., Inc., 1968), 274-297.
20. Lucy R. Lippard, "New York Letter: Rejective Art," reprinted in Lucy R. Lippard, *Changing, Essays in Art Criticism* (New York: E.P. Dutton & Co., Inc., 1971), 141-142.
21. Quoted in Jonathan Fineberg, *Art since 1940: Strategies of Being* (New York: Harry N. Abrams, Inc., 1995), 296.
22. Virginia Mecklenburg, *The Public As Patron: A History of the Treasury Department Mural Program Illustrated with Paintings from the Collection of the University of Maryland Art Gallery* (College Park: University of Maryland, 1979), 87.
23. See Cahill, *American Art Today*, p. 112.
24. See Howard Wooden, "Herman Maril," in *Collected Essays on 101 Art Works from the Permanent Collections of the Wichita Art Museum* (Wichita: Wichita Art Museum, 1988), 156-157.
25. Francis V. O'Connor, *Art for the Millions: Essays from the 1930s by Artists and Administrators of the WPA Federal Art Project* (Boston: New York Graphic Society, 1973).
26. Francis V. O'Connor, *Jackson Pollock* (New York: The Museum of Modern Art, 1967).
27. See Diana F. Johnson, "Art in Washington: Twenty Years," in *Washington: Twenty Years* (Baltimore: The Baltimore Museum of Art, 1970), 7-12.
28. Quoted in Arlene Corkery, "Some Recent Developments in Washington Art," in *Washington: Twenty Years* (Baltimore: The Baltimore Museum of Art, 1970), 17-18.
29. Ibid., p. 18.
30. Quoted in Bruce Altshuler, *The Avant-Garde in Exhibition: New Art in the 20th Century* (New York: Harry N. Abrams, Inc., 1994), 220.
31. Irving Sandler, "1967: Out of Minimal Sculpture," in Janet Kardon, ed., *1967: At the Crossroads* (Philadelphia: University of Pennsylvania, 1987), p. 41. See also Barbara Rose, "Remembering 1967," 32-39, and Lucy R. Lippard, "Notes on the Independence Movement," 22-31, in this catalogue of an exhibition presented at the Institute of Contemporary Art in Philadelphia, March 13-April 26, 1987.
32. For information on William Christenberry's previous teaching experiences and art activities see Gruber, *William Christenberry: The Early Years, 1954-1968*.
33. Samuel J. Wagstaff, "Introduction," in *Other Ideas* (Detroit: The Detroit Institute of Arts, 1969), 1.
34. Robin Reid, "Soothing 'Blades' Featured in Concert," article from unidentified newspaper contained in the artist's archives.
35. See Barbara Haskell, *BLAM! The Explosion of Pop, Minimalism, and Performance 1958-1964* (New York: Whitney Museum of American Art, 1984) and Thomas Crow, *The Rise of the Sixties* (New York: Harry N. Abrams, Inc., 1996).
36. Paul Richard, "A Naked Art Form," *The Washington Post*, October 28, 1969, contained in the artist's archives.
37. Meryle Secrest, "Game Opera: Playing Music by Chance," *The Washington Post*, December 12, 1969, contained in the artist's archives.
38. Paul Richard, "Sculptor's Retreat," *The Washington Post*, September 15, 1969, B1, B3.
39. Carter Ratcliff, "What It Is to Be There," in *Robert Stackhouse* (Wilmington: Delaware Museum of Art, 1991), 10-11.
40. Joseph L. Henderson and Maud Oakes, *The Wisdom of the Serpent: The Myths of Death, Rebirth, and Resurrection* (Princeton: Princeton University Press, 1990 edition), 36-37, 43-44.
41. Leslie Judd Ahlande, "Introduction," in *Contemporary Religious Imagery in American Art* (Sarasota: Ringling Museum of Art, 1974), 3-4.
42. Ibid., p. 20.
43. Renato G. Danese, "Introduction," in *New Sculpture: Baltimore, Washington, Richmond* (Washington: Corcoran Gallery of Art, 1970), 5.
44. Ibid., quoted in Danese, p. 6.
45. Paul Richard, "Evocative Wooden Form," *The Washington Post*, March 25, 1972, B7.
46. Benjamin Forgey, "Strange, Terrible Dreams," *The Washington Star*, undated review, contained in the artist's archives.
47. Susan Sollins, "New York Galleries," *Arts* Magazine, November 1973, contained in the artist's archives.
48. For an extended consideration of this conference and of Mary Beth Edelson's role in the planning and presentation of the conference in Washington, see Norma Broude and Mary D. Garrard, editors, *The Power of Feminist Art: The American Movement of the 1970s, History and Impact* (New York: Harry N. Abrams, Inc., 1994), 92-98.
49. Quoted in "Mary Beth Edelson," in Jules Heller and Nancy G.

Heller, editors, *North American Women Artists of the Twentieth Century: A Biographical Dictionary* (New York: Garland Publishing, Inc., 1995), 171. See also Linda F. McGreevy, "Mary Beth Edelson," in Delia Gaze, ed., *Dictionary of Women Artists* (London: Fitzroy Dearborn Publishers, 1997), 492-494.

50. Susan Sollins, "New York Galleries," in *Arts* Magazine, November 1973, contained in the artist's archives.
51. Paul Richard, "Homage Paid to Nameless Gods," *The Washington Post*, undated article contained in the artist's archives.
52. Benjamin Forgey, "Stackhouse Sculpture, Massive and Magical," *Washington Star-News*, November 19, 1973.
53. Carter Ratcliff, *Robert Stackhouse*, p. 13.
54. Martin Friedman, "Robert Stackhouse," in *Scale and Environment: 10 Sculptors* (Minneapolis: Walker Art Center, 1977), 30.
55. Jack Burnham, "Mary Beth Edelson's Great Goddess," *Arts* Magazine, November 1975, 78. See also, Randy Rosen, *Making Their Mark: Women Artists Move into the Mainstream, 1970-85* (New York: Abbeville Press, 1989) 16.
56. Martin Friedman, "Introduction," in *Scale and Environment*, X.
57. For information on the formation and activities of these groups, including the Black Emergency Cultural Coalition, see J. Richard Gruber, *American Icons: From Madison to Manhattan: The Art of Benny Andrews, 1948-1997* (Augusta: Morris Museum of Art, 1997).
58. Paula Cooper, in *The Art Dealers*, edited by Laura de Coppet and Alan Jones (New York: Clarkson N. Potter, Inc., 1984), 190.
59. Ivan Karp, in *The Art Dealers*, 144.
60. Roberta Brandes Gratz and Peter Freiberg, "Has Success Spoiled SoHo?" *Historic Preservation*, September/October 1980, 8-15.
61. Tom Armstrong, "Foreword," *200 Years of American Sculpture* (New York: Whitney Museum of American Art, 1976), 9.
62. Barbara Haskell, "Two Decades of American Sculpture, A Survey," in *200 Years of American Sculpture*, 187.
63. Martin Friedman, "Introduction," in *Scale and Environment*, 7.
64. David Bourdon, "Robert Stackhouse, "*The Village Voice*, September 13, 1976, 16.
65. David Bourdon, "Robert Stackhouse: On the Trail of Legend," *Arts* Magazine, December 1976, contained in the archives of the artist.
66. Jean-Louis Bourgeois, "Robert Stackhouse at Sculpture Now," *Art in America*, January/February 1977, contained in the artist's archives.
67. Marjorie Talalay, ed., *City Project 1977: Four Urban Environmental Sculptures* (Cleveland: Cleveland State University and The New Gallery of Contemporary Art, 1977), 15-16.
68. Ibid., 13-14.
69. Helen Cullinan, "Environmental Sculptures Shaping Up," *Cleveland Plain Dealer*, May 29, 1977, Section five, 17-18.
70. Nancy Rosen, "Introduction," *Artpark 1977: The Program in Visual Arts* (Lewiston, New York: Artpark, 1977), 2-3.
71. Ibid, 77.
72. Quoted in Friedman, *Scale and Environment*, 30.
73. Roy Slade, "Preface," *Sculpture at Cranbrook, 1978-1980*, (Bloomfield Hills, Michigan: Cranbrook Academy, 1980), no pagination.
74. Ibid.
75. April Kingsley, "Introduction," *Passings: Robert Stackhouse* (New York: Publishing Center for Cultural Resources, 1980), no pagination.
76. See, for example, Edward Lucie-Smith, "Graffiti Painting and Related Styles," in *Art in the Eighties* (New York: Phaidon, 1990), 63-67.
77. See Peter Frank and Michael McKenzie, *New, Used & Improved: Art for the 80's* (New York: Abbeville Press, 1987), 11-25.
78. Linda Cathcart, "The Heroic Figure," in *The Heroic Figure* (Houston: Contemporary Art Museum, 1984), 11.
79. Robert Hughes, *American Visions, The Epic History of Art in America* (New York: Alfred. A. Knopf, 1997), 594.
80. See Richard Flood, "Art in the Anchorage," in *Creative Time's Art in the Anchorage* (New York: Creative Time, Inc., 1983).
81. Sam Yates, "Robert Stackhouse, Dialogue with Sam Yates," in *Robert Stackhouse "Deep Swimmers," An Installation and Related Drawings*, with an essay by Donald Kuspit (Knoxville: Art and Architecture Gallery, University of Tennessee-Knoxville, 1985), 18.
82. Ibid., 8-9.
83. Robert Stackhouse, "Robert Stackhouse," in Frank Gettings, *Drawings 1974-1984* (Washington: Hirshhorn Museum and Sculpture Gardens and Smithsonian Institution Press, 1984), 223-224.
84. Linda Weintraub, *Land Marks, New site proposals by twenty-two original pioneers of environmental art* (Annandale-on-Hudson, New York: Bard College Center, 1984), 40.
85. Mary Swift, "Robert Stackhouse and Mary Beth Edelson," *Washington Review*, December/January 1990, 6.
86. *Stephen Antonakis, Michael Singer, Robert Stackhouse, Pat Steir, 19th Bienal De Sao Paulo, 1987*, exhibition guide contained in the artist's archives.
87. See *Sculpture: Walk On, Sit Down, Go Through*, Socrates Sculpture Park, May 17-September 15, 1987 (Long Island City: The Athena Foundation, Inc., 1987).
88. Susan Waller, "Robert Stackhouse, St. Louis Bones" in Debra L. Reinhardt, ed., *Laumeier Sculpture Park: Ten Sites-Works, Artists, Years* (St. Louis: Laumeier Sculpture Park, 1992), 61-63.

89. Christopher French, "Mary Beth Edelson, Martin Puryear, Italo Scanga, Robert Stackhouse," in *Mary Beth Edelson, Martin Puryear, Italo Scanga, Robert Stackhouse* (Washington: The Corcoran Gallery of Art, 1988).
90. Mary Swift, "Robert Stackhouse and Mary Beth Edelson," 5.
91. Carter Ratcliff, *Robert Stackhouse*, 23.
92. Mary Ann Marger, "Shipshape Show Drops Anchor," *St. Petersburg Times*, November 8, 1991, Weekend, 31.
93. Don Lynch, introduction by Robert D. Ballard, *Titanic: An Illustrated History* (New York: Hyperion, 1998), 198-209.
94. Robert Hughes, *American Visions*, 591.
95. For two contemporary surveys of the museum building environment evident in these years, see Douglas Davis, *The Museum Transformed: Design and Culture in the Post-Pompidou Age* (New York: Abbeville Press, 1990) and Josep Montaner, *New Museums* (New York: Princeton Architectural Press, 1990).
96. Barnett Newman quoted in Carter Ratcliff, "Barnett Newman: Citizen of the Infinitely Large Small Republic," *Art in America*, September 1991, 95.
97. Thomas Hardy, "The Convergence of the Twain," reprinted in Steven Biel, ed., *Titanica: The Disaster of the Century in Poetry, Song and Prose* (New York: W.W. Norton & Company, 1998), 25-26.
98. Ibid., 131.
99. From a series of interviews conducted with Richard Belger in Kansas City, Augusta and Washington, 1995 to 1998.
100. *Robert Stackhouse* (Laramie: University of Wyoming Art Museum, 1984), no pagination.
101. Robert Ballard and Rick Archbold, *Lost Liners* (New York: Hyperion, 1997), 146-185.
102. Ibid., 170-179. See also Frank O. Braynard and William H. Miller, Jr., *Picture History of the Cunard Line, 1840-1990* (New York: Dover Publications, 1991), 72-83, 118-119.
103. Roberta Lord, "A Dream Boat at KCAI," in "Robert Stackhouse, Kansas City Art Institute" (Kansas City: Kansas City Art Institute, 1996).
104. Kathleen Whitney, "Robert Stackhouse: The Ritual of Labor," *Sculpture*, May/June 1998, 18-19.
105. Ibid., 19.

SELECTED BIBLIOGRAPHY

Allen, Jane Addams. "A Feeling Kind of Artist." *The Washington Times*, April 10, 1989.

Artner, Alan. "Review." *Chicago Tribune*, February 23, 1979.

Blocher, Fred. "Sculpture Structure." *The Kansas City Star*, March 13, 1996.

Bourgeoise, Jean-Louis. "Review." *Art in America* (January/February 1976): 128.

Bourdon, David. "Robert Stackhouse: On the Trail of Legend." *Arts* Magazine (December 1976): 104.

Brenson, Michael. "Robert Stackhouse." *The New York Times*, February 24, 1989.

Clements, Paul. "Ship Shapes." *Museum & Arts Washington* (November/December 1990).

Cohen, Jean Lawlor. "Down to the Renwick in Ships." *Museum & Arts Washington* (March/April 1989).

Crutchfield, Margo A. "Introduction." *Robert Stackhouse, Encounterings: An Installation with Drawings*. Richmond: Virginia Museum of Fine Arts, 1990.

Davis, Douglas. "Washington." *Arts* Magazine (February, 1971).

Donohoe, Victoria. "Common Places Is Theme of Stackhouse Exhibition." *The Philadelphia Inquirer*, May 1991.

Erlich, Robbie. "Robert Stackhouse: Sculpture Now." *Arts* Magazine (December 1979): 26.

Forgey, Benjamin. "Review." *ArtNews* (January 1974).

Forgey, Benjamin. "The Hirshhorn's Big Draw." *The Washington Post*, March 15, 1984.

"Freiluft-Kunst in die Slums." *Der Spiegel* (August 8, 1977).

Gladsky, Kristen. "Robert Stackhouse's Works Build on the Minimalists - Sculptor's Repetitious Shapes Reflect a Nautical Theme," *The Kansas City Star*, May 18, 1995.

Hayakawa, Alan. "Stackhouse's Ships Are Vessels for the Imagination." *Oregonian* (September 30, 1982).

Hegemen, William R. "Minneapolis: Sculpture to Walk Through." *ArtNews* (1978).

Hoffman, Wendy. "Robert Stackhouse." *The New Art Examiner* (February 1978).

Kingsley, April. "Review." *The Village Voice*, May 28, 1979.

"Introduction"—. *Passings: Robert Stackhouse*. Roslyn, New York: Nassau County Museum of Fine Arts, 1980.

Kuspit, Donald. "Robert Stackhouse." *Robert Stackhouse "Deep Swimmers," An Installation and Related Drawings*. Knoxville: Art and Architecture Gallery, University of Tennessee, Knoxville, 1985.

Lord, Roberta. "A Dream Boat at KCAI", *Robert Stackhouse, Kansas City Art Institute*. Kansas City, Missouri: Kansas City Art Institute, 1996.

"Master/Apprentice: Stackhouse at KCAI." *New Times Arts and Entertainment*, March 7, 1996.

Marger, Mary Ann. "Shipshape Show Drops Anchor." *St. Petersburg Times*, November 8, 1991.

Morin, France. "Artpark 1977." *Parachute* (Autumn 1977): 38.

Mullinax, Gary. "A Voyage to Common Places." *Sunday News*

Journal, Delaware, April 21, 1991.

"The New Master of Drawing Power," *The Washington Times*, March 16, 1984.

Patton, Phil. "Review." *Artforum* (December 1976): 70.

Pearson, Deanne. "Review." *The Forum Magazine* (April 17, 1993).

Ratcliff, Carter. "What It Is to Be There." *Robert Stackhouse*, Wilmington: Delaware Art Museum, 1991.

Raynor, Viven. "Contemporary Art in Middletown." *The New York Times*, May 27, 1984.

"Review." *The New York Times*, April 23, 1982.

Robbins, Corinne. "Sculpture Now, 1974-79." *Arts* Magazine (October 1981).

Robert Stackhouse at Morgan Gallery/C.I.A.E. On the Cover, *Art Now International Gallery Guide*. (May 1992).

Ronck, Ron. "Abstract Meeting Reality." *The Honolulu Advertiser*, January 24, 1990.

Rub, Timothy. "Review." *Arts* Magazine (September 1984).

Russell, John. "Art: Thoughts of Spring and Grand Tour Views." *The New York Times*, May 27, 1984.

Sargent-Wooster, Ann. "Review." *ArtNews* (November 1976).

Shirley, David. "A Horizon Created of Wood." *The New York Times*, January 4, 1981.

Sidney, Lawrence. "Sculpting the Land at Oliver Ranch." *Garden Design Magazine* (December 1991).

Silverman, Andrea. "Robert Stackhouse at Dolan/Maxwell Gallery." *ArtNews* (May 1989).

Simons, Marlise. "Utopia Versus Reality in Brazil's Art Biennial." *The New York Times*, December 9, 1987.

Slade, Roy. "Report from Washington." *Studio International* (January 1972).

Sozanski, Edward J. "Ships and Snakes in Stackhouses' Mid-Career Works." *The Philadelphia Inquirer*, May 2, 1991.

"Stackhouse Commission Dedicated at University." *Hawaii Artreach* (November/December 1991).

Swift, Mary. "Robert Stackhouse and Mary Beth Edelson." *Washington Review* (December/January 1990).

Thalenberg, Eileen. "Site Work: Some Sculptures at Artpark." *Arts Canada* (October/November 1977): 16.

Thorsen, Alice. "Morgan Scores with Great Double Header." *The Kansas City Star*, March 18, 1993.

Waller, Susan. "Robert Stackhouse." *Alice Aycock and Robert Stackhouse, Sculpture at Laumeier*. St. Louis: Laumeier Sculpture Park, 1988.

Whitney, Kathleen. "Robert Stackhouse: The Ritual of Labor." *Sculpture* (May/June 1998).

Willig, Nancy Toblin. "The Nation...the Season at Artpark." *ArtNews* (November 1977).

Zinsser, John. "Stackhouse Sculpture and Watercolor." *The Washington Times*, May 11, 1989.

CHECKLIST

MORRIS MUSEUM OF ART EXHIBITION

ROBERT STACKHOUSE: MAJOR WORKS 1969-1999

Sky Song (Drawing Element)
1969
Graphite & Mylar on Paper
26½ x 36 5/16 (Unframed)
27½ x 39 5/16 X 3 (Framed)

Sky Song (Sculptural Element)
1969
Wood, Rope & Leather
40½ x 70 x 5½ (Unframed)

#5 (Sculptural Element)
1972
Wood
61⅝ x 9⅜ x 6

#5 (Drawing Element)
1973
Watercolor on Paper
14⅛ x 10¼ (Unframed)
22⅜ x 18¼ x 1½ (Framed)

"Sleeping King" with Shadow
1973
Charcoal on Paper
42⅞ x 42 7/18 (Unframed)
51⅛ x 50 7/16 X 2 (Framed)

Drawing for Ghost Dance #1
1974
Charcoal & Graphite on Paper
55 x 36 (Unframed)
59¼ x 40 X 2 (Framed)

Drawing for Ghost Dance #2
1974
Watercolor, Charcoal & Graphite on Paper
55 x 36 (Unframed)
59¼ x 40 X 2 (Framed)

Drawing for Ghost Dance #3
1974
Watercolor, Charcoal & Graphite on Paper
55 x 36 (Unframed)
59¼ x 40 X 2 (Framed)

"Sleeping King" Ascending
1975
Watercolor & Charcoal on Paper
36 x 54¾ (Unframed)
40¼ x 58¾ x 2 (Framed)

Snake Story
1976
Watercolor on Paper
10¼ x 14⅛ (Unframed)
18½ x 22⅛ x 1½ (Framed)

Seeing the Snake
1976
Watercolor, Charcoal & Graphite on Paper
57¼ x 98 x 2 (Framed)

Inside "Running Animals/Reindeer Way"
1977
Watercolor & Charcoal on Paper
59¾ x 39¾ (Unframed)
64 x 43¾ x 2 (Framed)

"Niagara Dance" Ship and Snake
1978
Watercolor & Charcoal on Paper
48 x 76⅝ (Unframed)
52¼ x 80⅝ x 2 (Framed)

2 Views of "Sailings"
1979
Watercolor, Charcoal & Graphite on Paper
42¼ x 58¾ (Unframed)
46½ x 62¾ x 2 (Framed)

From the Deep
1982
Watercolor, Charcoal & Graphite on Paper
84¾ x 118½ (Unframed)
88⅝ x 122½ x 2 (Framed)

Inside Four Structures
1982 (2/24/82)
Watercolor, Charcoal & Graphite on Paper
84⅜ x 120 (Unframed)
88 ⅞ x 124 x 2 (Framed)

Proposal for Brooklyn Bridge Centennial
1983
Watercolor, Charcoal & Pencil on Paper
25 x 22½ (Unframed)
29¼ x 26½ x 1½ (Framed)

Plans for Crosby Gardens
1984
Pencil on Vellum
18¾ x 23⅞ (Unframed)
27 x 31⅞ x 1½ (Framed)

Plans for Crosby Gardens
1984
Graphite on Paper
17 x 22 (Unframed)
25¼ x 30 x 1½ (Framed)

Working Drawing for Crosby Gardens
1984
Graphite on Paper
17 x 22 (Unframed)
25¼ x 30 x 1½ (Framed)

For "Deep Swimmers"
1984
Watercolor & Charcoal on Paper
Mounted on Linen
61 5/16 x 108 5/16 x 3 (Framed)

U.S. Capital Bones Not a Likely Prospect
1984 (7/18/84)
Watercolor, Charcoal and Pencil on
Paper mounted on Linen
60 x 107 x 2⅝ (Unframed)

"On the Beach Again" Australia
1985
Watercolor, Charcoal on Paper
Mounted on Linen
60⅛ x 107 x 2¾ (Mounted)
61⅛ x 108 x 3 (Framed)

Model of East River Bones/Laumeier
1987
Wood & Plasticine
6 x 46 7/16 x 19 (Piece)
48 x 48 x 20½ (On Pedestal)

Ruby Brazil
1987 (6/87)
Watercolor
60 x 95¾ x 2⅝

Dragon Fight
1987 (12/16/87)
Watercolor, Charcoal & Graphite on
Paper Mounted on Linen
60⅛ x 192¼ x 2¼ (Unframed)

Crosby Gardens Model
1988
Wood
6½ x 24 x 96

Gokstad (from Sources & Structures)
1988-89
Spit-Bite Etching
31 x 21 (Unframed)
39¼ x 29 x 1½ (Framed)

At Sculpture Now (from Sources & Structures)
1988-89
Spit-Bite Etching
31 x 21 (Unframed)
39¼ x 29 x 1½ (Framed)

(From Sources & Structures)
1988-89
Spit-Bite Etching
31 x 21 (Unframed)
39¼ x 29 x 1½ (Framed)

(From Sources & Structures)
1988-89
Spit-Bite Etching
31 x 21 (Unframed)
39¼ x 29 x 1½ (Framed)

(From Sources & Structures)
1988-89
Spit-Bite Etching At Sculpture
31 x 21 (Unframed)
39¼ x 29 x 1½ (Framed

(From Sources & Structures)
1988-89
Spit-Bite Etching
31 x 21 (Unframed)
39¼ x 29 x 1½ (Framed)

Inside "Encounterings"
1990
Watercolor, Charcoal & Graphite on Paper
25 x 18⅜ (Unframed)
33¼ x 26⅜ x 1½ (Framed)

Transtitanic
1992
Watercolor
225 x 58 x 3¼

Hot Stella
1992
Watercolor, Charcoal &
Spray Fixative on Paper
40¼ x 60 (Unframed)
44¼ x 64 x 2 (Framed)

Soundless
1992-93
Print Version - Spit-bite Etching
38 x 58 (Unframed)
39 7/16 x 59 7/16 (Framed)
Published by Tandem Press

On the Deep #2
1995
Watercolor & Charcoal on Paper
Mounted on Canvas
59½ x 40¼ (Paper)
60½ x 41¼ x 2½ (Framed)

Flexed Flyer
1995
Watercolor & Charcoal on Paper
Mounted on Linen
40⅛ x 120¼ x 1½ (Unframed)
40¾ x 119 7/16 x 3 (Framed)

Adrift
1996
7 Color Lithograph
44⅜ x 30⅜ (Unframed)
53⅙ x 37⅞ x 1⅜ (Framed)

Dick's "K.C. Way"
1996
Watercolor & Charcoal on Paper
Mounted on Canvas
39½ x 58 13/16 (Unframed)
40⅞ x 60⅜ x 2½ (Framed)

Blue Seeing
1998
Watercolor on Paper Mounted on Canvas
22¼ x 75⅛ x 1⅝ (Unframed)
23¾ x 76⅝ x 3 (Framed)

CHECKLIST

ADDITIONAL WORKS BY ROBERT STACKHOUSE

IN THE COLLECTIONS OF THE BELGER FAMILY FOUNDATION (NOVEMBER, 1998)

Great Rain Snake
1969
Oak
40'10" x 50¼ x 44

Recollecting Angel
1972-1996
Painted Wood and Wood Lathe
113½ x 32⅜ x 54½

Eye Shape/Boat Shape from Journey Series
1972
Oak & Redwood
21½ x 7¾ x 306½

Sculpture Study
1972
Charcoal on Paper
42 1/16 x 36 1/16 (Unframed)
50⅜ x 44⅛ x 1½ (Framed)

Boat Shape From Journey Series
1972
Oak & Redwood
11 x 210 x 13 (Without Pedestal)

Sleeping King
1973
Wood
90⅛ x 106 x 28½ (Unframed)

Abracadabra
1973
Charcoal on Paper
44 x 42⅞ (Unframed)
52¼ x 50⅞ x 2 (Framed)

Stacked Sleeping King
1973
Charcoal & Acrylic on Paper
42 x 117

Winged Goddess
1974
Lithograph
30⅛ x 22¼ (Unframed)
38⅜ x 30¼ x 1½ (Framed)

Recollection of a Great Rain Snake #3
1976
Charcoal on Paper
79½ x 72⅜ (Unframed)
83¾ x 76⅜ x 2 (Framed)

Two Studies for "Running Animals"
1976
Watercolor, Graphite, Charcoal & Pencil on Paper
72¼ x 46½ (Unframed)
76½ x 50½ x 2 (Framed)

A Working Drawing for Running Animals #1
1976
Watercolor, Charcoal, Graphite &
Colored Pencil on Paper
72½ x 46¾ (Unframed)

Speaking the Snake
1976
Watercolor, Charcoal & Graphite on Paper
52½ x 93¼

Running Tracks-Sculpture Study
1976
Watercolor & Graphite on Paper
35⅞ x 72¼ (Unframed)
40⅜ x 76¼ x 2 (Framed)

Niagara Dance
1977
Watercolor, Charcoal & Graphite on Paper
38 x 0 (Unframed)

Inside "Shiphall"
1977 (12/13/77)
Watercolor, Charcoal & Graphite on Paper
40 x 59½ (Unframed)

Cranbrook Dance
1978 (5/4/78)
Watercolor, Charcoal & Graphite on Paper
52½ x 83¼(Unframed)

Cheops Ship
1978
Watercolor on Paper
22⅜ x 30⅛ (Unframed)
30⅝ x 38⅛ x 1½ (Framed)

Working Drawing for "Sailings" #1
1978 (10/78)
Watercolor, Charcoal & Graphite on Paper
42¼ x 60 (Unframed)

Working Drawing for "Sailings" #2
1978 (10/78)
Watercolor, Charcoal & Graphite on Paper
42¼ x 60 (Unframed)

Working Drawing for "Sailings" #3
1978 (10/78)
Watercolor, Charcoal & Graphite on Paper
42½ x 60 (Unframed)

Working Drawing for "Sailings" #4
1978 (10/78)
Watercolor, Charcoal & Graphite on Paper
42¼ x 60 (Unframed)

Working Drawing For "Sailings" #5
1978 (10/78)
Watercolor, Charcoal & Graphite on Paper
42¼ x 60 (Unframed)

On "Sailings"
1979 (1/79)
Watercolor, Charcoal & Graphite on Paper
42¼ x 59 (Unframed)

"Sailors" at Sculpture Now, Installation
1979 (6/9/79)
Watercolor, Charcoal & Graphite on Paper
42½ x 60 (Unframed)

"Sailings" at the Hudson River Museum
1979 (1/23/79)
Watercolor, Charcoal & Graphite on Paper
42 5/16 x 60 (Unframed)

Working Drawing for "Sailors" #2
1979 (3/8/79)
Watercolor, Charcoal & Graphite on Paper
42¼ x 60 (Unframed)

An Outdoor Ship in the Air
1979 (12/5/79)
Watercolor, Charcoal & Graphite on Paper
32¾ x 42¼ (Unframed)

Working Drawing for "Sailors" #1
1979 (4/20/79)
Watercolor, Charcoal & Graphite on Paper
42¼ x 60 (Unframed)

"Sailors" Proposal
1979 (3/2/79)
Watercolor, Charcoal & Graphite on Paper
42¼ x 60 (Unframed)

Working Drawing for a Lithograph
1980 (11/80)
Watercolor, Graphite & Charcoal on Paper
30 x 84½ (Unframed)
34½ x 88½ X 2 (Framed)

China Clipper
1980 (9/20/80)
Watercolor, Charcoal & Graphite on Paper
30⅛ x 42⅞ (Unframed)
38⅛ x 42⅞ x 1½ (Framed)

Ship and Bulgarian Roof
1980 (6/80)
Medium
31½ x 47¾ (Unframed)

L. A. Jeffrey
1980 (5/14/80)
Watercolor, Charcoal & Graphite on Paper
42⅞ x 60 (Unframed)
46⅞ x 64 x 2 (Framed)

For "Passings" A Study of Two Ships
1980 (9/28/80)
Watercolor & Charcoal on Paper
30¾ x 42¼ (Unframed)
35¼ x 46¼ x 1½ (Framed)

"Passings" An Outdoor Installation
1980 (11/1/80)
Watercolor, Charcoal & Graphite on Paper
40 x 60 (Unframed)

Prudential Installation
1981 (9/9/81)
Watercolor, Charcoal & Graphite on Paper
32 x 95⅞ (Unframed)
36½ x 99⅞ x 2 (Framed

Canoe and Shadow
1981 (9/16/81)
Watercolor, Charcoal & Graphite on Paper
25⅞ x 80⅞ (Unframed)
30⅞ x 84⅞ x 2 (Framed)

Major Projects
1982 (2/11/82)
Watercolor, Charcoal & Graphite on Paper
84½ x 118 (Unframed)
89 x 122 x 2 (Framed)

Norse Burial Ship And P.C.V.A. Working Drawing
1982 (8/29/82)
Watercolor, Charcoal & Graphite on Paper
42⅞ x 60¹⁵⁄₁₆ (Unframed)

P.C.V.A. Project
1982 (8/28/82)
Watercolor, Charcoal & Graphite on Paper
40 x 60 (Unframed)

Working Drawing for "Mountain Climbers"
1982 (10/3/82)
Watercolor, Charcoal & Graphite on Paper
30 x 42¼ (Unframed)

"Bones" Installation
1983 (3/17/83)
Watercolor, Charcoal & Graphite on Paper
42½ x 96 (Unframed)

Chicago Sculpture International/Mile 2
1983
Watercolor, Charcoal & Graphite on Paper
39½ x 53½ (Unframed)

Dasher Boat
1983 (10/15/83)
Watercolor, Charcoal & Graphite on
Paper Mounted on Canvas
42 x 96¼ x 2⅞ (Unframed)

Cheops Ship In Its Burial Pit
1983 (1/30/83)
Watercolor, Charcoal & Graphite on
Paper Mounted on Linen
42¼ x 174 (Unframed)

Eye Shape/Boat Shape/From a 1969 Dream
1983-85
Watercolor, Charcoal & Graphite on Paper,
Painted Oak
64⁷⁄₁₆ x 149⅞ x 28³⁄₁₆ (Installed)

Ohio Prospect Bones
1984 (10/4/84)
Watercolor, Charcoal & Graphite on Paper
25¾ x 40½ (Unframed)
26¾ x 41½ x 2 (Framed)

Inside "Toronto Passages"
1984 (7/17/84)
Watercolor, Charcoal & Graphite on
Paper Mounted on Linen
60 x 107¼ x 2⅞ (Unframed)

Working Drawing for Print Project
1985 (7/4/85)
Watercolor, Charcoal & Graphite on Paper
29¼ x 41¼ (Unframed)

Print Study
1986
Watercolor, Charcoal & Graphite on Paper
41½ x 29½ (Unframed)
42½ x 30½ x 2 (Framed)

Indigo Way
1986
Watercolor on Paper Mounted on Linen
90⅞ x 167½ (Unframed)
91⅞ x 168½ x 3 (Framed)

Working Drawing for Pace Litho
1986
Watercolor & Charcoal on Paper
60 x 40 (Unframed)

Working Drawing for Pace Litho
1986
Watercolor & Graphite on Paper
40 x 60 (Unframed)

"Dreamers" and the "Great Rain Snake"
1986 (6/12/86)
Watercolor, Charcoal & Graphite on Paper
42¼ x 59¾ (Unframed)
46¼ x 63¾ x 2 (Framed)

Canoe in Passing
1986
Watercolor, Charcoal & Graphite on Paper
29⅞ x 41½ (Unframed)

Working Drawing for Philadelphia Print Project
1986
Watercolor, Charcoal & Graphite on Paper
29½ x 41½ (Unframed)

Sao Paolo Bienal Proposal
1987
Watercolor & Graphite on Paper
26⅛ x 40⅞ (Unframed)
34⅞ x 48¾ x 1½ (Framed)

"Ruby Birth" 19th Bienal De Sao Paulo, 1987
1988 (6/88)
Watercolor, Charcoal & Graphite on Paper
Mounted on Linen
60⅛ x 108⅛ (Unframed)

Two Diviners
1989
Watercolor, Charcoal & Graphite on Paper
40⅜ x 60 1/16 (Unframed)
41⅜ x 61⅛ x 2½ (Framed)

"Encounterings" Installation
1990 (8/90)
Watercolor, Charcoal & Graphite on Paper
40¼ x 60 (Unframed)

Inside Encounterings at V.M.F.A.
1990 (8/90)
Watercolor, Charcoal & Graphite on Paper
40¾ x 60 (Unframed)

Untitled
1990
3 Color Spit-Bite, Aquatint & Drypoint
54 x 101½ (Unframed)
58¼ x 105½ x 2 (Framed)

Naja's Deck
1991
Extruded Red Brass
4½ x 240⅝ x 26⅝

Aster's Leap
1991-93
Watercolor & Charcoal on Paper Mounted on Linen
120⅛ x 40⅛ x 1⅝ (Unframed)
121⅛ x 41⅛ x 3 (Framed)

"Soundless" Installation
1992
Watercolor, Charcoal & Graphite on
Paper Mounted on Canvas
30 x 40 (Unframed)
31 x 41 x 2 (Framed)

Divers / Six Views
1992 (3/92)
Watercolor, Charcoal & Graphite on Paper
30 x 42¼ (Unframed)

Encountering
1992
10 Color Spit-Bite Etching
35 9/16 x 51⅛ (Unframed)
39 13/16 x 55⅛ x 2 (Framed)

Spiral Stella
1992
Watercolor & Charcoal on Paper
Mounted on Canvas, Brass
60¼ x 60½ x 2 (Mounted)
61¼ x 61½ x 2½ (Framed)

Double Diviner
1992
Watercolor & Charcoal on Paper Mounted on Linen
60⅛ x 81¼ x 1½ (Unframed)
61⅛ x 82¼ x 2½ (Framed)

Soundless Trio
1992 (2/92)
Watercolor, Charcoal & Graphite on Paper
41 x 60 (Unframed)
42 x 61 x 2½ (Framed)

Hot Stella
1992
Watercolor, Charcoal & Spray Fixative on Paper
40¼ x 60 (Unframed)
44½ x 64 x 2 (Framed)

Three Sources
1992
Watercolor, Charcoal & Graphite on Paper
41 x 60 (Unframed)

Delaware Art Museum Sculpture
1992
Watercolor & Graphite on Paper
22⅞ x 30 1/16 (Unframed)
23⅞ x 31⅛ x 2 (Framed

Night Ruby
1993 (5/93)
Watercolor & Charcoal on Paper
30¼ x 22⅞ (Unframed)
31¼ x 23⅞ x 2 (Framed)

Descend #3
1993 (4/93)
Watercolor, Charcoal & Graphite on Paper
30 1/16 x 22½ (Unframed)
31⅛ x 23½ x 2 (Framed)

Fire Deck
1993
Watercolor & Charcoal on Paper
Mounted on Canvas
40⅜ x 60 (Paper)
41⅜ x 61 x 2½ (Framed)

Drifter
1993
Watercolor on Paper Mounted on Linen
120¼ x 80⅜ x 1½ (Unframed)
121¼ x 81⅜ x 3 (Framed)

Copper Naja
1994
Patinaed Copper, Wood, Screws
145 x 19¼ x 12

Red Iceberg
1994 (10/31/94)
Watercolor & Charcoal on Paper
27 x 79¾ (Unframed)
28 x 80¾ x 2½ (Framed)

Working Drawing for "Russian River Bones"
1994
Watercolor & Graphite on Paper
29½ x 41¼ (Unframed)
30½ x 42¼ X 2 (Framed)

Vertical Wyoming
1994
Watercolor & Charcoal on Paper Mounted on Linen
42 X 30⅛ X 1⅛ (Unframed)

Blue Iceberg
1994 (11/23/94)
Watercolor on Paper
27 x 79¾ (Unframed)
28 x 80¾ x 2½ (Framed)

Red Glass Study
1994
Watercolor & Graphite on Paper
9 1/16 x 12¼ (Unframed)
17⅞ x 20¼ x 1½ (Framed)

Blue Glass Study
1994
Watercolor & Graphite on Paper
9 1/16 x 12¼ (Unframed)
17⅞ x 20¼ x 1½ (Framed)

Working Drawing for Albrecht-Kemper Piece
1996
Graphite on Paper
17 x 22 (Unframed)
25¼ x 30 x 1½ (Framed)

Close "K.C. Way"
1997
Watercolor on Paper Mounted on Linen
108 x 60 1/16 x 1½ (Unframed)
109 x 61 1/16 x 3 (Framed)

CHRONOLOGY

1942 Born in Bronxville, New York, on July 31 to Gerald Murry Stackhouse and Phyllis May Holland.

1944 Grandfather, Hoyt Holland, purchases summer house at Peach Lake, near Brewster, New York. Robert spends summers here until age 16.

1954 Moves to Florida to live with his grandparents, Hoyt and Inez Holland. Lives with them at Lundy's fish camp, and attends junior high and high school in nearby Auburndale. Graduates from Auburndale High School in 1960.

1960-65 Attends the University of South Florida, Tampa, as a charter member of its first freshman class. Studies art under Harrison Covington. Also studies with Robert Gelinas and visiting artist, Friedel Dzubas.

1965-67 Attends graduate school at the University of Maryland in College Park. Thesis advisor is Herman Maril. Marries Dolores Novoa on December 31, 1966, in Tampa.

1967 MFA degree granted from the University of Maryland. Begins full-time teaching at Corcoran School of Art.

1969 First museum exhibition at the Detroit Institute of Arts, in "Other Ideas," installs *Blades*. Begins wood sculptures *Sky Song*, *Watching*, and *The Great Rain Snake*.

1970 Included in "Washington: Twenty Years" at the Baltimore Museum of Art and "New Sculpture: Baltimore, Washington and Richmond" at the Corcoran Gallery of Art. Divorces Dolores.

1971 Begins living with artist Mary Beth Edelson in Washington.

1972 First one-man exhibition at Henri Gallery in Washington, "Journeys Series."

1973 One-man exhibition at the Corcoran Gallery. Makes first lithograph, *Winged Goddess*. Makes first site specific sculpture, *Sleeping King Ascending*.

1975 Moves to New York with Mary Beth Edelson and her son, Nicholas. Renovates SoHo loft.

1976 First New York one-man exhibition at Max Hutchinson's Sculpture Now gallery, builds *Running Animals/Reindeer Way*.

1977-78 Completes sculptural installations at Artpark, in Cleveland, at the Walker Art Center, at the Cranbrook Academy of Art, and at the Hudson River Museum.

1979 "Sailors" exhibition at Sculpture Now.

1980 Camps out and builds summer house at Port Clyde, Maine, together with Mary Beth Edelson, her daughter, Lynn, and son, Nick.

1982 A major turning point when he completes first large-scale watercolors, beginning with *From the Deep*, surveying his subject matter of the first ten years. Receives second NEA grant for works on paper.

1983 *Mountain Climber* exhibited at Museum of Modern Art.

1984 *On the Beach Again*, first cast bronze commissioned sculpture, installed at the National Gallery of Australia. *Deep Swimmers* installation and exhibition at the University of Tennessee in Knoxville, organized by Sam Yates. Show traveled until 1986.

1987 Resigns position at Corcoran School, appointed Professor Emeritus; devotes himself to full-time art career. Begins series of projects including *East River Bones* (1987), *St. Louie Bones* (1988), *Les os du Quebec* (1989), and *Oliver Ranch Bones* (1989).

1988 First exhibition with Dolan Maxwell Gallery in New York. (Gallery's inaugural exhibition in New York.)

1991 "Common Places: Painting and Sculpture by Robert Stackhouse," presented at the Delaware Museum of Art, a survey of large-scale paintings and sculptures. "Soundless" exhibition and installation at the Contemporary Art Museum at the University of South Florida. First use of Titanic imagery and return to painting.

1992 First exhibition of prints at Pace Prints in New York.

1993 Beginning of significant relationship with the Morgan Gallery and the Belger Family Foundation in Kansas City.

1994 Moves studio from SoHo to Port Chester, New York.

1996 Visiting artist at the Kansas City Art Institute. Builds *K. C. Way*.

1997 Moves home and studio to Kansas City after ending his 27-year relationship with Mary Beth Edelson. Begins working relationship with Klein Art Works, Chicago. Initiates series of major sculptural installations including *Missouri Shift* (1997), *Blue Ryders* (1997), *Missouri Bones* (1998), *Angel Way* (1998), *Incomplete Angel* (1998), and *Michigan Swell* (1998).

1998 "Someways," first Belger Foundation sponsored survey exhibition, presented at the Albrecht-Kemper Museum in St. Joseph, Missouri.

1999 "Robert Stackhouse: Major Works 1969-1999" presented at the Morris Museum of Art. Related sculptural installation commissioned for Augusta State University. Permanent installation commissioned for sculpture garden at Nelson-Atkins Museum of Art in Kansas City. Moves into renovated 10,000 sq.ft. Belger Foundation studio space in Kansas City.

PHOTOGRAPHIC CREDITS

All photographs and reproductions, except those noted below, are drawn from the extensive collections of the artist and from the family photographic and scrapbook collections of Phyllis Stackhouse (especially the photographs in chapters 1 and 2.)

Extensive ongoing photographic research and assistance was supplied, throughout this project, by Dennis Morgan and the staff of the Morgan Gallery in Kansas City. The gallery's assistance in this and related phases of exhibition research and development has been greatly appreciated.

Photographs of individual works from the Belger Family Foundation, taken by Dan Wayne of Kansas City, Missouri:
Fig. 3.15, 3.16, 3.21, 3.22, 3.23, 3.24, 3.25, 3.26, 3.27, 3.30, 3.32, 3.35, 3.36, 4.1, 4.2, 4.3, 4.4, 4.5, 4.6, 4.7, 4.10, 4.14, 4.16, 4.18, 4.19, 4.20, 4.21, 4.22, 4.23, 4.24, 4.26, 4.27, 4.29, 4.30, 4.32, 4.33, 5.1, 5.2, 5.3, 5.5, 5.7, 5.8, 5.9, 5.11, 5.17, 5.18, 5.19, 5.20, 5.23, 5.26, 5.28, 5.31, 5.34, 5.35, 5.36, 5.44, 5.45, 5.46, 5.47, 5.48, 5.49, 5.51, 5.52, 5.54, 5.58, 6.1, 6.2, 6.3, 6.4, 6.5, 6.6, 6.7, 6.8, 6.9, 6.10, 6.12, 6.13, 6.14, 6.20, 6.21, 6.22, 6.29, 6.30, 6.35, and 6.36.

Photograph of Stackhouse article from *The Washington Post* (Figure 3.4) ©1999 used with permission, *The Washington Post*

Jeff Barnes
Fig. 2.1, *Palm Grove, Florida*, c. 1875, oil on canvas, collection Morris Museum of Art.

Mary Beth Edelson
Fig. 3.19, 3.20, 3.33, 5.42, and 5.43.

J. Richard Gruber
Fig. 2.8, 2.10, 2.11, 2.15, 2.16, 2.23, 2.25, 2.26, 2.27, 6.15, 6.16, 6.17, 6.18, 6.19, and page 144.

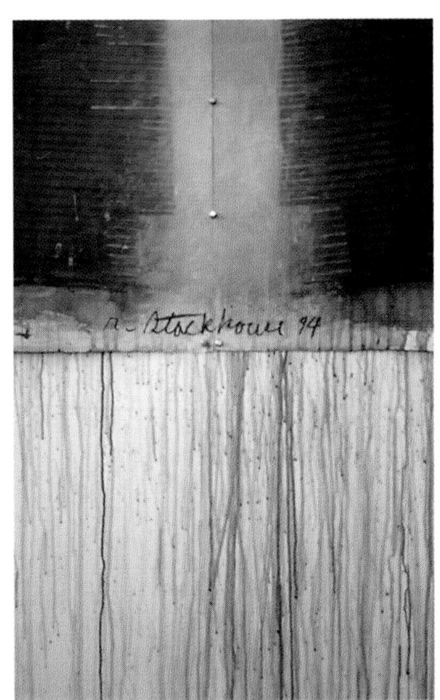